THE DEVIL'S RIGHT HAND

ALSO BY M. WILLIAM PHELPS

Perfect Poison
Lethal Guardian
Every Move You Make
Sleep in Heavenly Peace
Murder in the Heartland
Because You Loved Me
If Looks Could Kill
I'll Be Watching You
Deadly Secrets
Cruel Death
Death Trap
Kill for Me
Failures of the Presidents (co-author)
Nathan Hale: The Life and Death of America's First Spy
The Devil's Rooming House: The True Story of America's Deadliest Female Serial Killer
Love Her to Death
Too Young to Kill
Never See Them Again

THE DEVIL'S RIGHT HAND

The Tragic Story of the Colt Family Curse

M. WILLIAM PHELPS

National best-selling author of
The Devil's Rooming House

LYONS PRESS
Guilford, Connecticut
An imprint of Globe Pequot Press

Copyright © 2012 by M. William Phelps

Lyons Press is an imprint of Globe Pequot Press.

Text design: Sheryl P. Kober
Layout artist: Justin Marciano
Project editor: Kristen Mellitt

Library of Congress Cataloging-in-Publication Data is available on file.

ISBN 978-0-7627-6379-5

Printed in the United States of America

10 9 8 7 6 5 4 3 2 1

For any child dreaming
of the next great invention . . .

Table of Contents

Fear tastes like a rusty knife and do not let her into your house.
Courage tastes of blood. Stand up straight.
Admire the world. Relish the love of a gentle woman.
Trust in the Lord.

—JOHN CHEEVER, *The Wapshot Chronicle*

Vanishing Act

SAM ADAMS WAS RUNNING BEHIND SCHEDULE. IT WAS A WARM SUMMER afternoon in New York City, Friday, September 17, 1841, sometime near 1:00 p.m. The married printer, a man in his early thirties, hurried along Broadway in the financial district, close to the neighborhood of Park Row and Murray Street. Hanging around Adams's modest belly was his favorite gold chain, on which hung his pocket watch, key and seal attached. Although he was buried in debt, having been on the receiving end of several bad business deals recently, Adams wore moderately expensive clothing. "A black coat," his wife, Emmeline, later recalled, ". . . vest, gambroon pantaloons, a cotton shirt and black stock," which Emmeline had sewn herself. The reclusive, quiet, and religious man had a full shock of wavy black hair and oddly resembled future president Abraham Lincoln during his younger, beardless days. Adams was anxious to run a few errands and then head north a few blocks to Chambers Street. He needed to see about some money owed to him by a client for a nearly completed printing job. Frustration and contempt nagged Adams a bit on this afternoon; he believed one of his most trusted patrons was taking advantage of him. He felt he had been used and it was costing him his business. No more, the printer decided, would he lie down and be taken for a fool.

City Clerk John Johnson ran into Adams inside the Board of Foreign Missions near Murray Street. After a brief chat, Johnson went on his way, only to bump into Adams again on Chambers Street hours later, somewhere close to three o'clock.

"He was going from Centre Street to Broadway," Johnson explained, "on the side next to the post office. I did not speak to him then. He was walking moderately."

Johnson could tell something weighed heavily on Adams; rather, that Adams seemed terribly rushed. When they had spoken earlier, Johnson mentioned a proof for a "job [Adams] had been in the habit of printing" for the city.

"I'll bring it to your office," Adams told the clerk, further explaining that the job wasn't yet finished.

Adams had always been good about stopping for a chat, Johnson recalled days after they saw each other. In fact, there was not a man who had made the acquaintance of Samuel Adams who would later speak an ill word of him. Alfred Peckham had lived with Adams for two of the fifteen years he had known him, saying, "He was a remarkably mild, inoffensive man. But he frequently mentioned to me about his business and what trouble he had."

A fellow printer, Thomas Smith, said he "always considered [Adams] a very mild . . . man, so much so that [. . . he would not] insult [a person,] even if he received one."

"He [would] speak to me when we met, but *not* on this occasion," Johnson noted, speaking of that brief moment when Johnson watched Adams cross Centre Street on his way toward Broadway.

Indeed, something troubled the printer, and Adams was, despite his generally even-tempered manner, heading off to see it to the end. What Samuel Adams didn't know, however, and surely could not have, was that before he had a chance to even argue his case regarding the funds owed to him, he would be silenced.

One hundred miles southwest of New York City, a five-hour ride on horseback, perhaps a little faster by stage, a man who was rather famous for an apparent obsession with murder and death was itching to leave the City of Brotherly Love, Philadelphia. He would be dead himself under mysterious circumstances in a mere eight years, thirty-nine years young, just as he was becoming one of the most famous writers in America.

In September 1841, however, Edgar Allan Poe was living on the verge of homelessness, trying to make a living from his writing, editing a magazine and scribing letters to friends and family, dreaming of what was happening in the place where his heart was these days, and surely where he believed he could earn enough money from his writing to make a living:

New York literature may be taken as a fair representation of that of the country at large. The city itself is the focus of American letters. Its authors include, perhaps, one-fourth of all in America, and the influence they exert on their brethren, if seemingly silent, is not the less extensive and decisive. As I shall have to speak of many individuals, my limits will not permit me to speak of them otherwise than in brief; but this brevity will be merely consistent with the design, which is that of simple opinion, with little of either argument or detail.

Poe was wrapped up in the idea that storytelling, at its fundamental core, must maintain an adequate fidelity to life in general. He had no patience for dishonest writers who relied exclusively on the imagination; those who tried to trick their audience into believing that fiction not based partly in fact was what readers actually wanted. Poe combed the newspapers for raw material to mold into stories, and he took copious notes of circumstances in life that he found interesting fodder for his poems and tales. His parents had been actors. He experimented with drugs and certainly understood the power of alcohol. All of this, Poe realized, made life—and thus the stories writers told—more fascinating.

But Poe was also becoming increasingly critical of Charles Dickens's style of prose, which he felt seemed anchored and weighed down by the *ordinariness* of everyday life. The end of life—death, in all of its varieties and shapes—was what spurred the great poet and storyteller to put quill to page. He was fascinated with the beginning and conclusion of a life, not so much with what happened in between.

With his obsession with death, of course, came an understanding of God. Poe believed God to be a prime mover and not so much a caretaker. Poe's God was a watch-winder, one to whom he showed no particular devotion. Poe, in other words, was not one to hit the floor on his knees before bedtime.

"I have no belief in spirituality," Poe once wrote. "I think the word a *mere* word. No one has really a conception of spirit. We cannot imagine what is not."

In this same letter, Poe talked about the basic substance of life and its effect on the soul. Imparting what was, whether he knew it, a deist point of view, Poe believed that "unparticled matter, impelling and permeating all things, is God. Its activity is the thought of God, which creates."

The unmoved mover!

The enigmatic writer admitted that, at times, he could become "excessively slothful and wonderfully industrious." He explained how there were days when "any kind of mental exercise [was] torture"—moments during which, Poe noted, he simply retreated to the mountaintops and woods for "solitary communion."

Then there were those days when Poe suffered from what he called "a sort of mania for composition." His mind raced faster than his quill could keep up. "Then I scribble all day and read all night, so long as the disease endures."

In Philadelphia during that mild September 1841 afternoon when Sam Adams unknowingly (to either man) would become part of Poe's life, the poet with the ashen face of sadness was longing gracefully and compulsively for the city he wanted so much to call home again. This thought—of moving back to a place where he believed he could make a serious go of writing for money—consumed him; and yet, at the same time, as he would write a few years later, the idea of death being at the forefront of his prose persuaded him with equal force, if not more, to sit down and write these days.

"What we call 'death' is painful metamorphosis. . . . At death, the worm is the butterfly—still material, but of a matter unrecognized by our organs . . ."

On their own, these sentences made little sense to anyone but the reader to whom they were addressed; but in the context of what Poe was about to begin writing, and the literary mark on the world he would make, one can identify the fuel for his creativity and the shared human experience upon which he would channel some of his greatest work.

An honest, hardworking man, Samuel Adams undoubtedly wondered as he walked toward Chambers Street why the man he was about to confront— the appropriate word, we might mention here, for what was, essentially, an impromptu meeting—couldn't come up with the proper amount of money owed to him. Yet proper payment was only half of Sam Adams's concern. Earlier on that September 17, 1841, morning, he had become aware of something he had not shared with anyone along his midday stroll. Adams had visited with Charles Wells, a bookbinder he had used on occasion. Wells explained that Adams's client—a man by the name of John Caldwell Colt—had "ordered the books to be sent to Philadelphia" from a first print run Adams had been under contract to publish. Colt was a bookkeeper; he had written a book about accounting he promised would sell as well as a previous book he had written. Colt, Wells explained to Adams, was slated to have the books shipped to Philadelphia that morning. Beyond claiming himself an accountant and author, John Colt was the brother of soon-to-be internationally famous repeating-firearms inventor Sam Colt.

Adams was astonished by this new revelation. He considered it to be a fraudulent act on the part of Colt, and could not have cared less who John Colt's brother was, or how much money or influence the Colts supposedly had at their disposal.

As if unaware that the revelation might have bothered Adams, Wells then said, "I would ask that you should print a book for me. Take the pay in binding."

Wells was one of the busier binders in the city, and many of the local printers used him. It was a fair trade, Wells suggested. And it seemed from Wells's conversation with Colt earlier that morning that Adams was in the business of bartering for services—maybe one of the reasons why Adams's business was failing.

Adams didn't want to hear about any new business. Wells had bound the job in question, and Adams asked him about it.

"The sheets were sent off to the folding place," Wells explained. "They came [back] . . . and a portion of them were finished this morning."

Adams asked where they were.

Wells explained again that John Colt had "been in the bindery, and wished the books forwarded to Philadelphia. He had been there three previous times to then," Wells added, "and had made out invoices to the trade [of public] sale . . ."

Now, Adams realized, Colt had gone and taken things too far.

Samuel Adams told Wells he was heading over to visit with John Colt immediately to get to the bottom of this near-thievery.

Later, Wells talked about Adams's demeanor as he left that morning, remarking, "His general temper I supposed to be good, but never saw him under circumstances by which it would be tried."

These *were* trying circumstances, for certain. Enough was enough. Adams not only felt John Colt was claiming that the amount he owed Adams for this first print run was far less than what Adams had quoted but also that Colt was now going behind his back.

Adams told Wells to halt all work on the project until he could get to the bottom of what was going on.

Broken trust and money. Adams believed Colt had gone over his head and sold the books in Philadelphia at a profit margin larger than what they had agreed upon—and pocketed the profit. The four hundred volumes in question would have sold for between $125 and $150. Colt, Adams learned, was telling people he had made the sale in Philadelphia for $117.

And so off Samuel Adams went, down Centre Street toward the corner of Chambers Street and Broadway, where John Colt kept an office.

It has been said that Edgar Allan Poe "initiated the modern detective story" with the publication of "The Murders in the Rue Morgue"—some two years before the term "detective" was coined. Like many great literary success stories, "Rue Morgue," a story centered on the ghastly homicides of a mother and daughter, was rejected by several editors. Poe was editing *Graham's Lady's and Gentleman's Magazine* in Philadelphia at the time, which ultimately published the story in its April 1841 edition. With the publication of what is a straightforward whodunit murder-mystery, Poe made it clear to not only his audience but also the literati as a whole that he understood the difference between unfolding a good murder story on the page and pulling the reader into the minds of his characters, while laying out the psychology driving a murderer and the wonder of solving a case by the process of calculation. Poe addressed the question every murder-mystery fan—turning to fact or fiction—asks at some point: *Why do human beings kill?*

In the opening paragraphs of "Rue Morgue," Poe gives an indication as to how his unnamed narrator will accomplish these daunting tasks:

> *Yet to calculate is not in itself to analyze. A chess-player, for example, does the one without effort at the other. It follows that the game of chess, in its effects upon mental character, is greatly misunderstood. I am not now writing a treatise, but simply prefacing a somewhat peculiar narrative by observations very much at random; I will, therefore, take occasion to*

assert that the higher powers of the reflective intellect are more decidedly and more usefully tasked by the unostentatious game of draughts [checkers] than by all the elaborate frivolity of chess.

Chess was a metaphor Poe would return to throughout the story—and, in an understated way, an allegory to how he dealt with relationships in his everyday life. Poe's life revolved around writing and complaining (very little editing, incidentally). He pitied himself and the opportunities he was not given (and thought he deserved), routinely feeling sorry for each situation in which he found himself (whether self-inflicted or not). Like any aspiring writer, Edgar Allan Poe dreamed of earning a living from the letters he put together to form his stories. Poe was thirty-two years old in 1841. He had lived in Richmond, Virginia, and Boston by this time. He had been "classically educated" in Scotland and England between the years 1815 and 1820; he had attended the University of Virginia for eleven months, where he literally gambled away his chances of completing an education there. It was only after his legal guardian, wealthy Richmond merchant John Allan, refused to pay for the remainder of Poe's education at the university that the young man returned to Allan's home, met Elmira Royster, to whom he became engaged in 1826, and quickly took off once again. (Royster would eventually break it off with Poe and marry someone else.)

Poe's response to his surrogate father shutting off his flow of cash was quite disdainful, even for a man whose bullish and contentious reputation preceded him, and yet it was also scornfully Poe-etic in each carefully chosen word: "In a moment of caprice you had blasted my hope," young Poe wrote to the closest person he had ever known as a father figure.

Notwithstanding his abrasive nature, his cocky attitude, and the fact that *Graham's* was printing his stories and poems, Edgar Allan Poe was not happy in Philadelphia during the spring of 1841. The city was not doing anything for the man; and his job at *Graham's* was paying only enough for him to eat and feed his chronic alcohol habit. Poe had just gotten over an "illness of undefined character" that would "occur with increasing frequency until his death," one of his early biographers, George E. Woodberry, wrote. He longed to knock elbows with those writers in New York, whom he viewed as the best in the world. He had lived in New York (near Canal Street) during the early 1830s for a brief stretch, but the experience was anything but fulfilling. "I have no money—no friends," the poet wrote then.

Still, ten years hence, Poe was itching to return to New York, and he was on the threshold of producing those great works that would immortalize his reputation as a scribe. "The Raven" was right around the corner. So was "The Gold-Bug," a prize-winning, if obscure, story about a man, William LeGrand, who is bitten by a gold-colored bug and begins to act insanely, irrationally, and tragically. The plot deals with cryptogram solving, a secret message leading to a treasure.

But there was another story, one that would put Samuel Adams, John C. Colt, and Edgar Allan Poe on the same page, so to speak. It involved a dead body, a voyage aboard a passenger ship, and an oblong-shaped wooden box with a terrible stench. Poe would not publish the story for another four years, but "The Oblong Box" would tell a tale many believed simply fell from the imagination of a then-drunken, broke poet whose obsession with death was making him famous while at the same time slowly killing him. In this story, which epitomizes Poe's knack for taking an everyday life situation and twisting and turning it until every dark drop of drama has been wrung from its recesses, a man is on a passenger ship with friends heading from South Carolina to New York City. The narrator, early into the tale, notices an oblong-shaped crate in the quarters of his "acquaintance." The box is described as "six feet in length by two and a half in breadth." The narrator "observed it attentively . . ." The box made him curious. It was the shape that caught the narrator's eye as particularly "PECULIAR; and no sooner had I seen it," he adds early in the story, "than I took credit to myself for the accuracy of my guessing."

Not only was Poe patting himself on the back in that last passage, but in a stroke of genius, he placed this elephant in the room so that the tension and mystery in the remainder of the tale could be built around it.

There was something else the narrator noticed—that is, besides the odd, coffin-like shape of the box and the fact that its proprietor did not want the box taken from his stateroom. The box "emitted a strong, disagreeable, and, to my fancy, a peculiarly disgusting odor."

The impetus and inspiration for "The Oblong Box" came to Poe when he read about Samuel Adams long after Adams took that walk up Broadway toward Chambers Street and was never seen again. Poe couldn't have asked for better raw material; the true story of Samuel Adams's last day was as gruesome and unbelievable as the kind of fiction Poe was writing. With all the drama and sensationalism surrounding that meeting between Samuel Adams and John Colt and the day Edgar Allan Poe ran across the Colt/Adams story in the newspaper, there could have been only one teller of tales with the nerve and talent to turn those incredible events into a piece of art.

As Adams walked toward the Chambers Street and Broadway address he knew was not only where John Colt worked but also where he often slept, it is safe to say that he had only one additional task on his mind besides collecting money owed him and addressing the painful thought of being double-crossed: a face-to-face with the man he believed had stolen from him and, even worse, made him a fool. Adams knew there were going to be a few choice words, maybe a fist-pound on the man's desk, and a demand for an explanation.

John Colt, on the other hand, was under the impression that Adams had scammed *him*. On his way up to Chambers Street, Adams had run into another business associate who had told him there had been a miscommunication between Adams and Colt.

This calmed Adams some. It made him feel, perhaps, that Colt hadn't done anything intentionally wrong. It was possible that it was all a terrible mix-up. It was a good thing, Adams now surmised, that he was going to speak with Colt in person, even though he had no idea if Colt was even in town and at his office. The last Adams had heard, John Colt was in Philadelphia.

A vendor who had seen Adams would later explain, "I told Mr. Adams that Colt expected the proceeds; I thought it my duty to tell him . . ."

To that statement, Adams "did not show temper, but seemed surprised that there could have been a misunderstanding," the vendor added.

Adams was a man of very few words. What's more, "I do not recollect," said the vendor, ". . . that Mr. Adams was vexed when he left my store."

The vendor was under the impression, after speaking with Colt some days prior, that he—Colt—was "the owner of the property" in question (meaning the copyright holder). But Adams, when he and the vendor crossed paths that afternoon, explained that he was the one who held the copyright.

Samuel Adams ran his print shop at 59 Gold Street, on the corner of Ann, downtown. Just a little more than a half-mile away, on Chambers, past City Hall, about four blocks northeast of the modern-day World Trade Center site, was the Granite Building Adams had been so eager to visit. Adams had moved to New York seven years prior to this day. He began his career as a journeyman printer and soon "entered into [a] partnership with a Scotchman named Scatchard," an article written about him in 1841 reported. They opened a business under the name Scatchard and Adams. When Scatchard died a few years after the business opened, Adams continued running it by himself. After a fire had just about destroyed the business—"he lost nearly all his property . . . and partly by failure of those who owed him," the article continued—Adams ended up with an unnerving debt of $5,000, an enormous sum then.

Although Adams's wife did not know where her husband was heading on this afternoon, Emmeline Adams had endured a prophetic, night-marish dream the previous evening. The ghastly vision that woke her was the bloodied corpse of her beloved Samuel, dismembered and stuffed in a box—a dream, as things would soon play out inside John Colt's office, that would turn out to be astonishingly close to reality.

PART I

1

Clashing Foils

THE KILLER WAS MERELY A FUNGUS, AN AGGRESSIVE AIRBORNE MOLD botanists referred to by the scientific name *phytophthora ifestans*. This particular strand of the destructive parasite was dark in color, and shaped like an amoeba. With a body similar to that of a lesion, what was more commonly called "late blight" bore a mysterious—and perhaps prophetic—similarity to skin cancer. Yet it was easily ten times deadlier. Such a common, although devastating, organism, harmless to only a handful of plants, *phytophthora* sent millions of Irish to early graves, ultimately forcing surviving members of their families, with nothing more than the clothes on their backs and a bit of old-fashioned hope, to look toward America as redeemer.

During the early 1840s New York City went through the largest migration of Irish Catholics in history, all of whom were driven to the States by the great potato famine—or "potato blight"—back home. Most were good, wholesome, honest, hardworking people. Others were myopic, angry men, demoralized and desperate women and children in tow, starving, and on the verge of death, prepared to do whatever it took to survive. They arrived at Castle Garden, a former Revolutionary War post at the point of the city, and appeared on the docks up and down the Hudson and East Rivers, dirty and unkempt, bitter, broken and beaten, searching for a new life in a city considered to be the capital of the world. So enormous was this one single exodus that by 1850 Manhattan would be home to 133,730 Irish-born inhabitants—a number that by 1913 would swell into the millions.

With such a mass resettlement in such a short span of time, a tidal wave of violent crime erupted in the city. Such was the case in a section known as "Five Points," a neighborhood located in Manhattan's Sixth

Ward near Mulberry (today what we might call Chinatown and Little Italy, an area appropriately near the New York Criminal Court building). In his late-nineteenth-century book, *The Encyclopedia of New York City*, Kenneth Jackson made the claim that in this one small quadrant of the city there was one murder per day. Charles Dickens, on his first visit to the States in 1842—here on an American tour to, among other things, oppose slavery—was astonished by what he witnessed at Five Points. He said Five Points reeked "everywhere with dirt and filth." Crime was so rampant and brutal in this small section of the city—later called the first slum in America—that Dickens noted, the "very houses [are] prematurely old." The infrastructure alone, Dickens pointed out in his trademark dramatic, exaggerated prose, with its "rotten beams," was "tumbling down, and . . . the patched and broken windows seem to scowl dimly, like eyes that have been hurt in drunken frays."

Dickens referred to Five Points residents as "pigs," leaving his readers two questions, and ultimately, with one broad stroke of his quill, insulting native New Yorkers in the process: "Do they ever wonder why their masters walk upright in lieu of going on all-fours? And why they talk instead of grunting?" The well-known writer was so frightened during his first trip to the city he traveled with a police escort.

Thus, if nothing else, 1840s Manhattan was a fluid, rapidly growing metropolis, with thousands of immigrants arriving on an average day, roaming the streets and avenues that same night. Many of the children aboard the incoming ships, eager to reach American shores and take in all that the Promised Land offered, would be dead inside twenty years—casualties of the Civil War. But as the decade, which would eventually produce such infamous phrases associated with violence and murder as "the Gangs of New York" and "the Westies," dawned, many were unable to find work. The pot of gold they had perhaps dreamed of while watching the salty waves crash against the bow of their ships on the way here was nothing more than a mirage. An empty promise, filled by much of the same disenchantment they had fled.

⌒⌒

An accountant and self-described "teacher of writing," Asa Wheeler witnessed the mass migration into the city during the early 1840s firsthand while staring out the windows of his second-story downtown Manhattan office, as well as walking to and from his Thirtieth Street home every workday. America was coming out of the Age of Jackson, an era during which people became immensely interested in the process of electing and the power the presidency held. Some called this the Reform Era, when economic and social change swept across the United States, the epicenter of it all, of course, right there in New York City.

Himself an idealist, Asa Wheeler had carved out his own small piece of the American dream while working in the financial district near Five Points. The married, middle-aged man loved his work, prided himself on his uncanny ability to understand numbers and their power to raise a company above the fray or destroy it slowly like a cancer.

It was 2:30 p.m., on September 17, 1841, when Asa Wheeler looked up from his wooden desk and heard a rustle at his office door. Walking in was sixteen-year-old Arzac Seignette. The boy, Asa's pupil for the day, said hello, placed his hat on the table nearest to the desk, and sat facing his tutor. Across the street from the Granite Building, where the Tweed Courthouse and City Hall would soon stand, the trees swayed sluggishly against a gentle breeze. Men and women frolicked in the streets and along the green of the City Hall Park, as they often did on nice days in the city, looking forward to the upcoming weekend. The garb was Victorian: Men wore duck-tail jackets, pantaloons, top hats, gloves, vests, and bow ties; while the women, their hair up, donned bonnets, petticoats, heavy bell-shaped skirts made from Cartridge pleats with uncomfortably tight waistlines, dramatic boned bodices with V-shaped necklines and collapsed sleeves, as much jewelry as they could manage, flounces, white gloves to cap everything off, and shawls if the weather was cool.

New York was thriving, growing all around Asa. Boardwalked business fronts—like in small towns across the west—and cobblestone streets added to what was an English feel, which winning the Revolution hadn't erased. Much of downtown was in a state of recovery after the Great Fire of 1835 nearly gutted the city's wooden downtown district. On certain evenings, with the mist rolling off the East and Hudson Rivers, converging here on the southeastern tip, there was an unnerving strangeness, one that we'd now recognize as a Jekyll-and-Hyde atmosphere.

The corner street office in which Asa Wheeler tutored students like Arzac Seignette had a clear view of Broadway one story below. Seignette sat at a desk facing the busy thoroughfare, horses and carriages carrying New York elite from one end of Park Row and Broadway to the other. As Seignette got comfortable in his seat and the lesson of the day began, Asa Wheeler heard someone enter the building. It was near 3:00 p.m. The man walked past Asa's office and stepped into an office two doors down the hall. The proprietor of that office, John Caldwell Colt (JC), was also a bookkeeper. The Colt name itself was synonymous with status around the city. People knew John Colt, for sure. But they associated JC with his brother, Samuel Colt, an inventor working on several gun patents, many of which would soon revolutionize the world, including the soon-to-be world-famous Colt revolver. Sam Colt lived in the city but was in the process of opening one of the first state-of-the-art manufacturing plants in the United States across the river in Paterson, New Jersey. Like his great-grandfather before him, Major John Caldwell, one of the "richest and most prominent men" to hail from Hartford, Connecticut, by the time of his death in 1862, Sam Colt would amass a fortune worth a reported $200 million, which translates into billions today.

John Colt and Asa Wheeler had met in 1838, when JC was working his way through the business district in Manhattan, promoting a revolutionary way of double-entry bookkeeping he claimed to have developed. JC had published *The Science of Double Entry Book-keeping* that same year, a definitive textbook on the subject. The book was the talk of the industry. For maybe the first time, JC had explained the technical side of bookkeeping in lay terms and facilitated an understandable proposal of tracking where money came from and, maybe more importantly, where it went. The concept had been around since the 1200s, but no one had put it to use in such a simple, innovative way as JC had in the 1830s.

It was eight weeks prior to this particular September 1841 day when JC, looking for office space to rent, had called on Asa Wheeler, whom he knew to be occupying two offices in the Granite Building. This was the ideal location to fulfill the plans John Colt had made for his future. Here, downtown, he would be directly in the thick of the financial district and, equally imperative to his plan, close to many bookbinders and printers. JC had his second book on accounting printed and ready to ship.

"[He]," Asa later said, speaking of JC, "requested me to let him one [office space] for six weeks."

Colt was to pay Asa $10 at the end of four weeks, and $5 each for any additional weeks after that. September 4, 1841, was supposed to be JC's final day renting the office space.

But JC was still in the building nearly two weeks later, not making any attempt to leave.

The rooms "adjoin each other," Asa explained, describing the office space the men shared. "The entrance [is] on Chambers Street. Colt's room was the second door. The door swung in. My room was at the corner and there were folding doors in between that and the one occupied by Colt."

Colt's room had a window facing Chambers Street. Inside, Colt kept a few chairs, a table, a box, a trunk, a desk, books, paper, ink, pens, firewood, a small hatchet, a hammer, a saw he had borrowed the previous day, and plenty of essentials an accountant and author in mid-nineteenth-century New York might be inclined to use throughout his day.

Asa and JC met frequently in the hallway between the rooms and chatted. Because their rooms were connected via those double doors (a set of what we might call French doors today), they often walked in and out of each other's office space to borrow writing supplies or converse. Just recently, Asa had badgered JC about paying his end of the rent. It seemed John Colt—despite his so-called wealthy brother and his own success in bookkeeping and book publishing—did not like to pay his bills.

"Have these books," Colt told Asa one day before their chat that August, handing Asa several copies of his accounting book.

Asa Wheeler looked at them. "We were on good terms again," Asa said later, meaning he accepted the books as a "good faith" down payment for the rent.

But still, Asa told JC, "I need the office." The books were a token of peace; but Asa needed the space back. His tutoring business was growing. More students meant more revenue.

"One week longer?" JC asked.

Asa agreed.

That additional week, however, had come and gone.

As Asa was explaining the day's lesson to his student, Arzac Seignette, the session was interrupted by a tremendous boom coming from down the hallway, in the direction of John Colt's office. Asa didn't even know if JC was in his office. He had not seen him that day. Colt was said to be in Philadelphia conducting business.

"Heard a noise as if you laid hold of a man and threw him down without much trouble," Arzac Seignette said later, describing the commotion as it unfolded.

Asa Wheeler jumped up from his seat. Arzac Seignette stood.

"What was that?" Asa said to his pupil, probably more as a reaction than a query.

Arzac Seignette followed as Asa walked toward the door leading out of his office.

"I heard a noise like the clashing of foils and a violent fall on the floor," Asa Wheeler said, talking about what would become one of the most profound and memorable moments of his life.

"What is that?" Arzac Seignette asked his tutor as Asa opened the door to his office and walked into the hallway.

"I do not know," Asa said.

They loitered there about the hallway. Asa looked toward JC's office space. The noise had surely come from that direction.

2

Black Hats & Ink

ONE OF THE MORE UNFORGETTABLE RIBBON-CUTTING MOMENTS IN NEW York City occurred five months before that summery September day when Samuel Adams disappeared. Horace Greeley, a thirty-year-old entrepreneur and native New Englander, having been born and raised in New Hampshire, made history in April 1841 when he started the presses inside the *New York Tribune* building near Park Row, an immense structure that would sky upward of some 260 feet in the coming years. As it happened, New York City was becoming the media capital of the world—more than one hundred periodicals and twelve dailies already being published—and would continue to grow in that respect for decades to come. The newspaper Greeley opened, however, was not just a run-of-the-mill publishing venture. Having managed a weekly called the *New Yorker*, the well-known editor's *Tribune* would be a personal obsession, a bully pulpit for the publisher to voice his staunch objections to slavery and corrupt New York politics; to channel his unrestricted zeal for social reform; and to amplify his rather thunderous opposition to gambling, alcohol, tobacco, prostitution, and capital punishment.

Before the first edition of the newspaper hit the streets, Greeley let his New York readers know exactly what type of publication they were going to be purchasing for a penny, writing: "The *Tribune*, as its name imports, will labor to advance the interests of the People, and to promote their Moral, Social and Political well-being. The immoral and degrading Police Reports, Advertisements and other mutter which have been allowed to disgrace the columns of our leading Penny Papers, will be carefully excluded from this, and no exertion spared to render it worthy of the hearty approval of the virtuous and refined, and a welcome visitant at the family fireside."

Of course, the *Trib* did plan on running a bit of sensational news. Greeley was interested in the pulse of New York's economic and social heartbeat, approaching readers with passion and vehemence, while employing in-your-face reporting that shocked as much as informed. This, mind you, as one of the more innovative periods in American history erupted.

Starting a newspaper was a major gamble. New York was coming out of a desperate time—the panic of 1837, a bona fide economic depression. But it was sensationalism and controversy driving newspaper sales, and Greeley understood that. Murder and mayhem, fear and fright, would spawn sales (as they do today) of a newspaper Greeley promised would trumpet "Right Reason and Public Good," while overcoming "Error and Sinister Ambition."

That burning crusade for good Greeley lived by drove Asa Wheeler, as well. Asa was a man who believed in truth and justice for the average man and, it turned out, his nosy neighbor. Beyond his character faults, Asa Wheeler did not take lightly the idea that a man could, with status and wealth alone, pull one over on his fellows. That tremendous crash Asa Wheeler and Arzac Seignette had heard as they sat in Asa's office studying the day's lesson had brought the men to their feet and down the hallway toward JC's office.

Asa put an ear up to Colt's door, but "all was still," he later remembered.

So JC's landlord got down on bended knees and, closing one eye, looked through the keyhole.

"I found that the drop was down inside," Asa said. There was a piece of metal blocking his view. He could not see anything.

Taking his favorite pen out of his pocket, Asa finagled the pointy end into the keyhole and was able to push the drop to one side.

A ray of light met his pupil.

Again with one eye closed, this time Asa saw a shadowy figure, in silhouette, "in a position of bending down over something." The person stood close by the west wall inside John Colt's office, in his "shirt sleeves," and seemed to be staring at something on the floor that Asa could not see.

"On the table were two black hats," Asa said. "The person remained in the recumbent position for ten minutes."

Arzac Seignette stood behind his teacher. He asked what was happening, what was Asa looking at? Did he have any idea what had made that loud bang?

As Asa continued watching, the man behind the door, a man Asa did not recognize because he could not make out his facial features, walked over to a table in the room and placed "something" down, and then returned to the same spot ("in the same position") near the west wall.

The behavior Asa witnessed, coupled with the crash, made the accountant-teacher nervous. He was certain something wicked had taken place inside John Colt's office space.

"Come here," Asa instructed his pupil. They walked back down toward Asa's office. "You stand in my door and watch Mr. Colt's door till I go upstairs and find the owner of the building and procure advice or help."

It was now close to "the hour of dinner," Asa later said, somewhere in the neighborhood of six o'clock.

When Asa returned, he had a man with him. Arzac Seignette later referred to this man only as "Mr. Oakland," another tenant from the building.

Both Oakland and Asa tried to look through the keyhole and push the drop to the side, but this time the metal slide was stopped up by something.

Asa knocked on the door. "Who's in there?"

Meanwhile, two of Asa's students had entered the building, ready for the evening class, and stood with Mr. Oakland, Asa, and Arzac Seignette by John Colt's door.

"No person had gone into Colt's door," Arzac Seignette explained, "nor did I hear any voice in the room. Had not seen Mr. Colt that day and did not know him."

Twenty-six-year-old John Delnous, a bookkeeper who had been looking to rent Colt's office space after he vacated it, had arrived that evening to speak to Asa Wheeler about the office, only to find this dramatic commotion going on.

"John . . . John," Asa said, "please go find an officer and bring him here at once."

Delnous took off immediately.

A scholar from another section of the building, a man they called Seldon, had heard what he later described as "the sound like striking of foils on crossing each other." Seldon explained to the others as they stood near Colt's door, waiting for a police officer, that after the loud noise, he heard a "fall immediately . . . Did not think it was foils, but cannot compare it to anything else." Further, he explained, as he listened more intently after the crash, he thought he "heard a noise of struggling or something like that."

Outside on Broadway, the rain had kicked up, making the streets muddy, slippery, and messy. Asa and his crew decided that the best thing to do was to wait for the police. They could not barge into Colt's office without just reason or cause. The sudden sound of a crash was not enough.

John Delnous returned after going to fetch an officer. "They're engaged," he told Asa, "and would come in one half hour."

Asa sent his two students to tell the police it was urgent. They were desperate for help.

An hour later, the police sent word to Asa that "they would not dare to open the door," but insisted, Asa later said, that he and anyone else he could get to help him "keep watch" until the hour came to pass when they could spare an officer to send.

—◦—

The New York City police force—if it could be called such—of early- and mid-nineteenth century consisted of a mishmash group of angry vigilantes fed up with being victimized, citizens protecting their own property any way they could, and a small, inexperienced, full-time force of marshals, constables, and watchmen modeled after a structure England had installed back in the 1600s. Night watchmen patrolled city streets, mainly in the southern area of Wall Street and up at the Bowery toward the north, where the city's slaughterhouses attracted butchers from all over. The watchmen came out before the sun went down and walked the beat until sunrise. Mostly, these men were on the lookout for pickpockets, muggers, thieves, and gang-related crime. There was no ordered, organized police force, as we might think of it today, until the 1840s, when New York decided to adopt the modernized concepts the English had developed back in the mother country.

Most of the appointed officers were chosen by aldermen in various wards throughout the lower part of Manhattan. The criminals generally won most of the fights with these lawmen, who had the authority to whip and punish on sight (and site), but were outmatched in numbers and strength, not to mention guts. In a city of nearly three hundred thousand, the eight hundred "officers" chosen to keep order were no match for a growing band of prostitutes, vagabonds, gamblers, rabble-rousers, and ethnic gangs whose lot in life had become taking whatever they wanted by any means necessary.

The one standout in the early decades of New York's law enforcement community was a stubborn man, Jacob Hayes. The barrel-chested,

Napoleon-short, thickly framed cop had been appointed to a law enforcement leadership job in 1798. Hayes was twenty-six years old when he took over the post. He had come from a bloodline injected with obedience, discipline, and authority: Hayes's dad had served in the Revolution under the great general himself, George Washington.

"Old Jacob Hayes was another celebrity of New York," an article in the *Southern Literary Messenger* proudly proclaimed, not long after Hayes died, "no less conspicuous as a police-man . . . the most renowned thief-catcher of his day in America."

Hayes left behind a legacy of "exemplary character," that same article noted, both in "private life, being . . . generous and kind [and] . . . in his public capacity . . . inexorable and stern."

Hayes was the model of an ideal police officer that New York needed, a man on whom the city could base its police force.

"The detection of thieves was his ruling passion," the *Messenger* added, "and in this respect, no man was ever more amply gratified than himself. The delight of a terrier in a room full of rats was small compared with the joy of Jacob, when able to pounce on a gang of notorious criminals."

Hayes stood for integrity and justice within a city in desperate need of a cleansing. He understood that with his job came power, which was easily corrupted.

"The criminal law was the object of his fondest idolatry. He had no touch of pride, but he reverenced himself as its chosen instrument, its living incarnation."

If you were to picture one of these lawmen like Hayes walking the beat in early 1840s New York, maybe along the Bowery or at Five Points, consider a rough-looking gent wearing one of those black stovepipe hats towering higher than a doorframe, a white hanky tied around the nape of his neck, a set of gold or black buttons trailing down his full suit of dark blue, a billy club swinging from his hand. These guys walked proudly, twisting the waxed handles of their mustaches, whistling, their chests puffy and pushed out in front, a snide look about their faces, many waiting for someone to get out of line so they could drop him with the butt of their nightstick. This was an era of true cops-'n'-robbers; men chasing criminals on foot; the good guys (those who refused the bribes) looking to keep order in a city that seemed to symbolize crime and corruption.

During the mid-1830s, crime in Five Points had become rampant, violent, and widespread. In light of the escalation of unlawfulness, a great need for a structured, organized body of lawmen, same as in the Wild West, emerged amid the rubble of a sinking economy and a city-wide fire that decimated daily life for years—men who could intimidate and scare by the mere mention of what they would do to you if you got out of line. Things were beginning to get so bad in the city around this time, even a tough guy like bear wrestler Davy Crockett, describing a day he once spent in the city walking around Five Points, said that he would "rather risque" his chances "in an Indian fight than venture among these creatures."

Auctioneer and former New York City mayor Philip Hone, writing then, called this period in the city he loved, when the bottom literally fell out of the dollar, "[T]he most gloomy . . . which New York has ever known. The number of failures is so great daily that I do not keep record of them, even in my mind!"

It was none other than Jacob Hayes who escorted Charles Dickens, along with a fellow officer, around the city and into Five Points when Dickens came abroad for his infamous tour to the States. Dickens's harsh comments about the lawlessness and scourge he witnessed in Five Points followed him throughout his career, and yet in that same essay, Dickens spoke highly of this new police force Hayes and the city had put together, writing:

It is needful first that we take as our escort two heads of police, whom you would know for sharp and well-trained officers if you met them in the Great Desert. So true it is that certain pursuits, wherever carried on, will stamp men with the same character. These two might have been begotten, born, and bred, in Bow Street.

These were the same lawmen author Edward Spann referred to more than a century later in his book *The New Metropolis: New York City: 1840–1857*, as "haphazard" and "ineffectual," a group of violent policemen who had been "inherited from the previous century," part of an organization Spann called a "fledgling force."

Had there been a more organized, uncorrupted police force in the city, along with enough men to maintain New York City's growing populace and widespread crime problem, Asa Wheeler would have gotten the help he needed the moment he asked for it—and the mystery surrounding a single bump in the night would likely have been solved at that moment. Or, rather, the situation certainly would not have turned into the fiasco, the front-page fodder and raw material for Edgar Allan Poe's fiction that it would soon become.

Asa waited for an officer until nine o'clock on the night of September 17, 1841, but could wait no longer. His life had been disrupted by this episode inside John Colt's office, whatever had happened.

Wheeler and John Delnous sat in Asa's office and talked. They decided there was nothing they could do. It was obvious—or so they thought—no one was inside Colt's office and the police were not going to do anything about what they had reported.

So they left.

Not too long after, John Delnous returned.

"I remained for about a half hour," Delnous explained later, never saying if he had told Asa about his trip back to the office.

As he sat in Asa's office, listening behind the door, which was ajar just a crack, Delnous "heard someone unlock Mr. Colt's door from the inside, come out, lock it again. And go away."

There had been someone inside Colt's office the entire time.

But who?

Delnous wasn't about to play sleuth. He waited. Five minutes passed. He heard footsteps, a door open and close.

He ran down toward Colt's office.

"I heard someone in Mr. Colt's room tearing something resembling cotton cloth," Delnous said.

He moved in closer so he could hear better.

"The next sound was the rattling of water."

As he listened, Delnous thought he heard someone scrubbing the floor, placing a rag or cloth into a bucket of water every so often, then scrubbing once again.

Cleaning? Now?

What in heaven's name was going on in there?

3

Maiden Voyage

Sam Adams failed to return home on the night of September 17, 1841. The last time Emmeline Adams had seen her husband was at noon that same day. They had taken a pleasant lunch together.

"Do not know where he intended to go when he left home," she said, but "he did not return."

Emmeline woke up on the cloudy morning of September 18, 1841, and realized her husband was missing. It was unlike Adams not to return. That dramatic dream Emmeline had in the days before her husband disappeared, in which Sam Adams was murdered in a bloodbath, was likely due to the fact that murder in the city had become fodder for all the tabloids, the talk at meetinghouses, and the topic of the moment on street corners and businesses. There had been a high-profile killing that summer, a crime New Yorkers could not stop talking about, still unsolved. Fear lingered. An unspoken alarm came upon the streets: Who would be next?

It had occurred on the afternoon of July 21, 1841. Twenty-year-old Mary Cecilia Rogers, a stunning young woman, had stood in front of a cigar stand at 319 Broadway and beckoned customers to come in, much like a circus promoter outside his tents. Rogers had told her fiancé, Daniel Payne, "I am going to visit my relative, pick me up at six on Jane Street." She wanted an escort.

When Payne showed up, the woman city dwellers called the "Beautiful Cigar Girl" was nowhere to be found.

Mary had been a customer magnet for John Anderson's "snuff" business, with her fine frame and charming manner. She lived at 126 Nassau Street, her mother's boardinghouse, just a short walk from the cigar stand. Born in Connecticut in 1820, Mary was left fatherless when Mr. Rogers died in an explosion aboard a steamship, a tragedy that sent Mary and her mother to New York during that disastrous financial year, 1837.

Everyone who frequented that end of town knew the young maiden who sold cigars (pronounced "see-gars") by day and worked helping her mother clean and cook meals at night. "Amiable and pleasing," one boarder commented, calling Mary "fascinating." There was an "aloofness" and enigmatic appeal about the girl, drawing people toward her. Mary embodied a burlesque-like seductiveness that attracted more than repelled. So much of a city icon was Mary Rogers that the *New York Herald* published a poem, illustrating lucidly the consequence she had on those who crossed her path: "She moved amid the bland perfume/ That breathes of heaven's balmiest isle;/ Her eyes had starlight's azure gloom/ And a glimpse of heaven—her smile."

When Mary disappeared, the fear was that one of her suitors, the many men who had tipped their hats and smiled, undressing Mary with their eyes as they passed by the tobacco shop each day, had abducted the young woman and did vile and repulsive things to her before snuffing her out.

It was three days hence, July 24, when Mary's bloated and bruised corpse washed ashore on the banks of the Hudson River in New Jersey, near Hoboken. The worst fears of the city had been realized. It appeared Mary had been asphyxiated with a section of her own petticoat, a knot tied in a distinctive pattern, her body dumped in the water after the fact.

Philip Hone, who became the city's diarist during this period, stepped out from underneath his financial hat to write about Mary, certainly because her unsolved murder, as the summer of 1841 came to pass, was first and foremost on the minds of New Yorkers.

"[T]he body of a young female named Mary Cecilia Rogers was found on Thursday last in the river near Hoboken, with horrid marks of violation and violence on her person. She was a beautiful girl."

Hone called the tragedy a "shocking murder." George Walling, one of New York's more famous and respected police superintendents and chiefs (circa 1887), later opined on the most important transgressions of that century, calling Mary Rogers's murder one of the "great crimes that startled the country." Walling, who had the date of Mary's death wrong in his memoir, *Recollections*, said important men such as diplomat, newspaper publisher, and politician James Watson Webb, James Gordon Bennett,

James Fenimore Cooper, Washington Irving, and Edgar Allan Poe (who would write "Mystery of Maria Rogêt" as an homage to Mary) "were acquainted with the dainty figure and pretty face where they bought their cigars," adding how the "excitement following the murder . . . was conspicuously felt by the prominent New Yorkers of the day."

So, as the fall of 1841 approached, many in the city were on edge, waiting for their bumbling, keystone cop police force to find Mary's murderer. The *Herald* was out front with its criticism, calling Mary's homicide an "awful violation," saying that the criminal judges of the city were doing nothing more than "sitting on their own fat for a cushion bench," adding how it was the "the utter inefficiency of their police . . . leading fast to reduce this large city to a savage state of society—without law—without order—and without security of any kind" that was stifling any progress in finding the perpetrator who took Mary from the city.

———

Up at Chambers Street and Broadway, as the clock struck six in the morning on September 18, 1841, John Delnous, who had slept in Asa Wheeler's office, was awoken by a series of familiar sounds emanating from an unlikely source.

"Heard someone nailing a box," Delnous recalled.

It was the *rap, rap, rap* of a hammer banging on a nail, as if men were working.

"The noise awakened me."

Then the vibrating buzz of a saw cutting through a piece of wood, a man's elbow and forearm clearly hard at work.

Delnous got up, rubbed the sleep from his eyes, wandered over to the doorway.

The noises stopped.

John Delnous grabbed his hat and coat and headed out to grab a breakfast of coffee and biscuits.

He returned to the Granite Building an hour later. There was a crowd of people now standing around. One of them was Law Octon, the keeper of the building. Law knew John Colt, as did most everyone, but "had little acquaintance with the tenants." Law had stopped and looked into Colt's keyhole the previous evening with Asa Wheeler. He didn't think anything of what was happening. Just another day in the life of a tenant building, during a time when nosy neighbors ruled the roost. But when Law Octon walked into the building that morning, he saw a box of some sort, constructed from wood scraps, a crate, actually, sitting there "at the head of the first flight of stairs."

As Law walked over to the crate, John Colt emerged from his office. The box was in between the two floors of the building, on a landing. Colt grabbed hold of it, "threw it on its side," dragged it to the stairs, Law observed, "and slid it down." Colt stood in front of the box, using his shoulders and back as leverage to guide the thing down each stair in order to "prevent it going too fast."

John Delnous also noticed the box upon his return. He leaned down and saw that it was addressed to someone in St. Louis by way of New Orleans. "I wanted to ask about the key in the door," Delnous said to Colt, meaning what was going on the previous night when they were trying to look inside the office.

"Go look," Colt said. "The key is in the door."

John C. Colt did not look disheveled or nervous. Tired, yes. But he was a man here in the throes of doing some business with this box. Perhaps it was full of books.

Law Octon looked at the address, written in blue ink, and thought nothing of it. He watched Colt take the box down the stairs toward the main door leading outside, and then went back to work. The two of them, Law said later, never spoke.

Outside on Chambers Street, Colt walked west, toward Church Street. He left the box on a cart of some sort near the entranceway of the Granite Building.

"Are you engaged, sir?" Colt said to a nearby car man, Richard Barstow, who had been sitting in his carriage close to the corner of Church and Chambers.

"No, sir," Barstow said. "Where to?"

Colt explained that he had a crate he needed hauled to Maiden Lane.

Broadway was the first New York street lit up at night by gas lanterns, the type of antique posts on corners dotted about the city, those lights resembling glimmering stars from a distance on a foggy night. Maiden Lane was second. By the 1840s, Maiden Lane had already made its name as one of those soon-to-be-timeless Manhattan streets with a unique piece of history attached to it. In that devastating fire that ravaged the city in 1835, burning some 674 buildings to the ground, Maiden Lane was the first to go up in flames. Thomas Jefferson lived on Maiden Lane in 1790 for six months. It was the sole location in the city at one time (1827) where you could shop underneath a skylight-covered section called the "New York Arcade." Maiden Lane got its name during the Dutch-Manhattan days, when men would "drive the cows" from the north, down along the shores of the East River, and make that hairpin turn on Broadway (Boston Road then) near Maiden Lane, where the women washed clothes in a pond and hung the saturated linen on clotheslines. Cow Lane and Shortcut, it has been said, were names once considered; but Maiden Lane, where the ebb and flow of New York life converged, seemed far more appropriate. Colt had chosen Maiden Lane for his crate because there were several shipping companies there that could transport the package down to the docks and place it aboard a ship headed in the direction of the address.

Barstow followed Colt back to the Granite Building's front entrance.

"There was a spring cart opposite to the door," Barstow explained later, "standing sideways with the head toward Broadway."

While Colt stood by and watched, Barstow backed his buggy up to the doorway.

Colt walked into the building. Barstow followed.

"The box lay alongside the balusters," Barstow noted. "The car man who was there with the spring cart took hold of the box with me, and we took it up and we put it on my cart."

After Barstow and the other car man got the box situated in the back of Barstow's carriage, his horse waiting for the order to *giddy up*, Barstow asked Colt where exactly he wanted the box dropped off on Maiden Lane.

"I do not know," Colt said, meaning the name of the company. "It is at the foot of Maiden Lane. I will go along with you."

As it generally did, Maiden Lane bustled with crowds of people. Colt had no plan. He needed this crate shipped to New Orleans, a destination he had told no one about.

But Barstow noticed the crate was addressed to New Orleans, and he knew of a ship bound for that city. He indicated to Colt, who was riding along shotgun with him, that a ship heading for that location was docked and boarding freight. As they came upon it, he peered toward the ship as its pointed bow, like the beak of a parrot, gently swayed to the music of the East River.

The rain had started to fall aggressively. The streets were mud. Traveling toward the dock, Barstow noticed how dirty the box had become from the short trip and mentioned to Colt that it should be cleaned up before they put it down on the docks to be shipped.

Colt said he would do it himself. Barstow pulled up to the wharf near the end of Maiden Lane. Traditionally, this would have been Ferry's Wharf, located east of Water Street, on the waterfront. It was the same spot where Thomas Jefferson, when he had business on Long Island, took the ferry across the river. There was also Taylor's Wharf, located between Maiden Lane and Fletcher Street. Neither Colt nor Barstow ever said which wharf they had rolled up on.

The ship hovered over Colt's shoulder as he stepped down from Barstow's carriage and paid the man "two and sixpence" for the ride and his help. Before him was the mighty *Kalamazoo*, a 789-ton American vessel that had seen her time at sea. The ship routinely traveled to England, the Gulf of Mexico, Florida, and the Caribbean islands.

JC had found a transporter for his crate.

———

Back at the Granite Building, Asa Wheeler arrived for his day. He had learned his business ethics by working with his father in a shoe factory and brickyard the family ran on their New Hampshire farm during his youth. It was there, Asa later said, where he "acquired some knowledge of bookkeeping," by helping his dad manage the business. Soon, Asa went from getting his hands dirty in the warehouse and fields to working in an office. Teaching became a natural fit for the young farmer's son, who started to tutor farmhands in his spare time. At age sixteen, Asa left home and trekked through New England, looking for work in Maine, Vermont, Massachusetts, and Connecticut, finally settling in New York City some years later. Arriving in the city with what he said was five dollars in his pocket, Asa Wheeler, listening to his father's advice about "not running too much into debt," started to teach writing, penmanship, and book-keeping. After working for a year or so as the bookkeeper for a drugstore on Broadway, it didn't take Asa long to build a reputation "as a professor of penmanship." Young Asa had the patience and will required to teach. "He was introduced to the best families in the city to give instructions in writing, and also gave instruction in all the principal schools in town," an article about him reported, adding, "[He] was an indefatigable worker; he had never an idle or profitless hour." It was said that Asa Wheeler, at times, taught students from 4:00 a.m. to 9:00 p.m., an incredible feat of will by any standards. He started teaching full time with an office (or school) on Broadway and Murray Street reportedly above Tiffany's; then, because he needed more space, ended up at Broadway and Chambers, where he rented several rooms (offices) to other tutors.

Considering himself to be of the highest moral character, Asa Wheeler did not much appreciate John Colt's sluggish, often temperamental opinions about their work and profession. Colt was extremely vocal regarding his theories of bookkeeping. "[Colt] made some scathing criticisms about the teaching styles of the other prominent accounting authors of his day," wrote Dr. Jan Heier, an associate professor of accounting at Auburn-Montgomery University, with a Doctor of Business Administration degree from Mississippi State, who wrote about Colt's unique and purported groundbreaking bookkeeping ideas. "Colt discussed some interesting, though incorrect, theories regarding the origins of double-entry bookkeeping."

On this point about accounting, Colt and Asa Wheeler clashed.

"He was a high-strung fellow," Asa later said of Colt, "and quick to anger." Yet Asa could handle that. It was Colt's social and home life that rang Asa's bell from time to time. No one believed John Colt when he said he was married to Caroline Henshaw, the woman with whom he lived. That was probably one of the reasons why Asa Wheeler, when he heard that crash inside Colt's office the night before, was curious to find out what might have happened. With John Colt, one never knew what was going to happen from one minute to the next.

The first thing Asa Wheeler did after putting his belongings down on his desk that morning of September 18, 1841, was to knock on Colt's door.

With no answer, he tracked down a key to Colt's room. Asa's curiosity had gotten the best of him. He needed to see what was behind Colt's door.

Asa said he "only stepped one foot in and looked around." He did not want to go snooping inside Colt's office, or disturb anything, but he was certain something had happened and was determined to find out what.

The first thing Asa noticed was that the box over which he had seen the standing, silhouetted man the previous night was gone. More than that, the wooden floor around where the box had lain, in addition to a long path from Colt's desk to the area where Asa had seen the man standing, had been scrubbed.

"The part where I supposed I saw the man standing the day previous was more scrubbed than the rest."

Most intriguing to Asa Wheeler was that what appeared to be oil and ink "had been spilt round the base of the floor, and thrown in spots on the wall."

Asa wondered why. He closed the door—no one had seen him enter Colt's room—and retreated to his office down the hall. As he sat, Asa Wheeler considered how odd it was that the scrubbing was confined to the center of the room and "not quite dry."

Near 10:00 a.m., as Asa commenced his work, he was interrupted by a knock on his office door.

It was John Colt, just back from the wharf.

"Would your key fit into my door?" Colt asked.

This startled Asa Wheeler. He asked Colt to explain. Where was *his* key?

"I left my key at home," Colt said. "I wish to enter my room."

"I do not know," Asa said. He handed Colt his key. "But you might try."

Colt took Asa's key and walked toward his room, returning a moment later, explaining to Asa that the key did not fit. He'd have to head back home and retrieve his own. Before leaving, however, Colt "commenced to talking about book-keeping and writing, in which we were both engaged," Asa later said. He seemed manic. He carried on and on, making little sense.

"Mr. Colt," Asa asked at one point, changing the subject, "what noise was that in your room yesterday afternoon?"

"You must be mistaken," Colt said without hesitation, "as I was out all afternoon."

"There was certainly a noise," Asa insisted, "and it had quite alarmed us!"

Colt walked out of Asa's room without saying another word.

4

Family Ties

ADDRESSING ACQUAINTANCES AND POTENTIAL BUSINESS PARTNERS, John Colt explained that his brother, Samuel, was a successful and well-respected gun manufacturer and inventor. Sam and John were, after all, as tight as bricks, sharing a secret that could ruin Sam and further taint John's declining reputation. The truth was, during the fall of 1841, Sam Colt was nearly broke and under enormous pressure to acquire additional investors for his numerous inventions. Sam lived in New York City, but his Patent Arms Manufacturing Company in Paterson, New Jersey—opened in 1835 under $300,000 in investment capital of which Sam owned a third—was struggling to maintain a balance of finance, arms production, and base of customers who believed in Sam's weapons. Sam's revolver, which he had been working on since 1830 at the age of sixteen, one could argue, had not yet taken off. Beyond that, with a "lack of available machinery and manpower," wrote Colt biographer Bill Hosley, "cost-efficient production never stood a chance so long as the inventor continued to make design changes in the midst of production."

Sam and John had been raised in a nontraditional, struggling New England family. John Caldwell Colt (b.1810) was Sarah and Christopher Colt's third child, Sam (b.1814) their fourth. Christopher Colt was a speculator, a man who ventured into just about anything he thought would make him rich quickly. Sarah's father, the indelible Hartford businessman Major John Caldwell, who founded the first bank in Connecticut's capital city, didn't appreciate Christopher when Sarah first brought him home. There was a P. T. Barnum side of Christopher, who was said to have sold snake oils and elixirs out of the back of a wagon at one time. At the turn of the nineteenth century, Christopher was broke and jobless. He showed no future prospects, at least in the eyes of the highly successful Major Caldwell, who looked down upon the young man's reputation for gambling on gold and any other schemes that crossed his path.

Relenting to his daughter's pleadings, however, Major Caldwell signed off on the marriage—that is, providing Christopher became a working man in what had been a Caldwell family business tradition: the Triangle Trade. From Africa, slaves were shipped to the Americas; from there, sugar, tobacco, and cotton were forwarded to Europe; and, completing the triangle, rum, textiles, and manufactured goods were sent back to Africa. There were additional products involved, of course: whale oil, lumber, furs, molasses, silk, milk, rice, cloth, tools, gunpowder, iron, guns, flour, livestock, and a heap of others. But the Triangle Trade centered on the sale of slaves from Africa to the West Indies for sugar.

"Puritanical Yankees," Colt biographer Bern Keating wrote, "made fortunes trading human flesh and booze."

As did scores of others around the world. By the 1780s, close to an estimated one hundred thousand slaves per year were shipped to North and South America aboard more than eight hundred ships built and sailed for the sole purpose of trading human beings.*

Christopher Colt saw an opportunity and, according to Keating, jumped into it "heartily," becoming "satisfactorily rich" in no time. He found a trade that could, in turn, finance other ventures he was planning. But by the year 1820, both Christopher and his father-in-law, Major Caldwell, found themselves, like a lot of Americans, busted, having been victims of British privateers "waylaying," or pirating, their cargoes, along with a financial panic that occurred stateside in 1819, after growth in trade following the War of 1812 fell off. Essentially, there was tons of credit sitting atop a table with weak legs.

Sam and John's father took his growing family and moved from Hartford to Ware, Massachusetts, where he opened a silk mill. Not a year after the relocation, however, beginning a beaten path of tragedy and bad luck that would follow this family from one generation to the next, Sarah

---

* For more information about this vile part of American history, please see Emert, Phyllis Raybin. 1995. *Colonial triangular trade: an economy based on human misery.* Perspectives on history series. Carlisle, Mass: Discovery Enterprises. Emert's short book (64 pages) tells the history in great detail, using primary sources, giving readers facts and figures. Emert calls it—rightly so—the "triangle of human misery."

became ill. It was tuberculosis. JC was eleven, Sam just about to turn seven. Then, on June 16, 1821, Sarah died.

Christopher Colt found himself with six kids and no wife.

As Sam seemed to put his heart into the gun manufacturing end of his New Jersey–based business during the fall of 1841, his mind—and any little bit of money he had left—was elsewhere. He dabbled assiduously in inventions unrelated to firearms. One was a rather mysterious and closely guarded military project to create an underwater explosive, a mine Sam envisioned sitting in the ocean along the shores of America, protecting her from incoming enemies. Sam had also worked on a "failed telegraph communications company," and patented a powder cartridge design for use underwater—an offshoot of his wet mine—that won him an award and was "marginally profitable," noted Colt historian Bill Hosley.

Brimming with confidence in his wet mine, Sam Colt wrote President John Tyler, telling the commander in chief that his invention would protect the coastline of the United States and ultimately save the government a wad of taxpayer money:

> *It is with a little diffidence that I venture to submit the following for your consideration; feeling that I do as its apparent extravagance may prevent you from paying it that attention which it merits and but for the duty I owe my country in these threatening times, I should still longer delay making this communication. There seems to prevail at this time with all parties a sense of protecting our Sea Coast....*

Sam likely hired someone to write the letter while he dictated its contents; in many of the letters Sam Colt left behind, the uneducated inventor grossly misspelled even the simplest words. Nonetheless, Sam told the president he had been perfecting his idea for five years and promised the government would save "millions in outlay for the construction of means of defense."

While Sam was desperately trying to save a company drowning in debt and ill-fated manufacturing procedures, John Colt left the household Sam had set up on Broadway and Duane. The Colts had some rather high-class, wealthy cousins in New York, including Dudley Selden, the sole reason Sam had gone to New York with his models of a rifle and pistol back in 1835. Upon looking at Sam's models, Selden told his young relative to "draw up his application pictures" so they could see about patenting the weapons.

JC probably told friends, business associates, and family members he wanted to branch out and be on his own. In reality, he moved out of his brother's home for a different reason—namely, a woman, Caroline Henshaw. She was pregnant.

Miss Henshaw, as she was known, was "that rarest of combinations," according to a quasi-investigative piece in *Pearson's Magazine** written by Alfred Henry Lewis about the John Colt–Sam Adams debacle. Henshaw was described by Lewis as "warm," and having "large deep black eyes, hair the color of corn, the whole set off by a complexion compounded of cream and roses." It was easy to understand why the Colt brothers had fallen for the lady. She was beautifully fit and trim; she looked good on John's arm "at the occasional dinner at the Astor, or a more occasional show at Niblo's, or the Park."

But John Colt did not appreciate the notion that his family and the public disapproved of Caroline Henshaw, a dressmaker, spinster, and "general sewer," as Lewis referred to her. Some reports claimed the Colt family had chosen a mate who was "matched to a social degree" with the Colt family, and John was supposed to marry that woman instead. Caroline was from Cherry Street, which, despite having been home to George and Martha Washington at one time, was considered a "second-rate" region of the city which "smelled of plebeian," Lewis noted, knocking the working-class men and women who kept the city running. Along the chain of poverty, Cherry Street was just above "poor old Greenwich Street," famed diarist George Templeton Strong wrote in 1854, talking about how

---

* *Pearson's Magazine* was founded first in London and established in New York between 1899 and 1925 as a monthly publication "devoted to literature, politics, and the arts." Some later claimed it to be better known for "speculative literature," as you'll see in future chapters while reading some of the reporting Alfred Henry Lewis relied on for his story of John Colt's life and times, which Lewis wrote decades *after* the events took place. I quote from *Pearson's* to show how established the Colt name was in pop culture society; and to show how much influence the Colt brand had on people and, in addition, how, perhaps like the Kennedy family of the past fifty years, the Colt name was routinely attacked, even in its infancy. Lewis, according to his biography, was a "journalist and novelist who wrote about social issues." He was well respected and admired during his time. He wrote investigative pieces of journalism for several established and highly regarded magazines.

New York had become "one of the dirtiest cities in the world—and also one of its deadliest." The Colt dwelling on the "socially superior corner" of Broadway and Duane was not where the Colts wanted the socialites of New York to see a Cherry Street girl.

The family voiced their concerns, calling JC a "clod and an ingrate" for falling in love with a common seamstress who came from a part of town in which none of them would be caught dead.

Enraged by this, John Colt "turned his back as squarely on them, and packed off a bag and baggage . . ." and moved.

Where?

Greenwich Street, not far away from where Caroline lived. JC moved into a boardinghouse run by a woman called Mrs. Pickett.

Soon, JC and his future "bride" found their own place and moved in together.

Asa Wheeler did not report to his office on Sunday, September 19, 1841. Yet, he had already begun to investigate the situation regarding all that commotion in John Colt's office. He had called on the owner of the Granite Building the previous day to ask "his advice."

"This is a very, very delicate subject to meddle with," the man told Asa. "We had better wait until we see something in the papers."

Then on Monday morning, Asa showed up bright and early, thinking he might try to find out if John Colt was willing to talk more about what had happened the previous Friday. Outside, the weather had turned unseasonably hot and humid. Many newspapers later reported that a mini–heat wave had settled on the city. Late September was generally cool and crisp in New York, but temperatures were being reported in the mid- to upper-eighties and even low nineties, with the humidity making the simple act of walking a sweat-filled venture. This heat wave, brief as it would turn out to be, would seal John C. Colt's fate.

Asa was leaning against the folding doors between his office and JC's when Colt entered on Monday morning. JC's office, Asa observed, appeared clean. Like someone had spent the weekend tidying up, yet there was a certain austerity to it; the room felt staged.

As the men greeted each other with a smile, "[JC] commenced singing, which was very uncommon," Asa later remarked.

JC seemed to be in a good mood. He smoked. There were a "bunch of matches" spread out on a chair in the center of the room, which now smelled of sulfur.

"Would you like to smoke?" JC offered Asa, who declined.

"Very bad habit," JC offered.

"He said it caused him to spit blood," Asa recalled, "or he did it to prevent spitting blood, cannot say [recall] which."

Because JC suffered from tuberculosis, he was likely explaining to Asa that the smoking helped calm the blood spitting, a symptom of the disease.

Looking around the room, Asa noticed "thirty to forty specks on the wall." He never said what he believed the specks to be. But it looked as if ink had been tossed on the wall from a bottle.

"About that noise again, Mr. Colt," Asa asked.

"To tell you the truth, Mr. Wheeler," JC answered, "I upset my table. Spilt my ink, and knocked down the books, making a deuced muss. I hope it didn't disturb you."

Asa Wheeler walked away from JC and went to see about his work for the day.

John Colt fancied himself a writer. Bookkeeping was just one of many different ways JC had tried to make a living throughout the years. He had written technical articles about accounting and a well-received text on double-entry bookkeeping, published in 1838, which had sent him on the road throughout the country giving lectures and addresses about his trade. But it was fiction that stirred JC's soul; he wrote "sketches," short personal anecdotes and short stories. His dream was to publish these stories in the prestigious magazines of the day.

"Colt was not without his ambitions," Alfred Lewis wrote, "which were all literary."

Between 1836 and 1841, JC had submitted several of his short stories to magazines, one of which was edited by none other than Edgar Allan Poe. Alfred Lewis claimed that "*Graham's* over in Philadelphia had refused most consistently to accept, pay for, or print [JC's stories]."

So, in a strange coincidence within what would become a lifetime of strange coincidences, JC the writer was rejected by the man who would soon be writing fiction inspired by him.

The main reason for the rejection, Lewis observed, claiming to have gotten his information from the editors themselves, was because "the Colt literary output lacked quality, atmosphere, interest . . . and could lay claim to being pulselessly nothing beyond fairly good English."

This rejection was said to have "embittered" JC to the point of frustration and rage. It perhaps explains why, when the opportunity presented itself inside the pages of his self-published book on accounting practices and education, *The Science of Double-entry Bookkeeping*, JC tore into the elite educational establishment of the country, going off on tangents during his lectures and addresses, which he hubristically printed in the back of a book that had little to do with accounting and more to do with settling some type of personal score.

JC was in Cincinnati at a public meeting once, when he gave a lecture titled "An Address on Book-keeping by Double Entry." In Dayton, Ohio, some weeks later, he presented the same lecture again. But it was an address Colt had published in his book, which he never gave in public, that started people talking about how unstable and perhaps bitter the man had become. There were no other accountants, per se, traveling the country, giving angry lectures about the practices of book-keeping. It just seemed a bit over the top, even for a guy as volatile as John Caldwell Colt.

What became clear in his lectures and his writing about accounting was that Colt had waged a war, Dr. Jan Heier later said, which put him "at odds with the education establishment."

Still, Colt was making some rather cogent and sobering points, however couched in aggression and anger they were. For example, in that speech he published but never delivered, Colt talked about how "almost every branch of learning has had its advocate . . . but I can find no advocate on record of book-keeping." He went on to say that education, the "universal cry" and "common breath" of the world, "must be suited to the capacity of the youth, and the wants of man."

Colt was touting an idea that unless the "establishment" taught basic accounting practices in school (which was not being done), the youth of the day would grow up to destroy the country financially.

Dr. Heier called Colt's arguments "accounting apologetics." If nothing else, the man seemed sincere and passionate in his belief that accounting should be taken as seriously as any other school subject.

"There are branches of education useful to men at every stage," Colt wrote, "and occupation in life; and among the number there are few so easily to be acquired, that combine so many beneficial effects as book-keeping by double-entry."

Colt believed this one simple skill—recording where money came from and where it went—could save a company from financial ruin, staving off a monetary meltdown before it occurred. This was probably one of the reasons why, when Sam Adams accused Colt of fudging the numbers of their publishing deal, John Colt became so angry with him.

"Book-keeping is a science," Colt smartly wrote, "of daily and indispensable use, valuable alike to the rich and the poor, the young and the old, the statesman and the man of business."

From an early age, JC felt he had been born into a different kind of family, whose ambitions for self-promotion and self-reliance were part of the pedigree. He believed if you wanted something, you went out and took it: the Colt way. He had little patience for an under- or uneducated man. Education was, from JC's point of view, a tool to use along the path of success. And bookkeeping was an essential part of a man's way in the world.

"If education should be suited for the wants of man," Colt wrote, "then bookkeeping should be taught to all. For all men want a competency to live by; and no property is so secure as that in which the owner trusts not more in its preservation to a treacherous memory, than in a faithful and respected record."

And it would be a case of that "treacherous memory" versus a written record at the center of the search for a missing printer, Samuel Adams, when a strange, early-fall heat wave in New York City, the grounding of the vessel *Kalamazoo* in port at the foot of Maiden Lane, and one truly erratic and unhinged accountant, all converged.

5

Mankiller

HE WORE A TARPAULIN, A LARGE-BRIMMED HAT MADE FROM CANVAS THAT protected his face and head from driving rain or scorching sun. His checkered shirt and "duck trousers" looked sharp on the young boy. It was August 2, 1830. Boston Harbor. Standing near the bow of the *Corvo*, the sixteen-year-old child stared at the massive ship in front of him. Sam Colt was on his way to Calcutta, a trip—if we are to believe Sam's romanticized version of the story—that would change his life and greatly affect the world.

"The Captain & Super cargo will give him good advice," Colt family friend Samuel Lawrence wrote to Christopher Colt regarding Sam Colt's setting out on a trip aboard the *Corvo*, "if required & instruction in seamanship. He is a manly fellow, & have no doubt he will do credit to all concerned. He was in good spirits upon departure."

It had been a rough spell for Sam, JC, and the rest of the Colt children after their mother died from tuberculosis in 1821. Christopher Colt was depressed, at a loss regarding what to do, a single man with such a large family. On March 12, 1823, things got a little easier for Christopher after he married his second wife, Olivia Sargent, a mechanic-engineer's daughter from Hartford. Quickly, though, the Colt kids learned how different Olivia was from their mother, the tender, patient, and lovable Sarah Caldwell Colt.

Olivia "ruled" the Colt household, according to John. "[T]oo often the case," JC later told a reporter, "[Olivia] made it anything but a comfortable home ..."

One of the first things Christopher Colt's new wife did was separate the children, shipping them off to different relatives and friends throughout New England. Sam went first to a farm in Glastonbury, Connecticut, a quaint little town of rolling hills and rock ledges along the eastern bank of the Connecticut River, southeast of Hartford. Sam eventually ended up in

Amherst, Massachusetts, where he was educated at the Amherst Academy beginning in June 1830, for all of six weeks. Sam's course of study was navigation. Olivia wrote to Sam not long after his arrival, letting him know there was an opportunity to travel abroad and study navigation the only way one could truly learn such a thing: aboard the *Corvo*. Olivia was firm and unemotional in her suggestions, displaying a coldness her pen could not hide, doling out orders more than suggestions.

"Now when making a choice of occupation it is time to pause and reflect," Olivia preached. "You stand as it were upon an eminence, a given point of time to take your stand." She told Sam, perhaps seeing in him an entrepreneurial spirit and drive to succeed, to "give up the low frivolous pursuits of a boy—and determine at once you will pursue the steps of Manhood. Cultivate the Virtues that adorn and dignify the Man. Have a strict regard for Honesty and Integrity of character."

Olivia felt the need to explain that it was her job to "admonish" her stepson as he set out into the world by himself. She warned Sam that he would be "exposed to many hurtful temptations," and cautioned him to be prepared. In a sentence that could be construed as harsh, yet still contained sobering truth, Olivia cautioned Sam about his adolescent naiveté, writing, "[Y]our extreme youth will expose you to much that is eval [sic]—but I hope & pray you may be preserved blameless."

Olivia's letter reveals that Sam Colt, as a young man, was not the most obedient and devoted student or son and that Olivia, who had known Sam for seven years by then, was speaking from experience. Like any kid his age, Sam liked to cause mischief and test his parents' tempers. Yet Olivia made it plain that neither she nor Christopher would tolerate anything less than success from the boys. Two years before Olivia and Christopher sent Sam off on his travels, he had put on a rather dangerous and dramatic display of ingenuity, his inventive gene exposing itself at the young age of fourteen. It was July Fourth weekend. Sam thought it the best time to put on a public demonstration of his first true invention: an underwater mine. He printed handbills and passed them around the small town of Ware, Massachusetts. In the flyer, Sam made the guarantee that he would "blow a raft sky high" from a pond near his father's textile mill. So the crowds came, some curious, others no doubt hoping for a good laugh.

The explosion, it turned out, was immense, pushing water into the sky like Old Faithful. But the raft had not stayed in place over the mine and

Sam's spectators were simply drenched with water instead of watching a boat explode before them. In Sam's view, the demonstration was a success. He had proved that he could detonate a weapon under water. Christopher and Olivia did not view the spectacle as a boy genius spreading his wings, however, which was one of the reasons why they believed a trip abroad would serve the child well.

The creative gears inside Sam's head did not stop spinning. As he set out with the *Corvo* crew across the Atlantic, the teenager came up with one of the world's most industrious and perhaps significant inventions, this according to Sam's own recollection. As the legend goes, while Sam sat and watched the *Corvo's* captain steer her large wooden wheel, sixteen-year-old Sam Colt visualized the action of a revolving chamber: the cylinder turning, locking into place, a bullet ready and waiting to be fired. He saw rounds of ammunition spinning in a chamber, like the ship's wheel, ammunition, one after the other, ready for a hammer to be dropped on. So sure of himself and the idea that a chamber of rounds could spin on an arm and lock for a single shot at a time without reload, Sam claimed, he spent the trip whittling the first prototype of a barrel with five holes, a hammer to explode the gunpowder, and a spindle for the contraption to turn on—an invention that would revolutionize war and the battlefield.*

---

* It should be noted that Sam Colt had possibly seen an earlier version of the revolver—in some form of development—before he came up with the idea of the rotating chamber aboard the *Corvo* (if, in fact, this anecdote of his is true). It is unclear if Sam made his first prototype out of wood before reaching the shores of England, or after. The timing is important (and suspect). As Ellsworth Grant writes in his history of Colt Manufacturing, *The Colt Armory* [Grant, Ellsworth S. 1995. *The Colt Armory: a history of Colt's Manufacturing Company, Inc.* Lincoln, R.I.: Mowbray Pub., p. 16], "Although he later claimed he had not been aware of the existence of ancient examples of repeating firearms until his second visit to London in 1835, it is likely that [Sam Colt] had inspected them in the Tower of London in 1831, when the *Corvo* docked in the Thames." More substantial evidence backing an argument that young Sam had not come up with the idea entirely, Ellsworth goes on to note that Sam "may have" witnessed a "repeating flintlock with a rotating chamber breech invented by Elisha Collier of Boston in 1813 and patented in 1818." Collier's version of the revolving firearm weapon was "cumbersome," Ellsworth observed. So there was some work to be done on the invention. But the basic idea was out. Moreover, Collier's weapon was not automatic; the chamber needed to be "rotated by hand." Thus, Colt probably did not copy the design entirely, but surely, if he had seen it before leaving the port of Boston Harbor aboard the *Corvo*, Collier's design played a major role in his own invention. One has to then ask himself if a child of sixteen years would be of mind to consider all of this or simply come up with the invention on his own. Sam Colt was certainly an inventor at this age. When Colt returned to the docks of Boston in 1831 from his sea voyage to Calcutta aboard the *Corvo*, now a seventeen-year-old well-traveled boy on the verge of manhood, he had a wooden model "of his projected revolver" with him, Ellsworth noted. After getting the financial backing from his father, Sam constructed two working prototypes: one did not fire at all; the other blew apart, exploding upon first shot. Within some years, however, Sam would hold the first patent to this world-changing invention.

One writer later called John Caldwell Colt the "favorite son" inside the strange dynamics of the Colt family. It's hard to back up this claim. History tells us that all of the Colt children were treated equally, if not fairly, with the same jarring cynicism and coldness Christopher and Olivia saved for just about everyone else in their lives. They expected the kids to live up to a certain standard Sarah's side of the family held in society; anything less would be met with scolding, discipline, and disdain.

According to an early profile he was a "slim, quick, slight" and "reserved" man, the latter a bit of a stretch. "He stood straight as a lance," that same writer noted, "moved with an alert, springy step, and was not wanting in a highbred air with his dress . . ."

JC stood five feet eleven inches tall, had a "light complexion" against a "large head" and "oval face." His hair was a "profuse light brown, and richly curling."

It was JC's eyes, Alfred Lewis wrote, that set JC apart from others. They seemed to reveal a malevolent nature, what many would later view as a dark soul.

"Cold, hard . . . carrying in their gray depths a sinister shimmer like unto the gleam of a new bowie [knife blade]," Lewis wrote in the dramatic style of reporting often found at the turn of the twentieth century. Using history's greatest ally, retrospection, Lewis claimed JC's eyes, as he grew into a man few living in New York City could claim friendship to, told a tale of the "fires within." It was this buried rage, so encompassing and palpable in JC's conduct and manner, that "could emerge without moment's warning in a consuming, flaming whirl of passion."

Born in 1810, the first brother to Christopher and Sarah Colt's two girls, Margaret and Sarah Ann, JC was crowned a "passionate and revengeful" boy as a youngster growing up in Hartford. "[W]hile at school, in his boyish days, he was not unfrequently [sic] guilty of petty and disgraceful acts."

It would become obvious that JC grew jealous as his family expanded and he grew older, for he seemed forever to be chasing the success of his younger brothers. He began trying to carve out a place in history for himself at an early age, no doubt feeling pressured by the enormous accomplishments his three brothers were on their way toward achieving (James

Colt, the youngest Colt child, was a highly sought after lawyer in St. Louis and was said to have moved to the Midwest to get away from the family; his brother closest in age, Christopher Jr., became a powerful and wealthy merchant). Moreover, the male branch of the Colt pedigree held a garish incarnation the boys felt the need to live up to. JC's grandfather, Benjamin Colt, born from a line of Colchester, England, *Coults*, served with his fellow Colonialists in the Revolution. He survived that bloody conflict and eventually settled in Hadley, Massachusetts, working the land as a farmer. Benjamin married Lucretia Ely, of the famed Ely lineage (a family full of males who carved out their own triumphant and prosperous places in the New World), shortly thereafter. Christopher was born in 1780. When he was old enough to step out on his own, he migrated to Hartford from western Massachusetts to seek his fortune in international shipping and trading. There was a long line of thriving male role models for JC to live up to.

Christopher and Sarah had six children, equally spaced, two years apart, beginning with Margaret in 1806; and almost right away, it was clear that this family would not be strangers to controversy and tragedy.

Margaret was said to be ravishing in her beauty, "with rare accomplishments, fascinating manners, and many virtues." Yet, like JC, she was said to have harbored a terrible temper that she struggled to control in social situations. In 1824, when Margaret was eighteen (a second account puts her at twenty-one, the year 1826), she was in love and engaged to be married. But after accusing her lover of an "imaginary slight" (no doubt infidelity), Margaret could not let it go and she and her beau broke off the engagement.

Margaret's lover allowed her ample opportunity to apologize and admit her faults. But Margaret "was too proud to betray her feelings."

Eight months after the broken engagement, Margaret received an invitation to her former lover's wedding.

Margaret accepted the invitation, according to JC's account in a pamphlet later billed as *Confession*, "cheerfully." She was willing, apparently, to forgive and forget.

Christopher Colt was said to have purchased an expensive white gown made of satin for his daughter so she could attend what was supposed to be the social event of the season. Margaret was a Colt, after all. She would show up and prove the Colts were survivors; Margaret was to be "the belle of the evening," rubbing her newfound happiness in her former lover's face on his wedding day.

When the carriage arrived to pick Margaret up—she was said to be wearing the dress, "interspersed with pearls and brilliants"—she would not come out of her room. Word was that she had become "suddenly sick."

"So violent was the attack," JC said in *Confession*, "that . . . time was not even allowed to change her magnificent dress."

Margaret became violently ill as the night progressed. Family members asked her over and over what was wrong. Had she eaten something? Had she come down with a flu?

Finally, near death, Margaret admitted "she had taken arsenic," claiming the "moment she had received the invitation to the wedding, her fate was concluded upon." She did not want to live. "She could never summon the resolution to hear that the marriage of her former lover had taken place—much less to witness the ceremony."

Just a few hours after Margaret Colt became ill, she "was a corpse—a corpse dressed for a bridal party," JC later explained, "a victim of her own pride and ungovernable temper."

Margaret's death, JC said years later, "paralyzed" his "soul." Margaret was the spirit of the Colt children, and JC considered her to be his "one beloved sister, around whom entwined every tendril of his heart." He said Margaret was the "only being who had made the thought of being home endurable. . . . She could not fly into the world for refuge—but she found it in the grave." Her death affected JC so profoundly that upon hearing of it, JC claimed, he decided to join the military and "quit the country" entirely.

———

By Tuesday, September 21, 1841, Emmeline Adams could do nothing more than cry and plead for the return of her missing husband. Emmeline had feared foul harm from the moment Sam did not come home from work that first night. Yes, she'd had a prophetic dream, but the real reason for her worry was that Sam Adams was a man of fastidious habits. Adams was a Christian, a family man, and a dedicated husband. He and Emmeline had no troubles. They were not in marital discord. They had not been quarrelling. Still, it had been nearly four days that Emmeline had not spoken to Sam, and no one had seen or heard from him. She was certain the worst had happened.

Asa Wheeler and those who had heard the tremendous crash and boom inside JC's office (and, more importantly, that great period of silence that followed), not to mention the sawing and hammering throughout the night, were alarmed by a notice that went up around town—a missing-persons flyer—announcing that Sam Adams, a fine man of a good home, excellent standing, a respected businessman in the city who had last been seen walking into the Granite Building on Chambers and Broadway, had gone out one day and not returned home.

This notice, as Asa Wheeler ran into it while going about his day, was enough for the tutor, accountant, and landlord of JC to seek additional help from law enforcement. Putting the circumstances together, Asa figured he knew what had happened to Mr. Adams, although he was not yet ready to point an accusatory finger at JC.

"On Tuesday," Asa said later, "I saw the notice of Mr. Adams," and before running off willy-nilly to the police station, Asa went to see Joseph Lane, Sam Adams's father-in-law, whose name and address appeared on the flyer. Asa did not know Sam Adams personally. He took Joseph Lane's address on Catherine Street off the flyer and set out to speak with the man.

"Could not see him or Mrs. Adams," Asa explained. Neither was home. So Asa left word with someone at the house that he might have information regarding Sam's disappearance.

The situation had now become fluid. There was an energy surrounding Sam Adams's sudden disappearance and JC's odd behavior inside the confines of his office.

Sometime later (Asa never mentioned how long), Joseph Lane, curious and in quite a frenzy to hear what Asa had to say, showed up at the Granite Building. Lane had brought Sam Adams's accounting books with him for Asa to have a look at. If there was a connection between Adams and JC, some sort of a discrepancy between the two men—a motive for murder, in other words—Asa, an accountant and tutor, could find it.

"We need to see the mayor," Asa said after a careful forensic accounting examination of Sam Adams's books. He had uncovered a clue.

—⁓—

Mayor Robert Morris was one of those old-school New York Democrats, the son of a city merchant, who had an uncanny ability to relate to the struggles of the average city man. Morris came from a family that traced its American roots to the Revolutionary War. Most of them had lived in Morrisania, Westchester County; his grandfather was second chief justice of the Supreme Court in New York; Morris himself was educated by Elisha Williams, at one time a respected leader of the Columbia County bar. If there was a lawman in New York whom Asa Wheeler could have chosen to best figure out what to do in this situation, there was no better man than Mayor Morris—even though Morris, at one time a state legislator and assistant district attorney, had been embroiled in political controversy. If nothing else, Morris would not want to turn a blind eye and further contaminate his future in politics. He would have to see to the bottom of the case that Asa was putting together. Billed the "Tammany candidate" during the 1841 election, Morris had won by a majority of fewer than four hundred votes within some thirty-six thousand.

As their paths came to cross, however, neither Asa nor the mayor could have foreseen the onslaught of attention this case would receive or the conflict pointing a finger at a Colt family member would bring.

———

Asa was given an immediate audience with the mayor; and he quickly explained the circumstances leading up to his visit.

Morris, interest piqued, told Asa he would "immediately appoint an officer to watch the movements of Mr. Colt," explaining further that he was not going to allow JC to leave the city.

Exiting Morris's office, Asa Wheeler felt a bit more positive about the situation; he believed something was going to be done.

Meanwhile, as Asa worked his way back to the Granite Building, several events that would play a part in JC's imminent arrest on murder charges congealed. Number one, Asa Wheeler persuaded Horace Greeley's *Tribune* to insert an "advertisement" (a notice, actually), in the following morning's paper announcing that Sam Adams was last seen entering the Granite Building, along with several other important factors surrounding Adams's abrupt disappearance, being careful not to publicly implicate JC. Morris's office added to the notice, asking anyone with information—specifically any "car men" in the area of the Granite Building on that day or the following days—to come forward at once.

The notice reached the car man who had transported the box for JC and inspired the man to come forward. Based on the car man's information, several officers now involved in the investigation of Sam Adams's disappearance were sent to the wharf at the end of Maiden Lane.

It just so happened that over the past few days the unseasonable heat wave had shut down parts of the city, which gave the *Kalamazoo* good reason to hang in the port until business—and the weather—returned to normal.

With the rising temperatures and the confines below deck cramped with boxes and packages ready to be shipped around the country, several mates aboard the vessel reported a ghastly aroma emanating from the cargo hold.

As an inspection of the hold commenced, Asa Wheeler returned to his office.

Where an angry John Caldwell Colt was there waiting for him.

6

A Deathlike Hue

AFTER ASA WHEELER GOT SETTLED INSIDE HIS OFFICE ON THURSDAY evening, September 23, 1841, waiting on Mayor Morris and his team to make their move, JC came out of nowhere and, Asa recalled, "urged me to very politely come into his room."

Had JC somehow found out about his landlord's little trip across town to the mayor's office?

"He wished to have some conversation on the subject of bookkeeping," Asa explained later, "and obtain my advice as to the publishing of his work."

At least that's what JC told Asa.

To say the least, this was unnerving. Asa believed JC to be a cold-blooded murderer. Did he want to be alone with this evil man?

Asa made up an excuse instead of facing JC, saying later he "partly promised to go in" to JC's room, "but did not."

With any luck, JC would be confronted by the authorities soon enough and Asa would not have to deal with the situation.

Mayor Morris, meanwhile, had made a decision to arrest JC, "though any positive testimony against him," Colt's *Confession* rightly stated, "had not yet come to light."

True. At this time, there was nothing more than circumstantial evidence—and rumor—against JC. And even that could be considered a stretch.

The following morning Asa Wheeler was in the hallway of the Granite Building talking with another tenant, no doubt gossiping about the events taking up the time and energy of everyone in the building. "On Friday morning," Asa said, explaining how JC once again came upon him (and the other tenant), just as he had the previous evening, "he invited me in a very friendly and urgent manner to come into his room."

Asa Wheeler declined.

Mayor Morris showed up at the Granite Building sometime later. In the interim, Morris said he and several officers had deposed tenants inside the Granite Building, which subsequently led him to issue a warrant for JC's arrest. Along with Morris was an officer, A. M. C. Smith, a man they called Waldron, and another officer from the "Upper Police" whom they referred to only as "Justice Taylor."

"I was induced," Morris later said, "from something that had been told me, to go to the room in person . . . in order to arrest Mr. Colt."

They went directly to JC's office. JC was not there. On his door was a sign saying he had gone out and would return soon.

Morris stationed an officer at the head and foot of the stairs leading up to the second story hallway where JC's office was located.

Morris waited in Asa Wheeler's room next door.

After a short time, Asa Wheeler heard footsteps. JC walked up the stairs and down the hallway, heading toward his office.

Asa told Mayor Morris his man had arrived.

While JC was unlocking his door, Officer Smith grabbed him by the arms.

"It was expected he would make resistance," JC's *Confession* reported, "as he was reputed to carry a revolving pistol"—an allegation undoubtedly stamped onto JC's forehead solely for being the brother of the gun's inventor—"in his pocket."

JC, however, shocked the crowd of lawmen surrounding him and "submitted to arrest without murmur."

As JC was being contained, Smith noticed a change in the man's demeanor: a trance came upon JC. It was his skin tone at first, Smith explained, which turned from its "natural paleness . . . to a livid and a deathlike hue." It took JC a moment to collect himself before he could "speak audibly."

Morris introduced himself and the others with him, then asked JC to step inside his office.

They walked together and closed the door behind them.

"You are being arrested on suspicion of having killed Mr. Samuel Adams," Mayor Morris stated.

The officers searched JC as Morris showed his prisoner the affidavits he had drawn up to support the arrest.

"He assisted in the search and seemed disposed to yield everything," Morris commented later.

Nothing more could be done inside JC's office at this time. In addition and by law, JC needed a lawyer. So Morris had JC taken down to his 5 City Hall (Varick Street), House No. 32, office. Morris sent someone to call on Sam Colt and Dudley Selden, JC's distant cousin, a respected city lawyer who had served as a representative in Congress from New York (1833 to 1835). JC had some powerful people coming to his rescue, which was maybe why, after gathering his bearings and gaining a bit of his composure back, he seemed to be untroubled by the idea of being accused of a crime that could ultimately place him standing at the gallows.

Inside Morris's office, JC was asked to sit down.

"Where do you reside?" Morris queried.

"I do not live anywhere," Colt said. "I sleep in my room in the Granite Building, upon the floor, and get my meals at the eating houses."

"Were you in your room on the Friday evening last?"

"I don't recollect. It is very possible, however. I know I slept there."

"Were you engaged in that evening packing and nailing up a box— and did you send such a box away in the morning?"

"Most assuredly," JC answered, "I saw *no* box! Nor did I send any box away."

Morris learned Sam Colt was out of town, but Dudley Selden was on his way. As of that moment, Morris was under the impression JC had lied to them, which gave the mayor probable cause to have JC's office searched. In addition, JC was going to be "committed to prison" (the infamous Tombs) until he could be arraigned and formally indicted on one charge of murder.

Not much happened overnight; there was some difficulty in finding the car man who had transported the box for JC to the *Kalamazoo*, but he was eventually located.

"[The] superintendent of carts discovered the car man who was employed to take away the box from the Granite Building the previous Saturday morning," JC's *Confession* later reported. "He was taken before the mayor, where he stated that Mr. Colt had employed and paid him to carry a box from his room, corner of Broadway and Chambers street, to the ship *Kalamazoo*, laying at the foot of Maiden Lane on the morning of the 18th of September, and that he had delivered it accordingly."

The ship itself was still docked in port. Mayor Morris sent a team of officers, first thing Sunday morning, to board the ship, delay it further if need be, find that box, open it, and see what was inside.

———

When seventeen-year-old Sam Colt returned in 1831 from his trip aboard the *Corvo*, he set out on a new adventure, hoping to raise enough money to finance his invention of the revolving chambered pistol, a model of which he had carved out of wood and brought back to show prospective investors. Sam's father, Christopher Colt, was going to help (he gave Sam $1,000), but Sam needed to find a way to raise capital on his own if he ever wanted to see his invention get the respect he believed it deserved.

"Sam had to scrimp to make his living," Ellsworth Grant wrote in his biography, *The Colt Legacy*, "and to continue the development of the revolver, which he was certain would make him a fortune."

It was back home in Ware, Massachusetts, before his trip, when Sam had discovered an interest in what became, by the fall of 1832, his new passion: nitrous oxide.

Yes, laughing gas.

Presenting—and, quite shockingly by today's standards, offering— the gas to anyone who could pay for it during what was a vaudevillian-like sideshow was something, Sam figured, that could earn him enough money to further his idea of putting the revolving pistol on paper, obtaining a patent, and getting the weapon into production.

Sam the nitrous pusher called himself "Dr. Coult," resorting back to the Colt namesake. He printed pamphlets, announcing his sideshow as he traveled at first throughout New England. Sam promised to administer the gas to anyone who paid for it—a traveling drug peddler! In Portland, at the City Hall, a pamphlet Sam wrote explained in big, bold letters at the top pretty much what he was offering, announcing, "Dr. Coult" will ". . . administer the NITROUS OXIDE, or Exhilarating GAS . . . Exhibition to commence at 7 o'clock precisely."

The pamphlet went on to say how English chemist Sir Humphrey Davy had explored the "peculiar effects of this singular compound upon the animal system." Davy, Sam pointed out in small type, marketing his exhibition like a true pro, realized that when inhaled, the nitrous oxide made you "laugh, sing and dance." Sam went one step further, telling potential customers the gas had caused some to gain great, Herculean strength, but all the "sensations produced by it" were "highly pleasurable, and are not followed by debility."

Sam billed himself as a "practical chemist" and assured anyone who chose to partake that "no fears be entertained." Tickets to the event were fifty cents. He explained how he had witnessed the "extraordinary powers of the gas" in cities throughout the United States. For an additional price, Sam promised, he would give private demonstrations at a home or business and administer the gas at fifty cents per dose. On June 22, 1832, Sam placed an editorial notice in the *Boston Morning Post*, writing, "The exhibition of the singular and amusing effects of the nitrous oxide gas, when inhaled into the lungs, will be repeated this evening only, at the Masonic Temple."

The crowds came out. Sam traveled for approximately three years while pushing his sideshow of noxious oxide gas for kicks, getting people high from Charleston to New Orleans to Virginia to Montreal to Quebec, among other major cities and states. He claimed in one advertisement to have given the gas to some twenty thousand people on more than one thousand occasions.

If nothing more, the advertisements Sam Colt wrote and published proved how much of a showman and marketer he had turned himself into within just a few short years. Hence an 1834 ad published in a Montreal newspaper shortly before Sam's arrival there:

Nitrous Oxide Gas

Dr. Coult's Exhibition presents some of the most pleasing and laughable scenes one can well imagine. Although the peculiar effects of Nitrous Oxide keep the audience in a state of almost continual merriment, yet there is a great chance for the learned and curious to exhaust all their wits in sober contemplation on the causes and effects of Nitrous Oxide upon the human system.

The future gun baron's tour (for lack of a better term to describe what was a bizarre chapter in Sam Colt's life) not only sold his strange "feel good" gas, but also the man himself. It turned out to be the perfect learning experience for what was ahead. Sam would soon work harder than he ever had at selling one of his many ideas, thus revolutionizing the arms manufacturing industry. He had hired a man from Baltimore, John Pearson, to shape and engineer his revolver model into something Sam could then mass produce and sell. Pearson was Sam's gunsmith. In reading the letters Sam wrote to Pearson, one can see that, even at a young age, Sam was in charge of his destiny, directing Pearson about exactly what he wanted him to do.

It took him several more years, but by 1836, Samuel Colt, a mere twenty-two-year-old world-traveled entrepreneur, had a patent in hand for his revolver, which sent him sailing once again overseas, this time so he could patent the weapon in England and France. When Sam returned from securing those patents, he moved to New York City and persuaded wealthy distant-cousin Dudley Selden to invest two hundred thousand dollars in the gun corporation, which Sam called the Patent Arms Manufacturing Company.

As historian Bill Hosley so appropriately put it about the New Jersey location of the company, "Paterson was chosen because of its prominence as a manufacturing center, but more importantly because Colt had family there who were rich, well connected, and willing to invest in his dream."

Alfred Henry Lewis called the cargo area of a ship a "sacred thing," adding, "like the ten commandments," once a ship's hold has been packed, cargoes are not "lightly to be broken." Captains did not like to mess with the belly of a ship once it had been filled and signed off. Yet it was that cargo area in the bowels of the *Kalamazoo*, on Sunday morning, September 26, 1841, that turned out to be the center of attention as the mayor of New York City and his band of law enforcement officers held John Colt downtown on suspicion of murder. At the moment, Mayor Robert H. Morris did not have a body in order to make a true charge of murder against JC stick. He could assume all he wanted. He could point at JC and call him a killer. Say he was a liar. He could lock JC up. But without that body, Morris knew he had no case.

The *Kalamazoo*'s captain, a man they called Hawke, was said to be drinking at Lovejoy's Hotel when one of his mates ran down the wharf and into the pub to fetch him. Mate Tracey had suspected that the foul odor filling up the cargo area of the *Kalamazoo* was coming from a box set to be shipped to St. Louis, Missouri, via New Orleans. The addressee was one R. P. Gross, in care of a "Mr. Gray."

By now, several shipmates had zeroed in on the box and, with the help of Richard Barstow, the car man who had transported the item for JC, recognized it as the same crate JC had taken from the Granite Building and put on Barstow's carriage.

Tom Russell, a twenty-nine-year-old car man working with Barstow, had been on the *Kalamazoo* since early morning, pointing out the box he had helped Barstow put aboard the ship. The chief mate had told Russell there were plenty of boxes fitting the description he had given. So they sat and went through invoices looking for the precise number—this as Barstow walked the belly of the ship with another mate and located the box JC had paid him to transport.

"[T]he bills of lading for that day were examined," Tom Russell later explained, "and we commenced a search."

Below deck, it took six minutes, Russell said, to locate Barstow and the box. After everyone was certain they had the right package, they hoisted the heavy crate to "the middle of the deck."

Russell and the chief mate, after Captain Hawke had given the order, "knocked off the lid."

"First saw the awning," Russell explained.

The "stench" was so overwhelming and "bad," Tom Russell remembered, the car man couldn't take it and walked off the ship.

Several men now stood around the box, staring down into it, that awful smell wafting up around them in a cloud.

Someone pulled off the awning.

"[W]e discovered a dead body," the superintendent of carts (Russell and Barstow's boss) later recalled.

In the days that followed, the headlines of this discovery would be more sensational and dramatic with each passing day, yet every report seemed to hold a part of the ultimate truth. One writer penned this literary gem a day after the discovery, which did its job in getting the attention of the city:

> *[A] vessel bound for New Orleans was unexpectedly delayed after receiving the bulk of her cargo, and before closing the hatches the mate became aware of noisome effluvia in the vicinity of a box . . . exposing detached portions of a human body, which was subsequently ascertained to be that of Samuel Adams. It had been dismembered,*

salted, boxed, addressed, and shipped to a fictitious address in St. Louis via New Orleans.

Had JC murdered Sam Adams and cut his body into pieces over a mere disagreement? The way in which Adams's body was found indicated a clear and conscious decision to maim the man violently and hide the murder, thus giving Adams's murderer enough time to figure out his next move. All of which spoke to premeditation.

"[T]here was a rope around his neck," one of the car men standing, staring, when the crate was opened, later said, "and passed on around his legs, and his knees [were] drawn toward his head."

Samuel Adams had been hog-tied.

Morris and a team of law officers were inside JC's office at the time Sam Adams's body was discovered, searching for additional evidence of a murder. They had no idea what the others had uncovered aboard the *Kalamazoo*.

"Upon the floor, a shattered glass was found," JC's *Confession* stated, describing the search of his office in candid detail.

Beyond that, Morris located a hatchet, "the handle of which was newly scraped with broken glass—the end of the handle being covered with ink, the edge showing marks of blood."

On the walls, there appeared to be spatter of some sort. Morris and his crew believed it to be blood at first sight, but there also appeared to be ink covering it over.

Morris ordered his officers to "saw away" a portion of the floorboards, which were also covered with stains of what appeared to be ink.

While Morris and the others collected evidence from JC's office, Sam Adams's body was on its way to the "dead house" (city morgue), so the medical examiner could have it taken carefully from its present resting place and put out before him on a slab.

7

A Greenish Cast

THE BUILDING'S SHELL WAS MADE OF A TARNISHED GRAY STONE, ITS
"massive" presence in the city—almost like one of those tall English soldiers dressed down in red and black, a furry hat belted at the chin—overlooking the lower section of Manhattan, erected near the shores of the
East River on what would become Twenty-sixth Street. This was Bellevue
Hospital, one of downtown's most impressive edifices. The oldest public
hospital in America, Bellevue was founded in 1736 as "a six-bed infirmary
in New York City's first almshouse, on the site of City Hall Park." The
hospital was an icon at a time when monolithic structures in the city were
not even being thought about.

Facing the "lowest door on the building's front," you couldn't help but
notice the "gilt letters" announcing the entrance to a place no one wanted
to walk into: MORGUE.

"This door," historian James McCabe wrote in 1872, "marks the
entrance to . . . one of the most repulsive, but most terribly fascinating
places in the city."

Indeed. The Dead House of New York had been named after the
"famous dead house of Paris," McCabe noted. The inside of New York
City's main morgue, moreover, was an "exact imitation" of its Paris coun-
terpart, just a bit smaller.

Samuel Adams's body had not been taken out of the box aboard the
Kalamazoo on Sunday morning. The shipmates talked it over and decided
to spread "some chloride of lime over [the corpse]," put the lid back on the
crate, nail it shut, and chaperone it down to the dead house. The morgue
was, of course, where any mysterious dead body uncovered in the city
ended up: those unlucky souls found in gutters, back alleyways, along the

shores of the East and Hudson Rivers, and those men and women who died alone inside their homes, on the bar rail of a saloon, or any number of other ways and locations. A stray body stayed in the morgue between twenty-four and forty-eight hours (depending on the dead house's capacity). If no one claimed it, the city was forced to bury the dead man or woman at its own expense in an unmarked grave. Important to the case building against JC, "every article of clothing," McCabe noted, describing dead house policy, "every trinket, or other means of identification," found on a body, was "carefully preserved in the hope that it may lead to the discovery of the cause of death."

The deputy coroner, Abner Milligan, took one look at what was presumed to be Sam Adams's badly decomposed, nearly naked, deformed, and fiercely beaten body and realized he needed additional help with the inquest and examination. As it were, there was not enough of the body's head left so that anyone looking down into the crate could identify a face. Two physicians were called: Dr. Gilman and Dr. Kissam, local doctors the coroner utilized on occasion to help with the examination of corpses.

As historian McCabe later described it, the room the men stood in was about "twenty feet square," the floor made of brick tiles, the "walls rough and heavy." There was a partition of glass between the morgue and another room, making up two smaller rooms. This was where "the public" stood to identify the corpse of a missing loved one. During the era described by McCabe, there were four stone tables inside the rooms, each set on frames of steel. Overhead hung a protruding "moveable [water] jet," much like a detachable faucet on a modern sink, from which the coroner could shower down the bodies with cold water, washing any debris, rot, insects, dirt, and any other grime a body might have collected while it sat, waiting to be discovered.

"I found the body of a man," Dr. Gilman later said, talking about his first impression of the corpse he viewed inside the crate, "very much decayed. . . . The outer skin of the surface first changes color and decays—then the brain, which becomes a semi-fluid."

The body had not yet been washed down. Dr. Gilman noted the fact that there were "vermin about the body . . . but . . . saw nothing else."

Gilman and Kissam had been told the box was full of salt, that Sam Adams's body had been, effectively, salted over, likely to prolong the decaying process and the aroma of death that follows, giving the *Kalamazoo* enough time to transport the corpse, hopefully, without detection. But Gilman or Kissam found no salt. Which made sense. The salt had probably done its job, but condensation and humidity had melted it away. Sam Adams had been, by everyone's estimation, inside that crate for almost nine full days by that point.

The two doctors were not there when the coroner and his deputy took Adams from the crate and placed him on the stone slab. Viewing the corpse as he stood debating how to go about examining it, Gilman noted how "the body was excessively offensive and covered with [pests]."

One mate aboard the ship had reported seeing "white worms" inside the crate. When Gilman said pests or "vermin," he was referring to maggots (and perhaps blow flies, the evolution of the maggot), ham and hide beetles (which feed off the tougher parts of tissue, skin, and muscle during the latter stages of decomposition).

Gilman gave the order to cut the rope hog-tying Adams in the fetal position. James Short, who worked for the coroner as a hired hand, was given the pleasure of completing this ghastly job.

"Washed the body," Short said, ". . . cut the rope from the neck and the right knee, and also picked bones from the skull, washed them, and gave them to the doctors. The rope was a very thick one."

Adams's body stayed in the same curled-up position after the rope was cut. Postmortem rigidity had cemented the man into the shape of the box, making it difficult for the morgue workers to extend the body fully and lay it flat. As Gilman and Kissam looked on, they straightened the corpse as best they could for the examination.

What was left of Adams's head was observed first.

"The skull was fractured in several different places," Gilman said. "The right side of the forehead, the socket of the eye, and part of the cheekbone were broken in." The fractures were higher up on the head, on the opposite side. "The brow had escaped [injury], but above that the forehead [was] beaten in. The two fractures communicated on the center of the forehead, so that the whole of the forehead was beaten in, also the right eye, and a part of the right cheek."

This was obviously a savage, violent attack, aimed not simply at causing pain to and disabling Sam Adams but also at rendering him dead.

Gilman was detailed in his notes of the examination. As it got underway, he was particularly interested in the injuries Adams sustained to his

THE DEVIL'S RIGHT HAND

head. This was the cause of death—no doubt about it. The man the coroner presumed to be Samuel Adams had been beaten severely on the head with some sort of an object round in shape, but sharp, too. The hatchet they found inside JC's room had an axe head on one side, a ball peen hammer-like shape opposite it.

"On the other side of the head," Gilman said, speaking of the left side of what was a mishmash of decomposed tissue and skull, dried blood with strands of hair and other tenuous material stuck to it, brain matter quashed into oblivion, and what the maggots had left behind or hadn't gotten to yet. "Directly above the ear," Gilman continued, "there was a fracture [with a major] depression of the bone."

That bone was not detached; it was indented into the skull.

There was another fracture on the left side of the head above the ear, in which Gilman discovered "a round, clean hole . . . that you might put your finger through it."

Gilman said, "There was no fracture on the back part of the head," which was surprising, considering all the other injuries. "Two pieces, about the size of the head of an ordinary nail, were chipped or scaled off," however. "It was the part of the skull termed the *occiput*. The head was so much decayed that the scalp could be removed from the bone by a rub of the finger." Like the outer coating on a peanut.

Inside the cavity of the skull, Gilman and Kissam found nothing but "some pieces of bone," all of which were the size of half-dollars.

They moved onto the body.

On one of the legs—Gilman thought it was the left, though he gave no reason why he had a hard time figuring this fact out—showed a "dark mark near the instep, but whether from an old sore or a blow," he could not tell.

Then, they found something that would become important when officially identifying Sam Adams, a gold ring on one of his fingers, which was removed and handed to the coroner.

By their measurements, Adams was "five feet nine and a half inches in length. The body was that of rather a stout but not a fat man. The hair was long and black. . . . The whiskers were very small. The sore [on Adams's leg] was hard, dry, and almost perfectly black. The rope had passed from one knee to the other, and then to the head."

It was now well into the afternoon. Mayor Morris and his team of officers had arrived at the dead house. They brought with them several pieces of evidence they had uncovered inside JC's office. Morris had sent a second pair of doctors over to JC's office to conduct tests on some of the stains his officers had noticed inside the room. They could perhaps pinpoint which stains were blood and which were ink, cut those sections of the walls and floor out, and add them to the mounting evidence against JC.

Morris was certain the hatchet they uncovered was the murder weapon; that JC had bludgeoned Sam Adams in a fit of rage, nearly beheading the poor man, bashing his face in so badly it was unrecognizable. Could the doctors verify what looked to be evidence of this theory?

"All the blows on the head could readily have been made by the hatchet here produced," Gilman said, "except the round hole, which, I confess, I am at a loss to see how it could have been made by it, but it might have been so."

Kissam didn't feel the same way, saying, "[S]aw and examined the body [Gilman] described. The features were not recognizable. Do not know that the hole in the side of the head could have been made by a hatchet—would rather suppose, as Dr. Gilman observed, it resembled what would have been made by a nail. Never saw a wound in the head that had been made by a ball. Had this been a ball hole, would suppose it to have looked more regular."

Moreover, Morris had a witness—several, actually—claiming that the sounds they heard that Friday resembled the clashing of foils (fencing weapons). Two swords clanking, in other words. Did these fatal injuries such a claim?

Gilman couldn't equate the sounds with the injuries he examined.

"Do not think the sound in giving such blows would resemble the clashing of foils," the doctor said. "Have never been in an adjoining room when foils have been struck. There must at least have been five blows given—perhaps a good many [more]. If a ball had been fired from an air gun, it might have made such a hole as that in the head, and a person receiving it would be instantaneously killed, and unable to make any noise."

But they did not uncover "any ball in the skull." Seeing that JC was the brother of Samuel Colt, whom they all knew to be a prominent gun maker, supposedly on the verge of turning his company into one of the largest in the nation, there was the idea that JC had used one of his brother's pistols to shoot and then pistol-whip Sam Adams.

Asa Wheeler had told Mayor Morris a story detailing a conversation he had with JC two weeks before the discovery of Sam Adams's corpse. He and JC had talked about Sam Colt and his guns. It was the day before he and JC had bickered over the rent money, Asa explained, and JC's stay in the office being too long.

Asa had asked JC, "Is your brother the inventor of the patent pistol?" Asa had heard he was, but did not pay much attention. The idea Asa was trying to imply was that, if JC had a rich brother, he shouldn't be having such a hard time coming up with the rent money.

"He is," JC said. "Have you ever seen my pistols?"

"I have not."

"I have one in my room." JC turned, walked away, saying, "Stay here, I will go and fetch it so you can see it."

Asa waited. When JC returned a moment later, Asa stood from his desk and stared at the gun, taken in by it. He was impressed. "It had a beautiful pearl handle and 4 to 6 barrels—I think 6."

As Asa looked over the weapon, JC explained "a very ingenious mode for denoting with a cylinder."

Asa was intrigued by the notion that you fired one bullet at a time, and how the weapon itself presented the shooter with the next to fire, automatically.

"The barrels were about 4 inches in length," Asa said. "It had his brother's name on . . . at any rate, he said it was his brother's [invention]. He did not explain its capacity for propelling."

Inside the dead house they stood, staring at Sam Adams's caved-in face, discussing the blows to Adams's head and what type of weapon could have caused them.

"A single blow from a hatchet," Gilman concluded, "[is] sufficiently strong to drive in the skull, as we found it, [and] would prevent a person from crying out. The person would not probably bleed much. There would be more blood from such a blow than from a pistol ball."

Deputy coroner Abner Milligan searched through the box while the others carried on with the examination. Interestingly enough, Sam

Adams was found naked, with the exception of his bloodied shirt, which the coroner had cut off his body. Milligan found the remainder of Sam Adams's clothes—"a black dress coat, which had been much cut and worn; also a stock, which had been cut and smeared with blood on both sides; part of an awning; two pieces of matting about 18 inches square; and some oakum" (a tar and fibrous material used to build ships)—on the bottom of the box, along with "two quarts of common salt."

Clearly, Milligan realized, whoever had placed Sam Adams in the box had added these items in order to cover up evidence of a murder.

They eventually cleaned Adams's body and found no other wounds anywhere. Those injuries to his head—which had caved in the front part of his skull (his face), leaving the back nearly intact—were the only injuries the man had received.

An apothecary, a nineteenth-century term for caregiver or pharmacist, collected all of the items from the box, including Sam Adams's clothing and that gold ring the coroner had removed from his finger. He cleaned the items as best he could and then placed everything "in a cell at the Halls of Justice."

Milligan, who later explained this procedure, added, "They smell[ed] offensive still, never having been removed since the first day."

James Short, who had stood and watched the examination from start to finish, had washed most of the body down after the doctors said they were done.

"I will tell you the truth," Short recalled. "I saw salt on the body, and washed it off."

Short tried counting the "pieces of skull" but could not come to a conclusion as to how many there were. "I took them out of the skull, put them in a pail, washed them, and the doctors took account of them."

He described the first piece of skull as being the size of "the breadth of your finger." To Short, the skull wounds had definitely been made by some type of hammer. He was certain of it.

A coffin had arrived by this time. Short placed the body of Sam Adams into the coffin. Then he transported it down to the graveyard, which he said was "toward the Battery. . . . I do not know the streets of the city."

8

The Devil & the Gun Maker

SAMUEL COLT WAS PAYING HIS BALTIMORE-BASED PISTOL MECHANIC, John Pearson, $12 per week for his services, this after opening up a bank account for the gunsmith with $150. Full of entrepreneurial vigor and enthusiasm for his products, Sam was ready to begin mass-producing his weapons in the Paterson, New Jersey, plant he opened back in 1836. He had returned from a trip to England, Scotland, and France, where he secured additional patents. Yet he had enough brilliance and nerve to realize that in order to become the most celebrated, successful gun maker in the world, he would first have to sell himself as a devil-may-care (and successful) industrialist, unafraid to take risks. Sam knew marketing. He understood that image was just as important in sales as the product itself. Sam's cousin Dudley Selden, however, who had invested more money than perhaps anyone, "was growing impatient" with Sam's ostentatious ways of conducting business. Sam was throw-ing "lavish dinner parties" in the city for prospective investors, buyers, and friends, seemingly celebrating the triumph of the business without the revenue to back it up. He was running around the city as if he were some sort of manufacturing tycoon enjoying a windfall of cash that had washed ashore. As far as Dudley Selden could tell, sales were minimal, and Sam was accruing nothing but debt.

"I have no belief," Selden wrote, "in undertaking to raise the character of your gun by old Madeira."

Dudley Selden had gotten hold of Sam's enormous liquor bill and was appalled by what he saw. It was the Panic of 1837, New York was in a titanic economic meltdown, there were runs on banks, and panhandling was at an all-time high. One newspaper claimed "six thousand masons and carpenters and other workmen connected with building had been discharged." This was a small portion of what was said to be "one-third" of New Yorkers out of work during the panic. Staggering numbers, by any account. As the year progressed, the economic outlook went from bad to worse: The hardest times New Yorkers had ever known were ahead. What in the world was Sam Colt thinking, throwing parties and spending money as if he had it to burn?

Then something extraordinary happened. It was almost as if Sam Colt had been using a crystal ball to help him make business decisions. In December 1837, in the midst of the panic, Lieutenant William S. Harney, from the Second Regiment of the U.S. Dragoons, while stationed in the Florida Everglades fighting the Seminole Indians, wrote Sam a letter. Harney ordered one hundred guns, including fifty Paterson Colt pistols.

"I am confident," the colonel said in his brief missive, "that they are the only things that will finish the infernal war."

One could see Sam Colt, cigar hanging from his mouth, a glass of expensive liquor on a table in front of him, a thumb in his vest pocket, reading this letter, stopping every so often to jack up his pants from side to side, smiling, mocking those in the room who had ever questioned him: *I told you so!*

What seemed like a major victory for Sam Colt, however, turned into a struggle to obtain a contract for the deal—the beginning of a battle Sam would wage with the government.

Inside JC's Granite Building office on the corner of Broadway and Chambers, after Sam Adams's body had been examined and readied for burial on Sunday, September 26, 1841, a group of officers helped a local doctor (an early forensic technician) take a serious look at the evidence JC left behind. Mayor Morris had assigned the doctor and given orders that included scraping the stains off the walls and cutting out sections of the floor. The mayor had also obtained a lead from Sam Colt regarding where JC had lived during the past few months. Sam had told the mayor JC lived at "42 some street," as if he couldn't recall the name. It was actually Monroe, just walking distance from the Granite Building, across the street from City Hall Park.

"He thought Thomas Street," the mayor later said, speaking of his conversation with Sam a few days after JC's arrest, "but was not sure."

Upper Police magistrate Thomas Taylor, one of the mayor's chief investigators, took a walk over to Monroe Street and knocked on the door.

A woman, beautiful, young, and pregnant, answered. She called herself, Taylor later said, "Mrs. Colt."

It was Caroline Henshaw, JC's live-in companion. Henshaw had joined JC that past January. She was originally from Germany. JC had met Henshaw in Philadelphia. Although the circumstances of their supposed chance meeting are unknown, it is clear Sam Colt knew Henshaw first and met her in Philadelphia before JC had ever been in the city. What would become clear in the coming months, though no one else besides Sam, JC, and Henshaw knew it then, was that the baby Caroline Henshaw carried had been, in fact, fathered by Sam Colt. And it's not even clear if JC knew. According to all accounts given by JC, it was his child.

In any event, Taylor asked Henshaw, "What apartment does Mr. Colt occupy?"

Henshaw said JC had stayed in the apartment at times.

"Where is his trunk?"

Henshaw invited Taylor in. She left the room and came back some time later with an "ordinary black canvas covered trunk about two-and-a-half feet long."

A trunk was a man's life, where he kept all the possessions with which he traveled. A man like JC, who had been all over the Midwest before settling somewhat in New York City, had likely collected scores of personal items that would help police figure out who he was and what he had been up to. More than that, perhaps there was proof in the trunk of JC and Sam Adams having had a business relationship. Paperwork or something tying the two men together.

Taylor asked Henshaw if she had the key to the trunk. She said she would not open it without JC present.

So Taylor took the trunk and hauled it back to the police office by car man so he and the mayor could have a look inside.

Henshaw followed.

The mayor had a police officer grab JC from his holding cell, who then sat as Taylor opened the trunk in his presence. There was an address book, "some stamps with 'Colt's Book-Keeping' on them," and several note cards on which JC had jotted facts and figures to discuss during his lectures. Looking further, the mayor recovered a pocketbook with some folded papers inside which were "endorsed" with the words, "Hair of Sarah Colt, my mother, Margaret Colt, and Mary Colt, deceased." JC had locks of his dead relatives inside the trunk.

The mayor looked at the package. "There appeared to be some hair inside of it," he said.

Another package was inscribed to "my little old Aunt" and contained three letters. Inside the same packet of papers was a letter proving JC had, at one time, been discharged from the Marines.

JC had enlisted in the Marines near 1827. After three months' service, however, he wrote to his father indicating he wanted out. Christopher Colt could intervene on his son's behalf because JC was a minor. All Mr. Colt needed to do was write a letter asking for the boy's discharge and return home.

Christopher Colt refused, saying quite contemptuously, no doubt with Olivia standing over his shoulder, "Complete your enlistment in an honorable fashion so that you may look back upon it with pride and self-respect."

Undeterred by this setback, JC wrote the letter himself, forged his father's signature, and sent it off to his brother (James) in Hartford, demanding he send it to the Marines.

It worked. The Marines unleashed him.

The mayor and Justice Taylor thought the letter concerning the Marines discharge was the last meaningful possession inside JC's trunk until Taylor reached deep inside and came up with a watch, "a new and elegantly worked gold one." Surely nothing JC could afford, or, if he could, would keep in a dusty and dark trunk.

As Taylor produced the watch, JC "appeared to be more depressed than we had seen, leaning his elbow on the back part of his counsel's chair, with his hands over his eyes."

When asked, JC said the watch was his.

"Who is the manufacturer?" Taylor asked. A watch was an intimate purchase for a man. He was proud of where he had bought it. The watchmaker would recall the customer or at least produce a bill of sale.

JC said he could not recall.

John Colt was then placed back into his cell as Taylor hit the streets in search of the watchmaker who had produced this fine piece of jewelry. Taylor and the mayor were "in consequence of information," Taylor later said, meaning they had an idea where JC had gotten the watch, but wanted to make certain before confronting him with the accusation.

Taylor first went to a watchmaker on John Street.

Nothing.

Then onto Maiden Lane, the famous Platt & Brothers, who had not made the gold watch either.

Then Taylor decided to go with his gut—and call on Mrs. Emmeline Adams, to see if she recognized the watch.

It didn't take Mrs. Adams long to identify the gold item, saying, "I was in the country when he got it, and had been gone four to five weeks. The watch had been a subject of conversation. He sat on the foot of the bed on Wednesday night [the second to the last night she spent with him], took the key off my chain and endeavored with the pinchers to get the dents out. He was at 90 Chatham Street Wednesday night with me and had it."

Back inside JC's office, evidence was piling up. Several additional blood spatter droplets had been cut from the walls and floor and taken away.

"I took from the room," Mayor Morris said later, "articles as I thought would be necessary on the trial."

Among the blood spatter samples, Morris found "pieces of cloth, pieces of a towel, and pieces of a shirt . . . also pieces of a handkerchief, and a pamphlet . . . a ball of twine" along with several pieces of paper.

When they were finished, the mayor had his officers padlock the doors.

JC was indicted by a grand jury on Tuesday, September 28, 1841, who found a "true bill against Colt for murder." Not long after the indictment was issued, JC was brought before a judge and officially arraigned.

He pleaded not guilty and pledged to fight the charges with every bit of pleasure and energy he had, not to mention all the influence his brother and his family were going to jostle up.

The court set JC's trial for the "term of the Court of Oyer and Terminer" and placed it on the docket for early the following year. *Oyer* and *terminer* is a French legal term meaning a court authorized to hear and decide criminal cases. JC was facing the death penalty. If convicted, there was no doubt he would find a hangman's noose around his neck at some point.

And yet, as he sat inside his cell at the Tombs, meeting with his lawyers, discussing his opportunities (few and far between), JC made an announcement. He was ready to talk. He was prepared to give a full confession, he said, of what had ensued between him and Samuel Adams on that night. He asked for paper and pen. He would write it out himself and sign the document. But the *Confession*, although it would detail Sam Adams's violent death, was not going to be what everyone expected. Yes, JC said, he had killed Sam Adams. No, he claimed, it was certainly not murder. Something else happened inside his office on that night, and he was now ready to talk about it in detail.

PART II

9

The Sacrificial Lamb

IT WAS ALMOST CERTAINLY WRITTEN AFTER THE FACT AND PUBLISHED
to clean up JC's wicked image, quite likely subsidized by brother Sam's
connections. Nonetheless, a story was crafted claiming that on a danger-
ously cold morning in New England during the winter of 1822, twelve-
year-old John Colt, residing at his uncle's farm in Burlington, Vermont,
stepped out to feed the sheep and found a stray lamb "frozen to the
ground . . . nearly dead."

The sight of the suffering animal jarred JC, according to how his
uncle later told the story. So the young boy ran back into the house with
the anticipation of getting help from his uncle for the beast.

After listening to the boy plead for the animal, JC's uncle called out
to one of his farmhands and gave orders to slaughter the lamb immediately. It was on its way out of this life anyway. Put the animal out of its
misery and get it carved up for market.

"No," JC screamed, as he, his uncle later said, "implored for the lamb."

The farmhand soon came out of the house with a stick in his hand.
Walked over to the animal as it lay in the snow struggling to breathe.
Brought the stick up over his shoulder and prepared to plunge it into the
head of the animal.

Unnerved by the sight, JC got in front of the lamb, placing his body
between the farmhand's stick and the animal.

"I would rather be killed myself," young JC pleaded, "sooner than let
the lamb be killed!"

Just then, JC's uncle walked up and saw his nephew hunched over the
lamb, not allowing the farmhand to kill the animal.

Little JC said it again, this time to his uncle.

"Well," his uncle said in frustration, sizing up the situation, "you foolish fellow, take the lamb to yourself and do with it what you like."

Certain they would not sacrifice the animal, JC ran inside the toolshed and quickly emerged with an axe. Using the sharp end, he pried the lamb from the frozen ground, gently placed it in a wicker basket, wrapped it in blankets and straw, and carried it off to the house. After six weeks of tending to the lamb daily, JC was able to integrate the creature back into the farm and "return [it] to the stables," his uncle later said, where the lamb "throve well, though from its once frozen feet . . . [it was] always a cripple—and that great little cripple followed him about the farm."

This anecdote, as his uncle later told it, explained, at least in the eyes of JC's keeper at the time, a softness JC had shown as a child. The true heart the kid had to stick up for the animal was admirable, his uncle later reminisced.

If true, this story said a lot about who JC was when he arrived on his uncle's farm a twelve-year-old boy, and perhaps more toward how far he fell. If apocryphal, it showed the revisionist lengths the Colts would go to in order to polish the accused man's image.

Like his brother, John Caldwell Colt was determined to make something of his life when he left home, embarking on that trip north. It was 1823 when JC got his first taste of being away from the Colt nest. He had been officially educated in the three R's by the Reverend Daniel Huntington back home in Hadley, Massachusetts, until the age of nine, and then sent north, under the urging of Olivia Colt, to reside with his uncle in Burlington after his mother died and Olivia took over the Colt household. All we know of this uncle was that he was an "excellent man who appreciated his nephew's character," a narrative prologue to the *Life and Letters of John Caldwell Colt* reported, a document not written by JC himself, but later compiled in his honor and defense *after* his arrest. The document, some later believed, was likely an attempt to resurrect the idea that JC was an upstanding citizen who had been dealt wrongly by an aggressive mayor and New York City police force bent on hanging him as a murderer. More public relations work, perhaps, on Sam Colt's part— only this time for the sake of his brother and a gun-manufacturing business on the verge of making Sam one of the wealthiest men in America. The Colt name needed to be protected at all costs. Sam could not risk the chance now, with so much riding on the outcome of JC's case.

JC's uncle wrote to Christopher and Olivia not long after JC got settled in Burlington. He wanted to let them know they had raised a fine, decent boy. "I'll tell you what," Uncle wrote, "John is made of good stuff, and you need not give yourself any uneasiness about him." There was a bit of constructive criticism in the letter, too, but Uncle couldn't shame the boy without adding an implicit inclination that young JC would likely grow out of his bad habits. "He likes to have his own way rather too much, but then he is always more than half right. And where's the harm in giving him a little play?" Finally patting JC on the back, Uncle added, "He is kind hearted a fellow as ever was; and, take him all around, I never saw a better boy in all my life."

One of JC's earliest goals was to enroll at the U.S. Military Academy at West Point. Olivia said no, however. "She had decided that he should engage in mercantile pursuits," *Life and Letters* reported.

JC begged his stepmother and father for permission to enroll in a second military school, but they refused once again, telling young JC that his vocation was in manufacturing, the same as Sam. These rebuttals are probably among the reasons why, when the opportunity presented itself and JC thought himself a Marine, he talked his father into signing the papers but then bailed out first chance he got.

It was 1824 when JC returned to Massachusetts from Vermont only to be told he was being "placed in a store belonging to the Union Manufacturing Company" down in Marlborough, Connecticut, quite a ways from Hartford and even farther from Ware.

JC excelled in his job for Union, spending much of his time keeping track of the money. It was his first true taste of bookkeeping—a job he fell into and enjoyed from almost the moment he started. In fact, JC had done such a good job the company sent him to its Manchester office, where he was made the agent's assistant bookkeeper. As a celebration, Christopher Colt took his son on a trip to New York City, where JC found a new world, really, like that of which he had only read about in books. New York then to a boy of his age was glamorous and on a scale that failed to balance with anything the boy had ever seen. He was taken aback by how big everything appeared, how many people bustled about the streets, and how many opportunities there seemed to be for someone eager to step into the world and try anything.

"[New York City] seemed to him a paradise," *Life and Letters* reported. "On every corner for him were stores of knowledge and food for thought."

Seeing New York in all of its glory, an increased desire to "acquire an education" was born in the child. He couldn't return home and focus. His mind was south, in a city where action ruled.

Returning to Manchester, JC was antsy and uncomfortable. That fast-paced lifestyle in the big city beckoned. Somewhere near 1825, he packed his belongings and went back. Christopher hooked him up with his cousin Daniel Colt, and a job at a grocery store Daniel owned downtown. JC was in his glory. A boy in a man's world.

"My life," JC said in 1841 while awaiting trial on murder charges, "has been five times [more] this very imminently exposed, to say nothing of its frequent endangerment in hunting and horse-racing, where I was always rashly and foolishly venturesome from boyhood till I had occupation of later years, to keep me at my desk."

Throughout his childhood, JC claimed, he was prone to accidents and mishaps not all his own doing. If you believe what he later said, his younger days became one dangerous adventure after another. One time, he and a young lass were playing in a cider press barn, "drawing the juice of an apple out of a deep vat through straws." As they started to fool around, JC lost his footing and "plunged headfirst" down into the vat. "When the little girl got me out, my senses were gone, and she carried me home in her arms for dead."

He healed, of course. Then, later that winter while playing on the ice with friends, he fell through a soft spot and was taken down river in the choppy, cold waters, where "there I caught at the limb of a fallen tree, and drew myself upon the bank."

Telling these stories was a man in his later years inebriated with hubris, enjoying the mere art of telling tales from his youth. The stories fed an enormous ego JC had developed throughout his years.

The most dangerous incident he'd had as a young man came when JC was in Hartford one day with his father, where he claimed to have had a life-threatening encounter with a buffalo. From what JC later said, a caravan of animals had arrived in the city for some sort of event at the same time he and his father had. "Never before having beheld a buffalo," JC recalled, "I smuggled myself into a narrow passage, leading by a small door to an adjoining building." He was a curious boy, apparently, hoping to have a friendly meet and greet with a wild animal. "There I was," JC went on, "in front of the creature, and could command a complete view of its head."

As they stared into each other's eyes like boxers, the buffalo sensed danger, because the animal then "took, not for admiration, but defiance," and "forthwith plunged at me."

The buffalo, according to JC's account, nailed him "fast against the passage-door between his horns." And he was trapped. A small child between two husks, the hot breath of the animal on his knees, its eyes crazily rolling back in its head.

The buffalo's trainer saw what happened, JC said, and with several other men, beat the buffalo down with clubs.

But this only infuriated the animal, JC said, and "excited him to glare more fiercely and pin me tighter."

Through this entire episode, JC said he learned a great many things about himself. He never said how old he was, but one would assume that if this event did actually occur, he would have been nine to eleven years of age.

"Great danger," JC intoned, "sometimes gives one great self-possession."

He said he called out to the keepers to back off and "leave the buffalo to me to settle the difficulty."

So they did.

"I then patted the prairie hero, and stroked his neck, and talked soothingly to him, till, as if to consider what it all meant, he gradually unloosed his hold, and stepped slowly back."

JC began to walk out of the area. When he felt the coast was clear, he "bolted," but not before turning around and addressing his "shaggy-throated friend," yelling, "You don't catch me there again, I tell you!"

The person who later interviewed JC about this seemingly tall tale asked him if the incident had terrified him at all when he looked back on it.

"There you mistake," JC answered. "At first my peril gave me nerve; afterwards, delight. Indeed, I believe I am fortunate enough to have as little fear in my composition, as most men.... You ought never permit yourself to be agitated. The only rule in this world is, always to keep your cool."

Strange words coming from a man who, now faced with mounting evidence of murder building against him, sat down with his lawyer and began to dictate a narrative of what had happened between him and Sam Adams.

Confessions of the Way Life Used to Be

IT HAD BEEN BETWEEN THREE AND FOUR O'CLOCK ON THE AFTERNOON of Friday, September 17, 1841, when Sam Adams "called on" JC, arriving at the office JC rented from Asa Wheeler. All of those witnesses who had claimed to have seen Adams enter the Granite Building, never to be seen again, were right, JC explained to his lawyer from his prison cell. Yet, as JC told the story, confessing to Sam Adams's demise, it didn't happen the way the evidence suggested.

JC said he had no idea if Adams had planned to show up at his office, but when he walked into the room, JC was sitting at his desk, "engaged in looking over a manuscript account[ing] book." The busy accountant was working, deeply engrossed in a project that had consumed him, he recalled, for the "past two days." He was evaluating a company's worth, going over mathematical calculations that had stumped him.

Without saying a word, Adams walked into the office and sat down in front of JC on a chair "an arm's length away." Adams did not even take off his hat and greet JC.

"So near," JC said later, speaking of how close Adams sat near him, "that if we both leaned our heads forward toward each other, I have no doubt but that they would have touched."

With Adams in front of him, staring, not saying a word, JC decided it was a good time to speak of the account he had with Adams's printing business. There was that discrepancy between the two men regarding the books, an overdue bill, and the idea that JC had gone behind Sam's back and sold the lot for a profit. Adams, according to JC's later version, had given JC a detailed overview of the account "ten to twelve days before," which gave JC enough time to go over it line by line and see where Adams had made mistakes.

"This account is wrong," JC told Adams as the printer sat, glaring at him. JC was certain of the figures. He told Adams he'd rewritten the account the way it should have been in the first place, and thus reached inside his desk and handed Adams the revised version of the ledger. "Now, alter your account," JC told his printer, "as I have it there."

"No! You do not understand printing," Adams responded. JC never mentioned if Adams looked at the paper then or not. Only that he was defiant and noticeably angry.

So JC read the figures from his accounting log aloud, hoping it would convince Adams that he had indeed made an honest mistake. JC was so sure of himself and his figures that he offered Sam a deal. "I will give you ten dollars or some such sum," JC said, "if I am not right."

Adams took the paper and analyzed it. After a short time, he fixed the figures on the draft he had brought with him.

All seemed well. JC had convinced the printer that he was the one in error. Maybe now, JC thought, he could get back to work.

Then something happened. After he made the changes, Adams took a second look at the paper.

"I was right at first," Adams said. "You're trying to cheat me!"

Sam Adams stood.

JC stood.

"You lie!" Adams said, beyond several other remarks exchanged between the two men JC could not exactly recall. What was clear, however, was that Sam Adams was furious, and now, according to JC's version, looking to take out his anger on the man he believed had swindled him.

"Word followed word," JC later explained, "till it came to blows."

JC claimed Adams hit him with a punch "across my mouth and nose which caused my nose slightly to bleed." It was at that time, JC said (laying out his defense for a case his lawyers would soon argue on his behalf in court), when the words between the men took on a different connotation, and even later, when he had time to consider what had happened, he claimed an odd feeling came over him at that exact moment. "I do not know that I felt like exerting myself to strong defense," JC recalled. He wasn't sure if his next action was impulse or something he had made a conscious decision to do. In fact, he could not recall the strike he made against a man he now considered to be his enemy, saying, "I believe I then struck him violently with my fist."

Whatever he did do, John Caldwell Colt was positive the blow had incited more rage in Adams.

JC had been wearing a businessman's suit: ruffled white linen shirt of cotton with a low collar, a waistcoat with the lowered waistline of the day, and a puffy and wide cravat, which was tied traditionally in a necktie knot. JC had placed his waistcoat on a hook in back of the door. Sam Adams, he said, grabbed him by the cravat and shuffled him against the wall in back of his desk, pushing his side and hip against a table for leverage. Then Adams twisted the cravat "so that I could scarcely breathe," JC recalled. While doing this, Adams pressed JC's body "hard upon the wall and table." Adams was, essentially (if we are to believe JC), choking the accountant.

Sitting on the table beside JC—this, mind you, as Sam Adams continued tightening the handkerchief around JC's neck—was a hammer, an axe on one end and a ball-shaped metal head on the other.

"I then immediately seized hold of [the hammer] and instantly struck him over the head," JC explained.

Then a strange feeling of disconnect came upon JC. It was at that moment, he later remembered, in which "I lost all power of reason."

———

The job Christopher Colt was able to secure in 1827 for his son downtown with his cousin didn't turn out so well for JC. He was fired after Daniel Colt "detected" JC "embezzling" money. The accountant, it appeared, was dipping his hand in the cookie jar. And got caught.

So JC returned home, tail between his legs, where things did not go any better.

"The influence of his stepmother was at work against him," *Life and Letters* reported. "He left [a] home at which she made unendurable."

With tension tight as a drum inside the house, JC headed south. He had heard there was work in Baltimore. He was seventeen. Penniless. The chances JC had been given were blown, either by impatience, immaturity, or plain old criminal behavior on his part.

In Maryland, JC had no friends to speak of, but he was fearless and in desperate need of starting a new life. Not long after he arrived in town did JC find a job teaching mathematics at a seminary for ladies. From there, he became acquainted with a local high school and soon took a job as an assistant—to what he assisted was something he never mentioned.

Baltimore was booming at the time, as were many of the cities along the Atlantic coastline. Canals were being dug, shipyards built and buildings were going up. JC soon met a local contractor, who was "so charmed with his energy, acquirements, and excellent traits of character" that he offered JC a job as an engineer. This shocked JC; he had no engineering experience. He had never worked with his hands in this capacity, or with architecture and drafting. But he would give it a try.

Engineer, as it turned out, was a relative term. Definitely not the proper job description for what JC ended up doing along the Baltimore shoreline as the year 1828 came to pass. The correct job category would have been day laborer—JC was exerting his body out in the field, working "the labors of Hercules" to the great delight of his employer. He was an excellent worker. The money was what kept JC in the construction game as long as he stayed, yet after saving enough cash—and perhaps realizing a true education was what he needed in order to work with his mind behind a desk—he left the job abruptly one day and moved back north, this time to Wilbraham, Massachusetts, where he was resigned to devote himself to books. He began tutoring under the direction of future Wesleyan University president Wilbur Fisk, who was then the principal of Wesleyan Academy in Wilbraham. Things back home were too tenuous for JC to return. The effects of Margaret's suicide, which had crushed JC (and Sam), were still being felt. Olivia was causing more trouble inside the home than was worth putting up with. JC could not be around her under any circumstances, he lamented. The older he got, the more he realized Olivia was going to get her way despite the best efforts of any of the Colt kids.

Not having the mind to study, Margaret's untimely death lingering, and his father's mourning the perfect byway, JC convinced Christopher Colt to sign him up for the Marines, and the boy dropped his pen and paper in Wilbraham and took off for Norfolk.

That prospect didn't suit the character of the nomadic Colt, and after being turned down by his father, JC wrote that forged discharge letter and was back, then looking to set his feet in yet another new land and new opportunity.

This time heading west, JC decided on the mighty Mississippi. After reading about it back east, JC was now dedicated to pursuing the life of a professional card player, a gambler. JC knew numbers. He understood that a man's desire and behavior were evident in the way his eyes were cast. He felt he could beat other men at this game solely based on the fact that he considered himself stronger emotionally than any of his fellows.

The decision to head well inland and begin a new life at twenty as a gambler aboard the Mississippi steamboats would not necessarily work out the way JC had hoped.

Sam Adams lodged his top hat up and into JC's face while he held the man whom he believed to have stolen from him against the wall and desk. Adams's face was pointed down toward the floor, angling the hat that sat atop his head. JC had that "hammer," as he called it, in his hand, ready to, as JC later told it, defend himself. After all, Sam Adams was still twisting JC's necktie, causing the accountant to choke and gasp mightily for air.

Without realizing it, having lost control of his senses, JC claimed, he raised the hammer and sent it thrusting downward into the back of Sam Adams's skull.

"The seizing of the hammer and the blow was instantaneous," JC later said, trying to portray the scene as one of split-second self-defense.

He wasn't sure whether he knocked Sam's top hat off, though he was convinced that as Adams twisted the cravat harder, with more force, before the first blow, the lack of oxygen had led JC down that road of losing "all power of reason."*

Sam Adams never attempted to grab the hammer—and how could he? The man had taken a blow at point-blank range from the business end of a metal ball peen hammer. It made a hole in his skull and knocked him unconscious, sending his lifeless body to the floor (it may have even killed him instantly).

JC mentioned in his *Confession* only this one blow yet admitted there was a time between when he picked up the hammer and when he realized Adams was lying on the floor in front of him that he could not account for. This was when JC went into a mental blackout—and likely bashed

---

* As a crime expert who has studied this case from top to bottom, reviewing all of the evidence left behind, especially the medical examiner's reports and comments, I must say that this scenario JC gave of what happened inside the office is absolutely possible. Sam Adams was upset with JC. Adams, several people reported, had truly felt JC had ripped him off and, maybe worse, went behind his back. Adams's business was failing miserably. There's plenty of evidence to elicit a guess that Adams attacked JC on this day and JC reacted angrily and struck and killed him before he even realized what he had done.

Sam Adams's face in (as the evidence would later prove) with the axe and hammer sides of what was now a lethal weapon. JC could not recall what happened because he had no memory of it after rage took control of his senses. He later said that he might have "shoved" Adams off of him after striking him, but could not recall. There was only a "faint idea" of pushing the printer off him.

JC had snapped. He stayed in this trance until he heard a knock on his door, which "instantly startled" him back into the present moment.

It was Asa Wheeler, on the opposite side of the door, with his student.

JC walked over to the door, locked it, and turned the slide down so no one could peer inside.

Then he sat down behind his desk. "[F]or I felt very weak and sick."

According to JC's account, Sam Adams wasn't dead yet. Sitting and wondering what had just happened, JC looked over to where Adams lay still on the floor—"and seeing so much blood"—got up and walked over to him, where he stood staring down at a man who, struggling, "breathed quite loud for several minutes."

This must have been when Asa Wheeler moved the stock inside the key and looked.

As JC watched Adams gurgle and gasp for air that would never come, "poor Adams," JC later remarked, ". . . threw his arms out and went silent."

The printer was was dead.

"I recollect taking him by the hand, which seemed lifeless, and a horrid thrill came over me, that I had killed him."

Forgive Me, I Am Dying Now

JOHN COLT HAD A DEAD MAN AT HIS FEET WHO WAS NOW GROTESQUELY disfigured and bleeding all over the room. Sam Adams's face was unrecognizable. JC had blood all over his clothes. There was blood from one end of the office to the other. Spatter droplets were all about the walls and floorboards. Bloody boot prints. Handprints. There were people out in the hallway milling about. JC wondered, as he stood looking at the man he had murdered, if "the affray had caused any alarm" within the building.

John Colt walked over to the door once again, made sure it was locked, then turned the stock slide down for a second time (Asa Wheeler had pushed it up to look inside the room).

From there JC took a seat by the only window in the office. He needed to think things through and do something with Adams's body before someone figured out what had happened. JC was worried about the noise he and Adams, fighting, struggling for control, had made. There was that block of time JC could not account for—had there been screaming and yelling, too, he wondered, on top of the thrusting of each other against the wall?

The window near him was open about six or eight inches at the top, allowing a cold, damp breeze to trickle into the room. This helped clear JC's mixed-up mind. He sat, he said, for about a half hour near the window, taking in fresh air, staring down onto Broadway below. He held his head in his hands at times, shaking, trembling, wondering how he was going to get out of this mess. He even grabbed "the curtains of the window close, while they were within reach." A habit of JC's was to leave the "curtains about one-third drawn from the side of the window toward Broadway." He didn't want anyone from a corresponding building or rooftop looking in.

After a time, JC looked at Sam Adams. All the blood Adams had lost was now "spreading over the floor." Below JC's office was the apothecary's store, a pharmacy, and JC was worried the blood was going to seep through the floorboards of his office and drip down into the store.

"There was a great quantity, and I felt alarmed lest it should leak," JC explained.

JC stood, disrobed the cravat from around his neck, and tied it as tightly as he could around the neck of his victim, hoping to stop the flow of the blood, which was still coming out of Adams's head and face.

"This appeared to do no good."

Frantically, JC walked around his office looking for a piece of twine. Searching, he came upon a box that had once contained books and discovered an awning and a piece of cord attached, which he then "tied tightly round [Adams's] neck after taking the handkerchief off." It was at this time when JC stripped Adams of his clothing, figuring Adams might be identified by what he was wearing.

Near his desk, JC had a bucket "one-third full of water." There was a towel on a bench. Still worried about the blood leaking through the floorboards, JC took the towel and soaked up the blood, wringing it out into the bucket.

Finished some time later, the bucket was full of blood and water.

He then spread the awning out on the floor and pulled Adams's body onto the top of it, and rolled Adams's body up as best he could in it.

"I never saw his face afterwards."

JC then went back to cleaning the floor. When he believed he had finished, JC walked over to the window and sat down. He needed to settle himself and "think what was best to do" next.

As he sat, contemplating a plan, a knock upon the door startled him.

———

As it turned out, John Caldwell Colt wasn't cut out to be a gambler; he found winning poker games aboard steamships about as easy as trying to catch eels in the water with bare hands. Departing that scene on the

Mississippi, JC headed to Cincinnati, Ohio, where he met an "octoroon slave and mistress of a wealthy, young planter," according to Sam Colt biographer Martin Rywell. An octoroon slave meant JC had hooked up with a woman born of one-eighth black ancestry.

In 1830 slavery was rampant across the South, yet beginning to spread throughout the nation. The Civil War was several decades away. "African Americans were enslaved on small farms, large plantations, in cities and towns, inside homes, out in the fields, and in industry and transportation," said one writer.

Everywhere JC turned while in the South, he saw human beings in bondage, working the fields, being treated like animals. It appears from the evidence Rywell presents in his book, scant as it is, the Colts were not a family prone to treating human beings (Sam Adams's murder aside) with the disdain and scorn slaves received from their owners, and there is no documentation supporting a finding one way or another regarding how John Colt felt personally about slavery. Having grown up and lived in New England, of course, one would *assume* JC and his family were opponents of slavery; yet, in later years, as the Colt firearm business teetered on the edge of major success, it became patently obvious that Sam Colt, at the least, wasn't going to publicly contest slavery, especially if remaining out of the slavery fray meant building his business bigger and making more money. Agreeing with most Northern Democrats of his time, Sam Colt didn't necessarily view slavery as a moral issue, Barbara and Kenneth Tucker wrote in their important book, *Industrializing Antebellum America*. In fact, Sam "played on the fears of slave rebellion to sell guns to plantation owners," the Tuckers observed. Sam was the type of entrepreneur who saw an opportunity and exploited it, despite the implications of coming across as a proponent of what would ultimately divide a country and thrust it into civil war. This idea that Sam was riding on the back of the slavery movement to boost his profits was further bolstered by an article published in the *Journal of the American Institute* (1837), in which Sam was presented as a greedy slave monger: "Mr. Colt appeared to be near the scene of a sanguinary insurrection of Negro slaves," the article said. "He was startled to think of what fearful odds the white planter must ever contend, thus surrounded by a swarming population of slaves. What defense could there be in one shot, when opposed to multitudes, even though multitudes of the unarmed? The master and his family were certain to be massacred. Was there no way, thought Mr. Colt, of enabling the planter to repose in peace?"

Strong words, and Sam Colt never expressed any regret over their being published. The Tuckers took things a bit further, claiming the words had been, in fact, "printed with Colt's permission."

Sam believed—and openly promoted—the proposal that his invention of the repeating firearm was the perfect weapon to cast fear into and protect against those slaves who decided to get out of line or run away. In this respect, many of the newspapers later covering Sam's rise and fall in the business world called him a "Southern sympathizer if not an outright traitor to the Union."

In truth, though, Sam Colt was neither: He was a businessman, whose morality and apparent social stance were likely rooted in a staunch and passionate desire to see that his patents made money. Like JC, Sam harbored an inherent need to *be* somebody, to be noticed, to be the center of attention. But it was quite unlike Sam to get involved with a slave, as JC had, although she could have been considered white by all appearances. The situation spoke to the part of JC's character that craved constant disorder and drama; he adored the idea of people paying mind to him. He lived a life of varying degrees of narcissism, lapping up the notice of others and devouring the awareness of people talking about him, for good or bad.

Rywell claimed the relationship JC had with the Ohio slave resulted in JC's being challenged to a duel (by whom, Rywell never said), which sent JC running from Cincinnati and, ultimately, into the arms of a "new mistress."

From this period—about 1831—until we pick up JC's trail again in 1834, the only part of his life we know for certain is that JC traveled around the country: from Ohio to Vermont, to New Orleans, Michigan, Mississippi, Florida, Texas, and Louisville, where he began to develop the interest in bookkeeping he had harbored since his teen years.

"[I]n a year or two," *Life and Letters* claimed, "he amassed the materials for the work he had afterwards published."

In keeping with the spirit of that devious criminal vein running through him, there's a good chance JC stole many of—if not all of—the ideas about double-entry bookkeeping he had, as he put it, "collected" in Ohio. His first printed work, *The Science of Double-Entry Bookkeeping*, bears striking resemblance in scope, tone, and context to that of a book by James Arlington Bennett, a prominent lawyer who, in 1820, published what was at the time the double-entry bookkeeping bible, *The American System of Practical Book-keeping.** The concepts and layout of this book and JC's are very similar.

"Plagiarism is nothing new," said one prominent scholar on the subject of JC potentially stealing the ideas of Bennett. "The copyright laws back then were very fluid. I have read the book, and your assumption is probably correct."

While in Kentucky working out the accounting concepts he would later teach, lecture on, and publish, JC met a "Norwegian girl," Frances Anne Meir, a young lass he would soon find to be one of the more intriguing females he had ever met. JC never said where, but he was staying along the Ohio River (likely near Covington, just south of Cincinnati, splitting his time between Ohio and Kentucky). Frances, who had been married twice but lost both husbands to disease, was of "singular character, rare beauty, considerable accomplishments, and of a very romantic disposition." Because of these and other qualities JC found compelling, he became infatuated with the girl. Some evidence indicates a friendship blossomed between them because JC felt sorry for Frances. One writer who later spoke to JC about his life said JC "counseled her as a brother, and aided her with instructions." To wit, Frances was said to proclaim: "I know that I am not fit to become your wife, and it is happy enough for

---

* Of note, Friar Luca Pacioli, an Italian Catholic monk, wrote the first textbook on double-entry accounting in the 1494, today published as the *Ancient Double-entry Bookkeeping: Luca Pacioli's Treatise.* Luca is considered the father of double-entry bookkeeping. Luca was a mathematician who took his principles of numbers and applied them to bookkeeping. Some claim Luca taught Leonardo DaVinci all he knew about mathematics. As a sign of just how indelible and popular Luca Pacioli has become as a folk hero of mathematics and accounting, one need only to log onto Facebook and see that Luca has his own entry. John Colt undoubtedly studied Luca's treatise, as did any student of bookkeeping. Yet Colt's specific ideas bear greater consistency with the work of James Arlington Bennett's theories laid out in *The American System of Practical Book-keeping* some twenty years before Colt published his book. In fact, in his book, JC gives Luca a little poke, without naming him specifically, writing: "The principle of Book-keeping, as now understood and practiced, is laid claim to by the Italians, who date the time of its origin in the middle ages. But even the name, and the place from whence glimmered the first principle of the science of Double Entry Book-keeping, is unknown; that spot which would be held sacred by the whole commercial world, slumbers beneath the sea dirge; is heedlessly trod upon by the passing way-farer; and is wept for only by the dew drop of some straggling and unconscious flower." Further, JC commends the English and their "boundless and still spreading commerce" for inventing the science of bookkeeping the way in which he saw it moving forward.

me to be blested [sic] with your society, and to feel that you prize me as your truest friend."

Frances felt she was in the company of an important man (a reputation JC had surely built himself). According to *Life and Letters*, after a time of courting (or conning, rather), it was JC's "kindness [that] won her devoted attachment."

JC could charm the venom from a snake if he thought it would further him in life. The Norwegian girl showed the tiniest bit of resistance in the beginning of the relationship and this made JC want to win her over even more.

"He pursued toward her a course of virtuous resolution—hers toward him was one of concealed passion," added *Letters*, "to which she became a victim."

Frances had unremitting strength. "In her little hands," JC's interviewer claimed, "she would lift and extend an arm's length a weight of fifty-six pounds." She was athletic, JC said. And she could "hop eight feet, jump on a level ten feet and a half, and run like the antelope."

No sooner had JC learned that Frances was "in love" with him, than he spitefully turned around and told her his only desire had been friendship. He wrote to her, breaking the girl's heart. The high for JC was apparently in the pursuit.

It was a strange relationship; JC said later she knew they were only friends, yet one anecdote he relayed spoke of two adults acting as though there was much more. They had been out riding horses together along the Ohio River one late afternoon. The night sky was settling on the day. After stopping for a break, JC suggested they take the horses down to a small tributary and water them.

"They meant to rove until moon-rise," JC's interviewer wrote.

As they talked, Frances mentioned that she considered herself to be an expert swimmer. She said, "No man can out-swim me."

JC challenged her.

Frances smiled. Then took off all her clothes.

"And while [JC] stood pondering, he was suddenly aroused."

"Come on, you flinch!" JC said. Then he too disrobed and jumped into the water. They swam for a time, each trying to outdo the other, from riverbank to bank, laughing, yelling, screaming, having a joyous time. At one point, Frances pulled herself up on the bank and stood there, waiting for JC to emerge from an underwater dive. The moonlight had since come up and, according to JC's recollection, shone on a naked Frances as though someone had put a spotlight on her.

Realizing she was naked with the moon showing off her body, Frances said, in jest, "Oh, forgive me . . . I forgot!" and jumped into the water to hide herself.

Soon, they got dressed and rode back to town.

JC never admitted making love to Frances (on that night or at any other time), although the horseback ride and skinny-dip certainly expressed to Frances a growing sincerity and interest in her on JC's part. On top of this, JC was said to have given Frances a piano and hired her a tutor. He encouraged the woman to study books he had purchased and practice the piano.

Frances turned around and told JC she wanted to take up acting; her passion was the stage.

When JC heard this from a friend (he was in Ohio, Frances in Kentucky at the time), he became incensed. He had not hired a tutor and purchased a piano so she could cheapen herself with the exploits of the stage. He had an enormous resentment against the stage for a reason he never voiced.

"He renewed his earnest advice for her to devote herself to her music," *An Authentic Life of John C. Colt* read, "in a teacher and a composer, in the last of which she already made several brilliant essays."

Frances was talented. She excelled at the piano and JC saw her one day being a respected music teacher, which fit her personality, he believed.

After receiving a letter from JC in which he described in great detail how he felt about where he saw her life heading, Frances went silent. She would not write back to this man who had suddenly changed his opinions about her so drastically.

JC later promoted himself as Frances's mentor. He said he assumed she knew nothing more than friendship would ever come of the relationship. He thought Frances understood he was better schooled in worldly ideas because he had traveled. His brother was one day going to be a famous inventor. His family had wealth. It was mutually understood between them, he claimed, that JC was there for Frances as a big brother.

Not hearing from Frances stirred up JC's emotions. He soon sent a third letter, along with the items she had purchased for him as gifts throughout their friendship. In describing how bad it made him feel to send back her gifts, JC said, "And yet, I would almost as soon have parted with my soul."

Frances sent word that she could never explain to him how she felt about the last letter—in which he had scolded her. She didn't have the words to explain to him how angry and slighted that disturbing missive had made her feel. She was better off just dropping the subject and moving on and out of JC's life.

JC returned to town. He was back three days, he later claimed, before he and Frances saw each other. He had never called on her. There was one day when, without warning, she walked into his office "perfectly calm."

"I am very glad to see you," Frances offered. "I have brought back all of your letters!"

JC didn't see that she had them in her hand. He wondered what she meant.

Frances smiled. She took out a velvet case. Opened it. Turned it upside down and poured what was left of JC's letters—now nothing more than confetti—all over his desk. She returned the gifts he had given her: broaches, rings, chains, bracelets, each of them "pounded to very powder" and dumped on his desk next to the shredded portions of the letters.

JC said they laughed about the ordeal later that same day and spent several days together, joking and frolicking about town, arm in arm. Two old friends, he made it sound, catching up, forgetting about the past and moving on.

As JC got on with his life and Frances went about hers, moving into a boardinghouse nearby, they remained friends, but not lovers, JC said. Nor was their relationship anything like what it had been in the past. He had his life. She had hers.

Soon, stories made it to JC's office stating that Frances was using drugs and not eating and had secluded herself in her room. She was apparently spending her time pacing and talking to people who were not there.

JC offered to give Frances $300, he later said, so she could get on her feet and pick up with her music and "become independent and happy." He continued to pound into her psyche the idea that she had a future in music, if only she made it her focus in life.

In one letter to Frances, JC, who had, one could argue, shown this broken woman kindness and friendship, beyond leading her on, turned scathing, nasty, and angrier than he had ever been. He accused Frances in the opening sentences of running from "subject to subject as though [she] were half mad," adding that if she couldn't make up her mind about what she wanted to do with her life, it was going to destroy her. "It will sooner or later complete your ruin," he wrote, adding:

Forget the past entirely. Read the books I sent you. Spend all your time in improvement. Exclude yourself for a while from the world, abandon old friends. . . . You need in many great respects to improve your education. And so should you follow the advice I am so often given, you will be all together happier than you now are and perhaps more so than you have been in all of your life.

The man who had dropped out of the Marines, left school, tried gambling, petty theft, accounting, and roamed around the country for several years trying to figure out how to get rich quick went on to say that should Frances continue to insist on becoming an actress, which seemed to be the only trade that made Frances happy during this time of her life, then she was heading down a path of pity and scorn, of which, JC added, "the very devil must be behind."

Of note, JC was furious about the potential audiences Frances would have to perform in front of, perhaps because he had not run into friendly attendees at some of his lectures: men and women who had heckled and called JC names. He pointed out his concerns about the theater in that same letter, writing:

They [theater audiences] seem scarcely ready to believe their eyes—they applaud and go home; and judging others by the standard of their own barometer, they set the actress down to be as black a character as the inclinings of their own passions would make them, had they but the opportunity, or were removed from the restraints that artificial society has placed about them in the position they accidentally hold.

JC enjoyed ranting, maybe just to hear or read his own exhortations. He wrote in long-winded sentences and went on and on at times, sounding like a raving-mad lunatic. The woman was obviously depressed and in love with him, still feeling the pain of losing two husbands. She wanted to act in the theater. It seemed to be the only thing that would brighten what were surely the darkest days of her life. Yet JC rambled on about how bad a choice she had made for not listening to what he had suggested. In this letter, after his rambling passage about audiences, he carried on about how insincere and inhuman paying theatergoers were, men and women whom he referred to as the "rich and fashionables." He said people who attended plays had no sympathy or values, and "no feeling for others." He told the story of a play he had seen in Philadelphia once, where he met an actress who had a "hurricane brush over her short . . . career." Soon after she left the theater, rumors started about the woman. People in town said she was crazy and her mother was crazy. Was this what Frances wanted for a future—people chiding and making fun of her? JC wanted Frances to work in a noble profession. Continuing, he wrote:

> *If such could not escape such foul and impardonable [sic] reproach, what, my dear girl, are you to expect from the same tribunal, when you ask for bread, and at the same time ask to be considered respectable? Think these things over, Frances. God knows if I thought you would be happy in leading such a life, it would be to me a source of never-dying pleasure to promote that happiness as far as it comes within the reach of my humble capacity. Say no more about theaters. It puts me in the perfect chill to be forced to write such letters as this. Follow up on your music . . . and all will be well.*

He had a few more somewhat kind words for Frances and then ended the tedious missive, never offering himself as a friend or someone Frances could at least turn to if she felt things were getting worse.

Sometime later Frances got word JC was heading to New York. She sent a message to him hoping he would take her along. It was November 14, 1838, when JC sent a brief letter back, saying absolutely not. He and Nathan Burgess, his publishing partner, were going east together—without her!

Frances was taking a walk when she received the letter. After reading it, she rushed over to see her brother-in-law, who lived in town. She was said to tell him all about JC and her problems. She seemed out of it at times, "in a stupor."

Throughout the day, Frances talked in circles. Her sister and brother-in-law summoned a doctor. She was losing her mind. She refused any medicines the doctor offered. Instead, she called for a friend. She had wanted to dictate a letter to be sent to JC and needed her friend to write and send it. While speaking, she said her eyesight was failing, she was slipping away. That friend asked Frances what it was she wanted to say. Frances spoke directly to JC:

You say right, I do not love you; for women love but once, and the idol I worship is beyond my reach; but still, I love him yet. . . . I am grateful for the many favors I have received from you, and the interest you have displayed in my welfare. I have pretended to love you dearly, but in my heart, I did not. I have even admired your talents and respected your person, but your two last letters were of such a nature as to kill even those feelings. You will never see me again: for, a few short hours, and I shall be in heaven. Forgive me, for I am dying now. Frances.

Frances had done something even JC, as cunning and evil as his behavior often proved him to be, could not have considered an option. "Finding her love returned by friendship only," JC's *Life and Letters* reported, "[Frances] committed suicide."

She left JC with the sting of having had the last word. She had "taken one [hundred] and fifty grains of opium, upon receiving that last letter from [JC]." Frances lasted about a day after reciting the letter, finally succumbing to an overdose the following morning.

During this period of time while JC was with Frances, he had met and begun working with Nathan Burgess, whom he had first run into during his previous trip through town. Burgess and JC worked on a book they would publish within the next two years, *An Inquiry into the Origin of the Antiquities of America*, by John Delafield Jr.

The book was one of the main reasons why JC, with Burgess, moved back to New York. Throughout the time he worked on *Antiquities*, JC published his own book on accounting. According to Burgess, he and JC took a bath on the Delafield project.

"It was published [by] the Colt, Burgess & Co.," Burgess later said, "and we lost a thousand dollars by it."

Burgess didn't see any problems with his business partner. He liked JC.

"I am still indebted to Mr. Colt. He always treated me like a gentleman."

After that failed business deal of 1839 between Burgess and JC, JC struck out on his own. He was back in the city where he had once been caught with his hands in his father's cousin's cookie jar. Only now JC was older and wiser. He could settle down and open his own accounting office, teach, and write. But New York City was not going to be kind to John Caldwell Colt.

The tragedy of Frances's death had no effect on JC, or at least none that he spoke of. In fact, in all that was written about this incident in his life, John Colt never said anything about his feelings for a woman who had taken an overdose of opiates after he had basically chastised her to death. He never mentioned his relationship with Frances or her death to anyone. Nor had he ever showed any direct signs of being saddened by her passing. The entire matter of Frances taking her own life "could not have touched him too deeply," *An Authentic Life of John C. Colt* reported, "nor the less, because [he] endured in silence."

Back in Cincinnati, before trekking to New York during the spring of 1839, JC had advertised his services as a "former government accountant." He had finished his manuscript on double-entry bookkeeping and opened an office. This idea of having been part of the government's body of bookkeepers, Martin Rywell pointed out, was due to JC at one time being a Marine, and nothing more. There is no record of JC ever having worked as an accountant for the government in *any* capacity (as a Marine or civilian); and yet this advertisement, in all of its subtlety (or perhaps audacity), was typical of the con artist side of JC's character, something of which he had spent years refining. Before leaving Cincinnati and heading to New York, "John became the center of a hobohemian circle where unconventional artists, writers and pseudo-intellectuals congregated,"* Rywell wrote. It was likely during his Cincinnati counterculture days when JC had met and befriended Frances. JC's little brother Sam even headed west for a spell at some point and joined his brother inside this absurd group of people.

While on a business trip to New Orleans not long before leaving for New York, JC's business partner back in Cincinnati, Nathan Burgess, had made several bad choices, according to *Life and Letters*, forcing JC to close the doors of his company. "[JC] found that the affairs of the firm had been so mismanaged [in his absence] that he was obliged to close up his business with as little loss as possible."†

---

* According to UrbanDictionary.com, the term hobohemian refers to: "1: A homeless artist or musician, commonly found in cities; 2. An artistic hipster who often stays at the random homes of friends, family members and current lovers but never has any money or current mailing address."

† Here is JC, once again, shirking the blame—a mantra this man lived by. He never took responsibility for any failure.

12

A Silent Space of Time

JOHN L. STEVENS RETURNED FROM "AN EXTENDED TOUR THROUGH ASIA and the Holy Land" with images of fine art, large stone buildings carved out of sweat in the hillsides, and ancient architectural designs floating in his head. He had made drawings of an Egyptian tomb he had seen and brought them back to Hoboken, New Jersey, where he had lived all his life. Stevens published a book, *Stevens' Travels*, with illustrations and writings. Depending on whom you believe, it was one of those drawings by Stevens that became the seed from which sprouted the Halls of Justice on the grounds of the old Fresh Water Pond on Centre Street, there between White and Leonard, downtown (Federal Plaza and Columbus Park today). The city wanted a massive, imposing structure for a jail, with courtrooms and station houses for the growing police force, along with additional rooms for various aspects of law enforcement and legal work. It would be the epicenter of law and justice; the pulse and heart of a city taking a stand against crime. New York was in desperate need of a new jail in 1838, when work on what would be nicknamed "The Tombs" was finally completed.

"The old Bridewell was a nuisance," Edwin Burrows and Michael Wallace wrote in *Gotham*, a mammoth and exceptional book of New York City history, "and the Bellevue Penitentiary was too distant from downtown courts."*

---

* Charles Sutton, one of the wardens of the prison, wrote a book in 1874 titled *The New York Tombs: Its Secrets and Its Mysteries,* in which he describes the resurrection of the new jail similarly to how Burrows and Wallace did more than one hundred years later, offering insight, in the context of time, as to why the prison was built: "In 1830 the population of the city was 203,000. Crime had increased in proportion, and the need of a new Prison was keenly felt. The old City Prison, or Bridewell, just west of the City Hall, had become a nuisance, and was eventually torn down. The Bellevue Jail was too far out of town, too distant from the Courts, and accordingly, in 1833, it was resolved that a City Prison be erected further down town. The old Collect grounds were selected as the site of the new Prison, with a recommendation that it be built so as to afford the necessary accommodations for

Halls of Justice was the building's proper name; but because of its Egyptianlike presence in the city at a time when this sort of construction was rare, and the fact that in all of its grandeur and allure it looked more like a mausoleum, the Tombs felt more appropriate (and intimidating). Anybody arrested—didn't matter who it was or where the arrest took place in the city—would pass through the halls of the Tombs. Public officials and law enforcement liked this concept of a one-stop shop for law breakers.

Some scholars claim that John Haviland, a noted prison architect of the day who was given the job of drafting the plans, designed the Tombs from his own imagination, not relying on Stevens's work at all. Haviland was the go-to guy with the draftsman's pencil and ruler if you wanted a prison built in early-nineteenth-century America. Among scores of others, Haviland had designed the state prison in Trenton, New Jersey, some years before the Tombs, a building that surely showed signs of Egyptian influence.*

"Haviland is due the entire merit of having introduced this novel and complete style of prison architecture," wrote Charles Sutton a few short years after Haviland's death, "which soon attracted the attention of the entire civilized world."

Either way, JC was being held inside the Tombs as he awaited his day in court, which was said to be sometime in November 1841. As he sat in his cell, JC did his best to talk his way out of a hangman's noose. His lawyers listened and wrote. This *Confession*, as it would become known,

———

court rooms as well." I appreciate this passage, simply because it showcases how a decision—major as this one was then—had been made by city officials for practical purposes, not political, personal, or financial gain. Although corruption was certainly a major component of New York politics and the legal system at the time, this one decision to build a new jail seemed to me to be made in good standing with the needs of protecting those law-abiding New Yorkers who made up the soul of the city. (Sutton, Charles, James B. Mix, and Samuel Anderson Mackeever. 1874. *The New York Tombs; its secrets and its mysteries. Being a history of noted criminals, with narratives of their crimes.* San Francisco, Cal: A. Roman & Co., p. 48.)

* John Haviland was born in England on December 15, 1792. He studied with Elmes, "the well-known writer upon architecture." In 1815, Haviland traveled to Russia and entered the Imperial Corps of Engineers. According to a short biography written just after his death in 1852 (Simpson, Henry. 1859. *The lives of eminent Philadelphians, now deceased.* Philadelphia: W. Brotherhead., pp. 513–514), Haviland was "the first to introduce the radiating form in the construction of prisons; and he built the Pittsburg Penitentiary upon this plan." Also included in Haviland's long list of prison accomplishments are: the Eastern Penitentiary at Philadelphia; Halls of Justice at New York; the United States Naval Asylum at Norfolk; the New Jersey State Penitentiary; the State Penitentiaries at Missouri and Rhode Island; the Albany, Lancaster, Berks County Prison, Pennsylvania; the Deaf and Dumb Asylum, Philadelphia; the State Insane Hospital, Harrisburg; the United States Mint, Philadelphia; the County Halls of Newark and York, as well as numerous churches and private mansions.

was a good idea on the part of JC and his lawyers, if only for the way in which they went about putting JC's version—which sounded an awful lot like a claim of self-defense—out there. Dictating the details and presenting them to the court as a written document (i.e., a confession), would pre-empt a prosecutor's cross-examination. In this confession, JC could say anything he wanted. He didn't need to answer an opposing counsel's tough questions. Though, as it would become clear in the years that followed, what JC had to say, even if he was hiding some of the truth, allowed a deeper look into the psyche of this strange, nonconforming, bitter man.

"My horrid situation remained," JC recalled of that moment he sat near the window in his second-story office for a second time as someone from the building knocked on the door.

This one sentence, in which JC talks about himself as if he is in grave danger of some sort, exemplifies the characteristics of narcissistic personality disorder (NPD). He had just killed a man. Butchered him with an axe. Rolled him up in an awning. There was blood everywhere. Yet in his mind, JC had spun that circumstance around and turned it on himself by looking at how bad he had it. He mentioned nothing of his victim. It was all about JC and this unfortunate predicament he found himself in.

JC sat in that chair by the window, he said, "[f]rom this time until dark, a silent space of time of still more horrid reflection."

He was worried about what was going to happen to him. But he was also concerned this one incident would destroy his brother's chance of growing Colt Firearms into the industrial mega-business he had dreamed it to be.

As dusk fell, JC heard something outside. It was an omnibus, a trolley-like car pulled by a team of horses, passing by the Granite Building on Broadway. He heard people talking below. It was busy down on the street. And too dark now for JC to see anything.

He walked to the door, placed his ear upon its wooden back.

It was silent outside in the hallway.

"I carefully opened the door," JC explained, "and went out as still as possible, and I thought unheard."

Across the street from the Granite Building stood City Hall Park. JC, having left the building without being seen, ran into the pasture of the park.

Sam was at the City Hotel, mixing it up with the rich and powerful of the city, still trying to get his business over an economic hurdle. He needed a government order of pistols to rescue Colt Firearms. The building in Paterson his company had inhabited was costing money—money Sam did not yet have to spend.

"I crossed into the Park," JC added, "and went down from thence to the City Hotel, my purpose being to relate the circumstance to a brother."

Sam was talking business with two other gentlemen. JC was like a madman, looking in all directions, wearing bloody garb, the steely aroma of plasma (like wet metal) wafting up and reminding him of what he had done.

JC got Sam's attention, and as he recalled, "A few words passed between us and, seeing that he was engaged, I altered my purpose and returned as far as the Park."

This part of the *Confession* seems a fallacy. JC would not have spoken to Sam while covered in blood. He had no change of clothes at his office, that much is known. Save from wearing a coat to cover himself, JC perhaps fabricated this portion of his confession in order to involve Sam, who would soon be brought into the murderous affair.

The park, for JC, seemed like the best place for him to clear his head and think things through more cogently. What was he going to do with a dead man in his office?

He paced in the park. The one idea that kept popping up, JC claimed, was "going to a magistrate and relating the facts to him."

Confessing to what he had done.

"Then the horrors of the excitement, a trial, public censure, and false and foul reports that would be raised by the many who would stand ready to make the best appear worse than the worst, for the sake of a paltry pittance gained to them in the publication of perverted truths and original, false, foul, calumniating lies, all this, added to my then feelings, was more than could be borne."

It was a mouthful, written by a man who was focused, after he committed murder, on what effects his brutal crime would have on him alone.

What worried JC even more than anything was the cord he had tightly tied around Sam Adams's neck, "which looked too deliberate for anything like death caused in an affray."

Walking about the park as darkness settled on the city, JC thought hard and long about what to do next.

Then it came to him.

Light the Granite Building on fire and burn it to the ground.

———

Heading east during the spring of 1839 (probably running from creditors), JC rented an office space in New York "for the sale of books." By this time, he was into so many different business ventures (publishing and writing books, tutoring, business consulting) he realized going it alone in New York and focusing on his accounting work was the only opportunity he had to become rich and famous. But he needed to present himself as a professional, a businessman ahead of the curve.

"I have an infinite deal of pleasure," he wrote to a friend near this time, "in all these labors, which I shall never regret, even should I fail to receive any credit for them, or remuneration for what I have gone through, in producing so entire a revolution in the mode of treating a theme [accounting] so extensively important."

A reporter, one who probably would not qualify as such by the standards of modern journalism, later interviewed JC, who said he was thinking about politics and dreamed of buying land for farming in Missouri or Kentucky. JC explained how he wanted to "plant corn and plough politics." He spoke of one day "finding his way into Congress." Looking back, JC could not focus his efforts on one particular vocation; instead, he wandered from city to city, hoping to fall into whatever line of work he believed would place him in an elite crowd the fastest and make him the most money.

A fantasist, JC was unable to accept that he was nothing more than a laborer whose hobby was bookkeeping. Here he was now in New York, trying to make a name for himself in the shadow of a brother endowed by their father and a very wealthy cousin (Dudley Selden), looking for the shortest route to the good things in life. Apparently, though, JC was getting tired of the game. Mixing it up with the upper echelon of Manhattan's finest for a few months after arriving, realizing he was out of his element entirely, JC decided once again to take a different approach. No sooner had he arrived in town to find money and fame only an illusion was John Colt caught in the act and "indicted for being concerned in a burglary in

Wall-street." He had been apprehended in some sort of sting set up by law enforcement at the Astor House.* On his possession, night watchmen found "a great variety of skeleton keys," the same tools any seasoned thief would use and carry around with him to pick locks.

Not long after this incident, JC was arrested for breaking into the law office of Judge William Inglis. When caught, JC gave cops "an assumed name," and was never fully prosecuted. Let out on bail, he was said to have then holed up inside Lovejoy's Hotel, on the corner of Beekman Street and Park Row. It was here, according to JC's *Confession*, that he began to publicly display that repressed anger he held so deeply for so long a period of time. After not paying his hotel dues, the proprietor set out to evict JC and collect the amount. "He replied in a very threatening and surly manner," *Confession* reported. He was told he had to leave the hotel at once or pay his bill in full. To that JC responded "he would pay [the hotel proprietor] over his head with a poker if [he] didn't quit annoying him."

The other testimonial JC gave after his arrest for the murder of Sam Adams also glosses over this period of his life. *Life and Letters* claimed JC "was moral and temperate in his habits" after he arrived in New York, "but was on two or three occasions hurried into [excess] in wine by companions who took advantage of his general abstemiousness." That break-in on Wall Street was nothing more than a misunderstanding, JC explained, for he was drunk and led into it by his intoxicated mates.

"He was taken to the watch-house," *Life and Letters* reported, "and discharged when he had slept off the fumes of the wine the next morning."

---

* The Astor House mentioned here was the famed Astor Hotel. According to Matthew Smith's wonderful history of the city, *Sunshine and Shadow in New York* [Smith, Matthew Hale. 1868. *Sunshine and shadow in New York*. Hartford: J.B. Burr and Co., p. 310], on June 1, 1836, "the Astor House was thrown open to the public. It was then in the extreme upper part of New York. It soon became the most famous hotel in the nation. It has always been the centre of travel and trade. The omnibuses and street cars, connecting with all the ferries, places of amusement, and railroads, start from the Astor. The great rotunda is high 'change' daily for the eminent men of the nation. Political societies, clubs, benevolent organizations, and great corporations hold their meetings at this hotel." The Astor House was the type of establishment in the city where you went to be seen. You checked your pistol at the front counter and went about your business, schmoozing with the socialites of the day. JC had no place being there. This was where Sam Colt hung around, hoping to dredge up investors. With his book just about published, there can be no doubt JC saw himself in the same famous vein as his brother, Sam, and not being welcomed with open arms at the Astor Hotel was a slight and reflection of JC's failures. Robbing the place was one way to get back at the "establishment" itself, something JC undoubtedly took great pleasure in.

With New York City law enforcement on his back and a blizzard of legal trouble brewing around him, JC fled to Boston and Philadelphia, he later said, "to lecture." He was being paid respectable fees to speak about his knowledge of bookkeeping and several revolutionary business ideas he had sold as his own. Still, JC left New York not by his own accord; there's a good chance that Sam, who was close to making several important sales to the government that would grow his business substantially, told JC to get out of town for a spell, or at least until things settled down and Sam was able to secure those deals.

Just a year prior to JC moving back into the big city, Sam had traveled to Florida with one hundred of his revolving pistols (and some of the rifles he had been working on), where he met with William Harney. Sam ended up selling fifty of the rifles and a dozen pistols for a total of $6,250. Sam's Paterson factory was putting out about 5,000 firearms annually, so this was a good start. If Harney liked the weapons and the government understood the repeating firearm was going to help its soldiers win wars against the Indians, Sam understood his business would take off. Sam's primary purpose now was to make sure the military adopted his core beliefs. He would work exhaustingly on this prospect, as he had for the past several years. And the last thing he needed was the black sheep of the family being the butt of Astor House jokes and headlines for the penny presses.

13

Blood in the Gutter

TORCHING THE GRANITE BUILDING IN ORDER TO GET RID OF SAM Adams's rotting corpse inside his office, JC realized as he wandered through City Hall Park on the evening of September 17, 1841, was far too dangerous. "Fire the building at first seemed like a happy thought," JC later said, "and all would be enveloped in flame, and wafted into air and ashes." But the idea that so many others would go down with the building, JC felt, seeing there was "quite a number who slept in the building," not to mention the "destruction of property . . . caused me to . . . abandon the idea."

There had to be another way.

JC came up with the notion of making "a suitable box . . . leaded inside, so that the blood would not run out." After packing Sam Adams inside, JC figured, he could then find a proper place in the city to bury him. Yet once again, the narcissism JC harbored turned him away from this plan: "[T]he delay of all this, and the great liability of being detected" proved to be too much.

JC walked through the park for another hour or more. Nothing came to him. He could not go home to Caroline Henshaw. Seven months pregnant, the woman didn't need the stress of hearing about him having murdered a man. The less she knew the better off they both were in the long run.

So JC walked to the Granite Building and headed up the stairs toward his office.

"Wheeler's door was open," JC said later, "and he was talking to someone quite audibly."

JC passed quietly by Wheeler's door and "went into my room, entering undetermined, and not knowing what to do."

Whatever he did, JC considered, would have to wait until Asa Wheeler was finished teaching for the evening and "his lights [were] extinguished."

While he waited, a resolution to his problem suddenly hit JC like an old memory. "During this suspense"—that time when Asa Wheeler was still in the building with his students and JC was holed up in his room with Sam Adams's bloodied and butchered body—"it occurred to me that I might put the body in a cask or box, and ship it off somewhere."

The box inside JC's office was not likely going to work. "I supposed it too short and small, and entirely unsafe, as it was quite open."

Next door, in Asa Wheeler's office, JC heard voices. Wheeler was finished teaching for the evening. This worried JC. He felt "somewhat alarmed," thinking they were on to him.

It grew dark inside JC's office. "No time was to be lost." He needed to be quick about this plan. "Something must be done." He closed the shutters of the one window and lit a candle so he could see what he was doing. It was close to nine o'clock by this time.

Certain no one could see inside the room, JC picked up the box and placed it on his desk. Studying the inside of it more closely, he "soon saw there was a possibility of" packing Sam Adams inside the crate, "if I could bend the legs up, so that it would answer if I could keep some of the canvas around the body to absorb the blood, and keep it from running out."

He then stripped Adams's clothes off and threw them away so no one would identify Adams by his garments: coat sleeve, vest, pants, keys, and money, which "caused a rattling."

While doing this, JC covered the body with a section of the awning so he didn't have to look at it. With that done, he cut the awning into large strips and lined the bottom of the crate with them so the blood would not ooze through.

Realizing Adams would not fit into the box the way in which his body was positioned on the floor, JC took part of the awning cord and hog-tied the dead printer, later describing this part of the night in sobering detail:

> I then drew a piece of this rope around the legs at the joint of the knees, and tied them together. I then connected a rope to the one about the shoulder or neck, and bent the knees toward the head of the body as much as I could. This brought it into a compact form.

With Sam Adams's corpse hog-tied, JC picked him up off the floor and set Adams on a chair in an upright position. From there, he was able to hoist Adams over his shoulder and slip him into the box.

"The head, knees and feet, were still a little out, but, by reaching down to the bottom of the box, and pulling the body a little toward me, I readily pushed the head in and feet. The knees still projected, and I had to stand upon them with all my weight before I could get them down."

JC had stuffed Adams into the box, forcing his stiffening corpse (rigor mortis) to form the shape of the container. Then he carefully packed the awning all around the box, like tissue paper into a gift bag, though he said he "reserved" several sheets of the awning material to finish cleaning up the floor.

Instead of tossing Sam Adams's clothes somewhere along the street, JC decided to place them into the box with the body. After all, there was room. If someone found the box and opened it, did it really matter if the guy's clothes were there next to his decomposed flesh and remains?

After cleaning up as best he could, JC took that pail of water and blood left over from cleaning the floor and carried it down the stairs, eventually pouring it into the gutter of the street. He hurriedly went over to a pump and filled the bucket several times, tossing each full pail of water into the street to dilute the area he had bloodied. Then he took a bucket of water upstairs to dilute any remaining blood inside the office.

When he finished, JC opened the shutters of the window, placed the chair next to the window, locked the door behind him, and took off.

The Washington Bath House was just around the corner on Pearl Street and Broadway. JC needed to clean himself up; he had blood from head to toe. Yet, he claimed, he stopped first at "a hardware store" along the way to pick up some nails so he could finish hammering the crate closed. He had started to seal the box, but the nails kept breaking on him. He needed more to make sure the box was secure, with no chance of coming apart.

The store was closed. It was too late.

Arriving at the bathhouse, JC noticed it was "eight minutes past ten."

He "thoroughly" washed his "shirt and bosom." His garments were stained with blood.

Satisfied he had cleansed himself sufficiently, JC walked home to Monroe Street, arriving exhausted at five minutes to eleven. He lit a candle as soon as he walked in. Hearing him bustle about, Caroline Henshaw came out of their bedroom.

"Why are you so late?" she asked.

———

Martin Rywell portrayed JC's life during the period when he integrated himself back into the thick of New York City life during the winter of 1839–1840, after having gone off on a lecture tour, playing the part of the "proverbial barefoot shoemaker." JC was out there giving speeches on several new accounting concepts he had claimed to have developed, yet he could not manage to balance his own books. Any business venture JC had embarked on folded because of lack of capital and mismanagement of the money.

An accounting failure, JC displayed either great brashness or incredible delusion by taking his act to Philadelphia, which in 1840 was one of the top publishing markets in the country, along with New York City. Philadelphia was bustling, alive and politically active, it being fewer than sixty years since the end of the Revolution. Edgar Allan Poe was residing there, editing and writing. He had published "Tales of the Grotesque and Arabesque" that year. The first bank in the nation, established during the Revolutionary War, was in Philadelphia. John Wagner had introduced yeast that produced lager beer, which he had brought back to Philadelphia from Germany in 1840 (by 1850, the entire country would be making lager). There was even an earthquake reported that year in the City of Brotherly Love.

For JC, going into Philadelphia served two important purposes: One, nobody really knew him; and two, JC could pitch his ideas and concepts, meet with publishers, show his book off, and work his con artist magic on an entirely fresh crowd of people with money to spend. Times were tough for JC. He had published one book to wide acclaim and great success, but the idea of publishing an updated edition didn't seem to sit well with prospective clients and booksellers.

"[T]he small capital [he had] was no longer able to sustain him," *An Authentic Life* stated. JC felt he needed to return to the lecture circuit. Philadelphia had started out as a potential business environment, rich in new clientele and knowledgeable people. But JC struggled to get his book business going.

So he set out on another brief speaking tour, but then returned to Philadelphia and began hanging around a place referred to only as "Mrs. Stewart's house." Soon, the story goes, JC ran into a young woman. It was August 1840. She introduced herself as Caroline Henshaw.

"She was uneducated," *An Authentic Life* said of Caroline and "had no rank in society which could be injured by giving way to her wild fondness and the object of it only advanced her immediate interests."

In one version of their meeting and subsequent courting, JC took a liking to Caroline and soon taught her to read and write. A romance blossomed from there, or, as one of his biographers later put it, "In Philadelphia, a female in humble life had become acquainted with our subject under circumstances which excited the gratitude, that, in ardent hearts, as all history proves, so often grows into the reckless idolatry of passion."

But John Colt had expressed a desire long ago to remain single all his life. He wanted no part of marriage. He said it wasn't something he had ever envisioned for himself. Still, after spending time with Caroline, whom "he never deceived with false hopes, for she was perfectly aware of his having . . . resolved never to marry," they grew close.

Or had they?

There is some evidence indicating this "chance" meeting between JC and Caroline was perhaps staged by Sam, who had been in Philadelphia himself not long before JC arrived. It was Sam, some later claimed, who had fallen in love with Caroline, but since she was not up to his social caliber, as Sam was in the midst of building a business, dealing with foreign countries and heads of state and governments, he abandoned her, telling JC to go and fetch her for him.

In January 1841, Caroline Henshaw left Philadelphia and moved into the house of "Captain and Mrs. Haff" in New York City, where JC followed months later. Then she moved into her own place at 42 Monroe Street. JC told people he didn't live at either location, yet he slept in the same house as Caroline and reported to her on most nights. It was not as if they were "an item," out and about, arm in arm, perusing the streets and parks of New York like lovers. Their relationship, if it was a romance, had been hidden.

"The quarters of that city where they resided," *An Authentic Life* reported, "were not conspicuous ones, and they were there so privately, that scarcely any friend of our subject was aware of his being under such arrangements."

The reason for the privacy could have been that Sam was Caroline's secret lover. JC was the front. Sam was seen plenty of times leaving the abode where Caroline lived.

Caroline had a precarious nature. She was devoted to John Colt, who, by the time he was working out of Asa Wheeler's office space that year, was calling her his wife when anybody asked. This was because, of course, Caroline's pregnancy was beginning to show. Yet Caroline herself later gave away that JC could not have fathered the child, although at the time she claimed he had.

"Have known him fifteen months," Caroline said in January 1842, which would have put their meeting somewhere in October 1840, "knew him before I came from Philadelphia here, came on soon after him from Philadelphia, about three months after, had lived with him from 11 May to the time I understood he had been arrested."

Caroline was seven months pregnant when JC was arrested in September. Backpedaling in time, it would put conception of her child in the month of February. Caroline claimed not to have been with JC then.*

As the summer of 1841 became hotter and more humid as each day passed, Caroline's growing stomach was a constant reminder to both Sam and JC that this woman needed to be provided for. JC realized he needed to make money, quickly, perhaps the old-fashioned way this time. He had an update to his book ready for press. According to several sources, *The Science of Double-Entry Bookkeeping* had gone into eight printings. It was a successful textbook. JC had learned many new things since it was first published, and he had been preaching the idea of making bookkeeping and accounting a mandatory school subject while out on his lecture circuit. Under those circumstances, when he met Sam Adams during the summer of 1841, JC talked of printing a few new editions of the book, among them a "larger" volume he had called the "Teachers and Clerks edition," and another, somewhat smaller one that he referred to as the "School edition." Both would serve the needs of the educational establishment. If accounting was ever made a standard subject in schools across the nation, JC believed (maybe rightly so), he would own that market. Adams, who

---

* Sam Colt could have easily slipped into Philadelphia and fathered this child, as many would later speculate; and considering that Sam Colt would eventually hire the child to work for him (and Caroline would name him Samuel), one can be almost certain that Sam Colt was the child's father. With all of the evidence available, there is no question in my mind.

was not doing so well in business himself, agreed to become JC's printer, under terms of which have never been clear in the record left behind.

On August 30, 1841, JC attended a trade sale in New York that was promising. He did not, however, have books ready. Nor did JC have the savvy with New York publishers and buyers to make any major sales (John Colt was no Sam Colt when it came to marketing). There was another trade show on September 6, this one in Philadelphia. JC needed books ready—or a promise of delivery—for that show. At New York he had shown a sample of the revised text. In Philadelphia, he could sell the book in far larger numbers, set the price, and take the orders. *Life and Letters* explained the process JC used:

> *On there [sic] occasions new works go off in large quantities to the assembled dealers, who frequently buy from a sample, and pay either cash or bankable notes as soon as the goods are furnished, for which some two or three weeks are allowed.*

This was where the dispute between JC and Adams was born. JC took off for Philadelphia and sold his books at a larger profit than he and Adams had agreed—thus, Sam Adams believed JC was trying to scam him out of that extra profit, beyond, that is, already burning him out of an agreed-upon sum for the initial print run. At some point after the Philadelphia trade show, Adams got word to JC that he would not release JC's bookplates, which were said to be worth $500, until JC settled his account (the amount of which has also been in dispute): Adams put it at $71.15; JC at $55.80. Furthermore, without the bookplates, JC could not cut Adams out entirely by hiring a new printer.

"It appears also that our subject," *Life and Letters* reported, this statement regarding JC's motive, "was impatient about some delay on the part of his printer."

JC had sold books on order in Philadelphia; now Adams wasn't going to produce them.

"While [they were inside JC's office]," *Letters* continued, "[JC] was hurrying on the one side and procrastinating on the other, a suspicion on the seventeenth of September, 1841, was excited in the mind of Samuel Adams, that moneys expected by and belonging to our subject, and 'promised, it is said, by him to Samuel Adams, would be available.'"

It appears that JC had agreed to pay Sam Adams the difference, but then went back on his word.

So Adams, "under the excitement of this suspicion," went huffing and puffing down to JC's office on the afternoon of September 17, 1841, "to insult him," not knowing, of course, that he would soon meet the sharp end of an axe and end up inside an oblong-shaped box that, ironically, at one time contained copies of JC's books.

A murder we could say that began over $15.35.

Caroline Henshaw heard someone stirring inside the apartment at 42 Monroe Street. She got out of bed, put on a nightshirt, and walked out of her bedroom.

It was JC, of course. Unbeknownst to Caroline, he had just returned from killing Sam Adams, packing his body inside that wooden crate (still in his office), and cleaning up at the Washington Bath House.

Caroline asked JC where he had been and why he was returning home so late. It was after eleven now. JC was prone to habit: He had always, Caroline later recalled, returned "home before 10 o'clock." Yet for that entire week, she said, "[JC] had been absent . . . and his comportment was different after that night; he seemed strange in his conduct and declined to conversation."

According to JC, when Caroline pressed him about where he had been, "I made no excuse." He told her, "I was with a friend from Philadelphia. I shall get up early in the morning to see him off."

Caroline bought JC's lies. He urged her to get along to bed. It was late.

"I went to the stand and pretended to write till she became quiet or went to sleep," JC said.

Before putting out the light, JC undressed, spread his shirt out—which was still wet from the bathhouse washing—to dry, and went to bed.

Caroline said JC was a man who slept without his nightshirt open; he liked the freedom of tossing and turning and not having the bulky thing getting hung up on his neck, waking him, or heating him up so much that he sweated. On this night, however, and several that would follow, "[H]e slept with his night shirt pinned up."

14

Blood Brothers

THE MORNING AFTER HIS DEADLY ENCOUNTER WITH SAM ADAMS, September 18, 1841, John C. Colt was up at the crack of dawn: 5:30 a.m. sharp. He checked to see if his shirt was dry. It wasn't. He placed it inside a clothes basket underneath the bed and searched his room for a clean top and cravat.

While JC was putting on fresh clothes, fastening a knot in his handkerchief, Caroline woke up.

"Where are you going so early?" she asked.

"To the boat." JC had explained the previous night that he needed to see a friend off in the morning. "I don't think I'll return for breakfast."

With that, JC walked out of the room, down the three flights of stairs from the apartment, and into the dark and desolate morning that was Monroe Street.

First thing he did was walk down the block to the Granite Building, where, once inside, he "found all apparently as [he] had left it." He wanted to make sure no one had broken into his office in his absence and discovered what he had done. JC had no idea Asa Wheeler had gone to the police once already and was not giving up on the idea that something sinister had occurred.

From there, JC walked to Wood's General Store to buy the nails he couldn't get the previous night.

Wood's was just opening as JC came around the corner.

With a bag of nails, JC sealed the box and readied it for shipping. Only he didn't have a destination. He was certain he wanted the box shipped to New Orleans but needed to know that a ship in the local port was heading that way. So he walked down to the East River "to ascertain the first packet for New Orleans."

Finding the *Kalamazoo* just about ready to set sail for the southern coast, JC went back to his office and inscribed the box to a fictitious person and address.

"Moved it myself," he said of the heavy cargo, "but with great difficulty, to the head of the stairs—did not dare to let it down myself."

With the box containing Sam Adams's corpse sitting at the top of the stairs, JC walked outside to fetch a car man.

When he finished putting the box aboard the *Kalamazoo* with the help of that car man who later turned him in, JC was famished. It had taken him about an hour to complete the task. He was tired and hungry.

Certain no one was onto him, JC stopped by the eating room inside Lovejoy's Hotel and "called for a hot roll and coffee."

The killer had two cups of coffee, but "could not eat."

Suitably caffeinated, JC walked to his office, locked the door behind him, and inspected the room. It took him most of the morning, but he "wiped the wall," he later said, "in one hundred spots." He scrubbed and cleaned, desperate to cover up any remaining signs of the struggle he and Sam Adams had and the copious amounts of blood that drained from Adams's head.

Certain he had done his best to cover up the murder, JC walked home.

It was 10:30 a.m. when he walked through the door to the surprise of Caroline.

JC said all he wanted was a bath and bed. He was exhausted.

Caroline got a good look at her live-in companion and noticed "some spots" on the right side of his neck. Scratches and bruises. "A black mark."

Caroline asked JC about his neck. "What happened?"

He said nothing. He wanted to go to sleep.

She found this strange. "After he got into bed, I went to the bedside, it being unusual for him to be going to bed during the day."

Caroline tried to talk to JC.

But JC did not want to engage in conversation.

"He showed no [willingness] to state what had occurred," Caroline said later. "He appeared very stiff, as if he had caught a heavy cold, or something of that kind."

That rigidity, which many later claimed was unlike JC, continued, Caroline further explained, "until his arrest." JC thought he had done everything in his power to hide what he tried to brush off later in his *Confession* as a murder committed under circumstances that were beyond avoidance. JC had a right to defend himself, he claimed. In killing Adams, he was exercising that right. JC was saying in that rather long and detailed *Confession*—though he left out several important factors: namely, why he never told this story until *after* he was arrested and imprisoned—that Samuel Adams had attacked him first.

"This man, who came here a few minutes since and insulted me," JC explained to one of his interviewers post arrest, "is dead—dead by my hand. I did not mean to kill him, but he is dead. He would have slain me, or he would have proclaimed a triumph over me, and he perished in the attempt at one or the other—neither of which could I have brooked. Shall I rush forth and proclaim the truth? But suppose I do—will it be believed? Throughout my entire life I have been doomed to one series of misconstructions."

The interviewer who reported this proclamation by JC added, perhaps with a bit of ignorance, how it should "also be remembered that through-out [JC's] career rapidity and energy are his characteristics . . . [h]e was tenacious and sensitive, and, though gentle, his fortitude had no foundation in Christian forbearance." If "provoked," the interviewer added, by a "blow . . . from such a spirit, a blow in return" would have surely followed.

Sam Colt's brother was a loose cannon, a jack-in-the-box. JC had reacted to Adams without thought, without consideration for his actions or responsibility, and most assuredly without conscious and conscience.

With his lawyers, JC masterminded his *Confession* as the only way to get out of the hangman's noose awaiting him. And who could argue with the man for trying? The only other person involved was dead. If he hadn't bludgeoned the bloke with an axe, Sam Adams would have strangled him, JC contended. JC described a rage in Adams's eyes like that of which he had never seen on a man; he talked about a person who had turned into a monster there before him inside his office, this over a mere fifteen dollars and change; he mentioned how Adams was determined to punish him with death for the transgressions he believed JC had caused him. It was Sam Adams who went to JC's office in a rage, with the stress of a failing business plying him, working within his fragile psyche—not the other way around!

Still, when taken into the context of the evidence left behind, one would have to wonder if John Caldwell Colt was talking about himself in that *Confession* and the interviews that followed his arrest. JC had, unlike his brother Sam, believed from an early age that the world owed him a good living. Whereas Sam was willing to take calculated risks and work hard to live up to his grandfather's namesake, JC wanted things handed to him. Even after his arrest, when, certainly, Sam stepped in and took control of making sure his brother had a fair shot at beating the rap, JC was still spinning his life in a different—*poor me, I'm the victim here*—manner than much of the evidence would prove.

"The reluctance of our subject to mingle with the world," reported a section near the end of *An Authentic Life* the writer called "Reflections," "may have exposed him to misconstructions and prejudices of similar derivation, whereby, his own conduct has been not a little affected, and certain judgments upon his actions from the beginning of his course to its present awful juncture, warped from liberality."

The interviewer, however, went on to talk about the different sides of JC many had been witness to. Yet he wasn't willing to go after JC with any respectable, journalistic claw.

"I supposed, in the outset," the interviewer continued, "that John C. Colt had, as it were, two opposite characters—the one natural, the other super induced by circumstances. I sought, by the life into which I have just detailed, for a knowledge of the circumstances for which might thus have placed him in opposition with himself. I think I have gained the clue."

This was JC and Sam, once again, taking the truth of the man and polishing it to look good in the eyes of the public and potential jurors and judges.

"It appears to me," the interviewer went on, "that the unfortunate subject of these pages proved himself, in boyhood, a person of ardor and ingeniousness, fond of society, predisposed to strong attachments, joyous, active, benevolent and confiding, but excessive in his thirst for the approbation of others and in his reliance on himself." The reporter then added, in what was his patent hyperbolic jest, slathering admiration upon his subject (for a paycheck, no doubt), that, "however important [it] might be in any one's career, however humble, to those who follow, if every victim to error or misfortune could be faithfully dissected by a moral anatomist, the seat of the disease explored . . . the course of ruin [would be] made obvious."

JC, that same interviewer said without fear of exposing himself a fraud, was a fatality of the society that reared him; far more superior, too intelligent, and too ahead of his time to be taken seriously and viewed as the utopian educator his fellows should see him for.

The killer had done a good job, apparently, of building himself up into an icon, when, as a matter of fact, upon his arrest, he was broke, living like a gypsy, considered a scar of the Colt family, and shacking up with a pregnant woman whom he had claimed to be married to but was actually his brother's mistress.

A fake. John Colt had bounced around the country for a time trying to strike it rich, ended up back in New York, committed a few burglaries, then murdered the man who was printing a new edition of his book. How was Sam Colt going to put a shine on the idea that he had revolutionized—so he claimed—a machine used to kill people and his brother had, in fact, become a vicious killer?

What irony.

How would Sam Colt, who could sell water to fish, put a sheen on this tragic, potentially career-ending situation his older brother had gotten them into?

His brother's arrest and possible conviction would, Sam Colt knew, have serious implications on his firearms business. The company, during the fall of 1841, was already under the cloud of his brother's being lambasted a murderer by a tabloid press looking to sell newspapers. As he bartered with the military, which had been contemplating arming every vessel it had with Colt's repeating pistols and rifles, the media went on the offensive, piggybacking on widespread public disbelief in Sam's so-called super weapons. Back in June 1841, the Washington *Globe* printed a rather outspoken and harsh editorial as a deal Colt was trying to seal with the military was made public.

"In disgust," Bern Keating wrote of this critical period in Sam's life as a businessman, "[the *Globe*] . . . sneered at the backwardness of the military and likened them to French Canadian farmers who clung to the plow."

Not many wanted to give Colt and his invention the benefit of the doubt; this despite public displays the inventor had put on of a working weapon fired underwater. The military had published reports on Colt's firearms and believed in them, saying how "the Colt rifle was indeed loaded and discharged of sixteen shots—two cylinders—in two minutes, forty-nine seconds."

With the military on the fence, however, heeding to public outcry that Sam Colt was no more concerned for the welfare of the nation than he was with lining his pockets, the last thing Sam needed was to have his brother's name splashed across the front pages of New York newspapers, which were now calling JC an axe murderer, jumping on a bandwagon of guilt exploding as JC's trial neared.

"The Colt family moved as one for the rescue of the murderer," Alfred Lewis wrote. "It was as much their pride as it was their affection which furnished the impulse. . . . How . . . disgraceful would it be were he finally hanged in the Tombs' yard as a murderer!"

JC went after the tabloids, saying quite outspokenly from his Tombs prison cell, "The newspapers, *they* are the true mischief-breeders; they are the really unprincipled and remorseless murderers! By the pen there is more slaughter—and that of the most heartless and ferocious character—oh, infinitely more—than either by lead or by steel! . . . From my soul I hope . . . and, above all, that the slanderer's pen will not change a single heart or eye that [all of us] may value; for, of the numberless evils of newspaper corruption, the estrangements its reckless calumny produces are by far the most heart-withering!"

This outburst by JC was shocking to the interviewer, who suggested it came from a place inside the man's heart that was, "however hidden even from himself," rooted in "a disease."

It showed how JC could go from an educated-sounding intellect to, well, a crazed maniac during the span of a conversation. It only added credence to the argument that JC had snapped and killed Adams in a fit of rage.

"Nothing is safe but the plain truth," JC went on to say. "Even the 'hoax' which appears harmless may prove greatly the reverse in its consequences, especially to our reputation for integrity, insomuch as in its very nature, a 'hoax' leans to falsehood."

The bottom line, a more sober and grounded Sam Colt knew, seemed to be that if JC was found guilty and hanged for his crimes, how could he—Sam—walk the streets again with his "head in high society"?

According to Alfred Lewis, no sooner had JC been arrested than Sam began "pouring out the family gold like water." Sam hired two high-powered, expensive New York attorneys: Irish lawyer and activist Robert Emmet, and John Morrill, a former congressman. He reportedly paid the dream team $2,000 in cash and another $8,000 in stocks, but not from his

Patent Arms Manufacturing Company in Paterson. Instead, Sam offered the men stocks in his Submarine Battery Company and another enterprise he called the Waterproof Cable Company. Sam was determined to parlay his underwater mining operation into a moneymaking venture. If not the weapons themselves, then the cable that made underwater explosion possible would be worth a fortune. There was also word that Sam had sent a telegram to St. Louis, calling for their youngest brother, James, a lawyer, to make the trip back east to assist in JC's defense.

The last thing Sam needed at this period in his life was to be acting manager of JC's defense. Sam had problems of his own brewing. Cousin Dudley Selden had resigned as the Patent Arms Manufacturing Company treasurer in 1839, fed up with the way in which Sam had been running the business. Sam replaced Dudley with John Ehlers, a New York hardware importer and dealer, but their relationship began a slow evolution toward dissolution as 1841 came. By the summer of the year JC had committed murder, Ehlers had had it with Sam and his rather anomalous way of conducting business, especially the gunmaker's attitude, virtuous as it was, with regard to giving gifts in hopes of swaying contracts and investors. Near the end of August, John Ehlers went behind Sam's back and met with two stockholders to try to snatch up Sam's patent rights. The three of them soon authorized the sale of the patents to pay off some of the debt the company had accumulated over the years. Just two days before JC murdered Sam Adams, on September 15, three-fourths of Sam's interest in the company was said to have been sold off. When he realized what was going on behind his back, Sam hired a legal team to figure it out. With JC now in prison, a fight to save his company—a business in a state of limbo, pending litigation—gearing up in the New Jersey courts, and the pressure of launching a new line of products (the underwater mines and cable), Sam Colt had his hands full.

But Sam was never one to back down from a quarrel; he believed in fighting fire with fire. His life, truly, up to this point, had been built around contingencies and his ability to solve problems as they arose. Inventing was his nature; selling was his passion. These strong character traits had instilled in Sam a spirit to fight for answers. Thus, despite the many different diversions his businesses brought him, Sam took on a campaign to free JC, as JC himself invited reporters chosen by the family into his Tombs cell for interviews.

Beyond those men carrying pen and paper, none other than John Howard Payne was seen visiting JC on occasion. Payne, a staunch proponent for the rights of the Cherokee Indians, was the first American actor to appear on an English stage. He was also an admired and famous playwright and producer. "He spent time in debtor's prison," his Union College biography proclaimed, "was rumored to have been enamored of Mary Wollstonecraft Shelley, and he was a friend of Washington Irving and collaborated with him in the 1824 play, *Charles the Second.*" Yet Payne's most accomplished work by far—the composition that made him world renowned—was the popular tune "Home, Sweet Home," a song that nestled pride into the hearts of Americans far and wide: *Mid pleasures and palaces though we may roam, / Be it ever so humble, there's no place like home.*

Caroline Henshaw was said to also visit JC every day, staying with him until the prison told her to leave. Lewis Gaylord Clark, prominent editor of the *Knickerbocker* magazine, another one of New York's established and celebrated literati Edgar Allan Poe so heatedly and publicly despised, was seen entering and exiting JC's cell.

No evidence left behind indicates a purpose for which these men, so endowed with the respect of their contemporaries, had with JC. There is also no record of JC having ever mentioned these men or meeting them before he was confined in the Tombs. It was likely that Sam, who knew the men personally, sent them into the prison to "be seen" with his brother. Sam was forever trying to refine JC's tarnished image and vanquished reputation. Good PR was one of Sam's gifts; here he was utilizing every ounce of that talent, hoping each step he took along the way would have a promising effect and positive outcome on a prospective jury pool in a city undoubtedly paying close attention to the tabloid accounts of JC's arrest for Sam Adams's murder.

15

Catch-penny Abuse

HE WAS SITTING AT THE FOOT OF HIS BED, WRITING ON A CREAKY
wooden table inside his cell. It was October 1841. The way C. Frank
Powell described JC in *An Authentic Life* on this particular afternoon, it
was as if JC had not a care in the world:

> *I noticed his appearance intently. In height he is about five feet eleven; he
> is firmly built, though slender. His head is large, his face oval, his com-
> plexion light, his hair profuse, light brown, and richly curling; his nose
> aquiline; his lips in silence always compressed; his eyes of dark brown
> hazel, lighting up conversation, or in listening, with great expression.*

Regarding JC's eyes, or maybe more his attitude and demeanor, magazine writer Alfred Lewis, who spoke with many who had seen JC during
this period of his incarceration, framed the suspected killer's look a bit
differently. Perhaps Lewis carried on far too long in his description of JC's
eyes, but metaphor was indeed an appropriate device to speak of the man
behind those beady windows into the soul:

> *[T]hey were much too narrowly neighbors, were set much too closely
> together to inspire or permit common confidence of mankind. There was
> that in the expression of those eyes which distinguished their possessor, to
> even a casual appreciation, as not alone an uncertain but a dangerous
> quantity. . . . Altogether, Colt's eyes were the eyes of a man killer.*

For those who had never seen a prison, the Tombs was an awe-inspiring demonstration of what hardworking men, concrete, and steel could do in mid-nineteenth-century New York, a true testament to the building boom that was about to take place in this incredible city over the next century. Walking into the prison, C. Frank Powell was taken aback by the sheer immensity and precision of the construction alone. He shuddered at the sight of such a foreboding, solemn courtyard of men wandering about aimlessly, their lives now no more thrilling or significant than a herd of cattle being moved from one pasture to the next.

"Passing gate to gate," Powell noted, "through quadrangles of galleried stone prison-houses, we ascended to a bridge crossing one of these squares."

Once there, they met with a guard, who was behind two iron shutters, ready to lead them into the prisoner cell area where JC had been waiting.

Powell carried on in such a grandiose and flattering style as he described certain portions of his journey beyond the Tombs's walls, you'd think the man had been paid by the Colt family or JC's attorneys—which he likely was—to ruminate in print on a suspected murderer the reporter said presented a resounding "self-reliance, coupled with almost an incapability of admitting impressions from other minds into his." Powell referred to JC as "gracious and kind," this personal impression made upon him soon after they introduced themselves. A bit later in his introduction to *An Authentic Life*, Powell laid it on thick as wax, writing, "The prevailing characteristic of his countenance appears to be gentleness, and his bearing courteous and manly; the tones of his voice are sweet and mild, but firm."

Twentieth- and twenty-first-century researchers studying JC's life were a bit more objective in their approach to examining his character. Barbara and Kenneth Tucker, for example, made the claim that JC was as good an actor as he was a killer. Going back as far as, even, his teen years, the Tuckers claimed JC had a contemptuous relationship with his parents (Christopher and Olivia) after his mother died—that the Colt family as a whole were prone to depression, bitterness, and misanthropy. This seems more in line with how the lives of the Colt brothers played out. As to what JC did while he was in New York, the Tuckers were being kind when they wrote that JC had "bec[o]me involved with gamblers and criminals."

By JC's side inside his prison cell, he had a one-volume octavo edition of Dr. Oliver Goldsmith's works. This could have been a book about

Greece, England, or several other destinations Goldsmith had written about; it was never mentioned which volume JC was reading, or why he had such a text. Could he have been planning to say good-bye to the United States at some point?

JC's Tombs cell was between twelve and fourteen feet long, about eight feet wide. The three walls surrounding JC were made of stone and steel, the iron bars in front kept him contained much of his day. The walls were bare, save for a few hooks to hang clothes. Just above JC's head were pipes made of iron, where fresh water and heat flowed freely. The tiny bit of light JC wrote under came from a "slit in the ceiling at the end facing the door."*

This was JC's life. Sitting. Contemplating. Thinking—perhaps planning—of a way out of this mess he had gotten himself into. The first letter he wrote in October, which he addressed to a "Dear Friend" (someone in Boston), was the beginning of a campaign to free himself, not necessarily from the prison that confined him, but from the public furor that had come down upon him like a plague of locusts since his arrest. The New York tabloid media swarmed around JC and Sam, buzzing and salivating, as if they were the only game in town—and maybe they were. JC was portrayed as a gambler and womanizer, a perjurer who had lied his way into the Marines and then, to get out, falsified documents. Reporters had spent time digging into JC's past, publishing stories about his romance with that octoroon slave and his nomadic travels across the Midwest and South, looking for those salacious anecdotes that might act as some sort of a warning sign preceding the circumstances that had put him behind bars. The chance that JC was innocent was never discussed in the newspapers; it was assumed he was guilty until, by some miracle, he and his "wealthy" brother proved otherwise.

Opening the letter, JC wrote how good it felt to hear that his friend had been worried about his welfare, giving his addressee one of his trademark overblown sentences of self-assessed greatness: "From my knowledge of the past, I may rightly judge that your expressed kindness is but the overflow of your natural and wonted goodness."

It took JC but another sentence to express his growing disdain for the newspapers, adding, "I must assure you that it is a source of indescribable

---

* As an interesting aside, picture this prison not in contemporary terms—as our minds might be prone to do instinctively—but in light of it being a new facility. Thinking back, we might be inclined to picture a dismal existence inside JC's cell: dirty, unkempt, rotten and rank odors, rats, etc. But this prison was state-of-the art and had just been completed.

pleasure to take up one of your letters . . . and read [it], after looking over some of the morning prints, and seeing their mistaken zeal and error, or catch-penny abuse."

He blamed the press for feeding a public hunger for anything related to the Colt brothers. He blasted with a broad brush all reporters and editors: "The conducting of the press now-a-days is too generally reduced to a system from extorting money from whom they may, and the advancement of private ends, without the least regard to public morals or welfare."

JC certainly had a point. When the Brooklyn *Daily Eagle* published an update on the status of his forthcoming trial, the brief article opened by branding JC guilty as charged: "The trial of Colt, the murderer of Adams, has been postponed until the next term of the Court of Oyer and Terminer, which will not be until the first Monday in December."*

Continuing with his letter, JC claimed there were "new papers starting up every month" for the very purpose of tarring and feathering the Colt name.

"It is to be hoped, however, that the penny press," JC ranted, "like good wine that is at first thick and muddy, will ultimately work itself clear, to the great and lasting blessing of the country."

Near the end of the missive, JC warned his friend to "read no more of the clamorous stuff you see printed about me. You cannot [rely] on anything you see published as being true which relates to myself."

From that point forward he carried on, restating his contention that the newspapers were out to get him at all costs and would stop at nothing to see him hanged. He said none of it had an effect on his mood, however, but the mere idea that the printed articles "hurt the feelings of my friends" was what truly "caused" him the greatest "pain" of all.

Ending the letter, JC wrote, "All's well that ends well."

The next letter was dated October 28, 1841, addressed to a friend in Baltimore. No doubt the story had reached across the country by now, making JC out to be a vicious murderer who had used an "ax" to settle a score with a debtor—now at a time when Sam Colt was in the midst of finalizing one of the biggest deals of his career with the Texas Rangers. Moreover, word was that JC's trial was going to be postponed due to a witness not being available. Caroline Henshaw was close to having her baby. She had moved back to Philadelphia to be with "family" and was due to give birth

---

* Note the use of the Colt name only, not to mention the reference to JC as "murderer."

in early November to a child everyone believed to be JC's. The prosecution, headed by District Attorney James R. Whiting, who would go on to become a Supreme Court justice, and Assistant DA James Smith, needed Caroline to talk about JC's state of mind, the marks she saw on his neck, the fact that he was not himself after the murder, and how he had come home late on the night Sam Adams disappeared; these among other pieces of the puzzle Caroline would fill in.

This postponement, though, gave JC ample opportunity to work more on his image.

Opening the Baltimore-addressed letter, he picked up right where he had left off with the previous, disparaging the press: "Do not believe the thousand false statements you see heralded from day to day in the papers. Let them blow their blast. All you hear now is passion—passion."

For a good portion of the missive, JC spewed his venom at the publishers of newspapers and periodicals, calling them all devils feeding on his soul. Like any clinical sociopath might, JC never mentioned his victim—self-defense aside—and how much suffering members of the Adams family were certainly going through. He was concerned only with his own well-being and ultimate fate. In one passage, JC's hubris and, truthfully, loss of mind, was so blatantly obvious, it's no wonder those friends who heard from him at this time did not totally abandon him.

"The man that meets with misfortune nowadays," JC wrote, "becomes the victim of a certain portion of the press. If he is poor, his friends are brought in for a share, as mine have been, and placed upon the rack, and tortured until money is forthcoming."

The fact that JC saw himself as having no means to defend himself was astonishing; he had Dudley Selden, a lawyer, and brother Sam on his side, one man with unlimited funds and another with strong political ties.

"But in this case," he went on, waxing viciously on the press once again, "they will spill their ink to no purpose, for it is not only my misfortune, but that of my friends, as you know, to be without any very extensive means."

He signed the letter, "Your unfortunate friend, JC Colt."

The Patent Arms Manufacturing Company had a satellite office at 155 Broadway, downtown. According to Colt expert Herbert Houze in his splendidly researched, heavily illustrated book, *Samuel Colt: Arms, Art, and Inventor*,

Sam had "long suspected that Ehlers," the treasurer Sam had been having problems with, "was concealing sales in order to reduce the royalties due."

But Sam had a hard time proving his suspicions.

With what he viewed as backroom business practices going on between officers inside the Colt firearms company, without permission, Ehlers took (stole) some 550 weapons from the Broadway office when he left. This spurred Sam to draft an advertisement he thought he might print in the New York papers. This piece of writing is classic Sam Colt, displaying how undereducated Sam had been.*

A Jerman calling himself John Ehlers, about fifty years of age, five feet eight inches high, the upper part of his head balled short locks of yellow curly hair on the back & sides of his head, faice round, figure stout and ugly looking

The person above described has been imployed as the chief clerk & Treasurer ... & has of a suden absented him self without the knowledge of the President or stockholders of said Company after taking from there armoury ... from fifty to Seventy five thousand dollars worth of Colts Repeating Fire Arms ...

Sam went on to say in the ad that anyone coming forward with information about "the munstirous [sic: monstrous] movements" of Ehlers would be rewarded.

Sam's lawyers had a look at the planned announcement Sam wanted to publish in the city papers and smartly advised the gun maker to forgo the advertisement and allow his legal team to handle the matter.

Sam obliged.

---

* I've left the errors as Sam Colt wrote them (including missing periods and commas, etc.). It should be noted that Herbert Houze, in defending Sam, claimed Sam's chronic misspellings and often frivolous punctuation and horrendous grammar were due to the haste in which his letters were often drafted, and that Sam used a phonetic style of writing: Sam was merely sounding out his words and spelling them as they rolled off his tongue. Houze's evidence for this was that in Sam's later years, his letters were perfectly spelled and grammatically acceptable. A majority of scholars on this subject would agree, however, that as Sam grew the business and devoted more time to its day-to-day operations, he utilized a secretary to draft his later letters for him. I have to agree with this assumption. It's clear to me that, to respectfully disagree with Houze, Sam Colt was no wordsmith and did not have a solid grasp on the English language.

If there was one thing—that is, besides his brother's arrest and imprisonment on murder charges—consuming Sam Colt during this pivotal period of his life in New York City, it was an obsession with his submarine battery mine project, an invention Sam had dreamt of since his youth in Ware, Massachusetts, when he was just fourteen and put on that explosive display of an underwater mine in the family pond. His interest in expediting the project into production now was twofold: He needed money to defend JC and also wanted a side business to supplement his firearms operation, which had fallen on hard times and was close to closing its doors. The "Submarine Battery Company," as Sam named it, was about to be set up with capital exceeding $100,000. Sam was a gifted industrialist. His plan was to divide the company into some "2,000 shares each with $50.00 value," while he himself "retained 90% of the stock." According to Martin Rywell's research, Sam piloted this move by a plan to appropriate shares in the new company to his "father, stepmother, and brothers to create a dummy Board of Directors." Shrewd and conniving didn't begin to describe the way in which Sam Colt brought this venture into mainstream markets.

In the years ahead, Sam would go on to talk about what inspired him to invent such enormously violent machines and projectiles ultimately used to kill people. He tried selling the idea as a practical invention for the times, not telling anyone that he had conceived it as a child. It never occurred to Sam—or, rather, he did not voice his opinion about it if it had entered his mind—that while he was arming the world, especially what was quickly becoming America's "Wild West," giving people the opportunity with the squeeze of a trigger to kill their fellows, tragedy, death (even within his own family), and murder were taking place all around him, almost as if the universe was slapping Sam upside the head in some sort of celestial balancing act. In a letter Sam wrote to Congressman Henry Murphy (Brooklyn), a document which Rywell referred to as an emulsification "of the truth to make it more interesting," Sam explained how, after he had returned from Europe in 1836 during a sweeping, edifying tour of several countries, he became concerned with the "threatening aspect of affairs growing out of our French relations," adding that as he left Paris "everything seemed to render a War inevitable with the French and my desire was to aid my own Government in the struggle by placing at their services my own plans and inventions."

And so, according to Sam, that fevered inspiration he felt for this particular creation—the mine battery—was generated by his desire to make the safety of Americans a priority. This was the hard sell to his friend in Washington—the reason, Sam preached, why the government had to act *now* on this invention.

In October 1841, Sam wrote to the secretary of the Navy, Abel Upshur, who was on the fence regarding funding Colt's submarine battery invention. Sam admitted to the secretary how desperate he was not only for funding of the project as a basic military need, but also for money to help his big brother: "Circumstances of a nature too painful to relate have rendered it of vital importance that I should raise a som [sic] of money at once." It was as if Sam was trying to hide the fact that his brother had been arrested and charged with murder, and his firearms business was collapsing from underneath him. Upshur, a Princeton and Yale graduate, was not a man who made decisions based on the needs of those making the request. He was not about to help a man in need if it did not benefit the United States of America.

The other problem Sam had was keeping the invention secret. Sam was paranoid someone would beat him to the finish line and secure a patent before he had the chance. Sure, he was, generally speaking, in a more advanced stage of development than his competitors with most of his inventions, but there was always that nagging, nervous noise inside Sam's head telling him that he had better hurry up if he wanted to be first. No invention, essentially, is wholly unique, just as no idea is ever the first of its kind. Sam understood this concept. One could even argue that he mastered this concept. He knew that being first was sometimes more important than being the best. He could always tweak an invention once he obtained the patent, put it into production, and money started coming in. But once a competitor beat you, there was no prize for second place.

Realizing when he returned from France in 1836 that a war was, in fact, *not* inevitable and he could no longer argue international conflict as an accelerating factor—i.e., protecting the shorelines of America from a constant threat of invasion was no longer on the minds of politicians— Sam Colt needed to change his strategy. "It so happened that I scarcely reached Washington," he wrote to Congressman Murphy with a flair for the dramatic, "before a settlement of our difficulties with France was peaceably effected and finding there was likely to be no immediate call for my inventions in submarine fortifications I determined not to make my secrets known."

An additional problem, equally important, was obtaining that "stamp" from the government, with an advance attached, so he could stage several public tests (displays) of the apparatus. Sam wanted to show off his submarine battery defense mechanisms in New York Harbor, there out in the Hudson and East Rivers, as well as the Narrows, while he and several government officials, including military officers, watched from boats beyond. Here were Captain Christopher Colt's genes rising in his son: Sam knew that if he got the public behind his harbor defense torpedoes—projectiles, principally, that could protect any port from invasion—the government would have no choice but to jump on board and fund the project. And yet, here it was, heading toward the end of the year, JC's trial now about to begin after several delays, and Sam Colt was using every contact he had to get someone in Washington to come up with enough money for him to stage these dramatic displays of firepower.

Or was the money for JC's legal dream team?

That November, Sam traveled to Washington to meet with Upshur. Sam put on a presentation, orally, talking up his latest experiments with the weapon. He even resurrected Robert Fulton's ideas of a coastal torpedo from the eighteenth century, of which Thomas Jefferson himself, Sam pointed out, had been interested. Sam had known Upshur only by letter and a gentlemanly appreciation of each other's work. But here he was now, standing in front of the respected secretary, proposing his invention, showing him drawings and sketches and relating testimonials of his experiments. This impressed the secretary. "[I] went over with him the whole plans and secrets of my inventions," Sam later reflected, "which so far convinced him of their practicability that to remove the only remaining doubt he simply required me to make the single experiment of the blowing up of a vessel at a distance beyond the range of an enemy's shot."

The visit to the capital paid off. Upshur, although still unconvinced of the invention's capabilities and not yet willing to take the project in front of the Board of Navy Commissioners for evaluation, appropriated a $6,000 advance for what one writer later called a "sharply limited demonstration" from Colt.

This money was enough for Sam to draft certificates and initiate a public offering for the company (and maybe even keep JC's lawyers from walking out). Thus, as Colt Patent Arms seemed to be imploding under a cloud of bankruptcy and mismanagement, Sam was thinking about his future, on his way with this new project.

Returning to New York, though, that other sticky issue not yet cleared up hit him straight between the eyes: the fate of his brother.

16

Prison House

ONE OF THE MORE BIZARRE AND OVERWRITTEN PARAGRAPHS QUOTED IN Alfred Henry Lewis's account of Colt's life and times has JC walking the grounds of the Tombs courtyard. Lewis used the writings of a reporter, whom he referred to as "Dana," who worked at the *Tribune* at the time of JC's trial and "called upon Colt" in his cell. Lewis reprinted long excerpts of Dana's writing. Dana called JC "a bit flamboyant." During JC's imprisonment, Dana reported, the brother of the gun maker was treated with favoritism and given many of the luxuries a free man might have, recounting the days ticking down toward JC's trial as follows:

> When he is tired of reading, or smoking, or sleeping, he takes a stroll in the yard. It is necessary to dress for this, and his toilet takes considerable time. Finally he appears, booted and gloved. He may have his sealskin coat on, or he may appear in a light of Autumn affair of exquisite cut and softest tint. In his hand is a gold-headed switch, which he carelessly twirls during his promenade.

The reporter might as well have portrayed JC eating lobster and drinking champagne as the courts decided when he would be tried.

"Then comes his lunch," Dana went on to write, describing what was an average meal for JC while in prison:

> Not cooked in the Tombs, but brought in from a hotel. It consists of a variety of dishes—quail on toast, game pates, reed birds, ortolans, fowl, vegetables, coffee, cognac, with book and cigar. Such is the life on Murderers' Row, as lived by Colt, and a not unmerry life it is.

This was laughable, of course, but it showed how the Colt name had been besmirched by this horrific crime and how some would stop at nothing to continue to degrade the family and attack the dynasty that Sam Colt had spent years building and would soon push to phenomenal success. The Colt family name belongs in the ranks of other surnames in history recognized by mention only: Ford, Pullman, Kennedy.

Dana went on to describe the prison itself as dismal and dark, a man's world, where the worst criminals society had produced became, on the inside, the animals who ran the zoo (likely true). Yet, in the same breath, JC's cell was described as though it were somehow disconnected from that awful world: "As the keeper swings open the door of Colt's cell the odor of sweet flowers strikes you." This was not some arid illusion, Dana said, conjured for the purpose of prose. There *were* fresh flowers inside JC's cell in a vase on a center table, along with a "handsomely dressed little lady, with the golden hair and the sorrowful face"* the reporter had bumped into on the way into the prison, who had soon "left them." Regarding the flowers: "To-morrow they will be replaced by fresh ones."

This article Lewis excerpted was obviously inundated with narrative liberties, and it could be disputed and argued all day long. But the irony here was that had the tabloids done some true investigative reporting, the juiciest story of all, which would have changed everything for Sam Colt, was in Philadelphia: the true identity of Caroline's baby's father.

What was never in doubt or ignored as it pertained to the authenticity of JC's life behind bars at the time were the comments he made in the letters he wrote during those months of October and November, as the pendulum swung closer toward his day in court.

The evidence the prosecution planned to present was clear to JC as mortality stared him in the face. He maintained his self-defense-based innocence every chance he got and began to, surely under the direction of his legal team, think about a defense strategy, part of which included the *Confession* pamphlet.

Caroline Henshaw was still in Philadelphia, still pregnant, still waiting to give birth so she could make the trip back to New York to testify. JC began a letter to Caroline noting how he wanted to answer several of

---

* This could not have been Caroline Henshaw, who was in Philadelphia waiting to give birth.

her previous "inquiries" but could not do so until after his trial, when "I shall feel at liberty to write more freely." There's no doubt JC's lawyers told him to be careful with Caroline Henshaw and what he said. Everything, at this point, was going to be used to convict him. The press wanted it. The public demanded it. And an impatient, overzealous prosecution team was going to stop at nothing to see it to fruition.

JC explained to Caroline that his lawyers had told him they "are acquainted with all the facts" and "say I must leave all to them." Then, referring to his *Confession*, JC noted, "The best way of managing would be for me to state the facts, seal it up, and hand it to the court, and after the testimony is taken to open and read it." JC continued to expound on his idea to stand up in open court after testimony had been presented against him and proclaim his innocence by reading that prepared *Confession*. He made a point to say how "counsel" would probably think the move "too risky," but "the public press has excited the passions of the people to an alarming degree" (this was no understatement), which proved to him he had no choice, really, but to take such a dramatic step. He couldn't "go forth in the world a suspected murderer," something he viewed as "worse infinitely than much suffering." He wrote, "If I throw myself upon my peers they will be likely to believe me; . . . if I prove an alibi they will let me go, but always wrongfully suspect that I desired to kill my antagonist." Melancholy and pleading were there in JC's narrative voice. He went on to say that if only Asa Wheeler would stand up and tell the truth, he could be certain of acquittal. "But in this city I am so little known, it is to be feared that passion and not evidence will decide the case."

He carried on about how those who were set to testify against him were nothing more than a pack of lying charlatans looking to hang an innocent man who was of no consequence to them. He gave no reason why a long list of people he did not know would walk into court and lie about him. He failed to mention Sam Adams was a well-known printer in town, well-liked and highly regarded, and that many of those set to testify were friends of Adams.

Next, he began to saddle Caroline with the pity he felt for himself, laying it on with the slickness of a veteran snake oil salesman. This letter, it was very clear, had been well thought out and designed to reach Caroline and perhaps help to change her mind about what she knew. JC never came out and asked Caroline to lie; he simply used that old charm of his to manipulate. He told her it was his lawyer's understanding that the prosecutor had gone all the way to Washington and Congress to ensure he be hanged for the murder. "It would certainly be a feather in any lawyer's cap to get an innocent man hung."

Quite interestingly, JC signed the letter, "Yours Confidentially, JC Colt."

By his estimation Sam Colt had given the U.S. government a proposition it could—and should—not refuse. The inventor also knew that if he went public with his invention now, risking public discovery of this so-called secret "super" weapon, it would spurn a grassroots campaign overnight, pushing his submarine battery into action and production. Sam had a lab set up at the University of the City of New York, where he was in the process of testing elements in what one writer later called a "galvanic mine warfare system." Those stock certificates Sam had been working on were finished. What was thought-provoking about the company, in its early stage, was the idea that although it was not yet government-sponsored, Sam was able to finagle the notion publicly that it had been by announcing sales of stock certificates to Senator Samuel Southard and Major William McNeill. With those two names attached, the illusion was there that the government was not only involved, but also behind the project. And Sam, of course, was not the type of entrepreneur to correct a record that was going to help him raise more capital.

Sam still had some public relations work to do, however. Not everyone was convinced. To Edward Curtis, the collector of the port closest to the Narrows, that all-important stretch of waterway separating the boroughs of Staten Island and Brooklyn, connecting Upper and Lower New York Bay, Sam made a colossal declaration. It was near the end of October. Sam and Curtis were aboard the *Wolcott*, a cutter. Captain A. V. Fraser, of the U.S. military, just happened to be on the boat, too. Sam looked out into the water toward the harbor and told Curtis—being sure to say it within earshot of Fraser—that this invention of his he had been working on so industriously would one day defend an area such as the Narrows and essentially "protect the port 'against the whole British Navy.'" The most amazing aspect of this, Sam added (and there can be no doubt he took a grand pause before carrying on with this portion of his sales pitch), was how *one* man could operate the apparatus. Imagine: A single soldier protecting an entire port with enough firepower at the push of a button to annihilate any of the world's most staggering naval forces.

Obviously quite amused by this statement, in his description of the conversation, Martin Rywell called Sam a "stupid bureaucrat," conveying Fraser's response to Sam's outrageous allegation: "My 'Captain' . . . is one who is terribly inconvenienced by anything which interferes in the most remote manner with the monotony of his life."

With his joke, Fraser all but laughed at such a preposterous notion from a man who to him was nothing more than a dreamer and showboater who perfected guns others had, in fact, invented. Only men in uniform, with proper training and working weaponry, could defend a port against an attack. Military engineers, moreover, were busy completing a "national program of coastal fortifications," which they had proposed to build up and down the East Coast in several of the locations left behind by the Revolutionary War. It was a practical way to look at protecting the country. The legislation surrounding this effort had received "strong Congressional support following the War of 1812."

The message coming from those in Washington who had the power to make things happen for the brazen entrepreneur seemed to be: *Stick to making rifles and pistols.*

Still, the money kept coming in, there for Sam to use as part of JC's defense and developing his underwater missile. Sam kept pushing this idea that an underwater torpedo set off from shore soaring straight at a wooden schooner or cutter could rip the boat in two and sink it with little effort. It didn't matter how big the sloop was or how much military muscle it had on board.

As Philip K. Lundeberg later wrote in his short book (ninety pages) for Smithsonian Institution Press, *Samuel Colt's Submarine Battery: The Secret and the Enigma*, the officers and politicians could laugh all they wanted at Sam Colt. But this man, this inventor from the north with the belly laugh, fuzzy beard, and frizzy, curly hairdo, who had run an arms factory in Paterson, New Jersey, and had a brother in prison facing murder charges, this same bloke had something here with a mysterious weapon that seemed to promise more than it could deliver: "The history of nineteenth-century military technology contains no more baffling chapter than the dogged and long-obscured efforts of the New England arms inventor, Samuel Colt, to secure the adoption of his Submarine

Battery as a major element in the coastal defense system of the United States." Lundeberg called the device "an obscure yet potentially significant episode in the technological development of undersea warfare." A similar submarine weapon would be developed and used during the Civil War, yet as Lundeberg found, "Virtually no connection has been established between [Sam Colt's] galvanic observation mine schemes and the remarkable development of mining operations witnessed during the American Civil War as part of the Confederate system of riverine and coastal defense."

It was Sam's "favorite creation," most scholars later agreed. Besides digging him out of the hole of bankruptcy in New Jersey, it was a moneymaking opportunity with the potential not only to fund his brother's acquittal, but also to keep Sam's mind off those murder charges his brother faced (which could send JC to an early grave) and that other secret the inventor harbored: being the father of the baby Caroline Henshaw was about to give birth to.

———

JC amped up the rhetoric in his letter-writing campaign as the first week of November settled on the city with a blustery dose of cold winter air. Charles Dickens, perhaps as spiteful and bitter as JC regarding the people of New York, spitting his vicious venom, ridiculing the city and the social classes he thought below him, would later write: "In another part of the city is the Refuge for the Destitute: an institution whose object is to reclaim offenders, male and female, black and white, without distinction; to teach them useful trades, apprentice them to respectable masters, and make them worthy members of society."

The one thing Dickens found utterly appalling, for which the Englishman should be heralded, was human bondage. While writing to a friend back home, Dickens had put into perspective how he felt about the disgraceful practice embraced by a large part of America: slavery. "I am a lover of Freedom, disappointed."

In one letter before trial, John C. Colt continued to criticize the penny press, and with good reason. In New York, JC remarked, anyone who could fork over to an editor of one of these rags "ten prices of an ordinary advertisement," could publish whatever he or she wanted, no questions asked. This slithery, reptilian portion of the New York press corps was so corrupt,

JC repeated over and again to anyone who would listen, "[c]onsequently, the public must remain ignorant of my real character."

Part of JC's resentment, according to Andie Tucher's book-length examination of this period, which included JC's incarceration, *Froth & Scum*, stemmed from an unforgiveable journalistic leak. Several New York newspapers printed part of JC's *Confession*, after getting hold of excerpts, one would imagine, from the friend to whom JC had made his confession. The man who leaked the material had sealed JC's fate. That a jury pool had heard from JC himself that he had killed Sam Adams (although in self-defense) was too much of an obstacle to overcome in a courtroom.*

There was an angry, mob-mentality undertone to the "penny newspaper" accounts of JC's life, JC argued in a letter to a "friend" on November 2. Many of these newspapers, he wrote, had been branding him a "hideous monster." As soon as they found out how quickly papers sold when they spoke of JC as a murderer, the rags kept the stories coming and JC continued to be engrossed by how easily the public could turn on what a tabloid, however erroneously, printed about a man. Through all of this, though, he paid no mind to what he'd done to poor Sam Adams, routinely showing no remorse or compassion for the man or his family, never once saying he was sorry for what had transpired.

"All this is pictured forth," he wrote sarcastically, "for the good of the public—excellent creatures, they always have in mind so much good . . . —men with just knowledge enough to pervert misfortune into crime, without heart enough to feel its consequences."

Strange comments. Even if he had, as he claimed, killed the man while protecting his own person, there was still the gruesome and violent nature of the crime itself that JC was simply not interested in approaching.

JC explained in the letter that his trial had been postponed yet again—this time until December 27. He was eager to get this situation behind him, so he could "stand much more favorable before the public . . . than now." He had high hopes for an acquittal and, at times, didn't seem to doubt it was in his future. He felt that despite what was being printed about him, he could sway a jury with his argument that Sam Adams had come at him, made an advance, and JC was merely reacting to the behavior of a madman. "[S]till the evidence of that day will clear

---

* There's also the strong possibility that JC's camp released excerpts with the hopes of swaying jurors. If so, it was a huge blunder.

me from crime, at least in the minds of my friends (if there be any now that doubt)."

Quite interestingly, JC begged this particular friend not to believe any reports of him supposedly "being insane—wishing to kill myself!—the plea of insanity at my trial, etc., because you see such things repeated over and over again in certain daily papers."

He talked about a common phrase newspapers were now using to describe his crime ("murder, murder, murder") as being similar to that of a boy shouting "fire, fire, fire, but not with half the feeling; and in most cases entirely disconnected with sentiment." He called his cell "my apartment," describing it as "twelve feet deep, seven feet wide, and eleven feet from floor to ceiling." The one window to look out was "five by thirty inches, protected by glass, and admits a surplus of light." It was as if JC was referring to a room he had rented in the city somewhere, and not a prison cell. He did not see the disadvantage to being in prison other than the accusations being cast upon him. He claimed his bed was "far superior to what I had at many of our hotels at a charge of two dollars a day." Besides being confined, he said, "I am well off as any man in New York, and better than most." Even more compelling was the way in which he described the character of the men—"Captain Hyde and Mr. Purdy, and the rest"—in charge of watching over him: "My keepers . . . are excellent men—they have souls and feeling."

The one aspect of the judicial process JC hated more than most anything else was going to court. Not because of the proceedings, or the verbal public lashings he'd received as spectators watched him being shuffled into the building, but because of the crowds and menacing way in which many of the bystanders carried themselves in this very open and public setting. A "dense mass" was what JC likened the gatherings coming out to see him to. He had to walk between two men, who protected him from the swell and throbbing pulse of a mob he felt would crush him if given the opportunity.

JC thanked his friend for "your extended kindness in" reaching out and helping Caroline in Philadelphia.

Nine days later, JC wrote a letter to a different "friend." In this short missive, JC had somewhat confirmed what Dana would soon write about him (the overblown prose Alfred Lewis quoted many years later in his *Pearson's Magazine* piece). He explained that his food was being brought to him by way of a nearby restaurant and his comfort level was, once again, no worse than a stay at the finest hotel in the city. "Say to my friends that they must feel no anxiety for me!" he wrote. He was upbeat and feeling good about beating the corrupt powers that had put him behind bars and condemned him with nothing short of "blackmail." There were certain editors in town, he warned, willing to print anything. He felt good about the future and being exonerated. As soon as he was allowed his moment in court, the truth would be told and justice would prevail.

This letter, written on November 10, 1841, was the last letter before his trial, and it would be published as part of JC's *Life and Letters* just under a year later in the penny publication the *Extra Tattler*. JC's "confessions" were to be used in court, while—ironically—the *Life and Letters* document, written in the hopes of later absolving the Colt name and painting JC as a decent man wrongly accused, was published in one of those same papers JC was so sure had been out to hang him.

As his brother's day in court neared, Sam Colt felt a bit guilty that an unpaid bill by JC had been the catalyst of a crime that might soon place his brother on death row. According to Jack Rohan, who published his book *Yankee Arms Maker* in 1935, although "willing enough to help his brother within the limitations of his personal means"—i.e., food, shelter, and spending money, part of which, one could argue, was probably to make sure Caroline had been taken care of—Sam had flat-out "refused to dip into . . . [his] funds to pay Adams." And so, looking back, if Sam had only given his brother that measly loan, he would not have found himself having to pay to dig his brother out of this seemingly endless hole.

Part of Sam's not paying JC's debt had stemmed from Sam's having his own; the gun maker had spent a lot of time and energy keeping his creditors at bay. Rohan even said Sam had schooled JC on how to "make some reasonable arrangement" with Adams and work out a payment plan. "He had cause later to regret that he had not loaned his brother the money."

Theater of Murder

ON MONDAY, JANUARY 17, 1842, AFTER WEEKS OF PRELIMINARY PRO-
ceedings and gathering witnesses, JC was ushered with haste from a
parked carriage into City Hall. He walked between two guards, gawking
in awe at the crowds there to heckle and cast vengeance upon him. This
"immense" throng of onlookers and bystanders, there for the sole purpose
of greeting the Colt icon, "block[ing] the avenues to the Court Room,"
stood more than ten deep on each side, on top of surrounding the carriage. Men and women screamed at this man who, in their minds and
hearts, was guilty of murdering the beloved printer in cold blood.

"Hang him! Hang him!" the angry swarm chanted. They had been
waiting across the street in the park all morning for JC to arrive and
would, said one report, stay there all day long after he was brought into
the court building, "staring at City Hall . . . as if there were, in that occupation, amusement and the gratification of curiosity."

JC's trial was the "unparalleled" story of the New York century to that
point. Anyone who could "read, speak, or think, in the metropolis . . . even
in the country," was captivated with the murder of Sam Adams and trial
of John C. Colt, the "brother of the inventor Samuel Colt." The story was
so big it had usurped that other unsolved murder case making headlines
all summer and fall: the Beautiful Cigar Girl.

JC appeared quite "calm and collected," the *Brother Jonathan* tabloid
reported that same week, as he was escorted from the street to the inside
of the building, and even as he sat in court, waiting for the proceedings
to begin. A reporter for *Brother Jonathan* said JC was often seen "reading papers" while sitting at his table. A drawing of him during the trial
depicted an Edgar Allan Poe look-alike with a beehive knob of dark black

hair protruding off to one side of an abnormally huge head, a noticeable section above his right ear. He wore a black jacket, bow tie, white shirt, and, like any good suspect, whispered to his attorneys at times, while at others staring determinedly at the bench. JC needed to look busy and a part of a team there to defend him. He could not sit with a sour puss and be that bitter, wrongly accused man, angry at the system for condemning him before he had his chance to prove his innocence.

Alfred Lewis pointed out one of the more sardonic aspects of JC's trial by noting how it was being held in a building but "four hundred feet" from the "theater of the murder."

It was Wednesday, January 19, 1842, before the proceedings actually got on track. While the trial had started that Monday, January 17, a jury was not seated until Wednesday. Testimony and arguments got started then, after JC's lawyers pleaded with the court for a delay until Friday because of several issues they had with several of the chosen jurors. JC's attorneys argued that they had not had adequate time to question the three hundred potential jurors throughout the past two days.

The court denied the request and demanded that jury selection continue. On its first full day, the court went until "eleven o'clock at night" with a brief break for dinner. Out of a total of 336 potential jurors, both sides had agreed on eleven.

On Thursday morning, January 20, a twelfth juror was picked—and the prosecution began to lay out its case.

Born in New York City two years after the turn of the nineteenth century, Judge William Kent was forty years old when JC was brought before him for the cause of murder. His father, James Kent, had authored *Commentaries on American Law*, a rather liberal set of volumes known then as "the foremost American institutional legal treatise of its time." Judge Kent was an 1820 Union College graduate who had been instituted judge of the Circuit Court of New York City. Kent founded the Law School at New York University in 1838, according to his biography in John D. Lawson's *American State Trials*. Young and fresh and new to the bench, Kent was not about to be schooled here on how to handle his courtroom, something Dudley Selden, JC's acrimonious and dynamic lawyer, was looking to do during this trial. Selden, whom Lawson called a "prominent member of the New York City bar," had his own dealings ongoing with Sam Colt at the same time and was being stretched thin within the Colt family.

District Attorney James Whiting was new to the job. He had been appointed in May of the previous year. And here he was fronting one of the biggest cases the DA's office had ever tried.

If nothing else, many believed that the tactics both sides would use were going to provide plenty of drama for those lucky enough to attend.

Whiting's co-counsel, James Smith, gave a brief opening statement that sounded so remarkably modern that many lawyers of today could take a few pointers. The perceptive assistant district attorney stood and said,

> *This is the first time I have been engaged on the part of the People in a case affecting life and death. It is a painful task for me, for you, and for all here present to perform, but it is a necessary one. You have been selected out of a large number because you have declared you have no bias. Your sympathies must not be improperly exercised. You may feel them, but the jury box is not the place for their display. The prisoner is charged with murder—a murder unparalleled in the annals of crime. You will hear the evidence and it is for you to give it the weight you think it is entitled to. The counsel for the prisoner will no doubt endeavor to palliate the crime, but the violent character of the prisoner and the contrary one of the deceased which will be shown in the trial, leave but little doubt that the murder was willful and premeditated.*

It was such a refined and accurate opening remark, orated succinctly and patiently, hitting jurors between the eyes with a plea to focus strictly on the bare facts of the case. The idea that Smith mentioned how JC would somehow trivialize the crime and attempt to characterize the prosecution of the case as an attack on the Colt name was powerful. With only a few words, he humanized a case that had been so sensationalized in the press that many had no doubt forgotten there was an actual dead body, a man with a family, at the center of the proceedings.

Next, Smith gave a brief account of where JC had come from and what he had done for work: "Baltimore [was] where he taught mathematics for a while in a girls' academy. Then he became a surveyor. Enlisted in the navy. Soon got tired of this and was released at his father's request," a request made in a letter, the prosecutor failed to mention, that JC had written himself. "Then he was placed in a lawyer's office in New York—that of Dudley Selden, who later was to defend him on his trial for murder. After one year he entered the

University of Vermont, from there went west, engaged in land speculations. Lectured on chemistry in New Orleans and began teaching book-keeping there. Went to Cincinnati where he published his book on book-keeping and finally to New York City where he engaged in the same business."

The man JC had warned his pen pals about, who JC suggested would walk into the courtroom and crucify him with nothing less than lies and innuendo, Asa Wheeler, was called first by a prosecution team eager to see justice served. After giving the jury a description of his Chamber Street and Broadway office space in the Granite Building, explaining how JC had "called on" him to rent a room last summer, Wheeler was asked to describe those sounds he had heard on that day the prosecution believed JC murdered Sam Adams.

Wheeler offered few surprises. He spoke clearly and recalled conversations between himself and the accused as if they'd happened the previous day. He mentioned how odd JC had acted in the days after Adams went missing, how he had heard those thumps coming from the office next door to his, and how he then spied a box in JC's office he saw JC removing a day later. Shocking the courtroom, Wheeler spoke of his reaction to looking through the keyhole into JC's office only to spy the man he hardly knew leering over "something" on the floor. Stunning the gallery, Wheeler painted a dramatic picture of what that *something* could have been by stating emphatically, painting a picture of the missing man through a rhetorical device called synecdoche, "On a table were two black hats."

The prosecution had not resolved to showboating or asking this witness to speak beyond his proper place. After releasing Asa Wheeler, Whiting and Smith proceeded to bring in those witnesses who had either unknowingly helped JC dispose of Adams's corpse, or those who had seen JC on the day after he had committed murder. Each—the building's janitor, friends of Sam Adams, several carriage drivers (car men), and students of Asa Wheeler—added his piece of the puzzle, essentially sketching a narrative of a man who walked into JC's office and disappeared, and whose vanishing was followed by the appearance of a box, big enough for a man to fit into, whisked out of the office by none other than JC himself, who then tried to send to a fictional address in New Orleans.

Car man Richard Barstow said he "saw Mr. Colt in Chambers Street near Church, the morning of the 18th September, about nine o'clock. Asked me if I was engaged. Said he wanted a box to be taken to the foot of Maiden Lane. I agreed to take it." He explained how he completed the job while "Colt stood by." Then, Barstow reiterated, "[I] went back and asked him to what vessel I was to carry it. Said he did not know, but it was at the foot of Maiden Lane and he would go with me. Had noticed the direction and supposed the box was going to New Orleans. Stopped opposite a ship bound for there and pointed to the vessel to know if that was the one and he nodded assent. The vessel was the *Kalamazoo*."

Next, Barstow spoke of the weather and how he had dropped the box on the wharf, calling the delivery no different from "a box of sugar." He said JC paid him.

The prosecution asked if Barstow had ever seen the box again.

"A week afterwards," the car man said, "saw the same box again in the hold of the *Kalamazoo*. It was opened and contained a dead body. The box was then closed and carried to the dead house."

And yet, as JC and his lawyers sat, listening, shrinking into their seats, if anyone would have asked, they were not disputing any of this testimony. Where was the evidence, then, of actual murder?

As witness after witness entered, held his hat in his hands, swore to tell the truth, and took to the witness stand to defend Sam Adams's honor, all JC could do was sit and watch, awaiting his turn to speak. Selden's cross-examination of each witness did little to counter what appeared—at face value, anyway—to be unimpeachable, if mere circumstantial, evidence of a man covering up a murder. The prosecution seemed to be running on autopilot, nothing slowing its early pace or disrupting a particular accusatory momentum each witness was able to bring.

———

By the third day of testimony, the *Brooklyn Eagle* reported, "The same excitement prevailed about the Court." The *Eagle* had a reporter on scene and devoted substantial coverage to the case.

Most of the city's newspapers (and all of the tabloids) carried the direct testimony in its entirety, sometimes summarizing and paraphrasing long diatribes, while only briefly quoting, or not mentioning at all, Selden's concise cross-examination of each witness. Courtrooms at this time rarely ran with any particular cadence or back-and-forth, defense/prosecution parity. Much of the time, lawyers barked out questions and comments, confusing witnesses and beckoning them to banter on and on.

As the medical examiner and several physicians were brought in to testify about the condition of Sam Adams's body, along with those witnesses who had discovered the box on the *Kalamazoo*, the crate itself and the canvas in which JC had wrapped Adams's corpse was dragged into the courtroom and put on display to whispers and gasps. The presence of these dramatic pieces of evidence, legal writer Tom Smith considered, flooded "the room with a smell lessened little by the four months since the murder." Beyond that, the watch Sam Adams wore, which had become an important piece of physical evidence, in addition to the hatchet JC used to attack the man, were also put on display for jurors and showcased, like relics, for the gallery.

Throughout the span of three full days and sometimes nights, as each witness came and went, the *Eagle* reported, "The cross-examination developed nothing of importance." Mayor Robert Morris testified to some of the theatrics JC exhibited as the investigation into Sam Adams's disappearance pointed toward him. First, the prosecutor asked Morris to tell the jury who he was and when he had become involved in the case.

"Am Mayor of New York. Was applied to on Thursday, the twenty-third [September]."

Morris was asked to explain all he knew.

"Went over to the building and examined several persons," the mayor said in his deep baritone, more staged than pure,

among them the keeper *[Wheeler]*. *Associated Justice Taylor with me, who, on Friday morning, took depositions, and issued a warrant against Mr.* Colt. *Justice Taylor, A. M. C. Smith, another officer and myself went to the building to arrest Mr.* Colt. *His door was locked, and a label left on it that he would be back soon. Mr.* Colt *came to his door. I told him who I was and that I wished to see him in his room. We all went in and closed the door. I told him that he was arrested on suspicion of having killed Mr. Adams. The officers proceeded to search him. Prisoner assisted in the search and seemed disposed to yield everything. Sent an advertisement to the papers, asking any car man who had carried such a box from the building to the ship, to give notice at my office and succeeded in finding him. Went to the Coroner's office, and learned particulars as to the marks and on Sunday morning we got the box out.*

Selden asked when Morris heard about the salt in the box. This fact seemed to be important to Selden's strategy, although he did not illustrate with further questioning as to why he was so interested in it.

"Did not hear anything about the salt in the box till after the coroner's inquest," Morris said. This left the implication that Selden was trying to say (without coming out with the accusation) that Morris and the others had set their blinders on JC and never wavered from whom they wanted to blame for this terrible crime. The implied follow-up question was *Why didn't they follow the salt lead?*

"The two things were started simultaneously," Morris went on to explain in more detail—"to find the box and to find Mr. Colt's residence. Justice Taylor took charge of one branch and I the other. Colt's residence was ascertained on Saturday. We moved with as much secrecy as possible, in order to prevent a knowledge of these proceedings coming to the parties."

There had come a particular time during his testimony when the mayor discussed how they had uncovered locks of Sarah, Margaret, and Mary Colt's hair during their search of JC's trunk. As Mayor Morris and Selden talked about this, JC shuffled uneasily and uncomfortably in his chair. The mention of such family treasures was something that obviously bothered JC. "[O]n seeing which," the *Eagle* reported, "the prisoner seemed to be much affected, and wept for a long time."

Adding more heft to the anchor around JC's neck, a physician testified that among several items tested from JC's office, many of them contained the "presence of blood."

The doctor, quite sharp and articulate, said:

Saw spots on the wall. Preserved them for examination. An immense number of spots on the folding doors. Also took the hatchet, which was placed in my charge; also a piece of the floor, having a stain on it. Applied the test and the spots proved to have been blood. Blood was on the hammer side of the hatchet, which had been inked over, as also on the handle, near the eye of the hatchet, which had been inked. The spot on the piece of floor proved to be blood. Oil had been thrown round the base of the floor, under which was blood. There was also a piece of newspaper, which had much stains upon it. It was opened and showed much blood on it, and was also much torn. It was part of the New York Herald *of June 13, 1841.*

A bloodbath, in other words. Was the presence of so much blood the result of a self-defense crime scene or of a madman out of his mind, killing someone in a state of absolute murderous fury?

On the same day Mayor Morris provided his testimony, Emmeline Adams, Sam's widow, took to the stand amid a hushed room of sighs.

"Her appearance produced a great sensation," reported the *Eagle*.

The woman appeared tired and old, her face long and withdrawn from having to endure months now without the love and touch of a husband whom she had adored. It was that ring and Sam Adams's watch, Emmeline stated, by which she'd identified her husband.

"I did not see the body at the dead house."

When the prosecution finished with Mrs. Adams, the court asked Selden to move ahead with his cross-examination.

"We decline, Your Honor," Selden said smartly, waiving the defense's right to question the grieving widow of JC's victim. What good could come from the badgering of such a tired-looking and demoralized soul? Certainly nothing that could facilitate JC's cause for innocence.

On the sixth day of testimony, January 25, 1842, Asa Wheeler was recalled by the prosecution to set up a new theory, although questions would arise later as to why Whiting and Smith felt the need to do such a thing, other than the obvious reason of being able to drag in JC's famous brother. This new theory of the murder was steeped in the irony of Sam and John Colt's lives: One man was an accused killer, the other the maker of a killing machine. As a prosecutor, how could you not draw the comparison? How could you present your case without bringing in the notion that Sam Colt had built a life around weapons that killed people?

James Whiting asked Wheeler if he had ever seen a pistol inside JC's office. The court had made a decision before the proceedings began that day to allow the testimony. Wheeler described a conversation about guns he'd once had with JC. During the conversation, Wheeler testified, JC had actually brandished the weapon.

"We spoke of his brother," Wheeler said eagerly, looking toward the jury. "And I asked him if he (the brother) was the inventor of the patent pistol. He replied that he was and asked me if I had seen any of his pistols. Replied that I had not, he said he had one in his room and would go and get it and 'let you see it.' He went in and got it. It had a pearl handle and four or six barrels—I think six. Also explained to me a very ingenious mode of detonating with a cylinder. The barrels were about four inches in length. It had his brother's name on."

The gallery was not at all shocked by this testimony, but at the same time, many had not expected it. Wheeler's description spoke to a family whose livelihood depended on a society prone to violence. Wheeler had, without knowing, planted the seed that JC and his brother were both facilitators of death. The idea was that if Selden and his team paraded Sam Colt into the building and used his "status" to vouch for his brother's credibility, the prosecution was going to portray Sam as the man who invented a killing machine.

The witness following Wheeler said he had "purchased a pair of Colt's pistols, of the pattern shown. Tried some of them on board the *Belle Poule*. When merely propelled by a cap the ball was sent 160 feet, struck and dented a board, and rebounded ten or twelve feet. When fired at twelve feet the ball went through two thick covers of a book. The sound is like the cracking of a whip. Cannot say the sound is like the clashing of foils."

Even with the denial of the clashing-foils sound, as the day closed, many were left wondering: Had JC shot Adams and then pistol-whipped the printer? This seemed to be the scene the prosecution was trying to paint as Dudley Selden prepared to present his defense and the prosecution, thinking it had done all it could to prove its case of murder, was about ready to rest.

18

A Brother's Sins

JACK ROHAN PROBABLY USED A BIT MORE HYPERBOLE THAN NECESSARY. But while running the risk of overstating the obvious, the early-twentieth-century Colt biographer made an interesting point about Sam's work during the weeks of JC's trial, a time when it appeared the world was against the Colt family: "Sam's submarine battery . . . was exactly what every member of Congress would have ordered had he owned Aladdin's lamp."

This statement, a bit too enthusiastic, did hold a grain of truth. When Congress had a chance to take a serious look at Sam's proposal, the reaction wasn't a resounding *yea* from every member of the House, certainly not. But Sam had nonetheless won over enough hearts to warrant serious discussion about sending him additional funding for his experiments, which he desperately needed in order to forge ahead.

On the other hand, Sam had his enemies in Congress, who were prepared to fight him to the end. One of those men was none other than John Quincy Adams, "who saw [Sam] as a publicity-seeking charlatan." This opinion of John Quincy's, of course, could be validated: Any chance Sam was offered in front of the press, or any opportunity he saw to promote himself and his inventions, was never wasted. Sam adored the attention he received, no one can dispute that. Yet as Congress began talking about providing funds for his submarine torpedo, John Quincy got busy gathering proponents—many of whom were experts in their fields—to stand up against Sam and his underwater apparatus. "[M]any scientists viewed the battery as an auxiliary to coastal defenses, not worth the investment that would be necessary for harbors to be thoroughly mined." It was a tremendous commitment, essentially, and a major undertaking, had the government decided to fund the project without debating the pros and cons.

Despite having one of American history's most influential congress-men fighting him, a man who had been the sixth president of the United States, Sam saw John Quincy's negativity toward his mine company as nothing more than an obstacle he needed to figure out how to overcome. Unlike any of his siblings (and perhaps even his own father), Sam had the capability to rebound from disappointment with the wherewithal of an alley cat. Throw him and his ideas off a building and, while spiraling downward, the guy would figure out a way to land on his feet every time. Sam Colt never looked back. To do that meant certain failure. And fail-ure, for Sam Colt, was never an option.

While Dudley Selden made plans to dissolve Colt Firearms in Paterson, on top of dealing with the pressures of JC's trial, Sam contin-ued to woo the right players in Washington, persuading his advocates to accept his submarine mine and put the rubber stamp on the funding he needed. Money was at issue here. With enough money, Sam kept repeat-ing, he could arm the country in defense of an attack by any foreigner. As Jack Rohan wrote, however, this "elation" Sam surely felt over the possi-bility of getting congressional approval was consumed by the prospect of burying another family member by year's end and, beside him, a company he had put his heart and soul into since childhood.

"Although his political acquaintances had enough self interest in the financial success of the company to do their best for it," Jack Rohan added, "Sam operated on the theory that it would be easier for them to justify their actions if the device caught the public fancy."

But there was that jarring paradox staring Sam in the face once again: Putting on a public display Sam knew would garner the necessary sup-port would also mean giving away the secrets of his mine. Not to mention the cost of the display. Still, the more he thought about it, now with John Quincy trying to disrupt any momentum the project was getting in the House, Sam maybe had no choice but to stage a show in the waters off New York City.

Cultural historians have noted throughout the past fifty years that this era—1840 to 1850—was one of the more "violent and adventure-some years in [our] nation's" history. As Bill Hosley wrote in his expertly researched book, *Colt: The Making of an American Legend,* those ten unfor-gettable years were focused, for the most part, on "[i]ssues of race, guns and violence," all of which "had special meaning" to Americans, and Sam

Colt would exploit those issues with his inventive spirit and innovative nature to help define the generation and even change the way Americans viewed the process of manufacturing.

And yet, for every positive moment Sam Colt enjoyed during this hectic month of January 1842, there were three other reasons to give up. One week before JC's trial had started, for example, Colt Firearms secretary John Ehlers, that "Jerman" investor who had essentially swiped control of the company out from Sam's loose grasp, placed an advertisement concerning a meeting of Colt Firearms management to "dispose of all the goods and chattels" from the company and "dissolve its affairs and very existence." The timing was a bit of a jab. Ehlers knew Sam had his hands full already with JC and funding his submarine battery.

Then, if that wasn't enough, another hit came in the form of a letter:

Mr. Samuel Colt,

Sir: I am very sorry to say that your arms have proved an entire failure when put to the test of actual service. Lieut Sloan Comdg the Marines on the 13th Jany addressed me as follows: "I would respectfully suggest that Colts firearms be no longer used in my command."

The letter was signed by Captain McLaughlan, the one Marine Corps supporter Sam had in Florida. Sam's "repeater" pistol was not living up to expectations. There had been several "accidents," the apologetic-sounding captain—"I am perfectly satisfied that the principle of these arms is a good one."—had gone on to say in the letter. There had been "burst cylinders and barrels, jammed cap primers" and even one death, a young Marine, who died after the cylinder exploded in his face.

This bothered Sam, of course. But not for reasons one might expect. Knowing that McLaughlan's eventual report, which the captain had been forced to file under protocol, would put a damper on any future dealings Sam had with the government, Sam "whipped off" a letter to Commander Lewis Warrington, the president of the Board of Navy Commissioners. In that letter, Sam blasted Ehlers, a man he viewed as having ulterior motives; someone who had gone to such great lengths as having sabotaged Sam's entire gun-manufacturing endeavor. In his own unique way Sam had of taking thirty-six words to say what five could have accomplished, he wrote:

The chancery suit part of the wrangling over the dissolution of [my company] . . . had induced Ehlers to furnish to Government Arms imperfectly manufactured for the purpose of injuring their sail when they shall again come under my control.

The missive was replete with Sam's signature brand of paranoia and lack of emotional control. He seemed to suggest that Ehlers was not only dipping his greasy fingers into the safe, but that the man had done everything in his power to see that the company failed.

"Sam also wrote to his attorney," Bern Keating reported in his Colt biography, "explaining exactly the technique of metallurgic sabotage he accused Ehlers of resorting to as a guarantee of bankruptcy."

The reason why Ehlers had resolved to such underhanded, dangerous tactics—which now included, if you believe Sam, what could be construed as a charge of murder by some degree—was because "the company's assets," Keating so astutely pointed out, "would fall to him through a forced sale."

❧

On January 25, 1842, Dudley Selden's co-counsel, John A. Morrill (a stockholder, incidentally, in Sam's submarine battery company, with ten shares to his name), stood in open court and launched into the defense's opening argument. JC's legal team had begun its case. Former Congressman Morrill had an interesting public-speaking voice and was chosen to give the opening statement, most likely because he'd had that experience in Washington dealing with his counterparts on the floor of the House. In this court of law, his job was to redeem a man the press had already convicted, a man hated by just about everyone in New York City.

Morrill began by addressing the good men who held JC's life in their hands: "Gentlemen of the jury," he said calmly, with poise and control, "it now becomes the duty of the counsel for the prisoner— their solemn duty—to enter more minutely into the examination of the evidence which has been produced against the unfortunate individual who stands before you, a young man just entering into life, who has no friend around him but a brother, who is deprived by misfortune of the presence of his father—you know where his mother is, and also where are his beloved sisters."

Death surrounded this family like a curse, Morrill made a point to say. Still, the defense attorney was trying to imply that, despite death encircling the Colt legacy, none of it meant this man was a killer.

"While you have sympathy for him, I must admit that you must also feel the loss sustained by the widow of Mr. Adams . . .

> . . . one who has been bereaved by the loss of a tender and affectionate husband. The people ask that the laws shall be fairly administered, but while they do so, are sometimes carried away, and without thought will condemn an individual unheard. But the jury must lay aside these feelings, must lay aside feelings not only for the unfortunate prisoner, but for Mrs. Adams and for public prejudice. You must take hold of this case with clear, dispassionate minds, remembering to blend with justice the attributes of mercy. The counsel on the other side is all powerful, and it was necessary to fight the cause, as we have, from one step to another, knowing that 'trifles light as air' may have much effect on a case like this.

Here was a solid argument by the experienced lawyer who knew his place in a courtroom. Morrill was smart enough to spin a tale of woe and turn it into what could be, as he had said so clearly, misguided nothings blown out of proportion.

"A man will fight for his life," he continued, "and the counsel will contend not only for that life but for justice to the prisoner. It is with this feeling, and not with the view to detain the jury, that we have been thus minute.

"Gentlemen, John C. Colt, poor and friendless, a fellow citizen, comes before you charged with crime. He comes before you in defense of that life which is dear to all. He asks you to mete out to him justice—it is *all* he asks, it is all *we* ask. We seek but one thing: It is that we may have mercy according to law, and if he has such, we have no doubt that he will find a safe deliverance at your hands."

One reporter called Morrill's opening "eloquent." Surely the man was well-spoken; the argument he laid out well-executed and Morrill himself well-suited for the uphill battle he and Selden now faced. But one had to consider: Would any of these choice words sway a body of men sitting and listening, cloistered like monks inside this court building since the start of the trial?

Selden and Morrill called none other than Sam Colt to the stand first. The idea was to clear up any confusion the prosecution brought into the proceedings with its ridiculous "extra" theory that a Colt firearm might have been the murder weapon. Morrill and Selden had objected then to the preposterous notion, reading the entire indictment the prosecution had charged JC with, noting how "Adams was killed by blows from the confiscated hatchet." By reading Whiting's indictment out loud in open court, Selden made a point to Judge Kent that had the prosecution now wanted to say a Colt firearm killed Adams, it would mean the indictment was "improperly drawn." Selden and Morrill had built their defense around the "hatchet theory." They had not prepared to defend against the pistol as a murder weapon. The judge had allowed the new pistol theory evidence, which Whiting argued he had gotten ahold of only a few days before the trial started. Morrill and Selden, therefore, felt the need to call Sam to put on a display of his pistol and show how feeble a sound one of his weapons might make, crushing that "clashes of foil" argument early prosecution witnesses had told the jury they heard on the day JC killed Sam Adams.

"Am the inventor of Colt's patent firearms," Sam told the jury in his theatrically stagey, salesman's voice. Sam was a mere twenty-seven years to older brother JC's thirty-one. Sam had a way about him in front of a crowd, and this day turned out to be no different. He might have lived fewer than three decades, but the way in which he spoke and carried himself was that of a streetwise man of fifty. "Am acquainted with their construction," he stated to laughs from the crowd.

Sam was then "asked to show some experiments touching the power of the pistol with a cap." One courtroom observer talked about how Sam took one of his pistols, placed the balls "in the cylinder of one about eight or ten inches long, and propelled them by percussion caps, which he stated to be of great strength." The boom was loud. But Sam was able to catch "the balls in his hand as they came from the barrel." There was no charge in the weapon. It had been fired by mechanics alone.

More caps were placed inside the weapon. "He then fired at an open book at a few paces, which he struck, the ball penetrating nine leaves and indenting twenty-four. He also tried a patent pocket pistol at a distance, which made very little impression."

Selden asked Sam to throw the balls at the book in front of him.

The inventor did as he was told.

The impact was no different. Just about the same amount of pages had been crushed.

So the jury was left to question how one of Colt's pistols could have killed Sam Adams, how it could have left the gruesome injuries the man's skull had sustained, and how it had made a sound such as ten pistols being fired.

After being asked to talk about the type of weapons he had designed and manufactured in his factory, the gun maker said, "Never made pistols with more than one barrel except at first, about ten years ago, and then only kept them as models."

Sam's presence didn't seem to have the impact JC's lawyers had intended. Nonetheless, Sam showed support for his brother and even planted a seed that maybe there were people out there looking to cause his brother trouble by accusing him of things he could not have done. And if one was under the impression a Colt pistol killed the printer and JC had killed the man in self-defense, one had better consider the idea that perhaps another man had entered the office space and pummeled him, as well. The injuries Adams had to his skull were not done by any musket ball produced by Sam Colt. Sam's guns killed, sure. But they could not implode within a target and blow out; moreover, his ammunition was not made to enter a target and detonate.

After Sam exited the witness stand, Morrill called on one of the defense's doctors to support a claim that Adams's skull could not have been crushed the way it had been and "penetrated by a ball propelled only by cap." Doctor C. Zabrisky, a physician and chemist who had worked for Colt's Patent Arms Manufacturing Company, was certain a ball alone could not have done the job a model of Adams's skull had proven. The man could have been beaten *and* shot. But the more likely scenario, the doctor suggested, was that Adams had sustained much of his injuries not by JC's hand, but from a protruding nail sticking in the dead man's skull while his body was being transported to the *Kalamazoo* inside that box.

"I was never able but once even to indent a fireboard with a ball sufficiently deep to make it stick," Zabrisky testified. "The patent article, when fired with powder, makes more noise than common firearms," an inference to those clashing foils so many in the building had described.

"The impression did not appear to be so great at five feet distance as at twenty feet. Think it would be impossible for a ball to make a hole such as represented, in the head of deceased, by a ball from Colt's pistol, propelled by a cap."

With the presence of Dr. Gilman next, Morrill further argued his assumption. Gilman had examined Adams's head and body.

"Think it improbable that the hole was made by a ball of any description," Gilman admitted.

Then Dr. David Rogers was called to add credence to the same opinion, stating:

> *It is impossible to say what particular degree of injury would be necessary to create insensibility. In some cases, it is created by a very small-sized wound. In others, even where the whole front of the top of the head was broken in, as a wound caused by the falling of a block from a masthead, where the man preserved his sinuses throughout, and got well. A nail projecting into the box about an inch, I should suppose, must have penetrated the head of the body in any way it moved. The action of the body in carrying it to Maiden Lane, putting it on board the vessel, and afterwards carrying the body to the dead-house, might have been sufficient to drive the nail through the head.*

None of this, naturally, preserved or furthered JC's argument of self-defense. The injuries were not at issue; how they got there were.

Morrill and Selden were smart to have several material witnesses testify on behalf of JC conducting his own business with paper suppliers while painting Sam Adams as a hothead who walked about the city with a chip on his shoulder, a man looking for a fight.

Cyrus W. Field, a paper dealer Colt had used, spoke of how JC had his own account and routinely called on him for orders, but allowed others to make purchases for him. As Fields told his tale, a witness who was supposed to give a testimonial to JC's credibility actually backfired on the defense.

"Made paper to order and on account of Mr. Colt in July and August, 1841," Field explained to the certain shock of Morrill and Selden.

> *The terms were to be one half cash and one half a good note. . . . Soon afterwards, Mr. Adams came in, having in his hand a letter from Mr. Colt, dated Boston, and requesting I should let Mr. Adams have the paper. Told Mr. Adams the terms. The latter said Mr. Colt had always*

paid him and the books should not go out of his hands till the money was paid. I let him have ten reams. The balance of the paper was delayed in coming from Hartford and Mr. Adams was very anxious about it. On August 25th Mr. Colt came in and said it was too late for the trade sale, but, if I would give him time, he would take the balance of the paper and have the work perfected for the Philadelphia trade sale, getting his returns in time to pay for the paper. Mr. Adams thought the note of Mr. Colt would be good for the amount. The two lots came to $121.68 for which I took Mr. Colt's note at three months, which note is unpaid. The paper was sent to Mr. Adams' office. Understood the plates cost over $300.

Dr. David Rogers was then re-called as some movement in the courtroom caused a small commotion. Something was happening.

"The head of Mr. Adams was . . . brought into court by the physicians and coroner," *American State Trials* reported. Not actually into the courtroom, but placed on a desk in a room alongside the courtroom where proceedings were being conducted. It was a move on the part of Selden and Morrill that would have detrimental moral implications.

Rogers and the other doctors were asked to have a look at the ghastly display.

"Have examined the head of Mr. Adams," Rogers said some time later, sitting back down in front of the jury. "Am well satisfied from the examination and comparing the hatchet with the wound that the hole was made with the sharp side of the hatchet. It fits the wound precisely."

"We move, Your Honor, that the skull and axe should be shown to the jury," Prosecutor Whiting announced after the doctor made the implication it was the hatchet that had likely killed Adams.

"I object, respectfully, Your Honor," Selden interjected.

"However painful it is," Judge Kent offered, "justice must be administered and the head produced, if the jury think it necessary."

"We are only seeking truth," Whiting explained. "Desperate efforts are being made to break down the testimony. If it could be avoided I would gladly agree not to have the skull exhibited, but it was necessary, that the jury should see it."

All agreed.

A clerk went and retrieved the severed skull. It was then handed to Dr. Rogers by the coroner and displayed for the jury to see.

What a bizarre move on the prosecution's part. Here was the doctor, sitting in the witness stand, Adams's crushed and decapitated skull in his lap, wrapped in paper, set beside the court reporter's table. In fact, the place where JC sat with his lawyers was "within a few feet" of Sam Adams's skull.

Inside what was a "crowded to excess" courtroom, among spectators and onlookers, including Samuel Adams's friends and family, Dr. Rogers slowly unwrapped the paper to reveal a vile-smelling mishmash of bone fragments and dried tissue.

Some gasped. Others looked on with curiosity.

This was nothing but mere theatrics. Yet, given the time in American history that this bizarre courtroom move took place, when murder trials in general were more about drama and stage and spectators wearing their Sunday best in hopes of catching "performances," it's easy to understand why the prosecution did this. The behavior inside most courtrooms, especially in a city as populated as New York, was not too much different from that of the penny press reporting on it.

"Trial coverage was a staple in the so-called 'penny press,' and other daily and weekly newspapers," Dennis and Susan Hall wrote in their popular culture study titled *American Icons*. "Fact and fiction sometimes blended together in this journalism, but nobody seemed particularly concerned."

Part of the excitement stemmed from a craving the public had for trial stories in those fast-selling, widely popular fiction magazines of the day. Early pulp, we could call them. But to be able to witness this sort of melodrama in person was another thing entirely—and lawyers, both defense attorneys and prosecutors, played into this thirst for the spectacular drama that often defined a trial. The prosecution here knew the city was looking on, waiting with bated breath for every move coming out of City Hall; and this display of the skull would carry serious weight out in the social media of the day, not to mention with a jury whose eyes were bulging at the sight of such a ghastly piece of evidence.*

The Halls argued elegantly and sharply in their book that these types of sensational trials allow Americans to identify with who they are as a

---

* We do the same thing today inside the courtroom, only on a larger scale, which is then projected out into a mass media culture of tens of millions of people. Think of O.J. Simpson's trial and that "If the gloves don't fit, you must acquit" moment; the drumroll drama in the courtroom as OJ tried to force that glove onto his catcher's-mitt hand was palpable. And what about Casey Anthony? Need I say more on this!

people and "use them to make sense of their world because the courtroom trial in both fact and fiction is an established icon of their culture."

Not only did Dr. Rogers study Sam Adams's crushed skull as he sat on the witness stand, but he held it up for everyone to get a good look at. There, on display in front of everyone, was the victim's skinless skull, bloodied and dried and staring at them all.

But then Rogers took things a bit further, solidifying the prosecution's point that the murder was committed by a hatchet-wielding maniac: "He placed the corner of the axe in the hole over the left ear, which precisely fitted it," *American State Trials* reported. "He then put the hammer part in the fracture or indentation on the other side, which joined in it fairly as a mold. He then explained the wounds in front."

Were these the wounds inflicted by a man protecting himself?

Sitting uncomfortably, slithering in his chair, JC placed his hands over his eyes while Rogers's examination continued. He was doomed. The situation was about as bad as it could get for the accused murderer.

Born for Blood

JC could do nothing more than sit and stare at the floor, his hands covering his face. The severed skull was "interesting," said one courtroom observer, but also a "dreadful sight." Then Sam Adams's jaw, in two separate pieces, was unveiled for jurors, in what had become a courtroom circus. Jurors even passed the skull and jaw sections around as one of the doctors "went on to explain the nature of the wounds."*

One of JC's old friends from Ohio was called soon after. JC's former business partner Nate Burgess explained how he had taught bookkeeping with JC in New York after they moved from Ohio, where they had managed a publishing house that had failed. Other than that, all Burgess could say was, "Am indebted to Mr. Colt; he always treated me like a gentleman."

Selden stood and turned to the gallery, calling out several names from a list in his hand.

No response.

Then, "Is Miss Henshaw in the courtroom?" Selden asked.

The crier officially followed up, announcing, "Caroline Henshaw? Miss Henshaw?"

JC's so-called wife, the mother of "his" child (born the previous November), looked pleasantly comfortable sitting there. Her presence in the courtroom "created quite a sensation among the audience." The idea that a woman had lived with a man and had been impregnated by that man out of wedlock had "aroused acute public discourse," Andie Tucher wrote. This public image of JC bedding a woman whom many thought to be no more than a common whore was something JC's attorneys had a difficult

---

* In a world without crime scene and autopsy photographs to show the jury, displaying the actual pieces of evidence, however gruesome and theatrical, was perhaps necessary.

time contending with. They could bring in all the character witnesses they wanted. They could ask Caroline a thousand questions regarding how well JC had treated her. Yet, in the eyes of a contemptuous public, hungry for the next salacious penny-press story (and likely every juror sitting, watching this woman), Caroline and JC were nothing more than morally corrupt scoundrels. Caroline had been called everything from a despicable woman to a prostitute. Had anyone known then that the child she had given birth to—whom she named Samuel Colt "for his uncle"—was actually Sam's, JC not only would have been hanged there inside the courtroom, but Sam could have all but forgotten about his submarine mine business and that funding from the government he was so close to securing.

The pretty young woman had the apropos glow of a new mother; she looked happy, maybe more so because she and the baby had come through the pregnancy without too much trouble. Caroline wore a "dark bonnet, black veil, and light cloth cloak." The way she moved, the fashion statement she made, it almost seemed as though she was leading the procession of a funeral, a cloth tissue in one hand as the crier took a wooden chair and held it for the woman whose presence was hands down the most anticipated of the trial.

As she sat, Caroline threw back her veil in a melodramatically graceful manner, exposing her untarnished pale-white skin. She then proceeded to explain to the jury who she was and why she had been called. It took JC's mistress no time to paint a picture of a man who, for the fifteen months she had known him, lived under a routine that rarely ever changed—that is, except for the night in question, when JC arrived home later than usual.

"Have been acquainted with John C. Colt," Caroline began, "[and] lived with him from the eleventh of May to the time he was arrested. We first lived at Captain Hart's No. 42 Monroe Street. Mr. Colt was generally in from half past nine to ten o'clock in the evening. On the evening of the seventeenth of September he was not home at the ordinary hour."

This out-of-the-norm behavior was odd to Caroline, she further stated: "He was always home before ten o'clock."

After telling Selden how JC had slept for three consecutive nights in his bed shirt, which in her mind was another strange circumstance, Mr. Whiting asked the witness where she and JC had met.[*]

---

[*] Major trials during the mid-nineteenth century were sometimes more of a fluid Q&A type of conversation, not so much the direct-/cross-examination system we are used to today. Jurors, attorneys, and judges often shouted out questions as they came to mind, which might seem to us today as

"First became acquainted with Colt at Philadelphia," she said in her gentle tone, quickly pointing out that she "did not live with him before I came from Philadelphia." Then she talked about lying to many of JC's friends and the public by, "pass[ing] by the name of Mrs. Colt." Yet she gave no reason why she did this.

From there, Caroline spoke of her habits with JC, mainly walking at night around the city and going to bed (for sleep) together (at the same time of the night). Then JC's character was brought into question, Caroline responding quite categorically, "He was always very kind—very mild. Treated me kindly always; and do not recollect that I ever saw him in a passion."

She was asked about her baby.

"Am a mother by Mr. Colt," she said sharply, without hesitation (although, the witness did not say by which Mr. Colt, and no one had cause at this time to question her).

Whiting asked about Sam Adams, if Caroline had ever seen the accused with the dead printer. Then a juror piped in and asked if she knew Adams's watch was inside the trunk she kept in the apartment. The questions, it seemed, came from everywhere, all at once. Yet Caroline kept her composure, answering each with the courageous boundary and performance of an expert witness.

"Did not know there was a watch in the trunk when Justice Taylor took it," she answered. "Nor did I know then that he had been arrested. Did not know Adams. He was never at our house."

The one bit of doubt—if it came across as such—Caroline Henshaw provided to JC's defense argument might have arisen when she talked about the "black bruises" JC had on his neck when she finally saw him on that night he came home sweaty, in a mild state of mania. This could, if jurors looked at the case without that penny-press-aura corrupting judgment, lead one to believe JC *had* acted in self-defense. JC had scratches on him, too, Caroline told jurors. From all outward appearances, it seemed JC had gotten into some type of skirmish.

Selden had planned to call several character witnesses to vouch for Caroline's credibility and good standing, saying, "[My client's] relation

---

badgering a witness, but was expected on some level then. With a witness such as Caroline Henshaw, you'd assume many questions to arise; Caroline's character was on trial as much as JC's. She would have been asked repeatedly to explain why she had been committing what the lawyers would call "adultery" for so many months with a man now accused of murder.

with her was one of the acts for which he has been called upon by public sentiment to answer, but she was no prostitute except as regarded him. He did wrong and she did. But adverse circumstances alone caused them to live together in the illegitimate manner they did."

Judge Kent refused to allow any of Selden's so-called character witnesses to testify on Caroline's behalf, elaborating, "Unless the character of a witness is impeached, the testimony should be disallowed. It is unnecessary to produce evidence as to the character of the last witness."

Selden, sharp as a razor, however, was able to get a few of those witnesses onto the stand under a veil of testifying about JC.

None of this was going to make a difference. Society had judged this woman (and her roommate), and blamed *her* for falling in love with a man who was an impostor, a fraud and fake. JC's entire life up to this moment had been based on dishonesty, or so the record seemed to purport; yet, in his defense, regarding the situation of Caroline Henshaw, JC's loyalty to his brother Sam was unshakable. JC could have dropped a grenade inside the courtroom and disturbed the entire proceeding, putting a rubber stamp on a mistrial with the announcement that he was covering for his brother. But even as he was being backed into a corner and a guilty verdict seemed inevitable, John Colt stood behind his little brother and protected the Colt name.

There was a man sitting in the gallery who had himself testified already. He sat stoically with his top hat in his hands, wore a neatly pressed white ruffled shirt underneath a black vest, a bow tie tied perfectly as angel wings, and a plush black topcoat and matching pantaloons. He sat patiently, watching and listening. As Caroline was excused from the stand to a mild stir in the room, she stood, moved the veil back over her face, and was escorted out of the courtroom by this peculiarly quiet man who may have been her husband.*

Samuel Colt.

---

* One would have to deduce from the evidence left behind that Sam had suggested the arrangement between JC and Caroline when he found out she was pregnant with his child. Why JC never actually married Caroline seemed to be a mystery; yet, several accounts report that Sam was already married to the woman. "The inventor had met and married the young and unschooled Caroline some years earlier in Europe," Andie Tucher wrote in the well-researched and aptly sourced *Froth & Scum*, "Soon, however, he decided that so humble a bride was no worthy partner for him" (p. 173).

He was "easy, lucid, and spoke without confusion," Alfred Lewis wrote, describing JC's demeanor as he sat and acknowledged his guilt on Saturday morning, January 29, 1842. By Lewis's estimation, after studying the available research, JC made a terrible witness on his own behalf, a point with which few crime experts studying this trial would disagree. His pompous attitude and please-believe-me demeanor would not bode well with a gallery and jury who had made up their minds already. JC, conversely, could not hide who he was, or the failures of a wasted life. This was his destiny: death. He knew it. This so-called *Confession* his lawyer was about to read would only solidify that feeling among those chosen to decide his fate.*

Selden's co-counsel, Mr. Emmett, stood and faced the jury, saying, "We will admit that Colt took the life of Adams, and we now propose to tell you, as far as possible, how it was done. As the counsel for Mr. Colt, I state what he would if he were to stand up before you. It is not for you to receive it other than as a statement of facts, which you are authorized to reject or receive. I will read what would be the statement of Mr. Colt, were he called upon to give the facts in reference to it. We have a right, as none but the God above us saw the transaction, to show the manner in which the act was done. I shall speak in the first person."

Summarizing JC's *Confession*, the main argument made in this document was to insist that Sam Adams had called on JC that day and entered his office with an attitude, a man looking for a quarrel. They argued. It got physical after Adams called Colt a liar. In defending himself against Adams's advances, without looking, JC grabbed what he thought to be a hammer and struck Adams with it, hoping to hold the man back so he could explain the misunderstanding about the money in further detail. After looking down at the implement, this as Adams fell to the ground, JC realized he had in fact struck Adams in the head with a hatchet, unleashing a terrible rush of blood (the head bleeds more profusely than any other part of the human body). From there, JC said he panicked, hence the cleanup that followed and the way in which Adams's body was

---

* According to Alfred Lewis's account, JC read the *Confession* himself. In fact, Lewis goes on about JC's demeanor here during this period of the trial, writing, "He related the killing, with every subsequent detail of boxing up the murdered body, and was throughout as coldly unemotional as a snake." I have no idea where Lewis got this information. I could not find it. Quite to the contrary, the trial transcript from *American State Trials,* our best source for the trial, states that JC's attorney Robert Emmett read the *Confession,* even noting at the start of what was a long and tedious (one report says "he spoke for some hours") oration that he was reading it for his client.

found inside that now infamous wooden box those car men had taken to the *Kalamazoo* under JC's direction.*

When Emmett finished reading the statement over a chorus of whispers, keeping the courtroom buzzing with the similar background noise found in any city tavern nearby, the lawyer explained why they had read the document:

> *We had intended to state the facts to the public, but circumstances induced us to await the trial. When I first saw Mr. Colt he was a perfect stranger to me. After hearing the particulars, it was our intention to make the matter public, but decided otherwise. Mr. Colt consented to it only with the understanding that he should yet make the statement.*

"Are such a course of remarks proper?" Whiting asked.

"These communications were not admissible," said the judge.

Emmett would not give up. He cited laws and earlier precedents, as any competent trial attorney would. He reviewed all the evidence of self-defense, pleading with the court and the jury to disregard their prior judgments of this man and hear him out for a moment as to why this case, as complex as it had been, should not be about the man, but be focused on the evidence.

This was a solid argument, wrapped in truth and legalities. The lawyer knew his way around a courtroom.

Selden asked Emmett to take a seat. Maybe have a glass of water and gather his bearings. Anyway, it was Selden's turn now to address the court and jury. He wanted to put a bit more heft into Emmett's argument.

---

* I have to point something out here. As someone who has studied dozens of trials, both historical and contemporary, when it came down to the bare "legal" facts of this case, and one looked at all of the available evidence with a clear, objective eye, it does seem to me as though JC acted in defense of his own person—that is, if his *Confession* holds even the slightest grain of truth. It certainly wasn't premeditated murder; there was no cause or motive driving that theory. After all, Sam Adams sought JC out. At best, this case was maybe manslaughter or second-degree murder. Once you add the name—Colt—into it all, however, and toss in the bastard child of Caroline Henshaw, alongside Caroline and JC living in sin, JC's background as a cheat and liar, well, it's hard to convince a public bent on punishing the *person* and not the criminal *act* to think of this crime as anything other than a seemingly well-off man with the best attorneys money can buy looking to get out of a bad life and cover up a vicious, violent murder he had perpetrated. Funny how, in many instances, the tables are turned in this day and age; and how the penny press of yesteryear has become crime television, that opinionated-driven farce we see during prime time hours, where many defendants are subjected to routine prosecution by talking heads who know nothing about the cases in which they yammer on and on about.

"My remarks shall not extend to a length unnecessarily to trespass upon the time of the jury," Selden stood and said, which was a mistake, considering how long he would go. "For the statute gives to the jury the decision as to the *law* as well as the *facts*. The act in relation to concealing the body must not be connected with the idea itself."

The man had made an excellent point: How could one judge a self-defense argument by what the accused did *after* the fact?

"Even if you adopt the suggestion that breaking in the frontal bone was to conceal the body," Selden said, referring to the theory that JC had to crush Adams's jaw and skull in order to fit him into that box, "it can have no bearing upon the decision as to the guilt or innocence of the defendant."

Here was Sam's money being well spent—the reason the Colt brothers had chosen such an expensive team was because these lawyers knew how to frame an argument around the law. And if the jury had been the least bit unbiased, each man would have understood that Selden was not trying to pull a fast one here on anyone—but only pointing to what the *law* stated in reference to this case.

"Do you suppose," he continued, "it was a feeling of cruelty, for the purpose of mangling the body at his feet, as alluded to by the prosecution?"

Was JC acting evilly when he hog-tied Adams and crushed his face? Or was he simply acting in a practical (if not with an impractical mind) way, feverishly trying to cover up a horrible mistake, a temper he had allowed to get out of control?

The lawyer caught his breath and proceeded to give the jury an answer to his questions, stating:

I believe the wounds were given before the body of Mr. Adams was struck down. Mr. Colt would not have resorted to disfiguring the head to insure concealment; it was the last course that a man of mind would resort to. Adams lay prostrate at the foot of the prisoner—he fell, and the attention of those in the adjoining room was attracted by the noise—they listened—not a sound was heard, not a groan uttered. Where was the prisoner then? He was hanging over the body of his victim, contemplating the ruin that had been created. The transaction took place at half-past three, and it is said his room was watched till nine. Do you not believe that he knew the movements of those outside?

What sensations would likely be produced in his mind? No one put their hand upon the door for the purpose of entrance. He was in terror of his situation. He knew that no person had witnessed the act; that his situation, living in a state of profligacy, was against him—he had nothing on which he could fall back as to connection or character, and was not in a condition by which he could hope for credence in making his situation known.

JC knew, while staring at Adams's disfigured corpse, blood all over him, blood all over the floor, the walls and that hatchet sitting on the table, that the world would judge him on his living conditions, his past, and his name. There was no getting out of this without concealing the crime.

But then Selden, under the spell of his own excitement, made a crucial mistake. He asked jurors to walk in JC's shoes.

"There is no man but under such circumstances would have resorted to concealment rather than disclose what occurred. He determined upon the plan, and set out to put it in execution."

By making such a broad statement (judgment, really) of character and bringing into the argument the morality of the jurors, Selden ran the risk that the men deciding JC's fate might be appalled by such an unfair accusation toward them, thus placing each person in the room, hatchet in hand, now deciding his client's fate based on their own reaction to the crime and what each would have done.

Continuing a few moments later, he added, "Yet the means had nothing to do with the offence unless collected for that purpose. . . ." He resorted to the plan of placing the body in a box—it could not stay in his room, to attempt bringing it or throwing it into the sea, would be certain to cause detection, and it was disposed of in the best manner he thought possible. In relation to the catastrophe itself, Adams was standing on his feet, and fell dead upon the floor, and face to face."

As he wound down what had turned into an overstated diatribe, walking a fine line at this point of falling into a preachy state of finger-wagging, a speech by which he had made some interesting points, it was clear that reasonable doubt should be applied to this case, regardless of how long the lawyer had taken to make his point. The evidence did not back up the prosecution's case of murder.

A closing such as the one Emmett and Selden gave could not con-clude—or *should* not conclude, rather—without mention of Caroline Henshaw, and Selden got right to his point for bringing the woman's name back into the record, launching into an explanation that leaned again toward the reasonable doubt factor.

"The learned counsel said this morning that Caroline Henshaw's tes-timony was not entitled to confidence. That she was living in a state of adultery with Mr. Colt. If he means to apply that to her general course, he is much mistaken. I have seen those who pretended virtue guilty of vice—have seen the wife whose word was no better than that of the mistress. She may have been guilty on one point, but is entitled to credit as regards every other. Her testimony showed that she loved the prisoner, yet was determined to tell the truth."

Selden wasn't about to concede the gold watch being that of Sam Adams.

Caroline Henshaw had access to the trunk, and Colt knew it. He was aware that the watch was an elegant one, of peculiar workman-ship, and must be discovered in case he afterwards attempted to wear it. Is it likely he would have plundered another of such an article as that, and have committed murder in order to do it? Except what was shown yesterday, in respect to the articles found in the trunk, there is no evidence that Samuel Adams had anything about his person. He was not a man likely to have had money about him; he was pressed on all sides, and his books disclose it. There is nothing on the books that gives evidence of his having received a dollar of money.

Now for the quarrel. God forbid we should say anything against Mr. Adams, his character or his conduct. The name of John C. Colt is stamped upon the record of criminal jurisprudence; he has been represented as if he had been born for blood—has been persecuted and maligned; but it is not for us to visit the idea upon the unfortu-nate deceased. Adams went to Colt's room in a 'vexed mood,' having expressed surprise . . . that Mr. Colt expected the proceeds of the sale. Mr. Colt owed Samuel Adams only seventy-one dollars, but he con-tended that he owed him more. Out of that account words came up, which produced blows, and terminated in death. Mr. Adams had hold of Mr. Colt in a manner to prevent him crying out, and caused him to use the hatchet in self-defense.

Next, Selden broke into a long—much, much too long—soliloquy regarding the blood evidence and how none of it refuted the fact that JC had been protecting himself.

"When the wife was here," Selden said, referring to Mrs. Adams, "one of the salt men was directed to bring up the bloody garments and shake them under her very nose. Although the death of Adams had not been denied, the testimony must be brought up to make an effect on the audience. Even the grave was opened, and the head severed from the trunk. The physicians said they could examine it in another room, but it was necessary to place upon the table of a court the head, in order that you, gentlemen of the jury, might be influenced by the feelings observable among the multitude."

The attorney was on a roll now, hitting his stride, making sense, shaking down the prosecutor's pointless showboating and amateurish tactic of making a spectacle out of the court—prosecutorial actions and arguments that, had this trial taken place today, would have been shot down during a preliminary hearing.

Continuing, Selden said,

A charge was made that a pistol had been used, and the brain searched to find a ball. Could the prisoner have obtained the exhuming of the body to prove his innocence? The activity of the police has been brought into exertion, in a manner such as I have never known, in order to convict the prisoner, and his ease has withstood them all. He is entitled to the sympathy of a jury of his country. I ask only for the exercise of that principle of law, which says that where there is a doubt, it must be placed in favor of the prisoner. When there are two degrees in the statute—one that will cause a limited degree of punishment, and the other show excusable homicide, if there is a doubt as to which the case belongs, the jury is bound to present a verdict of acquittal. The jury has been kept aloof from external events, and can now see that what at first seemed murder, is but an accident. A prisoner is not bound to show justification. It is for the jury to decide.

He took a much-needed breath and then gave a concluding summation. Had it been another time, another court, another defendant, in another city but this one, Selden would have swayed a few minds:

Gentlemen, after nearly a fortnight's trial, the cause of the prisoner is now committed to your hands, a young man just entering into life, his prospects probably have been permanently blasted—but still it is for you to pass upon the facts. We leave his cause with you, requesting you to bear in mind justice as well as mercy is a portion of the attributes of the criminal law.

Then the man sat down next to his client. The gallery was aghast, in awe, maybe even disgusted by some of what the lawyer had suggested. Yet in terms of a closing argument, Selden had added serious lift to a remarkable job by Emmett.

Political gain—that was the message JC's lawyers had sent to the jury. This team of prosecutors, working under the guise of city officials, were thinking about their futures, how they would be held up on the shoulders of a city whose hatred for John Caldwell Colt and his bad behavior was being presented here as a spectacle.

A Bloodthirsty Heart

PROSECUTOR WHITING WAS GIVEN A TURN TO ARGUE ON BEHALF OF THE City of New York and the victim, Sam Adams; and the shrewd prosecutor wasted little time sharing the stark realities of the case, what became apparent when one took away all the fluff, pomp, and circumstance, and studied the bare facts. A good closing argument should include its share of assigning guilt—and Prosecutor Whiting, perhaps feeling his case slipping away, piled it on.

"Blood has been spilt," Whiting said with his booming lawman's voice, "shall we flinch in the performance of our duties, or fulfill our oaths? Not only do justice to the unfortunate person, but to ourselves and the country. The counsel has not attempted to show that the prisoner is *not* guilty, but I have been placed on trial, and charged with doing *everything* malignant."

The counselor's disgust for how Emmett and Selden had framed the charges and the prosecution's case was evident as Whiting seemed to grow angrier with each word. He was taken aback by the accusations lodged against him by Selden, especially.

"If I am such as they describe," Whiting continued, "the sooner you get another to fill the office of District Attorney the better! If doing everything to facilitate counsel for the prisoner, if ever having read the accounts in the papers, makes me guilty, then I am so—then have I persecuted their client to the death. If furnishing copies of all the affidavits, and showing favor to the prisoner, such as none ever was shown, then am I guilty. But I appeal to twelve honest hearts whom I see before me. I have done nothing since this trial has commenced but what was strictly enjoined upon me by my duty."

Walking away from the table behind which he stood, Whiting approached the jury with a question: "What do the counsel mean by their aspersions?"

Then, answering his own question with a sanctimonious tirade, he added, "As to the last gentleman who has spoken, if, peradventure, a little jealousy has entered into his feelings I will only say that if I ever go to the legislative halls, I will return to the people having performed all the pledges that have been enjoined upon me, and when I go from this trial to the bosom of the community I shall feel that I have performed the oath that I have taken."

In explaining himself and protecting his reputation, Whiting may have come across as pleading his own case, rather than pleading a case for justice.

> *As to the threats of the other gentleman, that I deserved impeachment, I can only say that his threats have no terrors. Perhaps I deserved blame, let not a hair of the prisoner's head be hurt, think not of me, they said I had a feeling of triumph, triumph of what—if it were in my power, I would unclose this man's chains and say 'go.' I would, after performing my duty, take that man's hand and hear from his lips that I had done no more than my duty. Has John C. Colt been unfairly dealt with? After making every effort to procure evidence, the counsel was offended because we proved the contents of the box! They observed that they intended to make a confession. That confession we do not hear of before, not even when the counsel first opened the case. Suppose we had been contented to do as the counsel spoke of. They had the confession in their pocket, and yet cross-questioned every witness that came up, and even stated, in opening, that we had not proved our case. Yet they charged us that we had kept the jury day after day.*

He paused here. Then: "I advise the counsel to beware how they sport with the lives of their clients; how they come to defend a case and still claim to have a confession in their pocket. Had the gentleman said, we do not dispute that he killed Adams, put him in a box, and put him on board a vessel, how long would it have taken to try the case?"

❦

Throughout the trial John C. Colt had maintained his composure. He had become frustrated at times and bowed his head, placing his hands over his face, while some reports have him grimacing and even crying. But other than those few reactive measures, most of the evidence left behind does not speak of any outbursts or strange behavior.

Five years prior to sitting and facing this jury of his peers, JC had run into none other than "Dr. Octagon," Orson Squire Fowler. It was at the Astor House one night amid a throng of people. Fowler had quite the reputation, even then, as an eccentric and strange broker of phrenology. Some considered Fowler no more than a con artist and carnival performer, trying to push street magic off as reputable science. In the years after he wrote about his analysis of JC, just before his death in 1887, Fowler was arrested for "practicing medicine without a license." When the doctor heard about the warrant against him, he commented, "I am surprised. I have never prescribed medicine to any of my patients." There was a specific doctor, Edward Storck, the chairman of the Board of Censors from the Erie County Medical Society in upstate New York, who claimed to have a letter written by Fowler in which the phrenologist had discussed prescribing medication for someone. "I would advise," Fowler explained to a *New York Times* reporter who had tracked him down before he was taken into custody, "Dr. Storck or any other man not to attack me, for he will surely get the worst of it."

Phrenology, by its simplest definition, is the "study of the shape and protuberances of the skull, based on the now discredited belief that they reveal character and mental capacity." A phrenologist might measure a man's head, in other words, feel its contours with his hands, and make an analysis of the man's character from that brief unscientific examination. Phrenology is said to have "characterized Enlightenment thought" during the nineteenth century.*

In the case of JC, phrenology—as O. S. Fowler moseyed up to the accountant and introduced himself, asking the gun maker's brother if he would mind an "examination"—would become something of a crystal ball. Many believed that by studying the shape of the skull the phrenologist could gauge an "indication of mental abilities and character traits." Franz Joseph Gall, the so-called founder of phrenology, "stated the principle that each of the innate mental faculties is based in a specific brain region ('organ'), whose size reflects the faculty's prominence in a person and is reflected by the skull's surface." Gall had "examined the skulls of persons with particular

---

* According to those who study phrenology today, "Historians connecting science, medicine, and culture have begun to recognize phrenology's significance as a medium through which a number of naturalistic and functionalist concepts reached a wide and popular audience."

traits—including 'criminal' traits—for a feature he could identify with it." So the idea that Fowler was now preparing to examine JC, at a time in JC's life when one could say he was bouncing around from city to city (before he had committed any serious crimes), at the height of his lying and cheating phase, is interesting in hindsight. Fowler wrote about this chance meeting, it should be noted, *after* JC had been arrested, charged, and put on trial. So his memory of the meeting was most likely tainted.

"I recollect perfectly well," Fowler wrote, "what I said to [John Colt], and also his phrenology developments."

Fowler observed that JC was one of the "most active and excitable" subjects he had "ever witnessed."

Obnoxious was probably the best way to describe JC then.

"[T]he whole organization [of JC's brain]," Fowler continued, "...the organs being *very sharp*, and indicating the utmost intensity and power of action. This, together with the great size and sharpness of Combativeness, Destructiveness, and Approbativeness, led me to dwell with great emphasis, and to lay especial stress upon his irritability, the suddenness and ungovernable fury of his anger, particularly when his *honor* was aspersed."

JC had a short fuse, could fly off the handle at any moment, others besides Fowler had reported. This was no great epiphany. Yet, the point was well made that had someone questioned JC's honor, well, that person had better watch out: He or she was going to see real rage.

Fowler made an important comment regarding JC's all-around appeal. JC was not, according to Fowler, a man who backed down from anyone. After introducing himself and making a quick exam, Fowler went on to tell JC: "You would not hesitate fighting a duel in defense of yourself or your friends, Mr. Colt. And [I bet] that nothing would frighten you. Your Conscientiousness is feeble—your sense of honor is more powerful than your sense of justice, and that I would trust your honor sooner than your oath. You would not do a *disgraceful* act, although you would not hesitate to do what was not right, *provided* you did not regard it as disgraceful."

Continuing, no doubt in the presence of many men, almost as a form of entertainment, Fowler told JC: "Approbativeness and Self Esteem are both very large, and Conscientiousness small." In retrospect, Fowler added, "Hence, the former became *perverted,* and hence also his revenge for every indignity offered to his honor, was unrelenting. Benevolence was large, so was Cautiousness, and his intellect very good. Veneration was small and Marvellousness utterly wanting. Calculation, Constructiveness, and Ideality were large, and Amativeness very large."

The most palpable trait standing out to Fowler on this day, so he later claimed, was JC's anger, as if it radiated from the man's pores. To believe Fowler, JC was a man walking through a crowd with pinched a face, vexed eyebrows, his demeanor armed and able and willing to do battle, his fists clenched, ready to deliver destruction at the drop of a hat.

Fowler stepped back when he was finished. Then he pointed at the accountant, saying quite brazenly, "Mr. Colt, I have one word of caution to give you. You are passionate and impulsive in the highest degree, which, with the great size and extreme activity of Combativeness, will make you desperate in a moment of passion. I warn you to avoid occasions calculated to excite it. When you find a dispute rising, turn on your heel and leave the scene of action; for when you come angry, your wrath is ungovernable, and you are liable to do what you might be sorry for."*

In his final analysis, Fowler made an extremely perceptive and accurate observation about the Colt brothers in general:

> *As far as I am informed, Destructiveness is a family trait. His brother, Samuel Colt, invents, but his inventions are all destructive—death-dealing weapons.*

—◆—

Prosecutor Whiting had made several conscientious points in his closing, however self-serving they may have seemed. It was pertinent information the jury needed in order to weigh all of the evidence. What the prosecutor had said in the beginning of his summation sustained the belief inside the courtroom that JC had tried to do anything he could to get out of this situation, and after all else failed, he decided to play the one card he had left: confessing to the crime.

---

* I cannot include this material from Fowler without sufficient warning (or maybe cautionary reading is a better phrase), saying that, again, Mr. Fowler wrote these remarks some time *after* JC had been arrested and charged, when it would have been easier for Fowler to fit his analysis into the context of what JC's life had become and the crime he was accused of by then. Nonetheless, it does show us how much of an impact JC's trial had on the culture. The fact that O. S. Fowler was later writing about a chance meeting with JC says a lot about the sensationalism surrounding JC's arrest and trial, and how it carried on even years after a verdict was reached.

Continuing, Whiting admitted his case was "circumstantial." He argued that JC and his legal team had had "time to write a confession, but it is at variance in all its main points with the evidence and the probabilities of the case." He talked about how a prosecutor's "duty is to ascertain the truth." He spoke of the jury being obligated to "perform" its duty, adding, "No man need to have his frontal marked with any better character .... If we maintain the laws against the lawless and against the bandit it is all the success we ask. Would to God I could look into the testimony this day and aid you to relieve this prisoner rather than convict him. But are we never to convict? What have you or I to do with the consequences?"

These were strong, opinionated words Emmett or Selden should have objected to, but they did not. Whiting was walking a fine line between facts and planting a seed of assumption into the minds of jurors.

With all that said, the prosecutor cleared up any confusion over his camp trying to sway the jury one way or another with mere suggestions, capitalizing on his earlier advice, noting:

You are to remove all doubts from your minds and pronounce upon the guilt or innocence of the prisoner—you owe that to your oaths, your country and your God. You come from the body of the community; I could have rejected every man from that box who had ever seen his face, but I did not press it. I would take twelve of his friends to try him, provided they were men of truth and integrity; you are simply to enquire into the circumstances of the case.

Next, Whiting attacked motive, which might have been the one thing his case had been lacking all along. Were jurors to believe that JC had murdered a man and mutilated his body to get out of such a small liability?

"If he killed Samuel Adams to get rid of a debt or without apparent cause it is murder! But if Samuel Adams went there armed—made an attack upon him and he found it necessary to use the hatchet in self-defense, it was justifiable homicide. . . . We claim this case to have come under the first class of murders. Killing a human being is not murder—it is the killing with an evil mind—with a bloodthirsty heart."

From this point forward, Whiting launched into a lengthy, often preachy denunciation, which centered on the law and God. Then he spent a half hour or more on the "facts of the case" from the prosecution's side of the fence, which were not at all different from what he had been preaching ad nauseam already.

Next, Whiting took to schooling jurors on JC's character, which was an interesting aside by the lead prosecutor: "This gentleman is represented to be everything mild, kind and affectionate—and yet when interrupted shows a diabolical temper."

A few moments later, Whiting made a feeble case against JC's argument that he had panicked and decided to cover up the murder for fear of no one believing it was self-defense: "Had there been no improper intention, he would not have locked the door."

As far as a murder weapon, "it does not matter when Adams came into the room, whether he was struck by the hatchet, or was shot—it is *still* murder," Whiting said. "When Dr. Gilman referred to the hole, the idea flashed upon my mind that a pistol had been used, and such appears still to have been the case. Why should every blow leave a fissure but this? All the rest exhibit such, but here is a clean round hole. I would ask the professional gentlemen how they account for the difference."

Whiting's tone was described as testy and even irritated. He could not let go of the fact that the defense had painted him as some sort of politically driven zealot who had brought charges against this man for his own climb up the political ladder. It appalled the prosecutor to think the jury would judge this case on the merits of such a transparent accusation.

"I have done everything that has been asked of me, and the remarks of the gentleman in allusion to me were made because he does not *know* me. . . . If, gentlemen of the jury, I have pushed this case too far, blame *me*; but, as a prosecuting officer, have I done so?"

As quick as he had started in on defending his own character, Whiting went back to the theory of self-defense and why it should be knocked down by the evidence alone, making a few elegant points.

"Had a quarrel taken place, as pretended, noise would not only have been made, but Colt would have been more likely, unless bent upon murder, to strike with a chair than a hatchet; and, even if he had done the latter, a high-minded man would have at once exclaimed to those around him, 'I have struck a blow which I shall regret all my life—and have shown contrition for the act.'"

Even during an era when the opening and closing arguments of a murder trial lasted far too long, Whiting probably pushed those limits even further. Passion and frustration seemed to take control of the prosecutor's senses. He was certain of JC's intentions and believed the trial, in all of its dramatic nonsense and histrionic hubris (from both sides), had come down to one important factor: Even if JC had not so much *intended* to kill Adams in those moments before Adams walked through his office door, when he decided to react with violence on that day, there can be no doubt he made a conscious decision in the moment to kill the man—and in that instance and its totality proved premeditation. Premeditation does not mean one has spent days, weeks, months, or even hours, planning a murder. The traditional view most courts agreed to under first-degree murder required that "no substantial amount of time need elapse between formation of the intent to kill and execution of the killing." One could, in theory, commit premeditated murder while running at someone with a knife, or in that split second before pulling the trigger. Many modernists see a problem with this, simply because when one looked into the particulars of first- and second-degree murder where intent lies at the center, premeditation can be applied to almost *any* situation, the fact being, even if one acts in a "split-second" judgment and kills a fellow in a fit of rage—i.e., JC's self-defense argument—it fell within the parameters of premeditation under the traditionalist view. "Most modern courts, therefore," lawyer Steven Emanuel, founder of the *Emanuel Law Outlines* series, wrote, "require a reasonable period of time during which deliberation exists."

Whiting finally concluded:

Gentlemen, I have endeavored to do my duty. If I have been too warm, appreciate it. But, as regards the excuse of the prisoner, if the memorials of the mother and sisters had been pressed closer to his heart, it would have been better for him. I believe that life was taken by John C. Colt. I believe if, by laying down his own life he could restore that man to his family he would gladly do it. I believe he would gladly give his life, but is that an excuse for taking the life of Adams? . . . If mercy is deserved it will be shown; but you have a simple duty to perform. I have endeavored faithfully to do mine. If erroneous, correct it; deal leniently and mercifully with the prisoner; do justly to yourselves.

Judge Kent was next to address the jury. He referred to what he was about to say as the "last scene." He asked jurors to "do away with the excitement thrown around the case by the speeches of counsel," encouraging each juror to focus on the law and the facts of the case, although Judge Kent himself would soon bring speculation and opinion into the record.

"Some allusion has been made to the excitement out of doors," Judge Kent said, nodding in the direction of the gallery and what was presumed to be a stirring populace of New Yorkers bent upon seeing JC die at the end of a noose. "I am inclined to believe it is overrated." Then, perhaps explaining some of the decisions he had made during the course of the now ten-day-old proceedings, he added:

Had I not thought so, I would have postponed the trial. It would have been strange if, in the city of New York, the public mind would not have been shocked by the murder, but I have no doubt that every justice has been done to the prisoner. The Court has kept everything uninfluenced by contamination from without, and I have no doubt but reliance can be had upon the sound heads before us. I was sorry to find some acerbity of feeling shown among the counsel, but I see no occasion for it. Never have I known more talent or industry displayed than in this cause. No blame is deserved on either side, and as to the District Attorney he has discharged his duty ably and eloquently, and without any feeling but that of his duty.

Kent broke into an extensive and tedious discourse on the law as it pertained to JC's case. He spoke of the various degrees of homicide and where JC's case fell into that matrix.

The degrees of homicides are four: justifiable and excusable homicide, murder and manslaughter. There is very little difference between the grades of the two former—the one is where an officer kills another in the performance of his duty—the other to prevent an attempt to kill where a man is allowed to defend himself even in taking life. If you think Colt killed Adams to protect himself from an attempt at murder or felony he is justified. It is also justifiable when a design is evident to inflict some great felony, such as to maim or murder, as where a man raises a large bar of iron to strike another. If you think this to have been the case, no blame is attached to the prisoner.

Put that way, Kent's statement seemed to be, indeed, an impassionate argument for JC's acquittal. But then he continued, clarifying his suggestions, bringing "mitigating circumstances" into the discussion:

Such as correcting a servant and death ensues, or a person in building lets fall a brick, and some person is killed—or where there has been some unexpected combat without dangerous weapons, and where it was not intended to take life. Words do not authorize one man to kill another, but wherein resisting an assault death ensues, and it is not intended to kill, nor done in a cruel manner, it is excusable homicide. If not justifiable or excusable, it is a murder or manslaughter. In the former there are no shades; in the latter four degrees. The first is premeditation, and where it is done with an instrument regardless of life. Where a person discharges a loaded pistol into a crowd, it shows a depraved mind, and where he takes life, it is murder. As to premeditation, I differ from the District Attorney as to a point of law. It was said that if a homicide was committed the law implies malice, such as the case where a black man cut a woman's throat in Broadway, but I cannot agree with that doctrine. You may say that Colt designed to take Adams' life, if so it was murder. But you must show premeditation. This is not necessary to have been previous to Adams going into his room. If you think he did it, not in hot blood, or in a fracas, it is murder. But if you do not think such, it is manslaughter, and you must bring it within one of the grades.*

From there the judge broke down each grade, giving analogies for every circumstance.

He talked about murder weapons not being one of the larger issues at hand.

He reflected on and on, making sure to let the jury know that JC's *Confession* would be "difficult to exclude," however, in another breath he referred to it as "irregular."

He said the *Confession* was "not" to be considered "testimony, and you (the jury) are bound to throw it out entirely so far as it goes to exculpate the prisoner."

---

* I have included these lengthy excerpts because this case was, in every aspect of the law, a murder case tried in the press, and I wanted to provide evidence of how the lawyers and the judge, at the end, began to backpedal and explain their many mistakes.

He said the case, when one boiled it down, "lies in a nut shell."

He mentioned several of the witnesses by name.

He said (quite strangely) that Adams's watch, found inside JC's trunk, "has also been admitted to have been taken."

Then he wrapped up this portion of his remarks by noting, "The question, then, is as to murder or manslaughter."

From there he broke into another rambling monologue regarding homicide in general and how it related to the "subsequent proceedings."

"In regard to the latter, they are of importance in judging of the character of John C. Colt, and throwing a reflective light upon his character. Dismissing his own statement, and what do we find? The chain of facts are remarkable, and show him to be an uncommon man."

When Kent finished with his analysis of witnesses, adding nothing more than girth to the enormous amount of information the jury had already, he spoke of JC's "conduct," which was one of the more important factors within this circumstantial case. How did JC act? And what did his behavior, after the murder, say about his guilt or innocence?

Kent asked jurors to consider several rhetorical questions. "Now, as to the occurrence itself, we must look again at the conduct evinced by Colt in packing up the body. Does this show an evidence of guilt? The law gives concealment as evidence of guilt. Is any deduction necessarily drawn from the fact but his desire to avoid punishment? Does this show that John C. Colt wished to avoid the State's Prison, which the law provides as the punishment of manslaughter? . . . The concealment was as likely to have been caused by a wish to avoid the punishment of manslaughter as well as of murder."

For the next half hour, Kent talked about Adams's wounds.

How "little discrepancy" there was as to "who first went to the police, and other small points."

He mentioned how much banter had been made about clashing foils and noises and how no one could ascertain from those noises whether he was hearing the "beginning of this controversy" or "ordinary conversation."

It didn't matter, Kent proposed, if "the blow was struck from behind."

Then he talked about Caroline Henshaw, whose testimony, he said, "appears to be worthy of confidence. That interesting young woman comes here under adverse circumstances. Her manner was childlike, she did not appear desirous of pushing her remarks, and the impression on my mind was decidedly in her favor. She stated that the mark [on JC's neck] was no larger than a sixpence, and she spoke with much caution. I believe her story, but the jury can weigh the fact."

The bottom line, Kent reiterated, "Was the case murder? You have heard the evidence. The desire of revenge is a prominent trait. A savage has been known to kill another to see how he would fall from his horse. It is hard to know the feelings that enter into the heart of a guilty man."*

After summarizing several more thoughts, Kent wrapped up his comments: "Do justice whatever may ensue. You are bound to spurn all excitements—must not cherish a mawkish sympathy—examine the subject coolly, bring in a verdict according to what you really believe, and do your duty to the prisoner, your country, and your God."

"Judge," Emmett stood and said right after, "I would ask you to instruct the jury that the case be excusable homicide unless the prisoner was armed with a hatchet at the commencement of the affray and had prepared it beforehand."

Kent paused. Thought it over.

"It shall be allowed."

The jury retired.

---

* Allowing Kent to continue here, he added: "But it is for the jury to think if there was any adequate motive. There appears to be no desire to preserve reputation, as Adams knew nothing against Colt, nor was there any old grudge—avarice may have entered his mind. . . . The watch was in Colt's possession. Suppose he killed him in an affray, what was he to do with the watch? Persons have been known to kill another for feeling; Colt may have been governed by such, but was it probable? Adams lay dead at his feet, and the possession of the watch is not inconsistent with the idea that he kept it someday to give it to his family. There appears to have been no grudge—very little motive for lucre, for the probability is that he would have selected a richer man."

This drawing of John Caldwell Colt depicts him holding onto a copy of the book that initiated an argument between Colt and his printer—a dispute over money that ultimately turned deadly.

PORTRAIT OF JOHN C. COLT.

In this drawing, commonly used during John Colt's trial by all the New York tabloid newspapers, we see Colt contemplating his troubling future and reflecting on a life that could have been.

FINDING THE BODY IN THE BOX.

After uncovering the bloodied and nearly decapitated corpse inside a box, authorities sent it to the city morgue, where a full inquest and autopsy was performed. The sensational case was front-page fodder for the New York tabloids as artists depicted the gruesome discovery of printer Samuel Adams's body in an "oblong box"—a true story that would inspire Edgar Allan Poe's short story by the same name. This illustration is from the 1874 book, *The New York Tombs* by Charles Sutton, warden of the prison.

Not long after John Colt gave his personal narrative of what happened between him and printer Samuel Adams, local artists began drawing pictures of the scenes—this infamous drawing, used in *The New York Tombs,* was called "The Blood in the Gutter."

THE BLOOD IN THE GUTTER.

John Colt wanted to marry his live-in girlfriend, Caroline Henshaw, before his death sentence was carried out. Present at this wedding (inside Colt's New York Tombs cell) was none other than Samuel Colt, the gun manufacturer and brother to the convicted murderer.

John's live-in companion gave birth to a baby after the trial—a baby named Samuel Colt. Speculation would follow the child as many wondered if he was the illegitimate son of soon-to-be world famous gunmaker Sam Colt.

BURNING OF THE TOMBS CUPOLA.

After John Colt was convicted and sentenced to death, a fire broke out in the Tombs prison. When guards finally reached Colt's cell, they uncovered the shock of their lives!

Sam Colt's first gun-making factory was located in Paterson, New Jersey. As this image proves, it was no modest business; Sam's factory was a large-scale manufacturing plant. Not long after his brother's trial, Sam was forced to close the Paterson factory and watch his dream—for the time being—fade away.

Young Sam Colt fashioned himself a colonel and took on the persona of a military man without actually enlisting in the army. Sam was the brains behind perfecting and marketing the revolving pistol; he wasn't quite the mechanically gifted inventor of the weapon. Yet from a young age, Sam Colt had dreamed of being a world-famous inventor, and he had the ideas to back up that vision.

By the time Sam set up shop in Hartford, Connecticut, he had refined his sales skills and perfected the weapon that would make him one of the richest men in the world, rich enough to build Armsmear, the enormous estate situated on the grounds of Colt Firearms in Hartford's south end.

When Sam Colt met production specialist Elisha Root, the two teamed up to change production-line machining and manufacturing. Root was the brains behind Colt's early manufacturing successes.

When John Coffee Hayes decided to use Colt's .34-caliber-five-shot pistol during a firefight with Comanche Indians, it was a decision that changed the course of gun-making history and, overnight, turned Sam Colt into a gun-manufacturing tycoon.

Before his untimely death, Sam enjoyed locking hands with the love of his life and walking along the grounds of Armsmear.

This portrait of Elizabeth hung inside Armsmear.

The first time Sam Colt met Elizabeth Hart, he knew he had kissed the hand of the woman he would one day marry. The two fell in love quickly and soon built a manufacturing empire like the world had never seen. Elizabeth Colt outlived not only her husband, but all of their children. Many believed Elizabeth was burdened with the feeling that Sam's "killing machines" were the impetus for the great tragedy that became their lives—that the universe had somehow paid the Colt family back for putting these weapons into public hands.

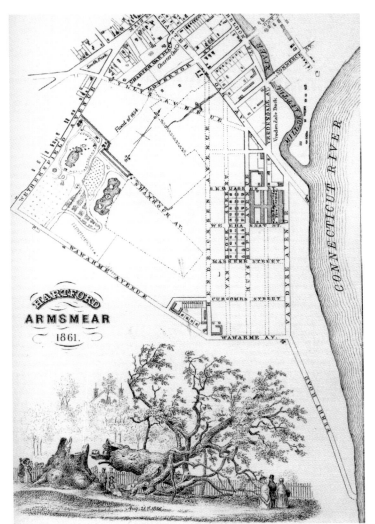

Armsmear was one of the most sprawling and—certainly—largest estates Hartford, Connecticut, had known; a piece of property some five hundred acres in size, which rivaled the estates of Sam and Elizabeth's friends in Newport, Rhode Island.

Called the "grandest residence in Hartford," partially modeled after the castles of European czars and kings whom Sam had befriended, Armsmear was designed by famed architect Octavius Jordan.

An advertising broadside of the Colt Repeating Pistol that made Sam Colt a household name and his wife one of the wealthiest widows in the world.

Sam's and Elizabeth's seafaring son, Caldwell Colt (left), died under mysterious circumstances aboard his yacht while in Florida waters.

21

"Death Hath No Terrors"

ACCORDING TO JC, DEATH DID NOT FRIGHTEN HIM. REGARDLESS OF the jury's verdict and what sentence he ultimately faced, to JC, death did not have a hold on him. "There is a world above this," he wrote to a friend, "and I believe a just one." He added that "man, at the worst, can only destroy the body," paraphrasing Matthew 10:28, or a variation of this biblical text. In killing Adams, he did nothing more, JC suggested, than "defend" his person "against a wanton, vile, and unpardonable attack." He would not have done things differently had he known the outcome would be the same. His actions that day were justifiable homicide. In JC's opinion, it did not matter what a jury thought of him, or how those men had come to their verdict; he knew in his heart and (all-of-a-sudden) pious mind that, for one, he was going to heaven when he died; and two, St. Peter was going to welcome him with open and comforting arms, simply because he had done nothing more than protect himself.

It was good that JC felt this way, because early Sunday, January 30, 1842, "Sabbath morning," noted one reporter, somewhere near 2:45 a.m., the jury sent word it had reached a verdict.

Near 4:00 a.m., Judge Kent called court back into session and took his seat upon the bench.

The jury walked in, all but a few looking tired, intense, morose, certainly knowing that a first-degree murder guilty verdict would send JC to the gallows. One report had them deliberating for a mere hour, although, court had ended the previous night somewhere near 6:00 p.m., so it was more like nine hours.

The clerk spoke first: "Gentlemen, what is your verdict?"

The courtroom, full to its capacity, breathless and waiting, turned toward the foreman.

"We find the prisoner," said the foreman ("in a faltering voice"), "John C. Colt, guilty of willful murder."

The worst possible outcome for JC.

"Is that your verdict?" one of JC's lawyers asked, referring to a poll being taken of each juror.

"[M]any of the jurors were deeply affected," reported the *Brother Jonathan* tabloid, "as they responded on the affirmative."

It was over. For the time being, anyway. Judge Kent, who had presented himself throughout, said *Brother Jonathan*, in a "remarkable" fashion, running the show with "clearness and impartiality" (quite laughable in hindsight), would wait until all of JC's appeals, to be filed immediately, had been decided before handing down his sentence. The public had gotten its wish, according to the tabloid. "Certain it is, that the miserable prisoner has less sympathy and pity expressed for him than almost any convict of whom the public have talked for years." If we are to believe *Brother Jonathan*'s reporting of the verdict, the streets were filled with city dwellers young and old applauding and jumping for joy at the prosecution's victory.

Until his sentencing, JC would be housed back in his cell at the Tombs, where an entirely new ordeal in the life of John Colt was about to unfold.

"Although I stand condemned by *twelve men*," JC wrote about ten days after the verdict, "do not think that it causes me so much pain as to imagine. No—no! Death hath no terrors for me."

He claimed his "great[est] suffering" was not for himself, "but for my friends. This will be to them a heavy blow."

In this same letter, dated February 6, 1842, he quoted several Bible passages and spoke of how heaven would be a place where he could find true justice for his actions. He blamed the "fiendish appetite . . . burning in the bosom of many witnesses." He accused all of creating falsehoods against him solely because of a dislike for the man, not the crime.

The letter was written in response to a friend who had sent JC a missive full of what JC referred to as "inquiries," answers to which, he said, if he was to sit and write them all out, "would fill a volume."

Yet JC started writing, anyway (as the month of February unleashed a fury of winter weather), and would not stop.

During its tentative run, the Patent Arms Manufacturing Company, Sam Colt's Paterson, New Jersey, gun-making business, made between "2,700 and 3,200 pistols in various models," according to Colt expert Bill Hosley, and "between 1,300 and 1,850 rifles, shotguns and carbines." By the time JC was convicted, despite Sam's efforts, and in spite of his more often detached business conduct, Patent Arms had gone belly up. It had survived six years. Did hiring such expensive defense attorneys for JC push Patent Arms over a cliff? Probably not. But the emotional and financial tightrope upon which it had to balance, not to mention the egg Sam had on his entrepreneurial face, all added to the company's demise. The more practical and probable reason for Patent Arms's closure was that Sam's ideas for pistols and rifles had been pushed into the marketplace before their time. America wasn't ready for the repeating firearm when he started the company in 1836; and, to boot, Sam could not find a way to manufacture the weapons at a cost-effective value. Hosley estimated the costs of manufacturing Sam's early weapons to be "between $45.54 and $57.33." Those prices by today's standards would come in at a whopping $3,000. On top of it all, the weapons themselves were far from perfect.

If what he did after the verdict was any indication of how Sam felt about his brother being found guilty, one would have to conclude it was business as usual for the gun maker. Patent Arms had failed. *Fine.* It was time to move on to something else, something with more potential. Sam had been laying the groundwork for the submarine mine company throughout JC's arrest and incarceration; now it was time to focus exclusively on that endeavor.

When Sam decided to put all of his resources into a project, he spared no shame in announcing to those who could help him get his invention into the mass market that without him and his latest creation, the world was going to miss out on his brilliance. Truth be told, this submarine mine Sam was now touting had been around since the Revolutionary War in some form or fashion. Still, Sam felt he was the one who had conceived and "mastered" it. Writing to the president, John Tyler, Sam claimed to have been working on the project since 1829 (which was, in a sense, true) as a curious fourteen-year-old blowing things up in his family's pond. But for the past five years, Sam went on to say, "I have employed my leisure, in study & experiment, to perfect the invention of which I now consider myself master; & which if adopted for the service of our Government, will not only save them millions outlay for the construction of means of defence, but in the event of foreign war, it will prove a perfect safeguard against all the combined fleets of Europe, without exposing the life of our citizens."

Sam was not bashful about displaying his hubris, for he certainly knew that if he was going to get anywhere with government officials, he needed to project confidence, self-reliance, and pride in his inventions. A few years later, still trying to defend his honor, Sam wrote Representative Henry Murphy:

> *The idea of Submarine explosions for the purposes of Harbour defence was conceived by me as early as the year 1829 while stud[y]ing in the laboratory of a bleeching and colouring establishment at Ware Vilage Massachusetts, and I made sundry experiments on a small scale at that time and repeated them in various ways for several successive years thereafter.*

Sam had a long history of taking the experiments and inventions of others and developing them into patentable creations from which he could make money. According to an article in the *Association of Ohio Long Rifle Collectors*, the revolving pistol, which Sam had patented in several countries, was invented not by a sixteen-year-old aboard a ship, a boy who had watched the captain steer its wooden wheel, as Sam had told the story, but by gunsmith Peter Humberger, who had taught the trade he learned from his father to his sons, Peter II, Adam, and Henry. The Humbergers claimed to have created the "revolving pistol" two years after Colt whittled that chamber and lock aboard the *Corvo* on a trip to India. In fact, the Humberger family felt Sam Colt stole the idea from them. "A documented example was their joint effort in 1832 to design and build a revolving pistol with double action trigger mechanism." It was almost two years after Colt's trip to India, but the Humbergers had been working as gunsmiths for decades. Peter Humberger III later told a story about his father, Peter II, and the day the revolving pistol was created on the Humberger Farm:

> *Adam, Henry and . . . Peter II met in his father's shop on the Peter Humberger Farm in Hopewell [Ohio] to hold a consultation about making a double-action trigger. He distinctively remembered that*

Adam and Peter appointed Henry for the task, as he in their estimation, was the finest workman of the three. This conference was held in 1832.

Henry Humberger had "completed the double-action and made a great many of the so-called pepperbox revolvers" that same year—1832—which would have put Sam in Ohio, traveling with his "Dr. Coult" laughing-gas sideshow.

Henry's "friends" urged him, reported that same article, "to apply for a patent."

"It amounts to nothing," Henry said of his creation, "except to shoot off [at] New Year's!"

As he was working on the gun, "anyone could visit his shop and watch the progress he was making." It was then that "Colt, of New York, heard of the revolver Henry Humberger had made and sent one of his workmen out of Somerset, who bought of Wm. Brown one of the original pepperboxes for Colt." It was said this same man "also visited the shop and watched the progress of the work, then almost completed."

Not long after, when the "very shrewed [sic]" workman assigned by Colt returned, "it did not take them long to finish a gun on Henry's model and apply for a patent."*

———

* *A Biographical record of Fairfield County, Ohio* (S.J. Clarke Publishing Company. 1902. New York: S. J. Clarke Pub. Co.; p. 444) gives credit for the revolving pistol to Adam Humberger, who, "resided in Somerset and is said to have been the inventor . . . although he did not get the credit of his invention." I might also add that, although possible, I would have to question whether Sam sent someone snooping over to the Humberger Farm—that is, if he didn't go there himself and disguise his identity. Sam was on the road with his Dr. Coult laughing-gas traveling sideshow and would have almost certainly passed through Hopewell en route to and from Cincinnati and Columbus. Knowing Sam, he visited the farm himself after hearing rumblings of the invention and told the Humberger clan he was "a workman for Mr. Colt," thus projecting a larger-than-life view of himself, already trying to make his name known. Regardless of the details, it is my view—after studying all of this evidence, including the fact that a Boston inventor was working on a similar revolver when Sam left the port of Boston aboard the *Corvo*—that Sam Colt did not come up with the revolving chamber idea while aboard that ship, watching the ship's steering wheel rotate. That story, to me, seems to fall right in line with the enigmatic and eccentric person, that caricature of himself, Sam became—a romantic myth perpetrated later on to fit this larger-than-life personality. You have to hand it to the guy, however: Sam had the gift of alchemy; he could turn any situation in his favor. And that instinct, the entrepreneurial spirit he embodied and perfected, would make him one of the most successful and wealthiest inventors of the nineteenth century, if not the most famous. Sam may not have invented the revolving pistol, but he perfected the weapon and save for the Paterson, New Jersey, failure, expertly marketed and manufactured the weapon in large numbers to fulfill the need of the marketplace. Success in the world of invention is not always about being the first; but is, as it should be, about being the best.

John C. Colt continued writing from his Tombs cell. It seemed the more time that passed the more he felt the need to explain himself. JC's letters during the month of February became a cacophony of Bible quotes, poems, and sayings of the day, all pointing to the one truth JC had come to throughout the past month: The press had convicted him long before he had the opportunity to prove his innocence; and the people of New York stood behind all those vicious lies. *Condemn* became a word JC leaned on again and again. There were glimpses into the mind of a man who could turn a phrase, which came from, simply, JC having written so much. "Justice is but a name; liberty but a shadow; give one wealth and I could put my foot upon the neck of the universe,"* he wrote one day near the end of February. Sentences like this told us a lot about where JC's mind was at a time when death seemed to be knocking on his cell door.

He held out optimism that the appeals court would see "the evidence of the least importance in the case, in strict justice, was in my favor. . . . I may now get a new trial and be justly dealt with."

The one subject JC almost never broached beyond a passing word in any of his writings left behind (something one might consider to be at the center of his thoughts), was his alleged son by Caroline Henshaw, Samuel Colt.

Like many convicts before him, and certainly many after, JC placed much of the onus on his lawyers for not allowing him to grant interviews to "several catch-penny sheets" before the trial. He dissected every aspect of his trial, effectively blaming everyone, including Sam Adams—but himself. He referred to Adams as an "unfortunate, foolish man," who had shown up that day "to my office in bad blood."

> *Because I defended myself against the abuse and assault of such a man as you may rightly judge him to have been from the subsequent conduct of his widow, I have been condemned without unprejudiced hearing, and am to be damned without ceremony.*

In one instance, he'd chastise his lawyers, reproaching each of them; and in the next, "I cannot blame counsel for the manner they conducted my trial, although my friends blame them for introducing my statement [*Confession*]."

---

* Although I could not find it anywhere, I would bet JC had stolen this quotation from a contemporary.

In a letter addressed to "Dear Friends," JC went through his *Confession* and spoke of how it was "incorrect" in certain areas. He was now upset that he never had a chance to edit it.

JC's letters were long because he had been answering questions sent to him by certain friends, some in Philadelphia and others in New York. On March 12, 1842, he received a "beautiful pack of questions, quite a number of which I have already answered." There were several queries, however, that JC went on to respond to in his omniscient way. The guy had an answer for everything. The questions themselves give one an indication as to how his friends felt about the crime and JC's conviction; the fact that they were asking such questions leads one to believe that JC's behavior after the murder had beckoned many to wonder if he was, in fact, guilty.

"When you had killed Adams," the first questioner asked, "how come afterwards [you went] to his shop, and why did you call on Mrs. Adams?"

JC answered: "It was five or six days after the catastrophe that I went to Adams' shop." He claimed to be looking for his "property," which he estimated to be worth $1,000, and wanted to make sure his plates had been put into Adams's vault to "preserve them against fire or other accident."

He denied ever going to visit Mrs. Adams.

"Why did you strip the body of its clothing?" another friend wondered.

"The clothing would have identified it years afterwards. Any simpleton, making up his mind to secretion, would have done so much."

"Why did you ship the body to New Orleans?"

"Because it was a warm climate, and the voyage to said city would take from seventeen to twenty days; and consequently agreeable to common course of nature, it would decay before any indication could be obtained to identify it."

He didn't realize it, but JC sounded like a man who had thought long and hard about killing a fellow human being, understanding there would be a price to pay for the crime if he got caught, thus making sane decisions afterward to cover up that crime.

The next question was whether JC had gone to see his brother Sam that night of the murder to ask for his advice.

JC denied going to see Sam.

In his next letter, JC said the one "thing" that had "sustained" him throughout his entire ordeal was the undeniable belief that his "conscience is clear."

"Thank God I do not feel myself culpable and never shall."

The time was getting to him, however. Considering what would soon take place in his life, JC offered a brief bit of insight, lamenting, "This misfortune is using me up fast. Every day now seems a month, and every month a year. . . . Even my hair has begun to silver, and a year more in that horrid confinement borne down and oppressed as I am, will make me old and white-headed."

This was quite a different sentiment from just a few months back when he spoke of his Tombs cell as though it was the king's palace. Now the walls were closing in on him. The air was dank and sour; the men tending to him no more his friends.

Still, it was here, at the end of this March letter, that JC realized how serious a situation he was in, writing:

> *Were it not for my child and the hopes of obtaining a new trial, and under a belief that it would terminate so favorable that I may yet live to triumph over much of that foul aspersion this great misfortune had placed upon me, my sorrows would not, I assure you, be farther prolonged from temporal considerations.*

The first of JC's court appeals had been decided on May 12, 1842. JC's attorneys argued on May 5 for a new trial based on juror misconduct. The judge denied a new trial. So JC's attorneys took that decision all the way to the Supreme Court in Utica, New York, where the judge's earlier decision was, on July 16, 1842, approved.

JC was running out of options heading toward the fall, this as his sentencing was coming up. He knew that if an appeal was denied, being found guilty of such an egregious charge and violent crime, there was a noose with his name on it in the gallows of the Tombs.

Back in June, someone had written JC and asked: "Do you read and believe in the Bible?"

JC had written of his surety in going to heaven, based on the fact that his conscience was cleansed and he had done nothing wrong. That was when, however, the future looked bright. Now, he would address those comments in a more realistic way, calling the Bible "a curious book. . . . As a book of history it is invaluable from its antiquity; and regarding it only as a fable, it certainly is the most curious book extant."

He went on to say that he didn't really understand the question or "what kind of an answer" the woman was searching for by asking such a question, adding:

> *If you wish to know whether I spend weekly so many hours upon my knees in a repetition of words and phrases, denoting in language ideas— or so many hours in conning over the chapters of the Bible, I must say that I do not. I only do those things when the spirit moves. I assure you that I have read the Bible more than once thoroughly, and often with love and admiration.*

The one piece of Scripture JC had connected with, as he put it, turned out to be "Christ's Sermon on the Mount, as given in Matthew, chap. 6 and 7, [which] may be read with never-tiring pleasure. There is in it a beauty and language enchanting the soul, and a purity of thought which carries man in conception beyond his nature. It has never been equaled by the eloquence of any other being."

What's interesting about this particular section of Matthew's gospel is that Christ gives his disciples the Father's rules and laws for living a moral life—the new commandments, if you will. Christ, knowing He is leaving to undergo his Passion, shares with the twelve what the Father needs and expects from each human being. Things along the lines of: "Be careful not to parade your uprightness in public to attract attention; otherwise you will lose all reward from your Father in heaven." Christ offers the "Our Father" prayer here. He says, "Do not judge, and you will not be judged; because the judgments you give are the judgments you will get, and the standard you use will be the standard used for you."

The idea that JC was thinking about Christ's Sermon on the Mount teaching as he looked toward his own mortality proves emphatically that he was considering a date with death and the implications the life he had led would have in the next world.

Yet, in the scope of what some said happened next, JC had a plan to get out of that, too—an incredible plot he would need Sam Colt and Caroline Henshaw to help him initiate.

PART III

22

Engine of Destruction

With all of his Patent Arms machinery sold at auction, Sam Colt was no longer able to continue producing weapons. So Sam wrote to William Ball in Boston and asked the manufacturer to "make samples of Colt arms" for him. Ball's company, N. P. Ames, had been contracted by the government to make swords, and by 1837, Ames was producing cannons. Sam needed to keep his pistol business running; he knew the time would come for his weapons. Right now, he needed to focus on the submarine battery—because the government, not at all thrilled about doing it, commissioned an experiment Sam had been wanting to conduct for the past year, giving him $20,000 to do it (this when, in June, "the Navy stopped honoring his drafts for the submarine mine"). The $20,000 Sam received might have seemed like a large sum of money; that is, if Sam hadn't found out that his competitor, a man named Robert L. Stevens, who was working feverishly on what he called a "harbor defense battery," received final legislation passage appropriating $250,000 for what was being called a "revolutionary iron-hulled Stevens Battery." The machine looked a lot like a submersible canoe, made out of steel. It could dive and speed toward an enemy sloop or schooner. The Navy stopped giving Sam Colt money because he had failed to deliver "various elements" proving progress.

Sam made the best of the $20,000. He gave New York Navy Yard Captain Mathew Perry a private demonstration of his galvanic detonating system, which impressed the military man and secured Sam a load of gunpowder so he could put on that display he had been clamoring about. Thus, being the stubborn (and consummate) salesman he was, Sam chose the appropriate date to conduct his public experiment and expose his latest creation to the masses: July 4, 1842 (fourteen years to the day he had first experimented with underwater mining back in Massachusetts).

Sam picked Lower Manhattan's Niblo's Castle Garden, for its proximity to the water near South Ferry, but maybe more so for the fact that it was an open-air theater. Sam knew his success would be based on anticipation and mystery, performance tools he had mastered as a sideshow entertainer during his Dr. Coult days. He would build up the public's expectations—of course, knowing he could deliver—and the payoff and impact of the display would have ramifications long after his show had come and gone. He wanted people to talk about what they witnessed. Public approval was perhaps more important than congressional support; the public, Sam knew quite well, drove innovation.

Congress allowed Sam to use an obsolete gunboat, the *Boxer*, which it had retired long ago. The Navy was set to supervise. Sam had made a deal with Niblo's to "split the gate from the demonstration," as Niblo's was charging to enter the theater and watch the show.

New York's mayor, the entire city council, along with thousands of people from all over New England and New Jersey were on hand for the festivities, some showing up with a personal invitation from the master of ceremonies himself. Sam was twenty-seven years old; it seemed he had Washington and the center of the world, New York City, at his fingertips. All this, it needs to be said, after failing horribly in business with his Patent Arms company. It was a remarkable example of the man's pliability, an inherent talent for coming out on top and perhaps knowing how far to push.

Sam sent invitations to several friends in the New York media, many of whom he had met during JC's trial. Included in the pack was the *Evening Post*, which gave the most impressive coverage of the event, capturing the true spirit of what innovator Sam Colt had strived to achieve by putting on the display in the first place:

Colt's sub-marine battery created much attention, and was witnessed by many thousands with great satisfaction. An old hulk was moored off Castle Garden fitted with temporary masts, from which were displayed various flags, with piratical devices, immediately under which the battery was placed, and the effect of the explosions was tremendous. The vessel was shattered into fragments, some of which were thrown two or three hundred feet in the air, and there was not a single piece left longer than a man could have carried in one hand.

The *New York American* weighed in, too, offering its take, similar in drama, putting Sam at the center of all the attention:

The case containing the combustibles was sunk under the hulk, and a wire conducted from it to the deck of the North Carolina, *distant some two or three hundred yards. At the moment fixed, (1 o'clock) Mr. Colt, on the deck of the* Carolina, *applied the acid to his plates, and quicker than thought, the doomed hulk was thrown into the air.*

Reports vary as to the status of the ship before Sam blew it to bits. Some claimed Sam's target ship was moving at three knots; others claimed it was anchored and still as a buoy. An article in the *Herald* reported that Sam's "battery" had been "placed under her bottom, the cable of the doomed vessel was cut, & when by the aid of the tide and the boats of the United States' Ship *North Carolina* [the sloop Sam was aboard], her speed through the water had been made about four knots an hour, the explosion took place."

If the sloop that Sam's electric current (torpedo) had hit were at anchor, "rather than a sailing craft," Martin Rywell wrote, "the skeptics contended as they were not convinced of the success of the experiment."

In addition to a cynical audience in attendance, Sam had his adversaries in the press, too, who had been on his back since JC's conviction. The *New York Sun* emphasized the notion that Sam's battery could only work as a stationary weapon of defense.

[I]t strikes us that the great difficulty in rendering the battery efficient must be the impossibility of placing it immediately under any vessel that it may be designed to destroy.

As Philip Lundeberg put it (accurately) in his article about Sam's battery published in 1974, Sam was more interested in drawing public attention to his invention than proving its merit and worth (and there was the subtle notion that Sam was holding back, scared to reveal all of the secrets behind his battery). If he could get people to talk about the battery, half the battle was won. As long as the government saw the necessity of the project and handed over more money, Sam had done his job. Writing to Secretary Abel Upshur the day after the experiment, Sam put his passion for the project—and the promise he was willing to make to the United States of America—into words, no doubt with the help of someone more educated:

> I will guarantee to fortify every Port upon our Seaboard against the combined Fleets of Europe, at a cost for each, less than that required to build a single steam ship of war; and when once fixed, my Engine of destruction may be used without the expense of fuel or soldiers, the cost of which, every year, exceeds the expense of making permanent Fortifications of my construction.

On August 20, 1842, Sam set out to prove his critics wrong. The concern of many was that Sam had strapped a weapon to the sloop and set off the charge from afar—that he had scammed everyone. Upshur did not have good news for Sam. The Navy did not have a "permanent weapons-resting establishment," and not even Upshur could convince his ranking officers that the money given to Sam would be well spent. Moreover, Sam's one major backer in Congress, Senator Samuel Southard, had died in late June. "[I]t soon became clear to the entrepreneur upon his arrival in Washington on 2 August," Lundberg wrote, "that strong opposition to his mine warfare proposal was developing in the House."

It was John Quincy Adams, Sam soon found out. Sam had reached out to Adams, asking for a sit-down, but Adams refused the inventor. In addition to those hurdles, the threat of hostilities between Great Britain and America had declined sharply throughout that summer and Congress reduced the size of the Regular Army.

If those skeptics in Washington would not come to him in New York, Sam figured, he would bring the show to them. By August 11, he and his crew were making preparations and setting cables up for a display on the Alexandria waterfront. This time, Sam was determined to prove that without his battery the shores of the United States stood at great peril, regardless of whether there was an immediate threat from foreign militaries.

On hand this time was none other than President John Tyler, the first vice president to take over the office after the death of a president. Along with the president and his entourage were eight thousand spectators. Described as a "sixty-ton ... boat," Sam's target on this day was somewhere along the Potomac. Sam later claimed to have fired his weapon blindly from five miles away, though many "experts think he was . . . stationed in [an] old Armory only a few feet from the explosion."

Speculation and rumor surrounding the display didn't matter this time. The fact that the president had taken an interest was enough to draw the needed attention Sam had been counting on. And the show, it turned out, went off as a success, as the *Niles National Register* later described it:

> *[A] steamer containing the President and members of the cabinet, with their suites, was opposite the spectators and its illustrious and precious freight received a very hearty greeting from the mouths of twenty-four guns. A few minutes afterwards the signal for the explosion was given by the discharge of a twenty-four pounder, and instantaneously as though a missile from the gun itself had borne the torch to a magazine in her, the old craft was sent in ten millions of fragments five hundred feet into the air, and then fell into the water with a roar like that of Niagara.*

Sam couldn't buy this type of press. If nothing else, the idea that President Tyler was there to see this exhibition had pushed his battery into the spotlight and, with any luck, it would stay there until Sam could make an argument in person to Washington policymakers once again.

⁓

While Sam planned additional demonstrations, the momentum of his project was brought to a complete halt on September 27, 1842, as JC went before Judge Kent to receive his sentence. Kent asked the embattled prisoner, now a convicted murderer, if he had anything to say for himself. "Why," Judge Kent asked, "[a] sentence of death should *not* be passed?"

JC handed a piece of paper to Kent, "which contained," *American State Trials* reported, "charges that the trial had been unjustly conducted and that the evidence had been trampled on by the jury."

The courtroom was jam-packed, with Sam there to support his brother. JC stood, assuming a "bold and careless air." He held his nose up to the bench, perturbed that justice had been overlooked in light of incompetence. He may not have said those words, but his demeanor and the charges he had made in the letter he submitted to the judge made his feelings implicitly felt all around.

"I am sorry that any unjust allusions have been made as to the conduct of the jury," Judge Kent told JC and the murmuring crowd in the gallery, bloodthirsty and itching for the utmost punishment. "It is due to justice, and it is due to one of the most intelligent juries that ever sat in a court of justice, that I should not allow them, in this, their proud tribunal, to be *insulted*, without entering a solemn protest against it." It was over. JC should accept responsibility and plead for mercy, throwing himself on the court.

"The jury were selected out of three hundred of our most respectable citizens," Kent continued,

> *taken indiscriminately from the city, selected under the most vigorous exercise of the peremptory challenge by the prisoner. And in every instance where objections were raised and allowed, it was in favor of the prisoner! Their demeanor in Court was such as to entitle them to the highest consideration of the tribunal in which they took part. They had been separated from their families and from their business, confined in a sort of prison for eleven days, and I never saw one of them exhibit the slightest impatience. On the contrary, they bore, with most exemplary patience, the tedious, even unnecessary, delays in the progress of the trial—calmly [and] honestly [and] unfalteringly earnest in their efforts to discover the truth from the mass of evidence spread before them. Had these men been followed to their rooms, we would have seen the same calm, unimpassioned inquiry characterizing their deliberations. As far, therefore, as the paper expressed dissatisfaction with the conduct of the Court and jury, it was the Court's conscientious opinion that the asseverations are untrue and unjust.*

Kent allowed his words a moment to settle on the room. Then: "I will now allude to the offence for which the prisoner has been convicted. No man ever doubted that it was a crime of the greatest magnitude and enormity. It was a crime, too, which had sunk deep in the community. Leaving out of view all the appalling circumstances, with which I will not distress the prisoner or myself in recalling, no doubt could exist but that the deed was executed under the influence of ferocious passions and sanguinary cruelty."

At some point JC asked to be heard, saying, "If the Judge had read the document he would find that [I] did not charge the jury with willful wrong, but that they were mistaken. As to any illusions made by the Judge,

[I] could assure him that [I] would rather leave his case with God than with man. [I] never did a deed in [my] life but . . . would repeat, had it to be gone over again. I am not the man to be trampled down in my own office, and look tamely on. It was not my intention to kill the man; but he made the assault, and must take the consequences. I am sorry the Court thought proper to make the remarks it has. For myself, I had intended to say something more; but, not expecting to be sentenced today, I was not prepared. I am ready to receive sentence, knowing that it cannot be avoided."

Kent took a breath. "Sentence will now be pronounced," he said without reservation or emotion. "With expressions of deep regret entertained by the Court at the callous and morbid insensibility exhibited in your last speech, and which shows that any further remarks would be lost. John C. Colt, the sentence of the Court is, that on the 18th of November next you will be hanged till you are dead, and may God have mercy on your soul."

The gallery cheered.

JC was removed from the courtroom.

23

Blood on His Hands

SHE WALKED INTO THE TOMBS, HER YELLOW MANE OF HAIR TUCKED away inside her "joyous bonnet," her face "aglow with happiness." Alfred Lewis claimed she wore an "otter muff, a green shawl, [and] a claret-colored cloak trimmed about with a scarlet cord."

Caroline Henshaw was not decked out in her Sunday best and smiling because of the future she and JC were to have. This was the last day of JC's life on earth. The gallows, that inevitable "death machine, was well oiled and all its hinges working easily." The executioner was seen, according to several reports, using bags of sand in place of JC's body to practice dropping the death trap's doors.

It was November 18, 1842—fourteen months since the day JC had murdered Sam Adams. Caroline Henshaw was dressed in these clothes, accompanied by Sam Colt, two sheriffs, and the Reverend Dr. Henry Anthon from St. Mark's Episcopal Church down in the Bowery. It was near eleven o'clock in the morning. JC's execution was set for 4:00 p.m.

Caroline and JC were about to be married.

A few days before this supposed pious event, JC's lawyers tried one last time to reach anybody they could by publishing a paper. According to Charles Edwards, who wrote about the last days of JC's life, the paper was directed specifically at the sheriff and contained a "solemn protest against the legal competency of the court before which [JC] was convicted and of the warrant under which he is held subject to execution."

It did nothing.

There was also some talk that Sam had tried to bribe a few prison guards, who would take part in an elaborate scheme to change places with JC and allow him to escape. Letters and pleas to Governor William

Seward to commute JC's sentence did not even warrant a response from the state's popular leader.

Meanwhile, JC prepared to take matters into his own hands. He contacted a physician he knew and asked for a book of anatomy.

The doctor declined the request, undoubtedly wondering, same as many others, what JC was now planning.

Inside JC's cell, Reverend Anthon, Sam, Caroline Henshaw, the two sheriffs, and Colt family friend and famed songwriter John Henry Payne stood as JC and Caroline, hand in hand, repeated the vows of marriage Anthon recited before them.

After the curt ceremony, JC handed the reverend $500 Sam had given him, telling the clergyman to use it to care for his bride and their child.

Following the ceremony, JC and Caroline were given some time to spend alone during what were JC's final moments of life. For that entire time, Caroline, one source claimed, mostly sat at the edge of JC's cot, "convulsed with tears."

There has been plenty of speculation surrounding the events that took place next in the lives of Sam and John Colt, not to mention much written about them. A few things we can be absolutely certain of: One, that JC again drew public attention to himself and created a maelstrom of controversy around the end of his life, giving more credence to the theory that the guy was a flagrant, clinical narcissist; and two, that Sam Colt would wash his hands of the situation and move on toward the greatest period of his life, unaware of course that an entire new wave of tragedy, death, and destruction was waiting for him.

The bizarre circumstances surrounding JC's death began a few days before he and Caroline were married—a marriage, some claimed, that was designed for a specific reason.

During those days leading up to JC's execution, "several attempts" had been made to break him out of prison. One friend had dressed in female clothing and visited the condemned prisoner hoping to swap clothing so JC could simply walk out of the prison in the disguise of a female. "Rooms were prepared in Brooklyn for the reception of Colt," *American State Trials* reported, "and every arrangement made so that he should be hidden when he again emerged into freedom."

The plot was apparently discovered, however, and foiled.

"On the party arriving at the Tombs and applying for admission they were informed that their conspiracy was well known, and they were advised to withdraw, and nothing would be said about the movement."

It was also reported that Sam had hired a city doctor to resuscitate JC's body after he was hanged, with the hope of bringing him back to life. *American State Trials* best described this strange plot to reanimate the Colt family killer:

> *A doctor of the city undertook to resuscitate Colt after he was hanged, in case the body was not too long suspended. This doctor asserted that Colt's neck was of such thickness that it would require a longer period than is usual in such cases before the unfortunate man would be strangled. A room was taken at the Shakespeare Hotel, where the body was to be brought direct from the Tombs, and there all efforts made for its resuscitation.*

After the marriage ceremony, somewhere near one o'clock on a bitterly cold November 18, 1842, day, JC received several visits from friends, all of whom he was greatly pleased to see. He "shook them cordially by the hand, and conversed with apparent cheerfulness with them for five minutes." The visitors, upon bidding their friend one final farewell, broke down in tears.

"Colt's wife, and his brother Samuel, also soon left, both deeply affected. The wife could scarcely support herself, so violent were her feelings and acute her sufferings. She stood at the door of the cell for a minute—Colt kissing her passionately, straining her to his bosom, and watching intensely her receding form, as she passed into the corridor. Here she stood and sobbed convulsively, as though her heart would break, until led away by friends."

"I want to see the sheriff," JC announced.

Dressed in full uniform, the lawman walked into JC's cell.

"I am innocent of the murder of Adams," JC pleaded in what he viewed as his final opportunity, "and never intended to kill him. . . . I hope that something [will] intervene to save [me] from being hung."

The sheriff stared at the desperate man.

JC "begged the sheriff not to execute the sentence of the law upon him."

"Banish all hope of that kind," the sheriff said sternly, "for you must die at four o'clock."

"I want to see Doctor Anthon," JC asked.

Anthon was summoned. He entered JC's cell some moments later. They prayed together for ten minutes.

The reverend doctor walked out and beckoned the sheriff once again.

"If there are any gentlemen present who wish to see Mr. Colt," the sheriff said aloud after visiting with JC, "and take their leave of him, he shall be happy to see them."

Everyone present, "with one or two exceptions, passed up to his cell door, shook him by the hand, and took their leave of him." There were several reporters on hand, standing in the foreground, observing, taking notes. To one of those, JC said calmly, "I've spoken harshly of some of the press, but I do not blame you at all; it was all my own fault. There were things that ought to have been explained. I know you have a good heart, and I forgive you from my soul freely; may God bless you, and may you prosper."

The guard in charge of walking JC to the gallows stood in front of him.

"Can I be left alone until the last moment?" JC asked.

It was close to two o'clock.

Two hours remaining.

The guard closed JC's cell door.

Forty minutes passed.

One hour and twenty minutes left.

JC had become friendly with several of the sheriffs and guards during his time in the Tombs. One of the men went over to speak with him near three o'clock.

One hour remaining.*

JC sat on his cot, his back to the cell door. When he heard the door open, JC turned and smiled at the guard. He stood. Shook the man "by the hand and kissed him, as he did several of those who had just previously bid him farewell in this life."

---

* It's important to note here that there is no source material describing where Sam or Caroline were at this time. Regarding the events that would occur next and the controversy that would follow (until the present day), we must point out that they could have walked off and been anywhere inside the prison within reason, standing there by JC's cell, or in a reception area waiting for JC's execution to take place. One would assume they were being watched.

"God bless you, and may you prosper in this life, which is soon to close on me," JC said to the guard.

Throughout the Tombs, "the excitement . . . increased tremendously, and the feelings of those in the prison were also worked up to a pitch of great intensity. No one, however, entered [JC's] cell till precisely five minutes to four o'clock."

The hour had come. There would be no additional good-byes or dramatic moments and good-wish embraces. Only tears. John C. Colt was a number in a system about to carry out a sentence.

As Reverend Anthon walked down the corridor toward JC's cell to escort him to the gallows, the man heard a panicked shout.

"Fire!"

Then, in front of the clergyman, "a rush of feet, attended by a clangor of bells" initiated chaos inside the Tombs. Part of the prison roof was in flames. Prison workers scrambled. Prisoners yelled and clanked metal cups against the bars of their cells, no doubt eager to be let out of their cages for fear of burning up.

Reverend Anthon appeared amid a crowd gathering at the end of the corridor leading to JC's cell. "In the midst of the riot," Alfred Lewis wrote of this moment, "the Reverend Anthon appeared, white of face, aimless fingers working, calling high and low for [the sheriff]."

Something had happened beyond the fire.

"Colt is dead in his cell!" the reverend screamed. "A dagger through his heart."

As the "tower over the vestibule of the prison" burned, bells and horns sounding, watermen doing their best to quell the flames licking upward into the sky (nowhere near JC's cell), somehow JC had escaped death by the gallows and—allegedly—committed suicide.

"On the keeper opening the door, Doctor Anthon, who was first, threw up his hands and eyes to Heaven, and uttering a faint ejaculation, turned pale as death, and retired."

JC lay on his back on his cot, his legs extended outward (as though sleeping), his bloody hands folded over his stomach, a knife's broken handle sticking straight up, its metal blade buried deeply into the center of JC's chest through his heart.*

---

* Some, including myself, would later question how JC could have stabbed himself in the heart and, at the same time, lie on his cot in such a state of repose.

"As I thought," said a guard staring at the dead prisoner.

"As *I* thought," said several others summoned to the cell.

"And going into the cell, there lay Colt . . . quite dead, but not cold."

As R. M. Devens captured the moment in his 1878 book *Our First Century*:

> *[John Colt] had stabbed himself about the fifth rib, on the left side. His temples were yet warm. His vest was open, the blood had flowed freely, and his hands, which were lying across the stomach, were very bloody; he had evidently worked and turned the knife round and round in his heart after stabbing himself, until he made quite a large gash. His mouth was open, his eyes partially so, and his body lay as straight on the bed as if laid out for a funeral by others. . . . The scene and circumstances were tragical to a degree altogether indescribable.**

---

* Gaylord Clarke, who was with JC and the gang on the day of JC's death, wrote an interesting account of the events that day, some of which does not juxtapose with several of the accounts written near the time of JC's death and shortly after. The anecdotes and stories chosen for this narrative are based on my own reading of the materials and how each line up with the next, this in the scope of the facts known to be true. Many times, especially when dealing with historical events of a dramatic nature, the years seem to add more theatrical nuance to the events; we sometimes lose our way inside the truth that seems to be so obvious. In my opinion, it is quite clear that JC died by a stab wound to the heart (whether he did it himself or had someone do it for him remains to be proven). That fire was a mere coincidence—or perhaps JC had it set by a fellow inmate so he could commit suicide without interruption (the fire started in the kitchen). Committing suicide before his execution falls in line with JC suffering from a chronic case of Narcissistic Personality Disorder. He was the keeper, in other words, of his own mortality. Right until the end. This was his one final, selfish act. That all said, however, I wanted to include Mr. Clarke's account in its entirety. Please see Appendix I for Gaylord Clarke's account of those final moments. I think the one clear difference is that the Reverend Anthon, according to Clarke, was not inside the Tombs at the time of the fire, but inside the rectory of his church. Lastly, this account by Clarke is the final word, collectively, found in *American State Trials'* coverage of JC's life, trial, and death.

24

A Dreadful Cup of Vengeance

SAM SAT IN HIS NEW YORK UNIVERSITY OFFICE "WEEPING," HIS HANDS over his face, the broad brim of his hat hiding the anguish burdening the inventor. He had given into the notion that another sibling was moving on to eternal life. Now it would be him, Christopher, Jr., and James left to carry on the Colt name.

A hackman (carriage driver) rushed toward Sam's office shortly after the Tombs fire broke out, bursting hurriedly into Sam's room, startling the inventor, announcing the news—and, according to one account, Sam's "expression changed to something nearly approaching joy."

"Thank God!" Sam supposedly jumped up and said. "Thank God!"

Why he said this and reacted in such a way was never recorded.

Outside the Tombs, a crowd gathered, whispering and gossiping. Many looked on as the fire, a majority of it contained to the top of the building, that cupola (or dome) over the building's entrance, was put out. The salient rumor working its way through the mob was that the fire had been set by someone connected to JC, so Sam (or someone Sam had hired) could slip JC out of the prison, replacing his body with a cadaver Sam had purchased. The idea that the body discovered inside JC's cell looked an awful lot like JC did nothing to stave off the growing buzz of a body swap.

The fire had destroyed the cupola and a small section of the Tombs entryway. Nothing more.

Questions, however, moved throughout the city with the swiftness of a flu: Who smuggled the knife into JC's cell? Did JC steal the knife from inside the prison? Was that marriage between Sam's purported bride and his brother a sham so that this conspiracy could be played out? Was that actually JC's body on his cell cot?

As of this writing, speculation still surrounds these questions.

The editor of the *New York Herald*, in a strangely worded piece, tried to facilitate the intrigue surrounding JC's death by asking several of the same questions in an editorial published the week of the fire:

> *In another part of this day's paper will be found the extraordinary suicide and death of John C. Colt, before the hour appointed by law for his execution, and the no less extraordinary circumstance of his marriage to Caroline Henshaw, and the firing of the cupola of the prison about the hour at which he committed the fatal act that closed his course on earth. We hardly know where to begin, or how to express the feelings and thoughts which rise up in the mind in contemplating this awful, this unexampled, this stupendous, this most extraordinary and most horrible tragedy. . . . The public will demand a full investigation of the circumstances through which such a catastrophe was permitted. How came Colt to ask for religious consolation from a clergyman and yet to commit suicide? The prayers said over him by the Rev. Mr. Anthon seem to have had little influence upon his mind when we look at the horrible termination of his life. Christianity had not penetrated or pervaded the last moments of his existence in the remotest degree. . . . Who gave Colt the knife? Persons who were alone with him in his cell yesterday were Rev. Mr. Anthon, Samuel Colt, Caroline Henshaw and Sheriff Hart. In addition to the above, David Graham and Robert Emmett visited him together, when no other persons were present. John Howard Payne and Lewis Gaylord Clark also visited him with Samuel Colt. Who gave Colt the knife?**

The governor would not order an investigation. The coroner, however, "did impanel a jury, hold an inquest and charge the county the customary fees," Alfred Lewis reported. This inquest, in Lewis's opinion, was "notable" for several reasons. Number one, not one man chosen for the panel (again, according to Lewis's unnamed sources) had "ever met Colt during his life; none of them so much as knew him by sight." Moreover, no one who had been with JC on that day was called before the panel. The coroner simply examined the body and shared his findings. In the end,

---

* See Appendix II for the middle section of this editorial, which is worth the read.

what conclusion could the coroner come to besides what was written on the death certificate: *death by suicide.*

"The rumor continued that the hastily assembled coroner's jury . . . contained not one person who had seen John Colt prior to that time," wrote Louis Goldberg and Willard Stone in an article the two wrote for the *Accounting Historians Journal.* Goldberg and Stone make a good point, stating, "This is difficult to believe after a widely publicized trial," continuing, "In addition, Rev. Dr. Anthon, who married John and Caroline, was stated to have been the first to discover the body in the cell."

No one in New York ever saw Caroline Henshaw again.

"After John's death," Goldberg and Stone reported, "Samuel provided for Caroline and the child."

Sam wrote to James Colt in St. Louis, asking his brother if there was room in Missouri for his bastard child and a woman he had no use for anymore. Sam truly was tired of Caroline, and although he never voiced an opinion one way or another, it's clear he was embarrassed by the whole situation.

James suggested the South, telling Sam he could not care for Caroline in St. Louis.

Sam ultimately thanked his brother for considering the request, mentioning how he had actually come up with a secondary plan since sending the letter: "She speaks and understands German and can best be cared for in the German countries," Sam wrote.

Indeed, Sam made arrangements for Caroline and his child to relocate to Germany. Caroline would soon change her name to Julia Leicester, and was ordered by Sam to tell anyone who asked that she was the "niece of Col. Colt," and that Sam Jr. was Sam's nephew, JC's child. Caroline would eventually meet and marry a Prussian Army officer, Baron Frederick Von Oppen, in a union the baron's family staunchly opposed. Many later presumed Sam had lost touch with Caroline and their child, but in the coming years Caroline would once again surface.

⌒⌒

Public opinion surrounding JC's death, be it suicide or at the hand of a fellow prisoner, spread rapidly and would not let up. One woman, writing the day after JC's death, had some rather potent and admirable things to say, while analyzing a case that would be talked about for more than a century. Her letter would be published in *The United States Magazine and Democratic Review* a year later (1843). "To-day, I cannot write of beauty; for I am sad and troubled," Maria Child began:

> *Heart, head, and conscience are all in battle army against the savage diatoms of my [time]. By and by, the law of love, like oil upon the waters, will calm my surging sympathies and make the current flow more calmly, though none the less deep or strong. But to-day, do not ask me to love governor, sheriff or constable, or any man who defends capital punishment. I ought to do it; for genuine love enfolds even murderers with its blessing. By to-morrow, I think I can remember them without bitterness; but today, I cannot love them; on my soul, I cannot.*

This was quite a controversial statement by a woman writing in the mid-1840s. Maria's opinions regarding the death penalty were rooted in her faith, a Christian virtue she obviously lived. Her piousness rose from the page, showing not only the power of the written word, but the gift Maria had in putting those words on paper. Bringing JC's name into the fold, she added:

> *We were to have had an execution yesterday; but the wretched prisoner avoided it by suicide. The gallows had been erected for several hours, and with a cool refinement of cruelty, was hoisted before the window of the condemned; the hangman was all ready to cut the cord; marshals paced back and forth, smoking and whistling; spectators were wai[t]ing patiently to see . . . [the] 'diegame.' Printed circulars had been handed abroad to summon the number of witnesses required by law: 'You are respectfully invited (to witness the execution of John C. Colt).' I trust some of them are preserved for museums. Specimens should be kept as relics of a barbarous age, for succeeding generations to wonder at. They might be hung up in a frame; and the portrait of a New Zealand Chief, picking the bones of an enemy of his tribe, would be an appropriate pendant.**

---

* If you wish to read the remainder of Maria Child's remarkable (and at times tedious) letter, a serious argument, nonetheless, against a society salivating at the sight of an execution, see Appendix III.

Maria went on to make the age-old argument that a man should not be condemned to death on circumstantial evidence alone. She summed up JC's suicide in a rather articulate analogy, appropriate for her time:

He was precisely in the situation of a man on board a burning ship, who being compelled to face death, jumps into the waves, as the least painful mode of the two. But they, who thus drove him "to walk the plank," made cool, deliberate preparations to take life, and with inventive cruelty sought to add every bitter drop that could be added to the dreadful cup of vengeance.

John was dead—now quite literally a memory, his body given to Sam for proper burial at what was said to be an undisclosed location.*

Or was it?

Alfred Lewis concluded his account of JC's life and death with the indelible, "And so the chapter ended."

Yet this would not be the end—far from it, actually. Sightings of JC would begin as quickly as word could spread. California. Texas. Connecticut. Massachusetts. Even several locations in Europe.

"He was sentenced to be hanged but committed suicide by stabbing himself in the heart with a knife," New York Police Chief George Walling wrote in *Recollections*, published forty-five years after JC's death. "This has been generally accepted as true by the public, but I have heard it declared over and over again, by those in a position to know, that Colt did not commit suicide; that the body found in his cell when the Tombs caught fire was only a corpse prepared for the purpose, and that he escaped in the confusion. The coroner, it is said, was aware of the deception. . . . Persons who knew Colt well are positive they have seen him since the time of his alleged suicide."

---

* There's a report (see: Wolf, Marvin J., and Katherine Mader. 1991. *Rotten apples: Chronicles of New York crime and mystery : 1689 to the present.* New York: Ballantine Books; p. 49) that JC's body was taken from the Tombs three hours after he was found dead and buried immediately in a graveyard behind St. Mark's Church, but this cannot be so, considering that an inquest into his death was ordered.

25

Moving On

SECRECY. IT WAS ONE OF THE MAIN WEAPONS IN SAM COLT'S ARSENAL of sales tactics whenever he engaged in a new venture. Writing to one of his closest supporters in Washington, Abel Upshur, near the time when JC committed suicide and Sam was trying to get the government to fund his battery project, Sam put into context the role secrecy played in the things he did these days, writing, "Everything on my part was conducted as privately as possible so much so that every reporter for [the New York] newspapers have as yet mistaken even the place I were stationed when I made the explosion."

There was a bit of smarminess and pride in his tone; the fact that he had fooled those same men who had written, in Sam's opinion, so many outrageous lies about his brother, was both comforting and triumphant. Sam loved the idea that he could fool people. Trickery was indeed a major part of the package Sam sold, regardless of the product, and likely one of the reasons why so many in the city held onto the notion that JC's body had been switched. It was an aura Sam had spent many years creating and perfecting around the family name; the public expected drama and mystery where the Colts were concerned.

The Potomac exhibition Sam had put on in August won over many of those naysayers who had questioned the battery project from the get-go—with the exception of John Quincy Adams. Yet a new name was also now on the list of Sam's government adversaries: Lieutenant Colonel Joseph Totten. Colonel Totten was a major military official, a ranking officer steadfastly determined to keep U.S. soldiers safe during firefights. It just so happened that Totten was chief of the Corps of Army Engineers. A thickly bearded man with a solid build and stern military look about him, Totten found his passion in construction and cement; he was responsible for the Totten shutter, a solid wall of protection from incoming fire for gun crews; definitely a government man you wanted on your side if you were pitching a weapon such as the one Sam had been trying to fund.

Although Sam had stored most of his supplies and equipment for his submarine battery in the United States Patent Office, an immense marble structure in Washington, he had yet to file for a patent on the project. He kept saying he wasn't ready; he needed to run more tests; and yet it all centered on getting more money and government backing during a time of peace.

Despite Sam's constant push for funds, Totten and Adams, two men who despised Sam and his contraption, sat on the board of the National Institute, part of a committee that discussed the nation's coastal fortifications and defenses. It just wasn't to be for Sam Colt and his battery.

But Sam needed this idea to work. He was already carrying an immense amount of debt because of his gun-manufacturing failure in Paterson. How could he, essentially, pick up his pistol production again and seek backers with such a dismal failure in his wake—regardless of whether it stemmed from those men he had trusted with his company—shadowing him?

"[I]t was apparent to John Quincy Adams that Colt's spectacular demonstration [in August] had powerfully influenced congressional opinion," wrote Philip Lundeberg, who called Adams a "doughty ex-president." Adams was determined to sink (pun intended) Colt and his battery, however, and went on to advise "the House . . . that further experiments 'would be but the throwing of so much money into the sea.'" There was a moral argument, too. War was one thing, Adams preached, but blowing up unsuspecting enemies without giving them the same fighting chance the opposition had was in no way a respectable act, even during war.

"He [Adams] was as fully conscious that the system would be useless to the United States," wrote Henry Barnard in *Armsmear*, "as if one hundred years had passed; but if it could be made successful, he was opposed to blowing up ships of war with submarine batteries; if done at all, it should be done by fair and honest warfare."

As Sam ran out of options, another soon-to-be-monumental figure, a man who had been borrowing cable from Sam throughout 1842, was on the verge of making one of the most profound discoveries in American history. Samuel Morse had an office not too far from Sam's near New York University. Morse was coming off a humiliating experience during one of his experiments with underwater cable at Governor's Island. It happened when a crew of merchantmen "innocently" and unknowingly cut Morse's cable, which terminated his experiment on the spot. He had worked diligently for that one moment, the anticipation and expectation of the display paving the way for what Morse had hoped was a large government check.

"Undaunted," Lundeberg wrote of this pivotal moment in American history, "Morse continued his private experiments at Washington Square, occasionally borrowing cable from Colt and making the discovery late in 1842 that two or more currents could be conducted simultaneously by a single wire, a commercially significant discovery that was eventually designated 'duplex telegraphy.'"

Morse took his show to Washington. Unlike Sam, though, the inventor was able to impress the leaders of the country, after staging several successful demonstrations on Capitol Hill. Even John Quincy Adams's acrimoniously public disagreement with the cable, in which he said he "believed that sending messages over a wire was the work of Satan," could not crush the excitement surrounding Morse's invention. This was a turning point in American innovation. It would change the way states communicated and wars were fought.

So impressed by Morse and his telegraph wire, Congress passed the Telegraph Bill on March 3, 1843, clearing the way for Morse to receive an endless supply of funding and governmental support for his experiments. The wire Morse had used was said to be Sam's creation, "fabricated," Lundeberg wrote, "by Colt's assistant, Robert Cummings." It was a simple lead-sheathed cable, its inner copper strands wrapped with cotton yarn and impregnated with asphalt and beeswax to protect it from liquid interference. In its simplicity and design, the cable was ingenious— yet again, however, not really one of Sam's creations.

Sam would not give up on his battery. He repeatedly tested the apparatus. Then, quite out of character, in May 1843, after Morse's star began to rise, perhaps when Sam realized his name being attached to Morse's underwater cable was not going to do him any good, the inventor came clean. Sam made a public admission unlike anything he had ever done; he gave credit where credit was due! Publishing a letter in the May 11 edition of the *Army and Navy Chronicle and Scientific Repository*, the tormented inventor wrote:

The first person who made any practical use of electricity for the purpose of igniting large masses of gunpowder was Mr. Moses Shaw, of Boston, Mass. His experiments were made as early as the year 1828. He applied it for the purpose of blasting rocks. An account of his method was communicated to Professor Silliman by the late Dr. Chilton, of this city; and it was published in the American Journal of Science and Arts, vol. xvi, 1829. Mr. Shaw at first made use of the ordinary electrical machine; but, finding it inconvenient in damp weather, he, by recommendation of Dr. Hare, of Philadelphia, employed the [calorimeter], a form of galvanic battery constructed by Dr. H., in which the plates are so connected together as to act as one pair.

Sam was admitting for perhaps the first time in his life, publicly, that he was not the first to come up with a particular idea his name had been attached to—but more importantly, scholars later pointed out, he was giving away one of the most important secrets of his submarine battery, offering it to the public, scarcely impervious to the notion that his competitors might steal his designs.

Whatever Sam Colt did, the man had a reason behind it. Be sure of that. He was putting this idea out into the public domain because he had found himself facing a barricade. There were men in top positions against him. He could not win a fight against Washington stalwarts, and he knew it.

Still, he would not be stalled or beaten. The next theatrical experiment Sam conducted started at Wood's Hole, Massachusetts, where Sam had located and taken possession of the *Brunette*, an abandoned ship on which the crew had reportedly "mutinied rather than continue sailing."

The *Brunette* was then navigated to Washington. The idea Sam had drafted was to blow the *Brunette* into smithereens with 150 barrels of gunpowder, surely enough to put on a display that would send word spreading around the country: If Americans wanted to protect the shores of their great nation, the only way to do it was with Sam's battery.

The Colt family was among the first enigmatic pedigrees that came into the New World with a history-making backlash of bad luck. Americans would be privy to this dynamic inside the Kennedy family in the century to come. The Colts, as an American dynasty, lived under a haze of universal recompense the cosmos sometimes felt compelled to dole out: an invisible rule of law that, to succeed in making killing machines—often put in the hands of human beings untrained to handle such weapons—there had to be a price to pay, a stipend, not to mention the struggle involved to get to the end of the race. Nothing came easy to the Colts. Ever. One could say, in retrospect, that some Great Being above was punishing Sam for being (or manufacturing) the devil's right hand.

It was shortly after JC's death and Sam's merciless, dogged determination to see that the battery project got governmental approval when Sam ran into an obstacle with an invention he had been trying to perfect: cartridges wrapped not in paper but tinfoil. Paper cartridges were prone to deterioration; liquid could easily penetrate through paper. Sam had conducted several experiments "with mixed results," but had persuaded the government to place "a large order" of the tinfoil cartridges for military use. Yet he soon got word that Washington had now reneged on the deal. So Sam abandoned the cartridge invention as the winter of 1843 settled on New York, and he refocused on his submarine battery.

The inventor just couldn't wrap his mind around the notion that the nation did not want to protect its shores with his battery. It seemed almost laughable to Sam that the government wasn't stepping up and putting $100,000 (the amount he expected to receive) in his hand to get this invention perfected and in use as quickly as possible. He believed the country was at risk, writing once that all Americans would suffer in the future if the government continued to "[starve] to death the inventors who can provide a safe and certain defense, at small cost."

A few months before Sam was set to put on his latest display in the Potomac, using the *Brunette* as his dummy casualty, a disaster took place just outside Washington that was going to greatly affect any additional progress Sam might have made or was making at the time.

The man they called the accidental president, John Tyler, took an invitation to send off the *USS Princeton*, a U.S. Navy warship that sailed with the largest naval weapon in the world. This massive ship with its massive gun was the pride and joy of the United States as the year 1844 dawned and plans were made to bring in the president to launch her into action. Firing a gun of such magnitude and might would send a message to the world. Work on this ship had been going on since 1841.

Swedish engineer John Ericsson had been hired by Captain Richard Stockton, who had been pursuing his dream of building the warship for decades, asking the Navy for appropriations since 1838. Stockton had in fact named the ship after his hometown, Princeton, New Jersey. The centerpiece of the ship was the Peacemaker, a ten-ton gun with a fifteen-inch bore, the largest in the world. Stockton called the safety of the ship with this weapon aboard during battle "something like a mathematical certainty." The ship had one deadly combination: "stealth and firepower."

In February 1844, the *Princeton* sailed from its home port, Philadelphia, where it had been built, into the icy waters of the Potomac, positioning herself for the cannon exhibition. Stockton had planned fourteen days of celebrations around the launching of the ship—a buildup, day by day, culminating in the president sending her off on her maiden voyage as those immense guns fired into the dark winter skies.

One of the only government officials unimpressed with her might was, of course, John Quincy Adams, being the curmudgeon he had become since his days in Washington as a prodigy of his father. Adams viewed the dramatic presentation, the festivities, and all the hoopla surrounding the *Princeton* to be a sideshow to the real reason for the ship: "the patriotic ardor [Washington had] for a naval war."

Warmongers, all of them, Adams would have been the first to say. Displays such as this were nothing more than dramatic nonsense undertaken to "fire the souls" of the president and Congress to initiate a war with some smaller nation.

On February 28, 1844, near noon, Stockton sailed with the ship as crowds gathered along the shores of the Potomac, the Peacemaker firing at huge blocks of floating ice, some reports claimed, as far as three miles away, turning each into slush with accuracy and panache.

The *Princeton* soon docked in Alexandria, awaiting a large crowd, including Sam's sole advocate in Washington, Secretary of State Abel Upshur, President Tyler, former New York state senator David Gardiner and his daughter, twenty-one-year-old Julia, whom the fifty-one-year-old president was more than smitten with and had been pursuing since they met five months after Tyler's wife had died. Dolley Madison was also invited aboard, as were dozens of other Washington socialites and important political figures.

The grand party was below deck, with food and drink and dance and talk of what such a flawless specimen of engineering could accomplish in the world for America. As the party carried on, a few party-goers pushed Stockton to fire the weapons again. He had put on a display from the shore, but his guests now wanted to experience the guns firsthand, as perhaps a sailor might.

Stockton refused. Too dangerous, he explained.

Abel Upshur told him to do it anyway. Everything would be fine.

Considering Upshur's request, Stockton presumed it to be an order.

Most of the women stayed below. The men, however, filled their glasses with champagne and went upstairs to watch.

As Tyler went to toast a comrade, an explosion like none other was heard on deck, and then a blinding light of white illuminated the sky, sending shock waves throughout the ship.

Something terrible had happened.

Tyler heard moans and screams and looked over to where the gun had gone off, only to witness a scene of utter devastation. The gun had backfired and blown up. The ship had been ripped apart. Pieces of flesh and bone and tissue scattered all over.

"Twenty feet of the ship's bulwark had been ripped away and bodies were strewn everywhere," a *Free Lance-Star* article reported. "The acrid smell of gunpowder mixed with the smell of burning flesh hung heavily in the air."

Abel Upshur, Sam's friend and ally in Washington, was killed, as was the secretary of the Navy. David Gardiner gave his life, but his daughter survived and ultimately married Tyler months later, on June 25, 1844. Sailors and crew members and staff had been killed. Many others were maimed and injured, including Stockton.

One could almost hear Adams laughing in jest at this horrible disaster. It certainly exemplified the sheer tragedy of war and the price America paid for producing weaponry of such great power; and maybe how pride and ego could be self-destructive.

Of course, this put Sam Colt in an even worse position in Washington than he had ever been. He had been pressing his battery, and Upshur was standing behind him. With Upshur dead and Sam's only additional supporter, Senator Southard (who had died only weeks before), gone, too, what was he to do?

"Though the Peacemaker accident had killed his most powerful and sympathetic supporter," Bern Keating wrote, "Colt bored ahead, for the international situation had warmed up again with pressure from the Republic of Texas for annexation as one of the United States."

Indeed, one step forward, two steps back—and perhaps three more forward for Sam Colt. He had landed on his feet *again* with an unstable Texas and Mexican border. The United States became "nervous," Keating pointed out, "about Mexican reaction if its errant province joined the Union and even more nervous that a rebuffed Texas would enter an alliance with Great Britain."

Instability among nations and the threat of war was what Sam needed, for both his battery and his pistol production to pick up again. And so Sam's next demonstration, with the *Brunette* already in place, was back on—and the inventor, for the first time in quite a while, enjoyed a new lease on potential success.

26

The Tail of a Lion

ON APRIL 13, 1844, SAM COLT STAGED WHAT WOULD BE THE FINAL theatrical demonstration of his submarine battery. This was it, Sam knew. He wasn't going to get many more chances to prove the value of his invention.

According to Bern Keating's account, Sam "sowed his mines on the Anacostia River bottom between the Old Arsenal and Greenfield Point and the navy yard." The ship Sam his sights set on, the *Brunette*, was a five-hundred-ton monster sailing vessel. They had renamed the *Brunette* the *Styx*, "for its death cruise," which Lieutenant Junius Boyle and a small crew, under Sam's direction, sailed over the minefield Sam had set up previously. The crowd gathered, watching in anticipation, surely with no more expectation than to see a great show of fireworks and hissing, showering water into the sky.

Boyle and his crew found their spot in the water and, after anchoring the ship in place, jumped into a small dinghy. Rowing away, Boyle fired a flare into the air letting Sam know the coast was clear; Sam could begin his exhibition anytime.

As was the case in his previous experiments, Sam was at an undisclosed location manning the minefield charges.

The mines were submerged in the water, anchored at the bottom, with cable leads heading toward the surface of the water, attached to what looked like bobbers (floating just below the waterline) full of gunpowder and charge. This was effective if the boat you were about to destroy had sailed over the device and you had a bead on where the device was actually located underneath the water. Within Sam's protected environment and controlled experiment, it was easy to detonate the charges because he knew when the boat passed over the mine. Still, Sam's point was that if you spread these mines over a wide area inside a harbor, no ship could get close without running the risk of being blown up. It was a good idea, but one the government was afraid Sam had not conceptualized all by himself and, at a time of peace, not too practical.

The one thing Sam had going for him was the buzz around this particular demonstration, good, bad, or indifferent. It didn't matter. The fact remained: Washington was talking about Sam Colt's battery, and that was exactly what the inventor wanted. Well publicized, one newspaper advertisement put it as plain as it could, adding a flare of excitement to the event:

> [T]he whole populace was in a fidget of satisfaction and impatience—everybody in every place, from the halls of Congress and the Executive Departments down to the boarding house kitchen and boot-blacks' cellars, were hurrying through the business of the morning to ensure an early dinner and a sight of the blow up.

Sam certainly had everyone's attention. The shores lining the river banks were packed with thousands of onlookers.

The best account of what happened next came from the *Daily National Intelligencer*, a Washington newspaper. In the days and months that followed this experiment, it would be widely reported that Sam either wrote the piece himself or "heavily influenced" the reporter, who had obviously either taken a bribe from Sam or admired the guy enough to write a puff piece. In his first-person account of the event, the reporter began: "I strolled down to the shores of the Eastern Branch about three o'clock; yet though it was more than an hour before the appointed time, I found thousands there before me, patiently waiting (under no very merciful sun, either) the destined hour to arrive."

The reporter walked up "an elevated bluff," and then stood in "delighted silence," a panoramic view of the water before him. After a breath, he described what he saw, in striking candor, praise, and excitement, as follows:

> The undulating shores on the opposite bank of the river, with their woods and farm houses, and cultivated fields; on the left, the navy yard, with its ship-houses and workshops; on the right, the arsenal, with Giesbury

point and Alexandria in the distance; close by, the wharves and river beach, covered with people; the nearer heights covered with carriages and vehicles of every description, with riders on horseback, companies of children, and anxious mothers trying to restrain them from venturing to the precipices.

The water itself, there below his gaze, appeared to be a "placid blue stream, gently rippled by a very light breeze, and glittering in the rays of a fervid, unclouded sun, covered with boats of all sizes, rowing or sailing to and fro—these objects combined in one wide *coup d'oeil*, present[ing] a scene which, for variety, interest and picturesque beauty, could scarcely be surpassed."

The stage was set. All of Washington waited, wondering how Sam's contraption was going to work. This was Sam's hour.

The *Intelligencer* reporter picked up the narration:

In the middle of the stream, and in full view, lay the object on which all eyes were fastened—a ship of about five hundred tons, very old, but newly painted, black with a white streak, her sails much patched and weather beaten, having at her mainmast head a red flag, and at the mizzen mast the American ensign floating beautifully in the breeze. She was at anchor, and near her were boats that seemed, from their motions, to be in communication with those on board. Presently a steamboat heaved in view and, taking her station at a convenient distance, began to let off steam; and before long, another and longer appeared, having her deck black with a crowd of people and bearing the national colors, having as it was understood, the President on board, accompanied by the Heads of Departments and other offices of Government. As all were now waiting with much impatience.

The anticipation, Sam was well aware, would sell the entire event. The longer he waited, the more tension that built, Sam himself nowhere to be seen, the louder the crowd would react to what Sam knew was going to be a series of explosions that would not miss their mark.

And then, with a mighty show of bravado only made possible by the one-and-only Samuel Colt, a gun was heard from the navy yard, followed by several others. Here was the opening, the prologue, the moment everyone had been waiting for: A seventeen-gun salute rang throughout the afternoon to let the crowd know that what was about to take place in the coming moments would be a historic feat unsurpassed by anything anyone had seen.

The reporter continued:

Every eye was turned toward the ship; but she did not move. A little boat advanced and removed certain buoys which had been floating near the spot where the battery lay; and soon after a low and peculiar sound was heard, when a most beautiful jet, of mingled water, fire and smoke, rose to a considerable height near the opposite shore, and as the water fell back in white translucent masses, the smoke, colored by the sun's rays with all the dyes of the prism, slowly melted into the air, while the grains of wet powder, ignited and smoking, fell in soft showers upon the bright surface of the river.

It appeared Sam had missed. The crowd watched as water spouts blasted into the air, rainbows abound, as if a whale had breached and sprayed a flute of misty seawater.

"This exhibition rose as if by the touch of magic," the reporter explained, "and seemed intended as a sort of prelude to convince the waiting multitude that there was a prospect of being paid for their walk."

Sam was toying with everyone—putting on a show.

His next charge seemed to also miss, discharging and blowing seawater into the air a bit closer to the target.

"Ah!" the crowd said in unison.

"What a pity! It was a failure after all!" a bystander yelled.

"Oh, he has missed her!" said another. "But it was very near."

But then, amid sighs and boos, whispers and shouts, maybe even some clapping and clamoring for more, Sam gave the crowd what it had come for:

The words were scarcely uttered when a third explosion took place— the bows and bowsprit of the ship, instantly shattered to atoms, were thrown into the air. The fore part of the vessel was lifted up almost out of the water, and then immediately sank, while the stern continued above water, and the mizzenmast was left still standing, though in an inclined position. The spars and sails hung in confusion, being suddenly blackened by the smoke, and the whole presenting a wreck in the highest degree picturesque.

Sam had blasted that five-hundred-ton box of wood into splinters.

The reporter called the next scene a "momentary pause of gratified suspense," as the audience stood stunned at the sight of a ship, split in two by a charge sent from an undisclosed location, sinking.

But then, amid the stunned silence of the crowd came roars, most on hand happy to have seen such a tremendous spectacle of firepower and harbor defense.

[T]he shores resounded with heartfelt plaudits, subsiding into long continuing murmurs of admiration. The gratification was unbounded. Nothing could have been more completely successful. There was no accident, no injury, no disappointment in any respect; the public expectation was not only met but surpassed; and when the boat containing the crew darted swiftly to the wreck, and with some difficulty restored the stripes and stars to their former station, it required no stretch of the imagination to fancy that we beheld a captive invader, which had been compelled to strike, and was now taken possession of as lawful prize.

Sam had proven the potential of his battery in front of a gallery of Americans prone to doubting Thomas syndrome: that seeing something in person, before stamping it with approval, beckons belief. The irony in it all, which no one had paid much attention to at first because the explosions were so powerful and impressive to the naked eye, was the location of Sam Colt during the demonstration. Where was the man of the hour? And why was he being so secretive about where he had stationed himself during these experiments? If he couldn't give up that secret and refused to make it part of the exhibition, what would stop everyone from walking away thinking that Sam had simply placed the charges onboard the ship itself?

It took days, but Sam came out and told the secretary of the Navy, John Mason, he had been positioned "on the opposite bank of the river ... more than two miles distant from the ship."

This was an incredible claim. Sending a ship to the sea bottom from two miles away, no doubt with the stealth of a burglar in the night?

Impossible!

Exactly. Where was the proof of such a claim? Where was the witness testimony to this stunning announcement by Sam Colt? If this were true, the submarine battery was as good as sold to the government. But how would Sam prove it?

News accounts—which seemed to be written by Sam himself— called the battery an "important invention . . . proved to be eminently successful . . . forever preventing the approach of an invader to shores thus guarded and rendered impregnable by the force of American science and enterprise."

Sam's adversaries in the military, however, took an entirely different approach to his latest demonstration and would not be swayed by newspaper articles likely influenced by the inventor himself. In the *Army and Navy Chronicle and Scientific Repository*, the totality of the public experiment by Sam was thus distilled into an exhibit no better than a hoax: "As experiments, these, as many others have been, were very beautiful and striking, but in the practical application of this apparatus to purposes of war, we have no confidence."

Sam could not win. No matter what he did there was always someone in Washington who simply saw through his snake oil salesman's approach and called things as they saw them. Nobody wanted to take Sam on merit alone. Sam, on the other hand, was too full of pride and fear that he would be robbed of his brilliance to come out and explain how he had done it.

Joseph Henry, at the time a famed American scientist and soon-to-be first director of the Smithsonian Institution, wrote to the secretary of war, William Wilkins, on May 3, 1844, outlining how Sam's invention should be viewed on Capitol Hill. Sam's continuous and brazen lobbying efforts to get his submarine battery into production under government funding and complete support were beating everyone down. Sam kept pushing; his adversaries pushed back. There was no middle ground. Sam wanted to be paid for the experiments he had put on, claiming that certain military officials had given him the green light to conduct the experiments in the first place.

Joseph Henry, however, scribed a fair warning to Sam: "Mr. Colt may, perhaps, not attempt to found his claims to originality on the invention of the galvanic process, to which he can have no title, but on a new application of this process to a method of harbor defence; and also on a new arrangement of subaqueous magazines for the same purpose."

Sam could not obtain a patent on the charge and bombs alone. He had no claim to the idea. But if he could prove his stealthy way of sending an ignition to the charges, well, the inventor had something the government might want.

Henry was saying, too, in not so many words, that Washington officials could see through Sam's way of pushing his invention into their faces by constantly changing its direction and purpose. Where was his darn patent application? Why hadn't he filed it?

The House piped in next. Too many questions arose within the confinement of what Sam had shown publicly. Sam had been too secretive about his invention and too sparse in giving credit where credit was due. Cannons set up along the shores, many in Congress agreed, would work in the same manner as Sam's battery. Why did the government need underwater mines?

Sam made one last effort to keep his invention alive. In his shoddy and broken style of butchering the English language, Sam Colt wrote to William Gibbs McNeil, an old friend and supporter who was now a civil engineer and who also had close connections in the military on Capitol Hill:

> *Movements are making to kill me off[f] without ceremony. A resolution was offered the other day in the House of Representatives. I presume at the instance of some officers of the Army hostile to my new mode of fortification, calling on the Secretarys of War & of the Navy for information as to the plans of my invention[,] the claims which I have if any to origonality &c, &c. The Navy department I think will treat the subject fairly but the Sec'y of War has refered the resolution to the Ordnance Department & the Engenear beauroughs, people of all others the least calculated to give a just repoart in a matter directly hostile to their own profession. Col Tolcot [George Talcott] & in fact nearly every officer of the ordnance department has been hostile to every invention I ever made & I can't hope for any other result in my present cace.*

Then he hit John Mason up with a snobbish letter (which he undoubtedly had some assistance proofreading), not helping his cause by showing how angry and bitter he was about not having been taken seriously:

[I]n no single instance have I failed in the use of my submarine battery, and that the combined results of my experiments proved beyond all doubt that it can be successfully employed with the most perfect ease and safety to destroy the largest class of ships of war when in motion passing in or out of harbour without the necessity of approach within reach of shot from guns of the largest calibre.

The battle between Sam and certain Washington officials went back and forth; Sam would not give up his so-called secrets without some sort of promise to fund the project. He wanted $100,000.

So stubborn were the opposing sides, Philip Lundeberg observed, that Sam and the antagonistic Washington officials worked "together . . . in postponing submarine mine development in the United States for nearly a generation."

The major battle was whether Sam was the first to invent such an apparatus. Washington didn't think he was, and so they continually asked for his plans.

Then, on June 8, 1844, startling just about everyone involved, Sam gave in and submitted a formal patent application, this after government officials asked Sam to submit his secrets to Henry L. Ellsworth, the commissioner of U.S. Patents.

Sam laid it all out. The most interesting aspect of his idea was something he called a "torpedo tower," a staging area along the shoreline where the master of controls hid from the enemy. Sam had it sketched as a hundred-foot-tall tower that allowed the shooter to look out at his target and see, effectively, the mines in the water—sort of like a modern-day video game. In this respect, the idea that a man could stand behind a barricade (ten stories high) and shield himself, hiding in plain sight from the enemy while looking out on the water, and when the time came, send a charge through a cable that was buried underground and ran into the water, was unique and innovative. No one had developed this concept yet. Sam might have used the ideas of others to construct the bombs and the way the mines hung underneath the water, but this tower was his invention alone.

Thus, Commissioner Ellsworth decided that Sam's "novelty [was] sufficient to sustain a patent."

Sam had won a battle, but certainly not his war with Washington, where the same mawkish sentimentality forever ruled: Never prove your adversaries wrong. It will bite you back every time.

"Unhappily for Colt," Lundeberg explained, "the committee did not limit its requirement to the criteria of originality, turning thereupon to the question of utility. In reviewing the War Department's objections, the committee found itself severely embarrassed by lack of tangible information."

The conclusion was that Sam had never *proven* he had ever used a tower in one of his experiments. Suffice it to say, he could have dreamed this up on paper to curry favor with those opposing him. The committee deciding whether to allow Sam's patent to be funded and fully backed by the United States decided that the "invention is entitled to the favorable consideration of government; but [t]here is not sufficient evidence, however, before the committee, to enable them to judge of the propriety of adopting it as a means of fortification; and they are therefore not prepared to recommend it for that purpose." They patted Sam on the back while walking him out the door.

Ultimately, the government tried buying Sam off with a ten thousand dollar settlement, but Sam could not come up with adequate expenditures to prove he had spent as much during his years working on the battery (1841–1844). Sam could not continue with experiments if the government would not back him. Yet he did enter into a financial battle royal with the Treasury Department over what he believed was owed to him—a fight that would go on until 1854.

In 1844, Sam wrote to a family member, clearly outlining how he felt about the entire matter of the battery and his fight with Washington bureaucrats, noting that he wasn't interested in picking up someone else's crumbs or showing up at the finish line behind his competition.

"[I]t is better to be at the head of a louse than the tail of a lion . . . if I can't be first, I won't be second in anything."

27

Saved by the Indians

SAM DID NOT GIVE UP ON THE FEDERAL GOVERNMENT COMING TO ITS senses and backing his submarine battery. His persistence and determination to succeed would not pay off with financial backing for the battery, but would soon be rewarded tenfold in another way.

Timing was everything, a concept Sam didn't understand as well as he should have. He had been pushing a defense weapon during a time of peace. He had been producing pistols under the same set of circumstances. Yet as the year 1845 progressed, fate took an interest in Sam's life again. The situation along the border between Texas and Mexico became increasingly unstable, and while brewing hostilities would change everything for Sam Colt, that old familiar Colt song was once again ringing throughout the air. No triumph for a Colt ever came without a price.

In St. Louis, Sam's brother James was nursing a leg wound that had saddled the lawyer inside his home. In their letters during this period, James told Sam he indeed wanted to help him with the various businesses Sam was pursuing, but was not up to it due to his leg, a terribly battered ego, and the financial stress all of his current problems had put on his estate. James Colt had entered into a duel with another man over a woman. He lost. Adding insult to injury, James faced charges for dueling, which was illegal. James's reply to Sam's request for business assistance was to ask *Sam* for a loan, claiming to have little money left after not being able to work, on top of doling out monies to his lawyers and doctors.

"Sam sent him a hundred dollars and advised him to avoid duels," Jack Rohan wrote.

In 1845, Sam's waterproof cartridges were well received in Washington, and an order under the state militia appropriation for fifty thousand dollars' worth was placed. Still, Sam ran into a bit of trouble while conducting business out of New York City. One night, he seemed to lose control of his senses, snapping and "striking [a man] several times in the face with his fist, blackening one of his eyes, knocking him down."

Sam had lost his temper, driving speculation in town that he was no better than his dead brother. New York didn't seem too receptive to the Colt name any longer. Sam had also lost a judgment against him in court for $1,200. He had exhausted all of his contacts and potential backers.

Struggling to pay his bills, even though he had landed that large contract with the government, Sam once again leaned on Samuel Morse, who had hired the gun maker to lay forty miles of underwater cable from Baltimore to Washington.

And then, when it seemed Sam was destined to fail on all levels once again, this despite a touch of good luck lately, lightning struck: Plains Indians and Mexican bandits—who were running wild along the borders and into the Lone Star Republic, which had been free from Mexican rule since 1836 and was on the verge of becoming a bona fide member of the United States—met up with mounted troops. Skirmishes broke out all over. Firefights and hand-to-hand combat ensued. For the Texas Rangers, the idea of firing a weapon and then having to reload got old rather quickly as Rangers faced swarms of Indians and bandits.

Among the Rangers was a twenty-eight-year-old Tennessean named John Coffee Hayes, a tough and rugged frontiersman, unafraid to fire a weapon at any man. Hayes had been appointed captain of the Rangers in 1840. During his time in the Rangers, Hayes was known as a fearless soldier who went after Indians and Mexican bandits with the fervor of a one-man army, bent on protecting his land from interlopers. During a fight one day along the Mexican border, Hayes happened upon a .34-caliber Colt five-shot pistol. It turned out to be a brilliant gun, satisfying Hayes's needs. The captain could hit five targets without having to reload.

"He was immediately struck with its possibilities," Bern Keating wrote, "and armed his entire company with the revolvers."

A second firefight that took place west of San Antonio during the summer of 1845 set Sam's future in steel without the inventor ever knowing what was taking place. On a balmy afternoon deep in the Nueces Canyon, a band of fifteen Texas Rangers came upon a tribe of about eighty Comanche Indians. Comanche had always operated under the assumption that the Rangers lacked adequate firepower and weaponry to stage any sort of major attack with much success; as long as the numbers were even on both sides, the Comanche knew they could beat the Rangers on a bad day. And when the Comanche were able to stage five or six times the number of Indians to Rangers in the theater of battle, there was no contest; they won every time.

This day would prove different, however.

The Rangers trotted upon the tribe, who were positioned along the Pedernales River. They dismounted with rifles in hand and began firing one shot at a time. This was just the sort of onslaught of firepower, the Comanche knew, they could dodge before making a counterattack. As soon as the Rangers went to reload, the Comanche would charge and assault. It had worked every time.

Hayes had also armed his Rangers on this day with the Colt .34-caliber five-shot pistol, however. So as the Comanche came at the Rangers, the Rangers mowed them down one by one, using Colt's weapons against vainglorious shouts from Hayes, "Powder-burn them!"

The Comanche were devastated. Hayes and his men were said to have killed or wounded half of their adversaries. It was an amazing display of firepower and the difference innovation could make on the battlefield: fifteen Rangers against a tribe of eighty Indians. Those Indians who survived rode back to camp and explained to their leaders how the Rangers had "a shot for every finger on the hand."

According to scholars who have studied this pivotal moment in American firearms history, it's clear that on the day Hayes and his Rangers assaulted those Comanche at Pedernales River, the "bow and arrow," Keating observed so astutely, "became obsolete overnight." There was no way the Comanche, or any other tribe of American Indians, could defend themselves against such a rapid-fire weapon. Sam Colt's repeating firearm had proven itself—without the animated and overly dramatic sales pitch of its patent holder.

For Hayes, realizing the power behind the revolving pistol on that day was the break the Rangers needed in combating the Indians and Mexican bandits. Hayes soon told his superiors he wanted to arm the entire Ranger force with Sam Colt's weapons.

Sam didn't know it yet, but his gun-making business was about to step back into action and start producing weapons.

Texas was annexed by a joint resolution on March 1, 1845. Soon-to-be-replaced President John Tyler assented to the proposition the following day. By July 4, 1845, Congress acted, announcing: "Whereas, the Congress of the United States of America has passed resolutions providing for the annexation of Texas to that Union, which resolutions were approved by the President of the United States on the first day of March, 1845 ; and Whereas, the President of the United States has submitted to Texas the first and second sections of the said resolutions as the basis upon which Texas may be admitted as one of the States of said Union, and Whereas, the existing government of the republic of Texas has assented to the proposals thus made."

The vote was 56–1 in favor of annexation. Making Texas a state was regarded by the Mexican government as "a barefaced steal of its territory," according to Jack Rohan. At the time, Mexico was a venomous country, run by thugs who would soon make "it plain that if the United States wanted to hold Texas, it would have to fight for it."

A war with Mexico seemed unavoidable, which became, for Sam's gun patents, the best thing that could have ever happened to the inventor. Add to that an explosion of construction going on in the Wild West (with word of a gold rush buzzing), and Sam Colt was sitting on the fortune he had always assumed, but not yet begun to realize.

Newly elected President James Polk, a rough-looking North Carolinian whose long white hair fit him rather well, sent troops into a territory deep in Texas along the Mexican border—the Rio Grande—to which Mexico had staked claim. This entire area—*Del Rio, Ciudad Acuna, Piedras Negras*—was a powder keg on the verge of exploding into war at any moment. Polk's plan was to present Mexico with a show of American might; place troops along the border in a statement of pressure. Once the force of America's military presence was felt by the Mexicans, Polk then "tried vainly to buy the northern provinces of Mexico."

Mexico was uninterested in negotiating any type of land deal. Texas was theirs. If the United States wasn't ready to give it up, Mexico, a country whose government was in shambles and being run mainly by bandits and hostile takeovers, was going to take it.

The Rangers had placed troops along a Rio Grande post, led by Samuel H. Walker. Thirty-one-year-old Walker, a Maryland native, had served under Hayes's regiment for the past ten years. Walker had an interesting history with Mexico. He had fought in San Antonio against the Mexican troops of General Adrián Woll and was captured there as a prisoner of war. Walker escaped but was soon captured again. As luck would have it, Walker drew the only white bean in what became known as the "Black Bean" incident, in which those remaining captives fatefully drawing black beans were all executed in front of Walker. Not long after, for a second time, Walker escaped his captors and hooked up with Hayes as he was manning the forts in San Antonio. A war with Mexico seemed increasingly inevitable. Walker joined a group known as Taylor's Army along the Rio Grande, where all of the action was now centered.

Sam Colt and Sam Walker had been writing to each other for some time, Walker praising, but also constructively criticizing Sam's weapons. Walker, along with Hayes, had experienced Sam's weapons during the Seminole War in Florida years before; they were both familiar with the capabilities of Colt firearms. Still, even though Sam Colt sensed some interest in his gun business, he could not have known that Sam Walker, one of the finest soldiers the Rangers had, would soon give him the enormous break he had been looking for since the late 1830s.

As the Rangers stationed at the Rio Grande monitored the situation under newly appointed Captain Sam Walker's division, on April 28, 1846, the Mexican Army staged a surprise attack, killing many American citizens and soldiers during what turned into a bloody and violent public battle. Polk waited a little over ten days, but on May 9, 1846, he had no choice but to officially declare war with Mexico: "As war exists, and notwithstanding all our efforts to avoid it, exists by the act of Mexico herself, we are called upon by every consideration of duty and patriotism to vindicate with decision the honor, the rights and the interests of our country."

Captain Walker had written to Sam before war with Mexico had broken out, further conveying his belief in Sam's weapons, explaining to Sam what Hayes and his men had accomplished with the .34 caliber back when they had fought off the Comanche, "boldly attacking them on their own ground," Walker noted excitedly, adding:

Colt Sir . . . The pistols which you made for the Texas Navy have been in use by the Rangers for three years, and I can say with confidence that it is the only good improvement that I have seen. The Texans, who have learned their value by practical experience, their confidence in them is unbounded, so much so that they are willing to engage four times their number.

Near this same time, Sam was busy setting up the Offing Magnetic Telegraph Association, still trying to work his contacts in New York, desperately hoping to align new investors to help him put together enough capital to incorporate the business. Morse was still part of Sam's life, feeding Sam work and describing the inventions he expected would be possible with his telegraph. Sam had propositioned investors with a design to lay telegraph cable from New York to New Jersey to Long Island, essentially connecting all three regions electronically. Messages, he and Morse preached, could be sent to and fro. There had to be some envy on Sam's part here: Morse's business was taking off at warp speed. Sam was settling for Morse's crumbs. Yet Sam could not have underestimated the energy building around him at the time; he must have known—or sensed, rather—that his time was coming. Lives of Americans were changing rapidly. The innovation happening around Sam was hard to keep up with. Ellsworth Grant, one of Sam's many biographers over the years, perhaps put this important period of Sam's life best, writing, "Although Colt was not destined to fight in the Mexican War, his guns were."

The world had finally caught up with Sam's advanced weapons.

The gun they were talking about in Texas was the five-shot Paterson pistol that Walker, Hayes, and the Rangers had found some success with during the past several years. In Sam's mind it was a good weapon, but there were ideas being discussed for a newer, more modern version of a pistol that might work more practically within the theater of war.*

Throughout this time Sam had heard whispers of what was going on in Mexico and Texas with his weapons; letters came from Walker and others describing how his pistols were winning many of the firefights for American troops. Being the consummate promoter and salesman he was, Sam Colt lobbied Captain Walker and pushed him to place large orders

---

* As an interesting aside, some have assumed that Colt's infamous and perhaps most popular pistol, the six-shot Colt .45, more commonly known as "the Peacemaker" (the same name given to the cannon aboard the *Princeton* that blew up, killing Abel Upshur and others), came out of this innovative time in American history, when the West was, as they say, won, the gold rush just beginning, and war with Mexico underway. And yet it would be twenty-five-plus years before the Colt .45 "Peacemaker" hit the market, a gun Sam Colt never saw, or had anything to do with.

for the Paterson weapons. The only problem for Sam was that in making promises to produce thousands of weapons, he was in a sense putting the cart before the horse: He had neither the machinery nor the space to manufacture guns on such a large scale. On top of that, he was broke.

Walker and Sam communicated back and forth, discussing various models Sam might be able to design. Walker was thrilled to be having a dialogue with Sam, building Sam's ego up to the point where Sam knew he needed to get a factory up and running as soon as possible. He felt the dynamism of his creations beginning to bubble. The stars were aligning.

"Without your pistols we would not have had the confidence to have undertaken such daring adventures," Walker wrote. "With improvements I think they can be rendered the most perfect weapon in the World for light mounted troops. The people throughout Texas are anxious to procure your pistols."

General Zachary Taylor, an American soldier in command of troops in Texas, wrote Sam and asked for one thousand Colt pistols within a period of ninety days. Walker wrote again and asked Sam if he could design a .44-caliber weapon that shot six rounds.

Sam promised Taylor the delivery. And realized then that the 1847 Walker Colt .44 revolver was about to become his next pistol. Sam put pencil to paper and designed the weapon as he reached out to family and friends for money. This was it: the opportunity he had been waiting for.

Christopher Colt, Sam's father—from whom he had been estranged for many years—turned Sam down. So he wrote back, saying, "I regret exceedingly that you cannot lend a helping hand to renew the manufactory of my Patend armes [sic.]." He went on to promise that any money sent would be "dubled [sic] every year while the war lasts."

The family had heard this all before with the debacle in Paterson. Many were now broke because of that venture. Here was Sam once again, the marvelous inventor, the pipe dreamer, screaming from the back of his chuck wagon, selling another vision.

Sam had four prototype weapons made with help and financial aid from Eli Whitney, who had been manufacturing muskets for the Army in his Whitneyville (New Haven), Connecticut, machine shop. Sam didn't realize it—and how could he?—but he was initiating relationships with a group of Connecticut inventors who were about to, on their own, change the world. Around him in the days ahead, as he began to get to know and work with Whitney, were the likes of Amos Whitney, the inventor of the Pratt & Whitney engine, and Elisha Root, who pioneered the art of production milling with his Lincoln Miller milling machine. If Sam wanted to build his company into a global phenomenon, which he certainly had tried to do during those early days in Paterson, he was now mixing company with the minds who could help him get there.

This new group of inventors and manufacturers, however, didn't much care for Sam's style of selling. They didn't appreciate that he lied to customers—especially when it pertained to delivery dates for the products Sam was farming out to these same men. And although Whitney helped Sam with his prototypes, "Whitney and a group of machinists and technicians," Bill Hosley pointed out, "eventually rallied behind the rival Smith and Wesson." In fact, Sam had tried to hire both Edwin Wesson and Eliphalet Remington, two names that would become synonymous with gun-making in the decades to come, to furnish him with the barrels and bullet molds he needed to complete his orders.

Walker kept pressuring Sam to send the weapons, and Sam continued to make promises he couldn't keep. The government even sent Walker north to work with Sam on the weapons, but Walker was quickly ordered back to Texas as hostilities with Mexico increased.

Despite the politics surrounding the manufacturing process, the Walker weapons finally arrived in Texas at Walker's base camp on October 5, 1847. The gun was formally named the Walker-Whitneyville-Colt revolver. Unfortunately, in what must have seemed like another shot in the arm of Colt-inspired bad luck shadowing Sam and his killing machines, Walker was gunned down—a Walker-Colt .44-caliber pistol in his hand at the time—and killed as he and a troop of Rangers made a charge on Huamantla, Tlaxcala, Mexico.

Regardless of Walker's death, however, nothing could stop Sam and his pistols. He had the war behind him, pushing his revolver along at a breakneck pace that even Sam's incredibly lacking management skills could not stifle.

Colt historian Bill Hosley summed up this extremely tenuous period in Sam's rise to fame and fortune, when government contracts were coming in but Sam, forever making promises he could not keep, had nothing but trouble producing the weapons at a rate he needed to, writing, "Cost overruns and production delays piled up . . . as Colt scurried about frantically, pushing, bullying, and pleading with anyone who could help to stop whatever else they had going and get behind this effort."

Sam went to every gun maker and machinist he knew or had heard of asking for help. Wouldn't you know it, Sam repeatedly told friends, no sooner had he auctioned off all of his assets from Paterson, than in came the contracts he had been waiting on all those years in New York.

In letters Sam wrote to Texas during this period, he claimed to have some fifty people working for him at a near nonstop pace, "as late as 11 or 12 o'clock at night."

And then an epiphany—that is, if we are to believe Sam Colt's reasoning for leaving New York: He decided to move to Hartford, Connecticut. Sam saw the potential, he had said, of the insurance capital as the perfect base for making good on the orders placed by the Rangers and American government. Hosley called Sam's move to Hartford (after a brief stay in New Haven) a practical necessity "based more on the availability of credit than on the civic pride Colt later claimed." Nonetheless, Sam had to realize that if you wanted something manufactured, Connecticut was a better place than New York City to get it done. There were foundries and machine shops all over Hartford. Steel was being cast in Springfield, Massachusetts (a twenty-six-mile hike), and several towns in Connecticut. Hartford was centered perfectly between New York City and Boston. But more than any of that, Sam Colt knew, there was money in the city—lots of it.

Sam's early idea was to "establish an Armory in Hartford," the *Hartford Daily Times*, reported. The *Times* was impressed by Sam's machine shop, noting how a large workforce of thirty was manufacturing guns with "ingenious machinery." Money trickled in for Sam, mainly from Elisha Colt, his uncle, an employee of the Hartford Exchange Bank with connections to people who could finance such a massive project. Some later claimed it was all a smoke screen—that Sam's new shop was much, much smaller, set up on paper to assuage those in Texas clamoring for his weapons, and that Sam had, once again, greased the palm of a newspaper reporter to fluff up his image.

"This was one wave Sam Colt was determined to ride," Bill Hosley wrote. "His rapid ascent to the top of the pyramid of American industry had begun."

28

House of Hope

COLT SET UP A SHOP ON PEARL STREET IN DOWNTOWN HARTFORD, JUST up the block from the Old State House and Bushnell Park. He had been living in New Haven since leaving New York in 1847, but was now, at thirty-three, back in the city where he had been born.

The Dutch called Hartford *Huys de Hoop,* or Fort Hope, "the House of Hope," in 1639, after settling in the central Connecticut location on the river. For Sam Colt, Hartford was not only a return to his roots but also a place where all of his dreams would soon come true—that is, once again, not without the cost of major emotional and physical damage. Hartford was undoubtedly the machining capital of the East Coast, if not the country, when Sam set up shop downtown. The building he found was a "medium-sized, three-story" tenement. By the spring of 1848, Sam and his gun-making operation were running at full steam, banking on orders still coming from Texas.

Design flaws and legal battles with Eli Whitney over who owned what quelled production of Sam's pistols somewhat throughout the year 1848, but one thing remained central: Sam had made a firm presence in Hartford on his own. He was still running on borrowed money, for the most part, but every day seemed brighter, and the orders bigger and, most important, continuous. Sam had found a home for his business and the business to fund that home.

Making quite a statement regarding Sam Colt's successful move to Hartford and the expansion of his business, one of his competitors, Edwin Wesson, soon opened for business on Pearl Street when he "erected a three-story brick building" directly across the street.

The banks of the Connecticut River offered Sam's vision of producing weapons in the style of a production line an added advantage: The river was an important means of transportation for steel and various other metals and machinery. In addition, the Connecticut River Valley, from Hartford up through Springfield and Holyoke, Massachusetts, and even points farther north into New Hampshire and Vermont, was "already a centre of arms-making, on its way to becoming . . . America's first centre of machine-based manufacturing." Sam could not have stepped into a better situation, the timing of his gun-manufacturing patents more than adequate. He had finally been able to bring all of his talents together with a public and government not only ready for it, but in great need of what Sam had to offer.

It would be years, though, before Sam turned a profit. One of the defining moments of his business, truly, took place in 1849, when he was "granted a controversial renewal of the patent protection that enabled him to beat back his American competitors." The Mexican War was over by then, a peace treaty signed. But once again, Sam had hit on the timing. The gold rush was booming, hence the "49ers" moniker attached to this period. All those prospectors out west were in great need of handheld protection. The Wild West was underway. Orders continued to roll in.

Sam had learned a few things, too, since his days in Paterson: namely, that relying on one's self in the business world was the only sure means to success. As it were, the government was breathing down his back after several of his competitors had gotten together and lobbied for an investigation into what Martin Rywell called a "monopoly of Colt's basic patent" that Sam had held. The idea behind this was that if Sam held the patents, the government could not manufacture the weapons in its own armories without paying Sam. It seemed unfair.

"The invention for the construction of these arms being patented," President Polk had written to the Senate, "the United States cannot manufacture them at the government armories without a previous purchase of the right to do so."

Sam had gotten smart. He was holding out.

"The right to use this patent by the United States," Polk continued, "the inventor is unwilling to dispose of at a price deemed reasonable."

Sam responded to this with a touch of his signature smarminess, writing, "They are close cronies," meaning Whitney and Colonel George Talcott from the Ordnance Department, who were leading the charge to prevent Sam from continuing, "both are my enemies."

Nothing could stop Sam and his rise this time around, though. The orders—thousands of pistols—continued to come in, and Sam, perhaps not as efficiently as he had promised, continued to fill them.

Years before he moved from Pearl Street to the more spacious Connecticut riverfront building of Solomon Porter's, a four-story, foundry type of structure entirely run by steam-powered engines, Sam wrote a friend in Illinois, extolling some of the lessons he had learned throughout his years:

> *I am working on my own hook and have sole control and management of my business and intend to keep it as long as I live without being subject to the whims of a pack of dam fools and knaves styling themselves a board of directors ... my arms sustain a high reputation among men of brains in Mexico and ... now is the time to make money out of them.*

This time around, there was no board of greedy investors digging into Sam's pockets, siphoning from the company or telling him what to do. Sam had an eye on everything. He was smart in allowing history to dictate how he managed the second incarnation of his gun-manufacturing business. He had even traveled abroad to France, Constantinople, Turkey, and other faraway, exotic places, sensing that war was brewing on the opposite side of the world where his weapons could be sold in larger numbers. He returned from this tour totally rejuvenated, with a suitcase full of weapon orders. In typical Sam Colt fashion, he'd sell arms to the Turks, then turn around, hop over and approach the Russians with a smile, telling them that the other side was arming itself against them. He played one country against the other in order to increase sales. It was a brilliant business tactic producing major results. Sam was no longer relying on one contractor—the U.S. government—for his business; he knew that in order to take the company over the top he needed to branch out, sell to the world, and make a name for himself all over the globe.

The trip abroad, coupled with a homecoming replete with "his pockets bulging with orders," as Jack Rohan put it, was one of the reasons why Sam chose to move across town into Solomon Porter's state-of-the-art manufacturing facility, essentially giving birth to the Colt Arms Manufacturing Company. That little machine shop on Pearl Street could not sustain Sam's rapidly growing business any longer.

Hosley called 1849 Sam's "year of new beginnings."

Still, Sam needed a confidant, a right-hand man. He desperately wanted someone whom he could not only trust, but a man who knew the business of manufacturing better than anyone else. Sam saw the potential. He understood the boom happening within the context of his patents, which had been renewed for an extension of seven years; he accepted that success was his if he made the right business decisions. He may not have put his finger on line production—in the same realm as, say, Henry Ford would in the years to come—but he certainly had a handle on the concept of mass production and what it meant for his business.

Sam found the person he had been searching for in a strange-looking man with close-set eyes, a large nose, and a stern, chiseled gaze of seriousness. Elisha Root would turn out to be a "central figure," as Hosley noted, "in the Colt legend."

Root embodied everything Sam wanted since the time he had started to invent. Sam had known Root since they were kids back in Ware, Massachusetts, and, if we are to believe the folklore surrounding the friendship, it was Elisha Root who had covered Sam with his own body, protecting him, as Sam's first underwater mine experiment blew mud and water into the air in the that little pond near Sam's childhood home.

In a letter to axe maker Root, Sam promised to pay the man what he was making, or a salary that Root thought was "fair and reasonable." Root could name his price, Sam was saying, adding, "the important thing is that you come to me at the earliest possible moment." Time was of the essence. Sam needed a manager on the floor with ideas to increase production. Elisha Root was that person, hands down.

In the end, Sam had "lured [Elisha Root] away from the Collins Axe Company by [giving] him the unheard-of-salary of $5,000 a year," according to Colt biographer Ellsworth Grant. Root had been instrumental in designing a production line factory to produce many of the axes ordered by the 49ers out west. He had mastered a way to produce quality tools in large numbers. That $5,000 salary Root reportedly made was later said to be double what Root was making at Collins.

Either way, Elisha Root and Sam Colt were a perfectly matched team. "He was a clever designer," Anthony Smith wrote of Sam, "and now had a skilled producer as superintendent; the two men's talents were entirely complementary."

Root wasted little time. No sooner had he stepped into Sam's new building near the South Meadows of Hartford along the riverfront than he patented several machines specifically designed to bore long, straight holes through steel (gun barrels). Root looked at business practically or even pragmatically: He was driven by the need to make the job easier for the machinist, mainly because he had come from that line of workers himself. If the job was not too hard or laborious, Root knew the machinist would inadvertently produce more.

What this did for Sam's weapons was drive the price down to nearly half the cost—for the customer—of the old Paterson models. Sam's new manufacturing plant, now with some seventy workers, was producing pistols for twenty-five dollars per weapon. His employees were earning fifteen dollars a week. Colt was paying everyone on time. Things were running about as smoothly as they could.

Still, production was stalled at about one hundred weapons per week off the line, quite a bit off the mark from the orders coming in.

Sam did not stop looking into the future; he began purchasing land around the factory. The idea of shipping his guns straight from the factory to a waiting steamer on the Connecticut River consumed Sam. From factory to customer, it was an incredible vision. So he bought up about five hundred acres of land along Wethersfield Road down toward the banks of the Connecticut River. It was a triangular-shaped tract of acreage leading down to a spacious section of the Connecticut River shoreline between Dutch Point and a lot owned by a man named Henry Barnard (one of Colt's first biographers). In total, Sam bought a third of a mile of property.

In his haste to acquire what many viewed as nothing more than swampland, however, Sam overlooked an important factor according to those nosy townies in Hartford and points beyond. Every spring, when the snows up north melted, the river crested up over the banks and into the city of Hartford, flooding a large section of the landmass Sam had just purchased, thus making it unusable, worthless in the eyes of the public. No one had built on this land because of the flood table. Was Sam Colt an idiot?

Some later claimed Sam was the shrewd businessman in the deal; that he acted nimbly and came across ignorant to get a cheap price on the land (which he did).

"He knew all about those floods," Jack Rohan wrote. Sam had traveled abroad to Holland and seen dikes put up to push the water back from the land as the rivers rose. He envisioned the same thing for his Hartford design. "And if the Dutch could keep the ocean out of their land with dikes, Sam was convinced that he could keep out the Connecticut River by the same method."

Immediately after purchasing the land (some reports claim it was 250 acres at a cost of sixty thousand dollars), Sam began building a dike along that Dutch Point/Barnard track of shoreline (approximately two miles long) to prevent the rising tides from flooding his factory. It was an ingenious idea and concept for its time and place. Sam knew the recorded history of the water table: In 1692, the Connecticut River had crested at twenty-six feet two inches; twenty-seven feet two inches in 1801; twenty-five feet three inches in 1841; and just over twenty-six feet in 1843.

"If his fellow citizens had regarded him as merely stupid when he bought in the South Meadow," Rohan added, "they were convinced he was crazy when he talked of building a dike."

One "tax payer" writing to the *Hartford Times* said, "The attempt to protect the South Meadow by embankments from the rise of the river is like shutting the hatches of a ship down, to keep it afloat, when the bottom is knocked in."

The editor of the paper fired back, saying how difficult a task Sam had set out to accomplish, "but he is a practical man, and is willing and able to take the risk; and in place of grumbling about his project, we ought to allow him to take the risk, and the benefits of the risk, if there be any in it."

Sam put a team to work constructing a dike twenty-five feet high, figuring that any spillover wouldn't matter much in the scope of blocking that initial wall of water and sending it downriver. He figured two-and-a-half stories was enough. Many Hartford residents were astonished by what they presumed to be bravado on Sam's part: that he thought he could thwart what was God's will of making that land along the riverbanks, what Rohan called the Lord's playground, heed to his demands. Sam was effectively playing God here—and many stood in line to protest such an act of blasphemy. The letters came in nonstop to the daily newspapers. Most expressed a concern that Sam had lost his marbles and should be declared insane.

Sam ignored the criticisms as best he could and continued work on a project he knew would take years to complete.

"He thumbed his nose at society and society's way of doing things," firearms historian Herbert G. Houze later said.

What no one knew, of course, was that Sam Colt, by this time, had mastered the art of design, be it a gun, a levee, an underwater mine, whatever he put his mind to. Sam's strength was in the dream—the ideas he conceived were ahead of their time, not by much, but enough to give the appearance that he was suffering from a tremendous bout of selfish, conceited pride.*

"Now, sir," Sam wrote to one newspaper, responding to a nasty letter printed about him and his grand idea to stop water from flooding the South Meadow, "I am not afraid to face the music or create it; and, if the City of Hartford will agree to relieve my property from increased taxation I will bind myself to exclude the river from the South Meadows, and more than all that, I will agree to dike the Connecticut Rover from end to end of the city, so that nothing less than Noah's flood can reach the houses which are now inundated."

The dike Sam was building would ultimately protect only his property—and there was Sam once again flipping his nose to make a point that he didn't give two bits what someone thought of his ideas, only that he be taken for his word. In the coming years, the city of Hartford would rely (and be saved countless times) by a dike spanning the entire contour of the shoreline from Riverside Park north heading south past the Barnard property Sam had purchased.

The other item of business Sam was now talking about as his Hartford business flourished, with orders continuing to come in and profits finally starting to add up, was the foreign market. Sam dreamed of taking over the European market of handguns by building a factory, modeled after his Hartford establishment, on British soil.

The only thing missing in Sam's life at this time was something he had thought little about since JC's death and the fiasco with Caroline Henshaw: a mate. A female companion with whom to share his life—someone who could complement his strengths and put him in line when he needed a swift kick in the arse.

---

* Something should be said here for the many ingenious minds of the world that have created those inventions that we take for granted today: electricity, the combustion engine, the rotating pistol chamber, the production line, etc. These inventors suffered from a form of narcissism that any inventor, envisioning the future, must have in order to move forward in spite of obstacles and public humiliation. We don't achieve greatness by currying favor and giving into public discourse and criticism. Think about someone during this period talking of flying to the moon or simply putting a two-ton piece of steel in the air with wings; that person would have likely been institutionalized.

29

Fortune Smiles

SHE WAS A PLAIN-LOOKING WOMAN, QUITE A BIT YOUNGER THAN SAM. In one photo that has survived the test of time, she is wearing a bonnet, her chubby, round face buried in the head covering, a cloak over her back and shoulders. Yet it was that plainness that Sam's future bride, Elizabeth Jarvis Hart, exuded that made her special and brought out her reverie and elegance. She was confident and feminine; smart and social; articulate and humorous. Elizabeth was the daughter of the Reverend William Jarvis and Elizabeth Hart. She had been born in Saybrook, a Connecticut shoreline community, on October 5, 1826. In 1852, as Sam and Elizabeth got serious about each other, she was just twenty-five years old, Sam then a weathered man of the world at thirty-eight.

"Unlike her entrepreneurial husband-to-be," Bill Hosley, the only historian to have written extensively about Sam's wife, noted, "Elizabeth was raised in affluence and enjoyed considerable social status as a descendant of a distinguished line of religious, military, and political leaders."

This extraordinary woman was the perfect accompaniment to Sam's life of inventing and dreaming and thinking about what was next. Sam had trouble living in the moment. Elizabeth would be the person to ground him; to teach him to enjoy the successes he had worked so hard to achieve; and to break out of his shell that complex man behind the world's most famous pistol.

Elizabeth's pedigree on her mother's side was part of an assembly of royal governors and military leaders from Rhode Island. These were wealthy people, a rippling effect of inheritance that had trickled down into the Jarvis-Hart household in Portland, a riverside community south of Hartford. This was a strong family, their values based in piety, respect, and obligation.

Sam and Elizabeth's paths had almost crossed once in the past, but many years ago. Elizabeth had gone to live with an aunt in Hartford during the 1840s and went to school in town. By then Sam was in New York defending JC and trying to save a sinking ship that was his first gun business. There is no record of exactly where Sam and Elizabeth met, but Hosley is probably right in speculating that their first encounter took place in Newport, Rhode Island, where Elizabeth's family took their summers in the opulence of "New England's fabled resort community."

There is no doubt that Newport was a playground for the rich, powerful, and politically and militarily connected, and that Sam was there during the summers of 1851 and 1852, rubbing elbows with those people who could help him build his business. By this time Sam was known internationally as the foremost gun maker with money flowing as freely as the reams of steel bar heading off one of his production lines.

Sam Colt had, essentially, made it.

"Stunning, poised, well-connected," Hosley added, "Elizabeth Hart Jarvis was obviously swept away by the . . . industrialist, not so much for his wealth . . . but his audacious charm."

Elizabeth grew into her late twenties a naturally gorgeous woman, and it was easy to see why Sam became so affixed to her. She walked with an air of pride and accomplishment her name carried, without coming across as pretentious or snobby. She was a strong-willed woman with dreams of her own—a trait Sam undoubtedly connected with intimately. Some later said it was Sam's "quick, high-tempered, impulsive" nature and his "honest, true, warm-hearted" spirit that won her over. But in Sam, Elizabeth had found a multifaceted man who lived up to the image of the person her family would approve of her marrying.

Looking back at Sam's rise, fall, and then second rise all the way to the top, in addition to what he learned along the way, it's not hard to see that he was a man of good heart and mind, more thrilled with the raw talent it took to sell than with what he was selling. He cared about people—especially his workers. He paid a fair wage, allowed long lunches and breaks, realizing his employees were the backbone of his company and the reason why he was able to thrive. More than that, Sam "never forgot to be generous," Henry Barnard wrote, "and his house was ever open to his friends with genuine hospitality." This included, Barnard added, the less fortunate and the sick, the "aged and the infirm."

By now Sam had that trademark look he would become known for: his thick, dark black hair parted at one o'clock, curls springing down both sides past his ears in bouncy coils; a salt and pepper beard, always perfectly groomed; his gaze determined and serious; a thick, plump face. He dressed in customary tweed three-piece suits, white shirt, and bow tie. He looked the part. Yet inside, Elizabeth found a much deeper, mellower man than one might presume by his outward appearances and zeal for making money. One "passion" of Sam's, Barnard pointed out in his memorial to Mr. and Mrs. Colt, *Armsmear*, a book named after the immaculate and immense estate Sam and Elizabeth were about to begin constructing, was his obsession with flowers, of all things.

"The greenhouses were a source of untold happiness," Barnard wrote.

The man could be as shrewd as one of P. T. Barnum's pitchmen, but according to Barnard, Sam was also as gentle as the New England summer breezes he loved so much, one of the many reasons why Elizabeth was so attracted to him. Sam was a complex character, in a world populated by bitter, cynical men, many mimicking their brethren for fear of going against the grain of society.

"There was a majesty in his forbearance," Barnard added, "that fairly awed me, and I often felt rebuked by it."

——•——

Sam could not escape the past. His own success had bred a following, and part of the distinction of being famous, for good or bad, was that your past affected aspects of your future. In 1853, the soon-to-be mega-famous novelist Herman Melville published a short story, "Bartleby, the Scrivener: A Story of Wall-Street," in *Putnam's Monthly Magazine*. Melville was coming off the heels of a dismal failure, a flop known as *Moby-Dick*, a novel nobody wanted to read.

"Bartleby" is about a lawyer—a rather impulsive, shameful man who is secretive about his own life for the most part and yet likes to meddle in the lives of others as a sense of enjoyment. He's successful and cocky. As his business picks up, he hires a legal aide, a secretary (scrivener). Bartleby is that person, a quiet, bookish type of small man who seems as if he is used to being pushed around by society. The story begins with an introduction:

I am a rather elderly man. The nature of my avocations for the last thirty years has brought me into more than ordinary contact with what would seem an interesting and somewhat singular set of men, of whom as yet nothing that I know of has ever been written:—I mean the law-copyists or scriveners.

He believes that the "easiest way to life is the best." It is a superb narrative voice: believable, authentic, literary, and entirely convincing. The lawyer is, in a sense, a voyeur, holing up in an office, watching the comings and goings of others in the same office, hiring people in order to study them, maybe even mess with their minds on some level.

In John Caldwell Colt's life, the impetus for Melville's story, the narrator would be Asa Wheeler.

Melville was not only inspired to write the story by JC's trial, but even mentions JC in the story. There's a tense scene between the narrator and Bartleby, who has refused to do what is being asked of him and, we come to find out, has been living in the office. He turns out to be a strange man of a ubiquitous nature. The narrator and Bartleby have entered into a dilemma and argument, and the narrator becomes unnerved. He finds himself at one point facing the realization that he is alone with Bartleby (a man they all thought they knew but had perhaps misjudged) in the office. Melville writes how the lawyer in the story (the narrator) identifies with JC's situation:

I was now in such a state of nervous resentment that I thought it but prudent to check myself at present from further demonstrations. Bartleby and I were alone. I remembered the tragedy of the unfortunate Adams and the still more unfortunate Colt in the solitary office of the latter; and how poor Colt, being dreadfully incensed by Adams, and imprudently permitting himself to get wildly excited, was at unawares hurried into his fatal act—an act which certainly no man could possibly deplore more than the actor himself. Often it had occurred to me in my ponderings upon the subject that had that altercation taken place in the public street, or at a private residence, it would not have terminated as it did. It was the circumstance of being alone in a solitary office, upstairs, of a building entirely unhallowed by humanizing domestic associations—an uncarpeted office, doubtless, of a dusty, haggard sort of appearance;—this it must have been, which greatly helped to enhance the irritable desperation of the hapless Colt.

Now two writers, both of whom would become household names and literary giants, had immortalized John Colt and the Colt family name forever in literature. Sam could not escape the tragedy or leave it behind, no matter how successful he became or how long he stayed out of New York City.

———

Work had continued on what was to become Colt's Armory, "the largest private Armory in the world" at the time, according to every Colt historian. This was not a mere building to house a production company; it was a vision of a future company that could produce weapons along a production line of machines doing one job all day and night long. More than that, Sam was planning an empire built around this armory: a city of its own, "Coltsville," it was to be called. "The compound was the most ambitious experiment in economic development and social engineering in the two-hundred-year-plus history of Connecticut's capital city," Hosley noted.

Sam saw a library, general store, technical college, housing, a post office, and just about everything a city would need to thrive on its own. George Pullman, maker of the Pullman railcar, would accomplish this same feat in Illinois, but not until the 1880s. Sam's city was a dream he'd had since childhood, said Colonel Henry Deming. As Hosley pointed out, though, Colt was inspired mostly by that failure in Paterson to control every aspect of his business. This was no boyhood dream; Sam knew that if he kept his business, and everything he needed to sustain it, in close proximity, he could watch over it all more closely and never lose sight of the end goal: total global dominance (which he had then anyway).

So many different opportunities and projects of Sam's were taking place that it was hard for him to be in one place for a long period of time. He'd pinch himself and wake up in London, overseeing his vision of opening there; then weeks later be in Russia, mixing it up with the czar; then in New York conducting business with investors; in Newport keeping the elite happy; and attending church services in Middletown at the Jarvis-Hart's Episcopal Church, just over the river from Portland, where the Jarvises now resided.

As his assets grew and cash flow increased, with "profit margins high" and his relationship with Elizabeth heading toward the altar, Sam never slowed down, traveling the world, making friends with emperors, dukes, and political leaders around the globe. Sam's weapons had helped countries win wars and others defend themselves against hostile takeovers and invasions. He sent machinery and workers to his London plant, where production didn't run as smoothly as it did back home, but was operating, nonetheless.

And yet all was not blissful euphoria for Sam during this central period of his life, when his ideas began to manifest into the reality he always envisioned they would. One of his weapons would be responsible for killing the daughter of America's preeminent novelist Harriet Beecher Stowe in Hartford; and, in 1854, as work on his dike was nearly complete, the river crested at nearly twenty-nine feet, flooding his entire factory and the surrounding grounds.

This flood, a foreshadowing of many more bad things to come, brought with it a second wave of tragedy that was about to take over Sam's life. He'd had tremendous successes. Yes, the London, England, plant fell victim to English laws, bad management, and political pressure, but his life since JC's death and the birth of his son, Samuel (now in Germany with Caroline Henshaw, receiving plenty of money from "Uncle Sam"), had been complete and free of much heartbreak. Colt Manufacturing's numbers were on the rise annually; his workforce grew each year by dozens of new employees. But the flood proved that even as Sam had forecast the unavoidable, his dike a means to prevent this sort of inevitable force of Mother Nature, no matter what he did or how much money he spent (or made), he could not escape from underneath that dark cloud that seemed to hover over the Colt family name.

—～✦～—

The Colt Armory was more than a factory or even the industrial capital of Connecticut. Sam had created a precedent for mass manufacturing of the future. Built along Van Dike Avenue, an area buttressed by the shoreline of the Connecticut River and Sam's dike, this incredible factory was on the cutting edge. Just across the street were the residences of the armorers, Colt's workforce. From there, heading up Shamrock Avenue, on both sides, north and south, was the immense property accompanying Sam and Elizabeth's mansion and the wide-open Armsmear grounds.

"Its extent," Henry Barnard observed, "is about one-third of a mile broad and two-thirds long." The mansion, perched up on a hill overlooking the river and Colt Armory, was fenced in by Wawarme Avenue to the south, Wethersfield Road (later to become an avenue) in back (east), with Charter Oak Avenue (to the north) closing it all in. This was Sam's vision from the beginning: a picturesque canvas of land surrounding his plant that he could begin to fortify with statues and greenhouses and plants and kids and anything else his heart desired; he added a lake, pond, bridges, flower and fruit houses, groves and graves, a swan and duck pond. Still, the crowning jewel of the entire estate was without a doubt Armsmear, the magnificent manor he and Elizabeth built. There were many religious reminders throughout the estate, Sam himself becoming quite the pious soul as he and Elizabeth became intertwined emotionally, spiritually, and physically.

Such a devout representation of the afterlife and a firm Christian belief found about the estate would be comforting to Sam and Elizabeth in the days ahead: because death and bereavement were about to become an annual part of their lives in unexpected ways.

30

Life Springs and Death Blows

A LONG COURTSHIP WAS FINALLY EFFECTUATED IN THE MARRIAGE OF Sam and Elizabeth on a hot, hazy, and humid New England afternoon, June 5, 1856. By that time work on Armsmear had been in full swing, sections of the enormous mansion built and rebuilt, torn down and reconstructed again several times, according to Henry Barnard's eyewitness account. The wedding ceremony was held inside the parlor of the Jarvis family's new Middletown residence by the same Episcopal bishop who had married Elizabeth's parents decades earlier. The night prior to the wedding, Sam had indulged his hundreds of Colt employees and many of his close friends and business confidants in what Bill Hosley called a "glorified bachelor's party."

The wedding was quintessential Sam Colt extravagance—the entire wedding party sailed from the armory in Hartford downriver to Middletown aboard the steamboat *Washington Irving*. As the boat, which had been "draped in bunting and flags" for the occasion, left the shoreline docking area near the armory, a "grand salute of rifles was fired from the cupola of the Armory." This was Sam showing his friends and family the worldly experience he had accumulated throughout his years of traveling abroad; he wanted them, as much as himself, to savor this moment, plant memories in the minds of those he loved in order to celebrate what was a union Sam (and definitely Elizabeth) believed had been made possible only through Divine Intervention.

Some estimated Elizabeth's dress and supplementary jewelry to cost in the neighborhood of $8,000, an extraordinary sum of money then, all of which was provided by Sam. The cake stood six feet high, with pistols and rifles made of an early form of fondant, and a young colt made of the same sugary substance capping the top. The reception was held in New York at the St. Nicholas, one of the most spectacular and expensive hotels in the city. The next morning, Sam and Elizabeth, along with Elizabeth's sister Hetty and her brother Richard, set sail for Europe, a translator Sam had used during previous trips by their side. Sam wanted to show off his new bride to the world. They ended up spending a month in London. Then the honeymoon became, essentially, a tour only a princess might be expected to take: Belgium, Bavaria, Vienna, Holland, and Russia. Wherever they went, Mr. and Mrs. Colt were treated as though they were the king and queen of America, most of the time greeted with warmer receptions than any diplomat of Sam's day.

Money was never an object, obviously—Sam knew, as well as most of the country had been anticipating by then, that America was heading toward a civil war, which was only going to send production and profit for Colt Manufacturing into an entirely new stratosphere.

Armsmear was completed in early 1857. The main structure and living quarters were modeled after the Italian villas Sam had visited throughout his extensive tours of Europe. One magazine called the estate "long, grand, impressive, contradictory, beautiful, strange . . . [I]t is a little Turkish among other things, with domes, pinnacles, and light, lavish ornamentation, yet . . . the feeling is English."

Many of the home decor influences Sam had witnessed throughout his years were put into this one impressive and opulent mansion that stood up to many of those he and Elizabeth had visited in Newport. This was Sam's master creation: an empire like none of its kind in Hartford, with sprawling grounds, horses, fruit trees imported from faraway places, sculptures and paintings and statues to remind Sam of how far he had come in the world and, also, how sophisticated his tastes now were. There can be no doubt this piece of property and the mansion that sat on it had been in Sam's head since his days of blowing water spouts in Ware. The entire estate—inside and out—was an homage, essentially, to just about every country Sam had sold weapons to and befriended. There was Oriental influence, English, Russian, Swedish, German, and Italian.

"Armsmear," Martin Rywell wrote, nailing the tone and feel of the place, "was a mold into which content could be poured."

Herbert Houze, in an interview later, added, "His stage was not Hartford; his stage was the world."

Sam had also bestowed some of his foreign influence on the Colt Armory by placing a large blue, onion-shaped dome, painted with gold stars, like those Russian and Arab buildings made legendary on the other side of the world he had seen during several trips, sitting on a series of Pantheon-like columns, standing atop the main armory building, which could be seen from just about anywhere in the city, and for miles if one traveled up or down the Connecticut River. On top of the onion dome was the symbol of the man who'd had it constructed: a gold orb underneath the statue of a "rampant colt" stallion, standing up on its hind legs, embodying the image of the weapon that had made its inventor a millionaire many times over.*

All seemed to be going well, this new Colt union a force to be reckoned with throughout the world. It almost seemed too good to be true for Sam—and maybe it was, because an avalanche of misfortune was just around the corner. Elizabeth gave birth prematurely to their first child, a son, on February 24, 1857.

"For ten months," Elizabeth later wrote, "the bright, loving little baby [Samuel Jarvis] made new sunshine in our happy home; but when he had made himself so tenderly beloved, he was, after a short but painful illness, borne so patiently, gathered into the arms of the Good Shepherd."

Elizabeth talked about their home—all of that wonder and grandeur surrounding them, the trappings of the fame and fortune Sam had acquired at their fingertips—becoming a "very, very desolate" place to be without the child's bubbly spirit around to liven it up.

After losing himself in a legal battle to keep his patents, filing for new patents on various new models of his pistols, Sam continued to build Coltsville, that small city around the armory, as Elizabeth later called it. They tried again to have another child. One year later, on November 24, 1858, "a little son was given . . . and home grew joyous again in the smile of the bright baby boy," whom they named for the child's two great-grandfathers, Caldwell Hart.

When no problems arose with the birth of little Caldwell, or soon thereafter, they tried again, Sam's new vision now including a herd of

---

* This incredible onion dome still stands today, 150-plus years after its designer placed it on top of the Colt Armory. Many of us in the state—and even tourists and those just passing through—drive by it weekly without as much as a second thought; yet the beauty of this symbol is in its history. The dome, in my opinion, represents all that Sam Colt dreamt of and envisioned as he settled in Hartford, Connecticut, and began to realize that time was catching up with him. He also had several similar domes (various sizes) placed atop Armsmear.

children following him around this massive piece of land that was his and Elizabeth's home. "Dark-eyed baby Lizzie," as Elizabeth later called her, was "the pet of all," no one more so than her doting father, who adored his daughter as though she was the only girl in the world.

The family vacationed in Nantucket and Martha's Vineyard that summer, 1860, Sam chartering a boat to take them from the armory grounds, downriver, into the Atlantic Ocean, and onto Cape Cod and its islands. He had what he wanted: a lovely wife and family. He was content. Caldwell was growing into a strong boy, Lizzie now just a few months old, right behind her big brother, the indelible "little queen" of the family. They had lost a son, but gained two children. Business was never better.

Yet no sooner had they returned from the Cape that summer than Lizzie fell ill.

"[W]hen the chill October winds were blowing," Elizabeth wrote years later, "our little Lizzie 'folded her pale hands' and closed the dear eyes forever."

This death, so sudden and so soon after the first Colt child, hit Sam "a death-blow," Elizabeth said, at the core of "his life-springs."

Devastated didn't begin to explain how hard Sam took Lizzie's death. On the day of the funeral, Sam stood stunned as Lizzie's body, covered with flowers, was presented in the house for mourners to pay final respects. The "agony" on Sam's gaze, Elizabeth later recalled, as the gun maker stood and "looked for the last time on the face so lovely in death" was intense, angry, deep, and tragic. Sam had entered a place of melancholy he had never been.

After paying his respects to Lizzie in private, Sam stood and looked out into the front meadow of the estate through a window, stunned, not knowing what to do. Had these deaths, so many now (with JC and his sister Margaret included), been part of some sort of celestial price for arming the world and putting killing machines into the hands of common men?

Soon, a "little train of mourners . . . slowly and sadly," Elizabeth remarked, walked toward the immaculate and grand entrance to Armsmear.

"The prayers were said," Elizabeth recalled, "the dust was given to dust by him who had poured the water of baptism on her fair young brow, and sealed her with the Saviour-seal."

After the funeral, Sam took a portrait of Lizzie and sat with it in his lap, "convulsed with such grief as one seldom sees."

The death weakened Sam greatly: physically, mentally, spiritually. It wrecked him.

"He," Elizabeth wrote, "who had borne unflinchingly every ill and burden of life, sank down before the open grave of the guileless babe, and for weeks did not leave his room."

That illness of the soul Sam suffered manifested into a physical fight. For the next three months, Sam stayed home battling gout, a debilitating disease, in which acid builds up in the joints of the body causing excruciating pain. Yet he had learned an important lesson from the past: The way to deal with severe pain—emotional or physical—was to lose yourself in your work. He had managed the company from Armsmear "when his body was suffering so unspeakably," Elizabeth noted, but his "mind and will were as strong as ever."

Hoping that a "more genial climate" would help calm his gout, but also hoping to get away from Armsmear and the business for a while, in February 1861, Sam, Elizabeth, and Caldwell sailed to Cuba. Sam had mentioned that the hot springs in Cuba might help with the pain. But he surely needed to just get out from underneath the dark shadow of Armsmear and the Colt Armory.

Caldwell was two years old by now and growing into quite the darling of his father's eye. Sam instilled the beauty and grace of sailing and commanding a ship in his son, showing him, even at a young age, that there was a certain freedom and spiritual reward in allowing the wind to be your guide and source of travel. Caldwell had sailing in his blood (Sam's grandfather), and the child was absolutely captivated by the sea.

Of course, there would be no rest for Sam upon his return: The Civil War had broken out as expected and, as Elizabeth explained, the war "brought to him increased cares, and while his physical condition required entire rest, he was making arrangements for doubling the capacity of his already enormous Armory."*

---

* As much as I could, I've resisted commenting on the political ramifications of Sam's gun business, understanding that it is a subplot to his life worthy of its own volume. Yet I want to point out here that there were rumors buzzing from one side of the country to the other as the Civil War broke out that Sam was selling his weapons to both sides. Some even went so far as to say Sam was a Southern sympathizer. But Sam's record, as Herbert Houze pointed out in 2006, speaks for itself. Sam armed the Union. He opposed slavery, "even bringing in a Boston abolitionist pastor to lecture his employees" (see Leavenworth, Jesse, "Arms, Art and the Man . . .," *The Hartford Courant,* September 20, 2006, p. D1).

It's quite clear the division in the country during this period took a toll on Sam; he wasn't thrilled about the expansion of his business based on American blood being shed. Elizabeth reported that on many nights the burden of what she called the "distracted state of the country" wore her husband down considerably. Sam was not an old man by any means at forty-six, but his body, day after day, began to give out on him. Still, within all of the ills he suffered, on top of the stressful periods of growing the business and losing two children, Sam kept his hat hung in Washington where he knew the path toward the future of his business would be blazed.

"He was always a democrat," Elizabeth said, "and a firm supporter of the policy advocated by [Stephen] Douglas, who was also his warm personal friend."

Another good friend of Sam's, a man Elizabeth did not name, made an interesting statement about him, saying, "Had he received a military education [hence the Colonel Colt moniker he sometimes was given], he would have been one of the greatest generals the world has ever seen."

This idea, that Sam Colt, who was often called Colonel Sam, could have made a name for himself as a military leader embodies the spirit of who the man was: Whatever Sam did, he would have strived to be the best and the one man in that field people remembered. This leadership quality, an inherent desire he had to achieve the pinnacle of success, staring adversity and failure in the face, was part of the complex Sam Colt DNA pattern. There have been very few men like him in history—innovators who, faced with one disappointment after the next, steadfastly dug their heels in and persevered. When the odds were against Sam Colt, it seemed to bring out the best in him. And yet, when it came to raising a family and weathering the darkness life brought his way, Sam could do no more than accept God's will, certainly in his and Elizabeth's pious sense of life, whatever it might be.

───～───

Elizabeth gave birth to Henrietta Selden, their second daughter, on May 23, 1861. This birth brought joy to Sam's heart and began to fill part of the void that Lizzie's death had left behind.

"Like little Lizzie," Elizabeth said, "she, too, at an early age, showed some absorbing love for her father, rejoicing his saddened heart with new hopes for the future."

The previous winter of suffering through bouts of gout had weakened Sam significantly. Losing Lizzie during that time and dedicating any free time he had to building up the business, making sure it was able to sustain the rapid growth it had been undergoing, was a major part of Sam's long days and nights. Indeed, Colt Manufacturing, the preeminent maker of pistols in the world, grew substantially during this period. Orders for pistols in 1856, for example, ended at 24,053, increasing by nearly 15,000 the following year, a short dip two years later, but then rebounding to a whopping 69,655 in 1861, with the addition of 3,193 orders for a rifle Sam had been perfecting. This number of pistol orders in 1862 would nearly double to 111,676, mainly on the strength of the Civil War, with an additional 8,500 muskets Sam was now making heading out the door. What drove profit margins more than anything was Sam's mastery of the production line that Elisha Root had initiated. Sam had developed the production line into a process: several machines dedicated to one particular job, all producing an end product.

Within all of that success, however, an underlying layer of gloom continually penetrated Sam and Elizabeth's lives. As Elizabeth herself later put it, even when that summer of 1861 brought with it so much good news and happiness, the "children bright and well, with almost every earthly wish gratified," a tempest of misfortune was there brewing on the horizon, one like that of which Mr. and Mrs. Colt had not yet seen. Later, Elizabeth put this period of their lives into perspective by asking one very pertinent question: "How could we dream of the fearful storm so soon to burst upon us?"

━━━

Sam caught a terrible cold that Christmas, which brought about "a slight attack" of that nagging gout condition he had been suffering from for well over a year. The gout was beating Sam; he had trouble admitting it, but it was disabling and taking him off his feet more than he was able to be his old self, hitting the road, selling guns, watching over the day-to-day operations of his enormous armory. According to Elizabeth, this particular bout was not as painful as those in the past, but had saddled Sam to bed, nonetheless, where he stayed throughout the Christmas holiday.*

The New Year came and with it Sam's health returned enough so that he was able to receive visitors. Sam had led a life up until then that was full enough to fill ten lives. There was an eerie sense of an end hovering there in the house that winter, like a bad aroma they couldn't get rid of, as Elizabeth and Sam managed to spend as much time as they could together, Elizabeth taking care of Sam while tending to the children's needs.

Sam took a visitor one day. The gentleman was an old friend of his grandfather. Sam was overjoyed to be able to sit up in bed and speak to the man.

"[He] seemed so proud to show him his boy of three summers and the little fairy-tale baby Hetty, whose bright sunny eyes and pretty curls was all hearts," Elizabeth later wrote.

By January 4, 1862, Sam was well enough to "sit up all day." Though he felt strong and probably could have with help, he was unable to walk anymore. Elizabeth and the Armsmear staff were confident that each day brought with it renewed fortitude and healing for Sam. He was a fighter. If there was one character trait that drove Sam Colt it was his tenacity. This disease would not beat him, Elizabeth and the staff insisted on believing. Elizabeth was a smart woman who had herself faced life's challenges with courage. Although she did not want to admit it, she knew what was happening.

"[O]ur hopes were very sanguine for his speedy restoration to health," she remembered later.

On January 4, Elizabeth went out. She did not say where. By now, Elizabeth Colt was known as the matriarch of Connecticut's capital city. Some would later call her "the queen . . . of Hartford society," and this was indeed Mrs. Colt's future. Elizabeth was not a woman who would stand behind her important husband fanning herself on hot days, wearing white gloves, a puffy dress, jewels and her hair up in a bun, afraid of saying things that might upset anyone of power; she was her own woman, had her own dreams, and certainly spoke her mind when she thought it prudent.

When she returned the staff rushed to greet Elizabeth. In her absence, she was soon told, Sam had requested a Bible. The book Sam had asked for wasn't just any Bible; it was the one his father had given him as a child.

---

* It is likely that either Sam lied about how much pain he was in was or had gotten so used to living with that pain by then that he was numb to it.

Sam wanted to fasten a piece of poetry he had cut out from a newspaper the previous summer to one of the pages in the Bible. He had a habit of placing things he had read that inspired him into his Bible.

But a poem—it seemed so unlike Sam Colt to do this.

This poem—"What! Leave my Church of England!"—"must have," Elizabeth remarked later, "touched an answering chord in his soul, as he had no particular fondness for poetry."

Sam didn't look so good that night as Elizabeth sat by his bedside and read to him as he fell sleep. As he drifted, Elizabeth, "noticing that he was much flushed, without saying anything," washed his face with a warm bath cloth and "brushed his beautiful curls."

As she continued with this loving gesture, Sam opened his eyes. "Thank you," he said, "for knowing just what I wanted."

The next morning, Sam woke to a smile. He was "quiet and cheerful," Elizabeth noted later. She sat and they spoke for quite a long time.

At one o'clock, several servants assisted Sam out of bed and helped him to dress. He wanted to spend some time with the kids.

While playing with the children, Sam had a momentary—or was it?—lapse of reasoning and lost his senses.

"His mind began to wander," Elizabeth explained.

What's clear here from the writings Elizabeth left behind about this day and those that followed is that Sam's level of consciousness and his intellect were breaking down in front of her and the children. He was not in his right frame of mind. Yet the truth remained that Elizabeth believed Sam was as "conscious of the change as" she had been. They understood what was happening.

Both considered the idea that it was a temporary condition, as it had been in the past; but there was no denying that Sam's health was failing. So they sent a telegraph to Sam's old friend, Dr. John F. Gray, in New York, summoning him to Armsmear.

"It was a painful evening to all," Elizabeth remembered.

Sam became even quieter the next morning, but "awoke calm and in his right mind."

Dr. Gray arrived. It was noon, January 7, 1862, a Tuesday. That night, a marvelous change in Sam's demeanor came over him; and, "for two or three hours he continued talking almost uninterruptedly and incoherently, when gradually it all passed off and reason resumed her sway."

The gout had entered into Sam's brain somehow and affected every sense. He was, slowly, losing his faculties.

Then a remarkable sense of peace—which would turn out to be the last—washed over the gun maker. It was as if Sam had been allowed one final moment of sanguinity with his family.

"[T]he clouds were lifted," Elizabeth wrote so beautifully, "and he looked off into the great unknown future with a calm serenity and . . . [b]eautifully and touchingly" spoke.

"Death is very near," Sam told his wife. "I trust in God's love and mercy. I have strived to do right according to my sense of right, though all things look differently to me now with death so near. I forgive all who have injured me."

He paused, then said something else, which spoke to a belief Sam had always maintained that people were against him, and his enemies had never stopped pursuing the violence they believed he was responsible for promoting with his killing machines. He explained to Elizabeth that God knew "how deeply he [Sam] had been wronged" throughout his life "in some shameful instances," but He also "knows, too, how much that forgiveness implied." Sam was not leaving the mortal world holding any grudges, in other words. He wanted Elizabeth to know that none of it mattered to him anymore. In spite of his detractors, he had succeeded in life *and* in business. He could die in peace.

In those hours when death closed in on Sam and he felt himself slipping further away each moment, he spoke of the children, "confiding our boy," Elizabeth recalled, "to my tenderest care and love; bidding me to keep that tender little one, so soon to be fatherless, from all evil—to teach him all the good—with the solemn earnestness only those can command who stand between the seen and the unseen, the living and the dead."

Within this whispered discourse regarding the children, Sam was able to make a rather startling statement, if Elizabeth's memory of this moment can be trusted: "Our bright, sweet baby is going, too," Sam muttered in a whisper, "and doesn't need to be kept from evil." It was as if Sam was speaking to "the Shepherd of the lambs," as Elizabeth referred to Jesus Christ, and then relating those prophetic thoughts back to Elizabeth in the exact moment Sam had received them from the Lord. The child, Henrietta, Sam went on to say, "soon would gather her untried soul into His own fold, to be blessed forever."

Sam bid his wife, whom he called "faithful" and "loving" in those final hours, farewell, "asking [her] to carry out all his plans so far as [she] might." He then motioned for Elizabeth to draw close so he could kiss her one last time. As he did this, Sam said, "When God wills, you should go to me beyond the grave, where partings never enter."

Elizabeth called it "reason," Sam's senses coming back to him for that brief moment, as he spoke again, finally uttering softly, "It is all over now."

Sam did not die that night. Or the next.

"He lingered on," as his wife put it, "through two more days of pain, with now and then a gleam of hope."

It was Friday morning, January 10, "when this great soul," Elizabeth called him, paying respectful reverence to the man she loved so much, "passed away to the untold mysteries of the spirit-land."

If Sam had mentioned his illegitimate son in Germany during all of what he shared with Elizabeth during those final days of his life, she never spoke of it. Caroline Henshaw had married Prussian nobleman and army officer Baron Frederick Von Oppen in 1857, a move that sent the baron's father into a whirlwind of bitterness toward the couple, the old man promising the baron he would be cut out of the family will and disinherited all together. Caroline had sent Sam a letter mentioning how the resentment between father and son had caused her great grief. She even asked Sam for a loan of $1,000 so the baron could leave the army. Sam had been sending Caroline, who had changed her name to Julia Leicester by then, money to educate and care for the child, who would have been twenty years old at the time of Sam's death—and now considering a move to the United States.

31

His Father's Son

THEY FORMED A PROCESSION LINE OF SOME 1,500 MEN LONG. "THE armorers," Elizabeth Colt called them. Sam's entire workforce, the armory closed for the day, each wearing a black armband, filed up the hill through the Colt's front yard. They walked slowly by the ponds and statues and gardens and exotic fruit trees Sam had imported from all over the world, and ended up in the elaborate horseshoe driveway, forming a line into Armsmear. They were here, of course, to pay final respects to a man they had looked up to and admired for so many years. All the flags in Hartford flew at half-staff on this day. The state was in mourning. An iconic figure had passed away. Carved on the side of the casket each mourner passed were the words that meant the most to Sam's widow: "Kindest husband, father, and friend, *adieu*." These same words would grace the front of Sam's gravestone.

The funeral was held on January 14, 1862, three o'clock sharp. Beyond the hundreds of employees from Colt Manufacturing, thousands of additional mourners passed through Armsmear for three straight days honoring the great manufacturing tycoon. Armsmear was packed to capacity most of that time. Although no one ever said why, the only soul that seemed to be missing was James Colt, Sam's brother.

"The funeral of Samuel Colt," Ellsworth Grant wrote, "America's first great munitions maker, was spectacular—certainly the most spectacular ever seen in Hartford, Connecticut . . . like the last act of a grand opera."

When the time came, Sam's casket was carried out to a gravesite on the grounds next to his children, Samuel Jarvis and Lizzie. Caldwell Colt, Sam's young boy, stood by his mother's side throughout the days of mourning. Elizabeth, the anchor of this broken family, was there to comfort the boy as best she could amid her own grief. A rancorous salute with musket fire was stricken from the ceremony at the last minute because Henrietta had taken critically ill.

"Hartford knew that day it had lost one of its noblest sons," Elizabeth later wrote. "[A]nd all felt then that he who that day had fallen was among those whose place could never be filled."

The tragic drama that had become Elizabeth Colt's life would not let up. Just ten days after Sam passed, little Henrietta, a fighter in her own right, was buried next to Lizzie and her father after she succumbed to illness. Sam had spoken of Henrietta's death during his final hours, giving Elizabeth that warning, and now, Rohan wrote, "His prophecy had been fulfilled."

Elizabeth had been pregnant at the time of Sam's death. It was not long after the funeral that she miscarried the child. And yet the worst was not over. Two years later, in 1864, the Colt Armory burnt to the ground—a fire that gutted the place, destroying machinery valued somewhere near $800,000 and "stock" of about half that value. More than those replaceable items, the fire had also taken "several remarkable original models" of Sam's weapons.

"No one learned the cause," Anthony Smith observed, "and inevitably there was talk of Confederate arson with the war still raging, but the presence of cotton waste near driving pulleys, and of floorboards deeply soaked in oil, were much more probable."

Sam was not a man who had believed in insurance and had never purchased a policy on the Colt building. Elizabeth being the more practical of the two, had, however, after his death, yet it was not enough to cover the cost of rebuilding. The business was said to be worth what would amount to about $200 million in today's money.

Elizabeth knew that she could not run the Colt Armory after she rebuilt the factory to "a facsimile of that destroyed . . . on the old foundations," this time entirely fireproof. Elisha Root died in 1865. So Elizabeth looked to William Buel Franklin, a man who knew the likes of Ulysses Grant and Thomas "Stonewall" Jackson, to run the company. Elizabeth was not ready to sell just yet, but she did turn over control to Franklin.

This opened up the opportunity for Elizabeth to focus her efforts on what meant the most to her tattered and torn heart: building a church. As Caldwell grew, Elizabeth saw to every detail while designing and building what was to become the Church of the Good Shepherd, right there on the Colt grounds.

She had come from a family of religious men and women, a devout Christian all her life. This church, built mainly for the armory and its workforce, was something that gave Elizabeth great joy as she mourned the loss of four kids and a husband within five years of her marriage.

Bill Hosley called the church "an artistic and technological marvel." Indeed, this massive stone building, with echoes of those basilicas in Europe Sam had visited and admired, was a place of worship to some 145 parents and children by the time its doors opened. Elizabeth also had a sewing school set up in a section of the parish so the children could learn how to make their own clothing. She wanted the people in whom Sam had put so much of his pride—his workers—to have the opportunity and an ability to fend for themselves out in the world. Self-reliance had always been one of Sam's virtues. Elizabeth would honor that by teaching it to those less fortunate.

The stained-glass "Apostle Windows" were imported and placed inside the church by 1868, making this marvelous edifice more than a holy structure of religious reflection and celebration; it was an assembly of immense and engaging aesthetics, bringing awe to those who viewed it for the first time. Elizabeth had built the church with her own money (there was never a mortgage on the building). This was her gift to the community of Coltsville and the surrounding Hartford region.

The three main stained-glass windows—the "emotional and artistic focal point of the church"—were designed by Elizabeth. These three windows were dedicated to Sam, Samuel Jarvis, Elizabeth Jarvis, and Henrietta. The souls Elizabeth had lost.*

Written along the frame of the windows was a passage Elizabeth had penned herself: "The Lord which is in the midst of the Throne shall Feed them and Lead them unto Living Fountains of Waters and God shall wipe away all Tears from their Eyes."

---

* It has been said that Elizabeth had Sam's face installed in the place of Christ's on one of the stained-glass windows depicting the crucifixion, but this does not sound like something Elizabeth, pious and devout as she was, would have done. Beyond a conversation I had with a journalist who was certain he had seen this, but could not recall where inside the building, I have not seen or heard of any additional proof. The fact that these windows were dedicated to Sam and the kids might have fueled that later speculation. What's significant about the dedication, senior warden of the church Jack Hale (circa 2010) told me, is the fact that Elizabeth had the window inscribed to "my husband, Sam Colt." First and foremost, in Elizabeth's view, Sam was a husband. "I had a cynical view of this once," said Hale, "and felt that Elizabeth was trying to rehabilitate Sam's image." But no more, Hale admitted. He now understands that it was because of her love for the man Sam Colt turned out to be.

With this church, Elizabeth felt she had turned things around for herself and her child; life could go on with meaning. And for some years, indeed, things were better—or, perhaps, stable. Collie, as Caldwell became known, celebrated his twenty-first birthday on November 24, 1879, and Elizabeth spared no expense in inviting "all the prominent society people of Hartford," an article in the *New York Times* said a day after the extravaganza. If the *New York Times* was writing about your birthday party, you came from an important pedigree. After all, Caldwell was the sole heir to the Colt throne. The party, which had been planned months ahead of time, began at 8:30 and ended somewhere near midnight. Elizabeth had ordered reams of stunning flowers and decked the mansion in tropical plants from one end to the other. The tables were festooned with gifts for guests and floral arrangements any bride would be jealous of. The Colt Armory Band and Adkin's Quadrille Orchestra provided the entertainment for the night. Above the entrance where each guest entered Armsmear upon arrival was a large number 21 done up in red roses. There was even a point during the night when "a group of young ladies and gentleman in costume, their hair powdered white, descended the staircase arm in arm singing Mother Goose rhymes," Ellsworth Grant reported.

The party was festive and ostentatious, *the* place to be seen on that night. All for Caldwell Jarvis Colt, who was preparing to take off to a life at sea as a yachtsman. Collie wanted to race those magnificent boats, which he had developed an obsession for throughout the years. Those Newport summers were imbedded in the boy. Sam had taught him to appreciate the sea and its value.

"Collie grew up a gay blade," said Jack Rohan, "a yachtsman of high repute and a sportsman of distinction . . . [and] showed neither taste nor talent for the business of his father."

Caldwell soon became the commodore of the Larchmont Yacht Club, a very private and very exclusive club located in Larchmont, New York, just over the Connecticut border in Westchester County. The boats competed mainly on Long Island Sound. Caldwell was the talk of the club, with his perfectly trimmed J-shaped (mutton chop) sideburns that connected to his mustache, penetrating blue eyes, self-assurance, demure and sleek manner. Caldwell personified the image of what a (rich) man against the sea looked like at the time. Sam would have surely been proud of his boy.

Caldwell named his yacht the *Dauntless* and, according to Ellsworth Grant, Caldwell's deck parties "were wild enough to inspire tales of orgies."

The ship was a 121-foot schooner, "luxuriously furnished," built in Mystic, Connecticut, and first owned by none other than James Gordon Bennett, founder of the *New York Herald*, a newspaper that had not written fondly of Caldwell's dead uncle, JC.

Caldwell had graduated from Yale. He was a smart kid, his heart in all the right places. He had a future ahead of him that rivaled any boy from the wealthiest and most prestigious families of the world. Like his father before him, Caldwell Colt had found his passion and dedicated his life to pursuing it. Yet, also like his father, he would not live long enough to see the true immensity of his desires come to fruition.

32

A Final Blow

MOST NEW ENGLANDERS BELIEVED THAT AS THE WINTER SEASON OF 1888 drew to a close in March, the worst was over. In fact, that winter had been milder than most and snow totals were rather low. That was all about to change, however, as Elizabeth Colt, heading into her golden years still a widow, thinking more and more these days about selling the company and dedicating her time to philanthropy, looked out onto the front Armsmear lawn on the evening of March 11, 1888, and watched as torrential rains pelted the landscape.

Waking later that night, or, rather, the next morning (March 12), somewhere near 2:00 a.m., Elizabeth was startled by the flapping window shutters and loose, rattling panes. The wind had kicked up significantly. And with it, the temperature had taken a tremendous nosedive. By daylight, the snow was coming down so heavily that it was hard to see a few feet in front of one's face. By the time it was over a day later, the Northeast was buried in three feet of heavy, wet snow, a deadly blizzard that had paralyzed all industry, stranding all of Colt's employees inside the building.

This storm, in all of its stealth, was a portend of things to come for Elizabeth. Tragedy was not yet finished with the heir to the Colt cathedra. During this time, Caldwell had traveled, pursuing with vigorous tenacity his desire to race yachts. Sam's illegitimate child, Samuel, had come over from Germany and was now working at the Colt Armory. Elizabeth was said to have spent a lot of her free time seeing to his welfare. Even when Samuel, whom Elizabeth was said to have adored, decided to marry a pretty young woman from Georgia, Elizabeth paid for the wedding and gave the couple a house across the street from Armsmear.

The worst of Elizabeth's pain came in mid-January 1894, when word reached Armsmear that Caldwell, who had been in Punta Gorda, Florida, sailing the *Oriole*, his winter boat (kept at his winter residence), had been found dead aboard the schooner under what appeared to be mysterious circumstances. This death meant that all five of Elizabeth's children had been taken before her. It seemed almost impossible to conceive that death had become her reality. What had happened to Caldwell? How could a seemingly healthy man of thirty-five die so suddenly and unexpectedly?

The report Elizabeth received was that Caldwell had been stricken with a severe case of tonsillitis and, as a complication of that ailment, suffered from heart failure. Rumors from suicide to murder circulated (in contemporary terms, think of a Kennedy death and the whirlwind of gossip following it until the facts are in—and even then the salacious stories continue). One story had the jealous husband of a woman Caldwell had been bedding aboard the boat killing Caldwell with a shotgun. Then someone said Caldwell had thrown a party aboard the ship, got drunk, fell overboard, and drowned.

Elizabeth had been planning the twenty-fifth anniversary celebration of the Church of the Good Shepherd as Caldwell's body was returned to Hartford. Now she had to scratch that jubilant event and make preparations to bury her last child.

Hartford Mayor Bill Hyde, who had known Caldwell since the two were boys hanging around together, eulogized his old buddy by calling Caldwell a "large-hearted man with generous impulses."

Caldwell's best friend, who had been with him when he died, wrote a letter to the *Hartford Courant*, hoping to put out all those fiery rumors bouncing around town. Regarding the gossip of suicide, which had "started at the North," William Prime wrote, "[t]his is absurd and pure fabrication. If it be so published it will grieve Mrs. Colt very much and ought to be promptly denied. When we went into dinner at 6 o'clock [on the night he died] I told [everyone] that Colt was dying & he died two hours later."

And so Elizabeth was left with nothing more than fading memories of her children and husband as the turn of the century neared. What had she done to deserve such misfortune? What would she do now? All alone, was there value in returning to the Colt Armory and watching over a business that, in all of its recompense, one might be led to believe, had given the family wealth and status, but at a debt no one could repay?

Elizabeth had learned from the past. Through the tremendous pain of losing Sam and Henrietta she had built a church. Now, with Caldwell gone, she would furnish the church with the "Caldwell Colt Memorial House," a parish home Bill Hosley called "one of the eccentric masterpieces of Victorian American architecture."

The building was completed in 1896. Famed architect Edward Potter, who had been retired for almost two decades, designed the structure after Elizabeth called on him and asked for his help (how could he refuse?). Looking at the structure from a distance in front, you can see how Elizabeth had insisted that the building have a nautical feel to pay tribute to the passion in her son's heart.

In total, Elizabeth had "spent the equivalent of $30 million building three of what today rank among Hartford's ten most significant architectural treasures."[*]

With no blood heirs to the Colt legacy, Elizabeth knew the time had come for her to give it all up, sell out, and walk away. She wrote in a letter dated 1901 that she felt Sam and Caldwell, had they been there with her, would have approved of the decision, concluding, "I have tried to honor their memories always."

That she did.

The company that had sustained the Colt name for nearly seventy years was sold to outside investors, a "group of Connecticut capitalists," as Jack Rohan called them. Beyond many demands, the one *must* Elizabeth insisted upon as part of the deal was that the company maintain the Colt name.

In any event, Elizabeth was out from underneath the confines of an industrial business, maybe even a shroud of darkness that had brought with it so much tragedy to the Colt family, beginning long before

---

* The trio of architectural wonders Hosley is referring to here are Armsmear, the Church of the Good Shepherd, and this parish house. But I need to say: Truly, I have only touched upon Elizabeth Colt's story and her significance as a socialite and businesswoman. She is a historical subject who deserves a biography of her own, showcasing her charitable heart and all of the groundwork she laid for the women's movements that would flourish in the years after her death. She was a woman who believed that what she had was worthless without giving back. As the first president of Hartford's Soldiers Aid Society, for just one small example, she was able to raise the equivalent of about $45 million in two weeks and also organized the first suffragette convention in Connecticut. I could go on and on with her accomplishments. Think about her life for a moment. She lost all those children and her husband. She didn't wallow and curl into a ball, moving away into seclusion, using all of her money to numb the pain of loss; she instead reached out and used her wealth to make people's lives better in the spirit of those deaths. We can be sure that Elizabeth Colt, with the faith of a true believer, lived the Gospels she so fervently held to her heart.

Elizabeth stepped in. She sold Colt for more money than she could spend in a hundred lifetimes—a figure that would translate today to hundreds of millions of dollars.

Sam and the children were exhumed from their graves at Armsmear and transferred to Cedar Hill Cemetery just up the road, heading south toward the town of Wethersfield.

Oscar Wilde wrote, "One can survive everything now-a-days, except death"—and Elizabeth Colt's strength and steadfast emotional durability certainly exemplified this popular quote. The Colt matriarch would have turned seventy-nine years old in September 1905, but as fate would have it, the beautiful and highly respected Hartford socialite was not to make that birthday celebration. It was August 23, 1905, when Elizabeth Colt died inside the home of her niece while vacationing in Newport, Rhode Island.

The will Sam Colt's widow left behind was thirty-four pages long. She left enormous amounts of money to many people, family and friends. She asked that Armsmear become a home for widows and/or orphans of deceased clergymen of the Protestant Episcopal Church and "as many impoverished but refined and educated gentlewomen as the buildings" would support.

The Church of the Good Shepherd was left with what would amount to about $28 million in today's money as a budget to maintain the integrity of the establishment. Elizabeth was adamant about keeping the building in a state of complete repair at all times.

As Bill Hosley—whose book, *Colt: The Making of an American Legend*, is by far the bible of Colt history—so proudly put it near the end of his text, "Elizabeth Colt's death marked the end of an era . . . [and she] had herself become a legend."

The matriarch of the Colt family, a woman who had essentially made Sam Colt the altruistic lad he became, not to mention the man he had always wanted to be, dubbed "the first lady of Connecticut" in all of her obituaries, endowed the city of Hartford with the wide-reaching and beautiful Armsmear grounds, a pasture of land that became Colt Park in the years after her death.

EPILOGUE

THIS BOOK HAS BEEN AN ABSOLUTE JOY TO WRITE. RESEARCHING THE Colt brothers' legacy has taught me many things about myself I did not expect to learn while working on a book. Sam Colt was an inspiration in determination and perseverance, a man whose life is a study in what a human being driven by the passion of his work can achieve. Despite being faced with bankruptcy, embarrassment, death, sickness, lawsuits (a subject I only touched upon in this book), a government rejecting him continuously, two powerful politicians attacking him and lobbying Capitol Hill not to fund his inventions, Sam Colt succeeded. Many of the great men and women who have made history and truly changed the world in which we live were eccentric characters not by accident; it is that eccentricity that made these men and women the geniuses they were. Look at Einstein. Copernicus. Aristotle. Edison. Ben Franklin. Madame Curie. Margaret Knight. The lives of these men and women were as interesting as their inventions and innovations; and yet, it is their failures that fed an unencumbered hunger for their projects to flourish, ultimately allowing us to reap the benefits.

For some time I wrestled with what to include in the narrative of this book. The challenge was to tell what is an epic story without clogging up the entire framework of the book with unneeded anecdotes and history we have all heard before. There are sections of Sam Colt's life, for example, I have glossed over (some parts I have skipped entirely), but with good reason: I wanted to keep the focus on the two brothers and how their lives interacted, coalesced, and juxtaposed with each other during the era in which they lived. I did not want to repeat what others have written about Sam before me. I hope I have achieved this goal.

In all of my historical writing, I have never tried to overstate the obvious or rehash what historians have taken to task before me. My goal has always been to make history accessible to the general reader, to present a story of an interesting historical figure that is both as close to the truth as I can uncover and exciting to read, maybe like a good old-fashioned novel. I have made it my focus to dig deep into the legend of a particular historical subject and find the facts to either support that legend or correct the record. I have never tried to change history; my aim has always been to delve into the fray and figure out exactly what happened—or, quite frankly, what the record has left behind. In actual fact, we are never going to uncover any more than, my guess would be, about 65 to 70 percent of *any* story. There is always an impenetrable layer of truth we will never know—and maybe that is the way it should be.

So much had been written about Sam Colt that it had always seemed to me, as a lifelong resident of Connecticut, having grown up directly across the river (in East Hartford) from Sam Colt's iconic blue onion dome and manufacturing plant, that there was not a lot left to be said about this family. But that all changed when I came across John Colt's story while researching my previous Globe Pequot Press/Lyons Press book about Amy Archer Gilligan, *The Devil's Rooming House*. I saw an interesting layer of the Colt story emerge: the contrasts between the two brothers and how their lives were interconnected and shaped by not only blood relation and a bastard child, but tragedy and the utter omnipresence of death as an intrinsic part of their lives.

The great "obvious" irony in the story of the two brothers—and I hope I presented this metaphor clearly in the book you've just read—is that one of these men crafted (we have to be careful not to say "invented") and mastered the first revolving, handheld killing machine and the other was a killer. And granted, that might be what the surface of this family saga begs us to contemplate in more depth as we compare the brothers' lives with each other; but consider all of the tragedy that took place within the Colt family (even before John's death and Sam's successes), continuing right up until the turn of the century, and even after, when Elizabeth sold Colt Manufacturing. I looked at this dynamic of the Colt story and could not help but think of the Kennedy family and how death and tragedy had penetrated that American dynasty not half as much as it had the Colts.

No matter what we believe, or what we place the foundation of our faith upon, we cannot deny that some sort of tragic karma, or dark cloud, followed this family around. With that in mind, I want to share something I feel is relevant to this part of the Colt discussion. If nothing else, it is certainly a strange and interesting side note (if that is indeed the right word) and coincidence (maybe a better word) in the tale of the Colt property known as Armsmear.

In 1999, along the southern end of Colt Park on Wawarme Avenue— an area overlooking a section of land where Sam and the kids and

Elizabeth once spent their days frolicking and enjoying life and, at one time, was close to the burial site of Sam and his three children, an area of the Armsmear grounds that Elizabeth and Sam passed daily—someone spotted what they thought to be an image of the Virgin Mary in the bark of a locust tree directly between the Colt building and Armsmear.

We've heard this before: the face of Jesus appearing on a grilled cheese sandwich; Mary's image in the unwashed window of an office building; a weeping statue of Christ; as I write this, a woman in Ohio claimed to have in her possession a pistachio nut with the face of Christ imprinted on it. Some see what they want and I guess we shouldn't judge their beliefs or faith; most of us simply go on with our lives with maybe a shake of the head while not paying too much attention, writing these incidents off as fodder for the *National Enquirer* or *World News Report* right next to sightings of Elvis and spaceships flying in and out of Area 51. As for this image in Colt Park, some claimed Mary had even appeared in the sky (near the tree) at certain times and in the leaves of the tree. According to those who saw the image first, Mary presented herself with her arms stretched in a welcoming gesture, a crown of twelve stars on her head.

Now, objectively speaking, regardless of whether the image—which has never been affirmed (or even acknowledged) by the Catholic Church as an actual Marian apparition—is what those who flock to this memorial believe it to be, a shrine soon went up and people from all over the world began making pilgrimages (and still do to this day). My interest in this as related to the Colt story is not in whether the apparition is genuine, or a figment of someone's pious, portentous imagination; it is simply to stop, consider the sincere religious beliefs of Elizabeth Colt, the emotional pain she suffered, the incredible warmth of this woman's heart, her charitable goodness, her dedication to the scriptures, the enormous amount of tragedy the Colt family endured, and point out that of all the locations in the world a Marian apparition has claimed to have taken place, here we have one on the Colt property, arguably a location that has produced weapons that have killed hundreds of thousands of people.

Within a few years the shrine grew. Hundreds of candles and rosaries and photos of lost loved ones and religious articles and flowers were placed at the site. A fence was built around the tree itself and a shed-like fixture built around the fence, protecting the area and all of the relics the faithful left behind. Someone placed a kneeler at the entrance to what had become an enclosed shrine to the Virgin Mary covered with dedications and religious articles of faith and beauty. I was there myself once. I did not see Mary, but I can honestly say that I felt a tremendous amount of positive energy and something acutely spiritual while standing at the site. It calmed me. Being there, I didn't want to question any of this (and questioning it, anyway, didn't really seem to matter). A sense of indifference and ambiguity washed over me. I could not deny it.

Many of the faithful in and around the Hartford region believe this Marian shrine to be a sign that God has presented Himself to this particular area of the world for some yet unknown reason. Again, my interest here, within the context of the Colt legacy, is not a pious one. I am not questioning what anyone believes. My aim is to only point out what happened on this piece of property once owned by the Colt family.

And then something happened.

Be it a cigarette butt tossed out of a car window, vandals, or Divine Intervention by the city of Hartford (which had been barking about removing the site for years), wouldn't you know, the shrine burnt to the ground.

Today the shrine once again stands, although it is not as large as it once was (but continues to grow). People stop, pray, leave an article of some sort, and yes, they still see Mary in the bark of that locust tree and the sky surrounding the site. They still believe. They still consider this sacred ground.

—◦—

The church Elizabeth Colt left behind serves a different community these days. The church's mission statement, in part, reveals a great deal about how the neighborhood around Armsmear has changed over the course of one hundred years: "The Episcopal Church of the Good Shepherd is a diverse community of faith and hope committed to worshipping and serving God in the midst of the city. The church is located in one of the [neediest] neighborhoods of Hartford. Within a one block radius of the church there are close to 1,000 units of publicly funded housing. Poverty, lack of education, crime, and violence are all challenges which the church has worked to address over the years. The parish membership forms a racially, culturally and economically diverse community drawn from throughout the greater Hartford region to this historic church."

The church is located at 155 Wyllys Street, Hartford. Services take place at 10:00 a.m. every Sunday. You can see images of this amazing structure on the church's website: www.cgshartford.org/index.html. Many things could be said for the way Elizabeth Colt made the Church of the Good Shepherd as a tribute to her husband's memory and, perhaps, as some have claimed, used this pious representation to "rehabilitate" Sam's image; yet there can be no mistaking the fact that Elizabeth Colt was a devout Christian who dedicated her life after the death of her husband and children to many great causes, changing the lives of many, many people.

ACKNOWLEDGMENTS

I'D LIKE TO THANK THOSE WHO WERE AN IMPORTANT PART OF THIS Colt journey and several others who have been a vital part of my history career as well: Everyone at Lyons Press, including: Keith Wallman, Janice Goldklang, Robert Sembiante, Lawrence Dorfman, Mark Carbray, Michelle Lusas Panek (my buddy!), and also, Kristen Mellitt and proofreader Steven Talbot, whose laser eyes caught many embarrassing typos and small errors; Dan Thayer; Denise Chandonnet, from Mass Lowell Lydon Library; all those at the Hartford Public Library who helped in their own little ways; Scott Galbraith, vice president of programming at the Bushnell Auditorium in Hartford; Dr. Jan Heier; Julia Sherwood Murphy, University of Pennsylvania Library; a big thanks to Gail J. Avino, circulation supervisor/ILL coordinator at Hall Memorial Library in Ellington, Connecticut, and all of the librarians at Hall who have supported me and helped me with my research; Sue Phillips, Hall Memorial director; at the Connecticut Historical Society: Diane McCain (and her assistants), Rich Malley, Elizabeth Abbe, and all those who work hard at this wonderful establishment and helped me dig through the plethora of Colt research (I am indebted to the society for having such an abundance of John Colt material); my business manager and agent, Peter Miller; Adrienne Rosado; Natalie Horbachevsky; everyone at St. Luke's in Ellington.

I want to extend immense thanks to Andrew "Fazz" Farrell, Anita Bezjak, Therese Hegarty, Geoff Fitzpatrick, and everyone else at Beyond Productions who have believed in me all these years, along with my *Dark Minds* road crew: Colette "Coco" Sandstedt, Geoff Thomas, Jared Transfield, Julie Haire, Elizabeth Daley, Jeremy Adair, and Peter Heap; along with my producers at Investigation Discovery: Jeanie Vink and Sucheta Sachdev. A special shout out to Henry Schleiff, president and general manager of ID, who has been behind my show since day one.

I greatly appreciate all of your help. I am grateful for everyone working on the series—you are all wonderful people, some of the most gracious and astute professionals I have *ever* worked with, on top of new friends. I look forward to the road ahead and where we're going to take this series!

In addition to being a great friend and the best serial killer profiler on the planet, John Kelly has become a mentor to me in both life and work. I love the guy. Thanks for doing the series, Kelly. You're the best.

I would be negligent not to mention all the booksellers throughout New England and beyond—those indy stores and the chains—who have supported me and talked up my books to their customers (thank you from the bottom of my heart); and my readers: you are the most wonderful people—thank you for sticking with me!

Lastly, my immediate family, who have stood behind me forever.

Appendix I

These excerpts are reprinted exactly as they were published, so forgive any mistakes—they are not mine.

Gaylord Clarke's account of JC's final moments.

I have no doubt that hundreds and hundreds of people, in this State, and in border States, are at this moment in the full and undoubting belief that John C. Colt, who took the life of Adams in 1842, is still in existence!— that he never entirely "killed himself," but that he was "spirited away" from the triple-barred and triple guarded "strong immures" of the Tombs, and is now in a foreign land, safe from further peril! Why, not two months since, I heard a magistrate from one of the lower counties of New Jersey say— a man accustomed to deliberate, and carefully weigh evidence, that "he has no more doubt that John C. Colt was among the living, than he was that he himself was alive!"—and I have heard at least fifty persons affirm the same thing. Few persons took a deeper interest in the case of Colt, from the very beginning, than myself. Firmly believing that the killing was never pre-meditated, but was the result of a quarrel and a blow suddenly given, when the parties stood face to face, with each other (and this was shown by the cast of the head, showing the mark made by the hatchet, which Dr. Rogers and a committee, of which I was one, took up to Albany, and laid before Governor Seward) I say, firmly believing all this, I never could consider Colt a deliberate murderer. Nor was he. He was convicted for concealing the body of his unfortunate victim. Does anyone suppose that if Colt had rushed out into the hall, after having struck the fatal blow, and said, "I have killed a man!—we have had a little difficulty—I have struck him with a hatchet, and have killed him!" does anyone now believe he would ever have been convicted? Never! But this apart.

I believe I am the only survivor of those who left John C. Colt in his cell at the Tombs, in company alone with his brother Samuel, some three quarters of an hour before the time appointed for the execution. The late Rev. Mr. Anthon, John Howard Payne, Samuel Colt, the unhappy condemned, and myself were the only persons in the cell at this time. It was a scene never to be forgotten. The condemned had on a sad colored morning-gown, and a scarf tied loosely around his neck. He had a cup of coffee in his hand, and was helping himself to some sugar from a wooden bowl, which stood on an iron water-pipe near the head of his bed. His hand was perfectly steady, as he held the cup and put in the sugar; and the only sign of intense internal agitation and excitement was visible in his eyes, which were literally blood red, and oscillated, so to speak, exactly like the red and incessantly-moving eyes of the Albinos. Our interview was prolonged for half an hour, which was passed in conversation with Dr. Anthon, Mr. Payne, and his brother. And when we were about to depart, and someone, looking at his watch, said that he thought he must be some ten minutes fast, poor John replied, "May you never see the time when those ten minutes will be as precious to you as they are to me! But, after all, we have all got to go sooner or later—and no man knows when!" As we closed the cell door, leaving him alone with his sorrowing, faithful brother, the unhappy man kissed us all on each cheek, and bade us "Farewell!" with emotion, too deep for tears—for not a drop moistened his throbbing, burning eyes.

We made our way with difficulty from the Tombs, by the aid of the surrounding police, who opened a space for our carriage through the crowd, which, in every direction, for two or three blocks, filled the adjacent streets, and reached, on Franklin street, nearly if not quite to Broadway.

I resided at that time in Seventh street, between Eighth and Ninth avenues, and Rev. Dr. Anthon lived in St. Mark's Place, in Eighth street. We deposited the good doctor at his door, and after calling at the same time to acquaint the family with the last sad scene we had witnessed, Mr. Payne and I were driven quickly over to the New York University, in the southern tower of which, in the upper story, Mr. Samuel Colt had his incipient pistol-manufactory, or rather his Invention and Improvement Office. As we entered, he was sitting at a table, with a broad-brimmed hat drawn over his brow, his hands spread before his eyes, and the hot tears trickling through his fingers. After a few moments' silence, at his request, I took a sheet of paper, and commenced, at his dictation a letter to his brother, Judge Colt, then of St. Louis. I had not written more than five lines, when rapid footsteps were heard on the stairs, and a hackman rushed into the room, exclaiming in the wildest excitement: "Mr. Colt! Mr. Colt! your brother has killed himself—stabbed himself to the heart . . . And the Tombs are a-fire! You can see it a burning now!" "Thank God! thank God!" exclaimed Mr. Colt, with an expression almost of joy.

We raised an eastern window of the tower, stepped out upon the battlement, and by a short ladder, stepped out on to the roof of the chapel, or main edifice, and saw the flames licking up and curling around the great fire tower of the Tombs.

There was something peculiar about the air—the atmosphere—on that day. One felt as one feels on a cold autumnal night, while watching, uncovered in the open air, the flickering of the aurora borealis in the northern sky. As early as half past three o'clock that afternoon, two stars were distinctly visible through the cold thin atmosphere. This was regarded at the time as a remarkable phenomenon.

Now everybody knows, or should know, that the body of John C. Colt was found exactly as described by the hackman; that life was totally extinct; that the corpse was encoffined, removed, buried, and "so remains unto this day."

The Tombs tower caught fire from an over-heated stove; and yet, all the doubters of Colt's suicide, whom we have ever met, contend that the burning was part of the plan; that it was hired to be set on fire, and that in the confusion the condemned man escaped.

APPENDIX II

THE MIDDLE PORTION OF THE *NEW YORK HERALD* EDITORIAL PUBLISHED AFTER JC'S SUICIDE.

Taking all the horrid circumstances of his end into consideration, we have every reason to believe that Governor Seward will order an investigation into the facts, and ascertain that no one is to blame for such a death but the unfortunate being himself. Toward him that was, none can have any feeling but that of pity, commiseration, and deep anguish of heart. From the first moment of his trial, to the last pulsation of his existence, he seems to have been under the influence of a false system of morals, a perverted sense of human honor, and a sentiment that is at utter variance with the mysterious revelation of Christianity, or the sacred institutions of justice in civilized society. The perverted principles of honor and respectability that spring from modern philosophy and human pride have precipitated him upon the fatal precipice. These principles, arising from materialism in philosophy and unbelief in all revelation, are too rife in the world, and may be looked upon as the principal cause of all the licentiousness, private and public, which seems to overwhelm the whole institutions of civilized society in one mass of uproar, confusion and despair. We cannot say more to-day, nor could we say less at this momentous crisis. We have no doubt Governor Seward will order an investigation at once into this most unheard-of, most unparalleled tragedy....

Appendix III

Selected excerpt from Maria Childs's letter.

This bloody insult was thrust into the hands of some citizens who carried hearts under their vests, and they threw it in tattered fragments to the dogs and swine, as more fitting witnesses than human beings. It was cheering to those who have faith in human progress, to see how many viewed the subject in this light. But as a general thing, the . . . spirit of murder was rife among the dense . . . which thronged the place of execution. They were swelling with revenge, and eager for blood. One man came all the way from New Hampshire, on purpose to witness the entertain [event]; thereby showing himself a likely subject for the gallows, whoever he may be. Women deemed themselves not treated with becoming gallantry, because tickets of admittance were denied than; and I think it showed injudicious partially; for many of them can be taught murder by as short a lesson as any man, and sustain it by arguments from Scripture, as ably as any theologian. However, they were not admitted to this edifying exhibition in the great school of public morals; and had only the slim comfort of standing outside, in a keen November wind, to catch the first toll of the ball, which would announce that a human brother had been sent struggling into eternity by the hand of violence. But while the multitude stood with open watches, and stinted ears to catch the sound, and the marshals smoked and whistled, and the hangman walked up and down, waiting for his prey. Lo! word was brought that the criminal was found dead in his cell! He had asked one half hour alone to prepare his mind for departure; and at the end of that brief interval, he was found with a dagger thrust into his hurl. The tidings were received with fierce mutterings of disappointed rage. The throng beyond the walls were furious to see him with their own eyes, to be sure that he was dead. But when the welcome news met my ear, a tremendous load was taken from my heart. I had no chance to analyze right and wrong; for over all thought and feeling flowed impulsive joy, that this "Christian" community were cheated of a hanging. They who had assembled to commit legalized murder, in cold blood, with strange [confusion] of ideas, were unmindful of their own guilt, while they talked of his suicide as a crime equal to that for which he was condemned. I'm willing to leave it between him and his God. For myself, I would rather have the burden of it on my own soul, than take the guilt of those who would have executed a fellow-creature. He was driven to & fearful extremity of agony and desperation. . . .

To me human life seems so sacred a thing, that its violent termination always fills me with horror, whether perpetrated by an individual or a crowd; whether done contrary to law and custom, or according to law and custom. Why John C. Colt should be condemned to an ignominious death for an act of resentment altogether unpremeditated, while men, who deliberately, and with malice aforethought, go out to murder one another for some insulting word, are judges, and senators in the land, and favorite candidates for the President's chair, is more than I can comprehend. There is, to say the least, a strange inconsistency in our customs.

As we walked homeward, we encountered a deputy sheriff; not the most promising material, certainly, for lessons on humanity; but to him we spoke of the crowd of savage faces, and the tones of hatred, as obvious proofs of the bad influence of capital punishment. "I know that." said he; "but I don't see how we could dispense with it. Now suppose we had fifty murderers shut up in prison for life, instead of hanging em; and suppose there should come a revolution; what an awful thing it would be to have fifty murderers inside the prison, to be let loose upon the community!" "There is another side to that proportion," we answered; "for every criminal you execute, you make a hundred murderers outside the prison, each as dangerous as would be the one inside." He said perhaps it was so; and went his way.

As for the punishment and the terror of such doings, they fail most keenly to the beat heart; in the community. Thousands of men, us well as women, had broken and startled sleep or several nights preceding that dreadful day. Executions always excite a universal shudder among the innocent, the humane, and the wise-hearted. It is the voice of God, crying aloud within us against the wickedness of this savage custom. Else why is it that the instinct is so universal?

The last conversation I had with the late William Ladd made a strong impression on my mind. While he was a sea-captain, he occasionally visited Spain, and once witnessed an execution there—he said that no man, however low and despicable, would consent to perform the office of hangman; and whoever should dare to suggest such a thing to a decent man, would be likely to have his brains blown out. This feeling was so strong, and so universal, that the only way they could procure an executioner, was to offer a condemned criminal his own life, if he would consent to perform the vile and hateful office on another. Sometimes executions were postponed for months, because there was no condemned criminal to perform the office of hangman. A fee was allowed by law to the wretch who did perform it, but no one would run the risk of touching his polluted hand by giving it to him; therefore the priest threw the purse as far as possible; the odious being ran to pick it up, and hastened to escape from the shuddering execrations of all who had known him as a hangman. Even the poor animal that carried the criminal and his coffin in a cart to the foot of the gallows, was an object of universal loathing. He was cropped and marked, that he might be known as the "Hangman's Donkey." No man, however great his needs, would use this beast, either for pleasure or labor; and the peasants were so averse to having him pollute their fields with his footsteps, that when he was seen approaching, the boys hastened to open the gates, and drive him off with hisses, sticks, and stones. Thus does the human heart cry out aloud against this wicked practice!

The testimony from all parts of the world is invariable and conclusive, that crime diminishes in proportion to the mildness of the laws. The real danger is in having laws on the statute book at variance with universal instincts of the human heart, and thus tempting men to continual evasion. The evasion, even of a bad law, is attended with many mischievous results; its abolition is always safe.

In looking at Capital Punishment in its practical bearings on the operation of justice, an observing mind is at once struck with the extreme uncertainty attending it. The balance swings hither and thither, and settles, as it were, by chance. The strong instincts of the heart teach juries extreme reluctance to convict for capital offences. They will avail themselves of every loophole in the evidence, to avoid the bloody responsibility imposed upon them. In this way, undoubted criminals escape all punishment, until society becomes alarmed for its own safety, and insists that the next victim shall be sacrificed. It was the misfortune of John C. Colt to be arrested at the time when the popular wave of indignation had been swelling higher and higher, in consequence of the [circumstances] with which Robinson, White, and Jewell, had escaped. The wrath and jealousy which they had excited was visited upon him, and his chance for a merciful verdict was greatly diminished.

The scale now turns the other way; and the next offender will probably receive very lenient treatment, though he should not have half so many extenuating circumstances in his favor.

Another thought which forces itself upon the mind in consideration of this subject is the danger of convicting the innocent. Murder is a crime which must of course be committed in secret, and therefore the proof must be mainly circumstantial. This kind of evidence is in its nature so precarious, that men have learned great timidity in trusting to it. In Scotland, it led to so many terrible mistakes, that they long ago refused to convict any man of a capital offence, upon circumstantial evidence. . . . (the letter goes on and on, but focuses on other crimes unrelated to JC).

Endnotes

Prologue: Vanishing Act

x   **"A black coat," his wife, Emmeline, later recalled:** Colt, John Caldwell. 1842. *Trial of John C. Colt for the murder of Samuel Adams.* New York: Benj. H. Day; p. 5.

x   **"He was going from Centre Street to Broadway":** Ibid., p. 6.

xii   **"New York literature may be taken as a fair representation":** Poe, Edgar Allan. 1849. *The Works of Edgar Allan Poe,* Vol. III. New York: WJ Widdleton; p. 24.

xii   **" I have no belief in spirituality":** Woodberry, George Edward. 1885. *Edgar Allan Poe.* American men of letters. Boston: Houghton, Mifflin; p. 212.

xiii   **"unparticled matter, impelling and permeating all things":** Ibid.

xiii   **"a sort of mania for composition":** Ibid., p. 211.

xiii   **"What we call 'death' is painful metamorphosis":** Ibid., p. 212.
Additional works helpful to me in understating Poe and his mind-set while he was living in Philadelphia were: "Edgar Allan Poe," Biography.com, www.biography.com/articles/Edgar-Allan-Poe-9443160 (accessed Apr 9, 2010); The Literati of New York City: Some of the Honest Opinions at Random Respecting Their Authorial Merits with Occasional Words of Personality. [S:1 - GLB, 1846] - Edgar Allan Poe Society of Baltimore - Works - Misc - The Literati [part I] (txt-2); and Letter, Poe to Mr. Lowell, New York, July 2, 1844.

xiv   **"ordered the books to be sent to Philadelphia":** Lawson, John Davison. 1914. *American state trials; A collection of the important and interesting criminal trials which have taken place in the United States from the beginning of our government to the present day.* St. Louis: Thomas Law Books; p. 467. (*American State Trials*).

xiv   **"I would ask that you should print a book for me":** Ibid.

xiv   **"The sheets were sent off to the folding place":** Ibid.

xiv   **"been in the bindery":** Ibid.

xiv   **"His general temper I supposed to be good":** Ibid., p. 467.
I'd like to underscore something about the quotations above: There were several versions of the testimony from John C. Colt's trial. Court reporters were not at all then what they are today. We can assume, then, that the testimony was paraphrased and rewritten several times. I used all of the resources for the trial I could find, checking each against the other, and deciding on which quote was the most accurate.

xv   **"Yet to calculate is not in itself to analyze":** Poe, Edgar Allan, Stuart Levine, and Susan F. Levine. 1990. *The short fiction of Edgar Allan Poe: An annotated edition.* Urbana: University of Illinois Press; p. 175.

xvi   **"In a moment of caprice you had blasted my hope":** Ackroyd, Peter, and Edgar Allan Poe. 2008. *Poe: a life cut short.* London: Chatto & Windus; p. 32.
For my analysis of, and quotations from, "The Oblong Box," I used: Poe, Edgar Allan. 1975. *The complete tales and poems of Edgar Allan Poe.* New York: Vintage Books; and Poe, Edgar Allan. 2004. *The collected tales and poems of Edgar Allan Poe.* Hertfordshire, Ware: Wordsworth Editions.

xviii   **"I told Mr. Adams that Colt expected the proceeds":** Lawson, *American State Trials*, p. 467.

xviii   **"did not show temper":** Ibid.

xviii   **"I do not recollect":** Ibid., p. 468.

CHAPTER 1: CLASHING FOILS

The information in these opening paragraphs was gleaned from my study of several invaluable sources, among them are: Burrows, Edwin G., and Michael L. Wallace. 1999. *Gotham: A history of New York City to 1898*. New York: Oxford University Press; Dolan, Jay P. 2010. *The Irish Americans: A history*. New York: Bloomsbury Press; Jackson, Kenneth J., ed. 1995. *The Encyclopedia of New York City*. New Haven, Conn.: Yale University Press; pp. 572–573, 582; BOOKRAGS STAFF. "Reform Era and Eastern U.S. Development 1815–1850: Education: Overview." 2005. May 9 2010. www.bookrags.com/history/reform-era-education/; and "The First Slum in America." *The New York Times*. 2001 September 30.

4   **"everywhere with dirt and filth"**: Dickens, Charles. 1842. *American Notes*. London: Chapman and Hall; p. 90.

4   **"Do they ever wonder why their masters walk upright"**: Ibid.

4   **"teacher of writing"**: Lawson, *American State Trials*, p. 459.

4   **"richest and most prominent men"**: Hosley, William N. 1996. *Colt: The making of an American legend*. Amherst: University of Massachusetts Press; p.14.

6   **"requested me to let him one"**: Lawson, *American State Trials*, p. 459.

7   **"adjoin each other"**: Ibid.

7   **"The entrance [is] on Chambers Street"**: Ibid.

7   **"Have these books"**: Ibid.

7   **"We were on good terms again"**: Ibid.

7   This conversation/scene, beginning with, **"I need the office,"** please see: Ibid.

8   For the **"clashing foils"** part of this scene, please see: Ibid., pp. 459, 505, 469.

CHAPTER 2: BLACK HATS & INK

9   **"*The Tribune*, as its name imports, will labor"**: Parton, James. 1889. *The life of Horace Greeley, editor of "The New-York tribune," from his birth to the present time*. Boston: Houghton, Mifflin & co.; p. 190.

10   **"Right Reason and Public Good"**: Ibid.

10   **"all was still"**: Lawson, *American State Trials*, p. 459.

10   **"I found that the drop was down inside"**: Ibid.

10   **"In a position of bending down over something"**: Ibid.

10   **"On the table were two black hats"**: Ibid.

11   **"Come here"** . . . **"You stand in my door"**: Ibid.

11   **"No person had gone into Colt's door"**: Ibid., p. 461.

11   **"the sound like striking of foils on crossing each other"**: Ibid.

12   **"They're engaged"**: Ibid., p. 459.

12   **"they would not dare to open the door"**: Ibid.

    In drafting my paragraphs about the NYPD and New York law enforcement, I relied on several great resources. Among them were: Allan Nevins, "Horace Greeley," DAB, 7: 528–34; Van Deusen, *Greeley;* www.nyc-architecture.com/GON/GON021.htm; Parton. *The life of Horace Greeley;* pp. 156–160; *Munsey's magazine*. 1800s. New York: F.A. Munsey & Co. [etc.]; p. 444; and Lardner, James, and Thomas A. Reppetto. 2000. *NYPD: A city and its police*. New York: Henry Holt and Co.; pp. 3–10.

13   **"Old Jacob Hayes"** (and subsequent paragraphs relating to Hayes): *Southern literary messenger*. 1848. Richmond, Va: Jno. R. Thompson; p. 514.

14   "[T]he most gloomy . . . which New York has ever known": Ellis, Edward Robb, and Jeanyee Wong. 1997. *The epic of New York City*. New York: Carroll & Graf.; p. 242.

14   "It is needful first that we take": *Munsey's magazine*. 1800s. New York: F.A. Munsey & Co. [etc.]; p. 444.

14   These were the same lawmen: Spann, Edward K. 1981. *The New metropolis: New York City, 1840-1857*. New York: Sur; p. 39.

15   "I remained for about a half hour" (and following quote): Lawson, *American State Trials*, p. 461.

15   "I heard someone in Mr. Colt's room": Ibid.

15   "The next sound was the rattling of water": Ibid.

CHAPTER 3: MAIDEN VOYAGE

16   "Do not know where he intended to go when he left home": Lawson, *American State Trials*, p. 466.

16   "I am going to visit my relative": *New York* magazine, Nov 14, 1988; pp. 41–42.

17   "Amiable and pleasing": Stashower, Daniel. 2007. *The beautiful cigar girl: Mary Rogers, Edgar Allan Poe, and the invention of murder*. New York: Berkley Books; p. 16.

17   "She moved amid the bland perfume": Ibid., p. 22.

17   "[T]he body of a young female named Mary Cecilia Rogers": Philip Hone. 1936 . *The Diary of Philip Hone*, ed. Alan Nevins. New York; p. 555.

17   "great crimes that startled the country": Walling, George W. 1887. *Recollections of a New York chief of police*. New York: Caxton Book Concern; p. 28.

18   "sitting on their own fat for a cushion bench": Lardner, Reppetto. *NYPD: a city and its police*.

18   "Heard someone nailing a box": Lawson, *American State Trials*, p. 461. The subsequent quotes following this one, detailing this scene at the Granite Building, can be found in Ibid., pp. 459–462. (These trial transcripts are very comprehensive and dramatic. Witnesses recounted every nuance of that morning and the days following.)

19   Broadway was the first New York street: This paragraph was constructed using a variety of sources, including: Wolff, Stephen. Memories of Maiden Lane: *Like Billy Pilgrim, Wolf walks backwards through a long, varied story*, Volume 79, Number 36, February 10–16, 2010; Burrows, and Wallace. *Gotham*; and no byline given, Maiden Lane: How the Famous Business Street Got Its Name, *New York Times*, January 9, 1921. These sources, along with several others, helped me create a sense of place early in this book. They are great resources if you are looking to learn the true history of New York.

20   "There was a spring cart opposite to the door": Lawson, *American State Trials*, p. 462.
      The subsequent scenes between JC and Barstow, including the dialogue between the two men, were drafted from Barstow's testimony, which can be found in Ibid., p. 462; and *The Life and confession of John Caldwell Colt: who stands indicted for the murder of Mr. Samuel Adams, on the 17th September, 1841, together with full details of the murder and all the facts known relative thereto*. 1841. New York: Printed for the Publisher, at 162 Nassau Street; p. 2. (From this point on, this document will be referred to, more simply, as *Confession*.)

For information re: the *Kalamazoo,* see: Hunt, Freeman, Thomas Prentice Kettell, Isaac Smith Homans, and William B. Dana. 1848. *Hunt's merchants' magazine and commercial review.* [New York]: Freeman Hunt; p. 201.

21 **"acquired some knowledge of bookkeeping":** In the years that followed the murder of Sam Adams and John Colt's arrest, there were several articles published about the main witnesses who testified against John Colt. Credibility was everything in a nineteenth-century courtroom. The better standing you had in the community, the easier it was for jurors to believe you. Witnesses were judged by their work, their love life, and the way they treated people. In Asa's Wheeler's case, I've taken the liberty to talk about his life in general because ultimately Asa Wheeler becomes the chief witness against JC. For his biography, I found an enormous amount of information (in which the quotes here are drawn from) in: unauthored, *Colt: A Celebrated Murder Case Recalled,* Brooklyn Eagle, Aug. 5, 1879, p. 3.

22 **"[Colt] made some scathing criticisms about the teaching styles":** Heier, Jan R. 1993. A critical look at the thoughts and theories of the early accounting educator John C. Colt. Accounting, Business & Financial History. 3(1):21–36. www .informaworld.com/10.1080/09585209300000032. (accessed 07 June 2010).

22 **"He was a high-strung fellow":** *Colt: A Celebrated Murder Case Recalled.*

CHAPTER 4: FAMILY TIES

24 **"lack of available machinery and manpower":** Hosley. *Colt: The making of an American legend,* p. 21.

25 **"Puritanical Yankees":** Keating, Bern. 1978. *The flamboyant Mr. Colt and his deadly six-shooter.* Garden City, N.Y.: Doubleday; pp. 4–5.

26 **"It is with a little diffidence":** Ibid., pp. 48–49.

27 **"draw up his application pictures":** Ibid., p. 16.

27 **"that rarest of combinations":** Lewis, Alfred Henry, "The Broadway-Chambers Street Murder," *Pearson's Magazine.* 1899. New York, N.Y.: Pearson Pub. Co.; p. 42.

28 **"one of the dirtiest cities in the world":** Spann, *The new metropolis.* p. 134.

28 **"clod and an ingrate":** Lewis, "The Broadway-Chambers Street Murder," p. 42.

28 **"turned his back as squarely on them":** Ibid.

28 **"[JC] commenced singing":** Colt, 1842. *Trial of John C. Colt for the murder of Samuel Adams.* p. 2. This document, published in the *Sun* (January 1842) at the time of Colt's trial, is a much more detailed account of the proceedings than John Davison Lawson's *American State Trials,* which I cite throughout my notes. Each document complements the other. The *Sun's* coverage of the trial was much more extensive, and certainly more sensational. The dialogue in these scenes is taken verbatim from both accounts. When witnesses testified during nineteenth- and twentieth-century trials, they often went into great detail while describing the events in question.

29 **"Colt was not without his ambitions":** Lewis, "The Broadway-Chambers Street Murder," p. 43.

30 The quotes from Dr. Jan Heier are drawn from his excellent article on John Colt's controversial bookkeeping opinions—1 Heier, Jan R.. 1993. A critical look at the thoughts and theories of the early accounting educator John C. Colt. Accounting, Business & Financial History. 3(1):21-36. www.informaworld.com/10.1080/09585209300000032. (accessed 07 June 2010)—and an interview I conducted with Dr. Heier on June 3, 2010.

30 **"almost every branch of learning has had its advocate":** Colt, John Caldwell. 1853. *The science of double entry bookkeeping, simplified, arranged, and methodized: containing, also, a key, explaining the manner of journalizing, and the nature of the business transaction of each of the day-book entries together with practical forms for keeping books.* New York: Lamport, Blakeman & Law; p. 215.

31 **"There are branches of education useful to men at every stage":** Ibid., p. 217.

31 **"Book-keeping is a science":** Ibid.

31 **"If education should be suited for the wants of man":** Ibid., p. 220.

CHAPTER 5: MANKILLER

32 **"The Captain & Super cargo will give him good advice":** Houze, Herbert G., Carolyn C. Cooper, Elizabeth Mankin Kornhauser, and Samuel Colt. 2006. *Samuel Colt: Arms, art, and invention.* New Haven [u.a.]: Yale University Press [u.a.]. www.loc.gov/catdir/toc/ecip0518/2005024430.html., p. 38.

32 **"[T]oo often the case":** Colt, John Caldwell. 1842. *Life and letters of John Caldwell Colt; condemned to be hung on the eighteenth of November, 1842, for the murder of Samuel Adams,* a collection put together and annotated by the *Extra Tattler*, October 21, 1842, p. 2. I attribute this quote to John Colt, however, it is taken from the narrative section of the annotated *Life and Letters*, and so it is a summation of a quote John Colt gave to a *Tattler* reporter.

33 **"Now when making a choice of occupation":** Houze, Cooper, Kornhauser, and Colt. *Samuel Colt: Arms, art, and invention*, p. 37.

33 **"blow a raft sky high":** no byline available, "Sam, the Man Behind the Gun." *Time*, March 2, 1962, 102 pages, Vol. 52, No. 9, p. 57.

35 **"favorite son"** (and subsequent description): Lewis, "The Broadway-Chambers Street Murder," p. 41. As well as subsequent quotes.

35 **JC stood five feet eleven inches tall:** Colt, *Life and Letters*, p. 5.

35 **"Cold, hard . . . carrying in their gray depths a sinister shimmer":** Lewis, "The Broadway-Chambers Street Murder," p. 42.

35 **"passionate and revengeful":** *Confession*, p. 5. The additional biographical information of the Colts included in this paragraph is from a variety of sources; mainly, Rywell, Martin. 1955. *Samuel Colt, a man and an epoch.* Harriman, Tenn.: Pioneer Press; p. 74; and Goldberg, Louis, and Willard E. Stone. 1985. "John Caldwell Colt: A notorious accountant." S.l: s.n, The Accounting Historians Journal, Vol. 12, No. 1, Spring 1985, pp. 121–22.

36 **"with rare accomplishments, fascinating manners, and many virtues":** *Confession*, p. 2. One has to take JC's description of Margaret's dramatic suicide with a grain of skepticism, seeing that JC was himself staring down the barrel of death as he dictated his life and confession. So you would think there was a bit of hubris and theater playing in his mind, along with a modicum of selfish pride to make his situation look good, and that of whatever it was he talked about either sympathetic or irrational. Each of the Colt children had a flare for the dramatic, and each, in his or her own way, wanted to be viewed as a player on a stage, hence the narcissistic nature each child expresses throughout his or her life. Being the center of attention was, in terms of Colt DNA, something each of the children tried to attain at any given opportunity.

37 **Margaret's death, JC said years later, "paralyzed" his "soul":** Colt, *Life and Letters*, p. 4.

38 **"On Tuesday"..."I saw the notice of Mr. Adams":** Colt, *Trial of John C. Colt for the murder of Samuel Adams.* p. 2.

38 **Could not see him or Mrs. Adams:** Ibid.

38 **"We need to see the mayor":** Ibid.

39 **"Tammany candidate":** New York State Historical Association. 1895. *The memorial history of the city of New York: biographical.* New York: New York History Co.; p. 378.

39 **"immediately appoint an officer to watch the movements of Mr. Colt":** *Confession,* p. 7.

CHAPTER 6: A DEATHLIKE HUE

41 **"Urged me to very politely come into his room":** Colt, *Trial of John C. Colt for the murder of Samuel Adams,* p. 2.

41 **"He wished to have some conversation":** Ibid.

41 **"partly promised to go in":** Ibid.

41 **"On Friday morning":** Ibid.

42 **"I was induced":** Ibid., p. 3.

42 **"It was expected he would make resistance":** *Confession,* p. 8.

42 **"submitted to arrest without murmur":** Ibid.

42 **"natural paleness ... to a livid and deathlike hue":** Ibid.

42 **"You are being arrested on suspicion of having killed Mr. Samuel Adams":** Colt, 1842. *Trial of John C. Colt for the murder of Samuel Adams,* p. 3.

43 **"He assisted in the search and seemed disposed to yield everything":** Ibid.

43 **"Where do you reside"** (and the subsequent remainder of the conversation): *Confession,* p. 8.

43 **"[The] superintendent of carts discovered the car man":** Ibid.

44 **"Sam had to scrimp to make his living":** Grant, Ellsworth S. 1982. *The Colt legacy: The Colt Armory in Hartford, 1855–1980.* Providence, R.I.: Mowbray Co.; p. 16.

44–46 These paragraphs about Sam Colt's nitrous oxide gas demonstrations were drawn from his pamphlet, which can be found in a number of texts, including: Barnard, Henry. 1973. *Armsmear: The home, the arm and the armory of Samuel Colt. A memorial.* New York: Alvord, Printer; p. 150.

45 **"Dr. Coult's Exhibition presents some":** Ibid.

46 **"Paterson was chosen because of its prominence as a manufacturing center":** Hosley, *Colt: The making of an American legend,* p. 17.

46 **"sacred thing":** Lewis, "The Broadway-Chambers Street Murder," p. 44.

47 **"[T]he bills of lading for that day were examined":** Colt, *Trial of John C. Colt for the murder of Samuel Adams,* p. 3.

47 **"First saw the awning":** Ibid.

47 **"[W] e discovered a dead body":** Ibid.

47 **"[A] vessel bound for New Orleans":** Haswell, Chas. H. 1896. *Reminiscences of New York by an octogenarian (1816 to 1860).* New York: Harper; p. 374.

48 **"Upon the floor, a shattered glass was found":** *Confession,* p. 8.

48 **"the handle of which was newly scraped with broken glass":** Ibid.

48 **"saw away":** Ibid.

CHAPTER 7: A GREENISH CAST

49   **"a six-bed infirmary in New York City's first almshouse"**: no byline given, "Bellevue Hospital," a history, www.med.nyu.edu/medicine/aboutus/affiliates/bellevue.html.

49   **"lowest door on the building's front"**: McCabe, James Dabney. 1872. *Lights and shadows of New York life, or, The sights and sensations of the great city a work descriptive of the city of New York in all its various phases: with full and graphic accounts of its splendors and wretchedness, its high and low life, its marble palaces and dark dens, its attractions and dangers, its rings and frauds, its leading men and politicians, its adventurers, its charities, its mysteries, and its crimes.* Philadelphia, Pa.: National Pub. Co. (*Lights and Shadows* from here onward); p. 839.

49   **"This door," historian James McCabe wrote**: Ibid.

49   **"some chloride of lime over it"**: Colt, *Trial of John C. Colt for the murder of Samuel Adams*, p. 3.

50   **"every article of clothing"**: McCabe, *Lights and Shadows*, p. 839.

50   **"twenty feet square"**: Ibid., p. 9.

50   **"I found the body of a man"**: Colt, *Trial of John C. Colt for the murder of Samuel Adams*, p. 4.

51   **"the body was excessively offensive and covered with [pests]"**: Ibid.

51   **"white worms"**: Ibid., p. 6.

51   **"Washed the body," Short said**: Ibid., p. 7.

51   **"The skull was fractured in several different places"**: Ibid., p. 4.

52   **"On the other side of the head"**: Ibid.

52   **"There was no fracture on the back part of the head"**: Ibid.

52   **"some pieces of bone"**: Ibid.

53   **"All the blows on the head"**: Ibid.

53   **"[S]aw and examined the body [Gilman] described"**: Ibid.

53   **"Do not think the sound in giving such blows"**: Ibid.

53   **"any ball in the skull"**: Ibid.

54   **"Is your brother the inventor of the patent pistol"**: Ibid., p. 6. (Including the remainder of this short scene between JC and Asa Wheeler.) The detail that Wheeler gave during his appearance at JC's trial on the witness stand is impressive. Asa gave jurors entire conversations he had with JC and others. He talked about every move JC made that week and the entire situation of JC's arrest and the discovery of Adams's mutilated corpse.

54   **"A single blow from a hatchet"**: Ibid., p. 4.

55   **"a black dress coat, which had been much cut and worn"**: Ibid., p. 3.

55   **"in a cell at the Halls of Justice"**: Ibid., p. 7.

55   **"They smell[ed] offensive still"**: Ibid., p. 5.

55   **"I will tell you the truth"**: Ibid., p. 7.

55   **"pieces of skull"**: Ibid.

55   **"toward the Battery"**: Ibid.

CHAPTER 8: THE DEVIL & THE GUN MAKER

56   **"was growing impatient"**: Grant, *The Colt legacy*, p. 18.

56   **"I have no belief"**: Ibid.

56   **"six thousand masons and carpenters"**: Burrows and Wallace. *Gotham: A history of New York City to 1898*, p. 617.

57	**"I am confident," the colonel said:** Grant, *The Colt legacy*, p. 18.
57	**"42 some street":** Colt, *Trial of John C. Colt for the murder of Samuel Adams*, p. 4.
58	**"He thought Thomas Street":** Ibid.
58	**"What apartment does Mr. Colt occupy?":** Ibid.
58	**"Where is his trunk?":** Ibid.
58	**police office:** Ibid.
58	**"some stamps with 'Colt's Book-Keeping'":** Ibid.
59	**"There appeared to be some hair inside of it":** Ibid.
59	**"Complete your enlistment in an honorable fashion":** Rywell, *Samuel Colt, a man and an epoch*, p. 74.
59	**"a new and elegantly worked gold one":** Colt, *Trial of John C. Colt for the murder of Samuel Adams*, p. 4.
59	**"appeared to be more depressed than we had seen":** Ibid.
59	**"Who is the manufacturer?":** Ibid.
60	**"in consequence of information":** Ibid.
60	**"I was in the country":** Ibid., p. 5.
60	**"I took from the room":** Ibid., p. 4.
60	**"pieces of cloth, pieces of a towel, and pieces of a shirt":** Ibid.
60	**"true bill against Colt for murder":** *Confession*, p. 12.
60	**"term of the Court of Oyer and Terminer":** Ibid.

CHAPTER 9: THE SACRIFICIAL LAMB

65	**"frozen to the ground":** no byline given, *Extra Sun!!! Life, letters, and last conversation of John Caldwell Colt.* 1842. This document has also been published under the title *Life and Letters* . . . What I like about this document, and one reason why I give it so much credence in analyzing JC's story in its entirety, is that it is a collection of letters and testimonials. There is some biased narrative within it (like much of what was written then), but for the most part it is composed of letters written by JC and letters written to JC, along with interviews and quotes from various people in JC's life at the time. Yet, in all fairness, the document did include some rather biased storytelling designed to clean up JC's malignant image.
65	**"implored for the lamb":** Ibid.
65	**"I would rather be killed myself":** Ibid.
66	**"Well"** . . . **"you foolish fellow":** Ibid.
66	**"return [it] to the stables":** Ibid.
66	**"excellent man who appreciated his nephew's character":** Ibid.
67	**"I'll tell you what":** Ibid.
67	**"He likes to have his own way rather too much":** Ibid.
67	**"He is kind hearted a fellow as ever was":** Ibid.
67	**"She had decided that he should engage in mercantile pursuits":** Ibid.
67	**"placed in a store belonging to the Union Manufacturing Company":** Ibid.
67	**"[New York City] seemed to him a paradise":** Ibid.

CHAPTER 10: CONFESSIONS OF THE WAY LIFE USED TO BE

70	**"engaged in looking over a manuscript account[ing] book":** Lawson, *American State Trials*, p. 476, was instrumental in creating this scene of JC and Adams's meeting.

However, there are no fewer than four additional manuscripts and publications that have printed the same information. This *Confession* of JC was part of his trial and also printed in many of the newspapers, and it was later turned into a book with an introduction and prologue. The words are nearly identical in every account.

70   "So near," JC said later: Ibid.
70   "ten to twelve days before": Ibid.
70   "This account is wrong": Ibid.
70   "No! You do not understand printing": Ibid.
71   "I will give you ten dollars or some such sum": Ibid.
71   "I was right at first": Ibid.
71   "You lie!" Adams said: Ibid.
71   "Word followed word": Ibid.
71   "I do not know that I felt like exerting myself to strong defense": Ibid.
72   "so that I could scarcely breathe": Ibid.
72   "I then immediately seized hold of": Ibid., p. 477.
72   "I lost all power of reason": Ibid.
72   "The influence of his stepmother was at work against him": *Extra Sun!!! Life, letters, and last conversation of John Caldwell Colt,* p. 3.
73   "so charmed with his energy, acquirements, and excellent traits of character": Ibid.
74   "The seizing of the hammer and the blow was instantaneous": Lawson, *American State Trials,* p. 477.
75   "shoved" Adams off of him after striking him: Ibid.
75   "[F]or I felt very weak and sick": Ibid.
75   "poor Adams," JC later remarked: Ibid.
75   "I recollect taking him by the hand": Ibid.

CHAPTER 11: FORGIVE ME, I AM DYING NOW

76   "the affray had caused any alarm": Lawson, *American State Trials,* p. 478.
76   "the curtains of the window close": Ibid.
77   "spreading over the floor": Ibid.
77   "There was a great quantity": Ibid.
77   "This appeared to do no good": Ibid.
77   "tied tightly round Adams's neck after taking the handkerchief off": Ibid.
77   "one-third full of water": Ibid.
77   "I never saw his face afterwards": Ibid.
78   "octoroon slave and mistress": Rywell, *Samuel Colt, a man and an epoch,* p. 74.
78   "African Americans were enslaved on small farms": no byline given, "Conditions of Antebellum Slavery: 1830–1860," www.pbs.org/wgbh/aia/part4/4p2956.html.
78   "played on the fears of slave rebellion to sell guns to plantation owners": Tucker, Barbara M., and Kenneth H. Tucker. 2008. *Industrializing antebellum America: The rise of manufacturing entrepreneurs in the early republic.* New York: Palgrave Macmillan; p. 87.
78   "Mr. Colt appeared to be near the scene of a sanguinary insurrection of Negro slaves": Ibid.
79   "printed with Colt's permission": Ibid.

79   "Southern sympathizer if not an outright traitor to the Union": Ibid., p. 88.

79   "new mistress": Rywell, *Samuel Colt, a man and an epoch*, p. 74.

79   "[I]n a year or two": *Extra Sun!!! Life, letters, and last conversation of John Caldwell Colt*, p. 4.

80   "Plagiarism is nothing new": Dr. Jan Heier interview, June 11, 2010.

80   "Norwegian girl": *Extra Sun!!! Life, letters, and last conversation of John Caldwell Colt*, p. 4.

80   "counseled her as a brother": C. Frank Powell. 1842. *An authentic life of John C. Colt, now imprisoned for killing Samuel Adams, in New York, on the seventeenth of September, 1841*. Boston: s.n. Dickinson.; p. 46.

81   "He pursued toward her a course of virtuous resolution": *Extra Sun!!! Life, letters, and last conversation of John Caldwell Colt*, p. 4.

81   "In her little hands": Powell, *An authentic life of John C. Colt*, p. 47.

81   "They meant to rove until moon-rise": Ibid.

81   "No man can out-swim me" (as well as the rest of this scene by the water): Ibid.

82   "He renewed his earnest advice for her to devote herself to her music": Ibid., p. 49.

82   "And yet, I would almost as soon have parted with my soul": Ibid., p. 50.

83   "I am very glad to see you": Ibid.

83   "pounded to very powder": Ibid.

83   "become independent and happy": Ibid.

83   "subject to subject as though [she] were half mad": Ibid., pp. 48–49.

84   "Forget the past entirely" (and the following excerpted sections of JC's letter in this chapter): Ibid. (letter was printed in its entirety as a footnote). This is an important document in the scope of JC's life. It explains a lot about who he was when he believed the person to whom he was corresponding to be below him intellectually and emotionally. He, unlike his brother Sam, never spoke from the heart; whatever JC said or wrote was generally influenced and refined to figure in the person to whom he was communicating with. He was never, essentially, himself.

86   "You say right, I do not love you": *Extra Sun!!! Life, letters, and last conversation of John Caldwell Colt*, p. 4.

86   "Finding her love returned by friendship only": Ibid.

86   "taken one [hundred]and fifty grains of opium": Powell, *An authentic life of John C. Colt*, p. 52.

86   "It was published [by] the - Colt, Burgess & Co.": Colt, *Trial of John C. Colt for the murder of Samuel Adams*, p. 8.

86   "I am still indebted to Mr. Colt": Ibid.

87   "could not have touched him too deeply": Powell, *An authentic life of John C. Colt*, p. 52.

87   "former government accountant": Rywell, *Samuel Colt, a man and an epoch*. p. 74.

87   "[JC] found that the affairs of the firm had been so mismanaged": *Extra Sun!!! Life, letters, and last conversation of John Caldwell Colt*, p. 4.

CHAPTER 12: A SILENT SPACE OF TIME

88   "an extended tour through Asia and the Holy Land": Sutton, Charles, James B. Mix, and Samuel Anderson Mackeever. 1874. *The New York Tombs; its secrets and its mysteries. Being a history of noted criminals, with narratives of their crimes*. San Francisco, Cal: A. Roman & Co.; p. 48.

Endnotes

88   "The old Bridewell was a nuisance": Burrows and Wallace. 1999. *Gotham: a history of New York City to 1898*, p. 636.

89   "Haviland is due the entire merit of having introduced this novel and complete style of prison architecture": Laxton, William. 1838. *The Civil engineer and architect's journal.* London, p. 227.

90   "My horrid situation remained": Lawson, *American State Trials*, p. 478.

90   "[f]rom this time until dark": Ibid.

90   "I carefully opened the door": Ibid.

91   "I crossed into the Park": Ibid.

91   "A few words passed between us": Ibid.

91   "Then the horrors of the excitement": Ibid.

91   "which looked too deliberate for anything like death caused in an affray": Ibid., p. 479.

92   "I have an infinite deal of pleasure": Powell, *An authentic life of John C. Colt*, p. 53.

92   "plant corn and plough politics": Ibid.

92   "indicted for being concerned in a burglary in Wall-street": *Confession*, p. 5.

93   "He replied in a very threatening and surely manner": Ibid.

93   "was moral and temperate in his habits": *Extra Sun!!! Life, letters, and last conversation of John Caldwell Colt*, p. 4.

93   "He was taken to the watch-house": Ibid.

Chapter 13: Blood in the Gutter

95   "Fire the building at first seemed like a happy thought": Colt, 1842. *Trial of John C. Colt for the murder of Samuel Adams*, p. 479.

95   "a suitable box": Ibid.

95   "Wheeler's door was open": Ibid.

95   "went into my room": Ibid.

96   " his lights [were] extinguished": Ibid.

96   "During this suspense": Ibid.

96   "I supposed it too short and small": Ibid.

96   "somewhat alarmed": Ibid.

96   "No time was to be lost": Ibid.

96   "soon saw there was a possibility of": Ibid., p. 480.

96   "caused a rattling": Ibid.

96   "I then drew a piece of this rope around the legs": Ibid.

97   "The head, knees and feet, were still a little out": Ibid.

97   "a hardware store": Ibid., p. 481.

97   "eight minutes past ten": Ibid.

98   "Why are you so late?": Ibid.

98   "proverbial barefoot shoemaker": Rywell, *Samuel Colt, a man and an epoch*, p. 75.

98   "[T]he small capital [he had] was no longer able to sustain him": Powell, *An authentic life of John C. Colt*, p. 56.

99   "Mrs. Stewart's house": Ibid., p. 57.

99   "In Philadelphia, a female in humble life had become acquainted with our subject": Ibid., p. 56.

99   "he never deceived with false hopes": Ibid., p. 57.

99   "Captain and Mrs. Haff": Ibid.

100   **"Have known him fifteen months":** *Extra Sun!!! Life, letters, and last conversation of John Caldwell Colt*, p. 8.

100   **"Teachers and Clerks edition":** Powell, *An authentic life of John C. Colt*, p. 58.

101   **"On there [sic] occasions new works go off in large quantities":** Colt, *Life and Letters*, p. 4.

102   **"under the excitement of this suspicion":** Ibid., p. 5.

102   **"home before 10 o'clock":** *Extra Sun!!! Life, letters, and last conversation of John Caldwell Colt*, p. 9.

102   **"[JC] had been absent":** Ibid., p. 8.

102   **"I made no excuse":** Lawson, *American State Trials*, p. 482.

102   **"I went to the stand and pretended":** Ibid.

102   **"[H]e slept with his night shirt pinned up":** *Extra Sun!!! Life, letters, and last conversation of John Caldwell Colt*, p. 9.

CHAPTER 14: BLOOD BROTHERS

103   **"Where are you going so early?":** Lawson, *American State Trials*, p. 482. (I should note here that with all the conversations—i.e., dialogue—in this book multiple sources were used. I always went back and re-sourced each conversation with additional documents. For the most part, the reason why I was able to re-create so many conversations is the product of great resource material left behind and trial transcriptions that are very detailed. Witnesses often recalled what was said and what their response was, offering me, the researcher, a prime opportunity to re-create scenes with actual dialogue given to us by the memory of a particular source.)

103   **"found all apparently as [he] had left it":** Ibid.

103   **"to ascertain the first packet for New Orleans":** Ibid.

104   **"Moved it myself":** Ibid.

104   **"called for a hot roll and coffee"** [and next paragraph] **"could not eat":** Ibid.

104   **"wiped the wall":** Ibid., p. 483.

104   **"some spots":** Ibid.

104   **"He showed no [willingness] to state what had occurred":** *Extra Sun!!! Life, letters, and last conversation of John Caldwell Colt*, p. 9.

104   **"until his arrest":** Ibid.

105   **"This man, who came here a few minutes since":** Powell, *An authentic life of John C. Colt*, p. 64.

106   **"The reluctance of our subject to mingle with the world":** Ibid., p. 60.

106   **"I supposed, in the outset":** Ibid.

106   **"It appears to me":** Ibid.

107   **"In disgust," Bern Keating wrote:** Keating, *The flamboyant Mr. Colt and his deadly six-shooter*, p. 41.

107   **"the Colt rifle was indeed loaded and discharged of sixteen shots":** Ibid., p. 40.

108   **"The Colt family moved as one for the rescue of the murderer":** Lewis, "The Broadway-Chambers Street Murder," p. 47.

108   **"The newspapers, *they* are the true mischief-breeders":** Powell, *An authentic life of John C. Colt*, p. vii.

108   **"however hidden even from himself":** Ibid., p. viii.

108   **"Nothing is safe but the plain truth":** Ibid.

108   **"pouring out the family gold like water"**: Lewis, "The Broadway-Chambers Street Murder," p. 47. Rywell's *Samuel Colt, a man and an epoch*, p. 76, was also helpful to me in constructing this particular paragraph.

110   **"He spent time in debtor's prison"**: no byline given, "Union Notable: John Howard Payne," Union College 2009, www.union.edu/About/notables/Payne.php.

Chapter 15: Catch-penny Abuse

111   **"I noticed his appearance intently"**: Powell, *An authentic life of John C. Colt*, p. vi.

111   **"[T]hey were much too narrowly neighbors"**: Lewis, "The Broadway-Chambers Street Murder," p. 42.

112   **"Passing gate to gate"**: Powell, *An authentic life of John C. Colt*, p. vi.

112   **"self-reliance, coupled with almost an incapability of admitting impressions"**: Ibid., p. vii.

112   **"bec[o]me involved with gamblers and criminals"**: Tucker and Tucker, *Industrializing antebellum America*, p. 29.

113   **"slit in the ceiling at the end facing the door"**: Powell, *An authentic life of John C. Colt*, p. vi.

113   **"From my knowledge of the past"**: Colt, *Life and Letters*, p. 4.

113   **"I must assure you"**: Ibid.

114   **"The trial of Colt, the murderer of Adams"**: *Brooklyn Daily Eagle*, "The Trial of Colt," November 3, 1841, p. 2.

114   **"new papers starting up every month"**: Colt, *Life and Letters*, p. 4.

114   **"It is to be hoped, however"**: Ibid.

114   **"read no more of the clamorous stuff"**: Ibid.

115   **"Do not believe the thousand false statements"**: Ibid., p. 3.

115   **"The man that meets with misfortune nowadays"**: Ibid., p. 6.

115   **"But in this case"** . . . **"Your unfortunate friend, JC Colt"**: Ibid.

116   **"A Jerman calling himself John Ehlers"**: Samuel Colt, "Absconded" (August – September 1841). Samuel Colt Papers, Box 8, File 4, Connecticut Historical Society.

117   **"Submarine Battery Company"**: Ibid.

117   **"2,000 shares each with $50.00 value"**: Rywell, *Samuel Colt, a man and an epoch*, p. 68.

117   **"threatening aspect of affairs growing out of our French relations"**: Ibid.

118   **"Circumstances of a nature too painful to relate have rendered"**: Keating, *The flamboyant Mr. Colt and his deadly six-shooter*, p. 55.

118   **"It so happened that I scarcely reached Washington"**: Rywell, *Samuel Colt, a man and an epoch*, p. 70.

119   **"[I] went over with him the whole plans and secrets of my inventions"**: Letter, Colt to Representative Murphy, 3 June 1844, Colt Papers, box 5, Connecticut Historical Society.

119   **"sharply limited demonstration"**: Lundeberg, Philip K. 1974. *Samuel Colt's submarine battery: The secret and the enigma*. Smithsonian studies in history and technology, 29. Washington: Smithsonian Institution Press; p. 29.

Chapter 16: Prison House

121   **"called upon Colt"**: Lewis, "The Broadway-Chambers Street Murder," p. 48.

121   **"When he is tired of reading, or smoking"**: Ibid.

121 "Then comes his lunch": Ibid.

122 "As the keeper swings open the door of Colt's cell": Ibid.

123 "I shall feel at liberty to write more freely": *Extra Sun!!! Life, letters, and last conversation of John Caldwell Colt*, p. 6.

124 "galvanic mine warfare system": Lundeberg, *Samuel Colt's submarine battery*, p. 29.

124 "protect the port 'against the whole British Navy'": Keating, *The flamboyant Mr. Colt and his deadly six-shooter*, p. 55.

125 "My 'Captain'. . . is one who is terribly inconvenienced by anything": Ibid.

125 "national program of coastal fortifications": Lundeberg, *Samuel Colt's submarine battery*, p. 5.

125 "strong Congressional support following the War of 1812": Ibid.

125 "The history of nineteenth-century military technology": Ibid.

126 "In another part of the city is the Refuge for the Destitute": Dickens, Charles. *American Notes*.

126 "ten prices of an ordinary advertisement": *Extra Sun!!! Life, letters, and last conversation of John Caldwell Colt*, p. 7.

127 " hideous monster": Ibid.

127 "stand much more favorable before the public . . . than now": Ibid.

128 "being insane—wishing to kill myself": Ibid.

128 "murder, murder, murder" (and the following quote in this paragraph): Ibid.

128 "your extended kindness in": Ibid.

129 "Say to my friends that they must feel no anxiety for me!": Ibid.

129 "willing enough to help his brother": Rohan, Jack. 1935. *Yankee arms maker: The incredible career of Samuel Colt*. [Illustr.] New York: Harper and Brothers, p. 138.

Chapter 17: Theater of Murder

130 " block[ing] the avenues to the Court Room": Weld, H. Hastings, John Neal, George M. Snow, and Edward Stephens. 1842. *Brother Jonathan*. New York: [Wilson & Co.]; p. 136.

130 "Hang him! Hang him!": Ibid.

130 "unparalleled" (and the following quote): Ibid.

131 "four hundred feet" from the "theater of the murder": Lewis, "The Broadway-Chambers Street Murder," p. 48.

131 "eleven o'clock at night": These paragraphs depicting the opening moments of JC's trial were constructed with a number of sources, this quote in particular derived from: Weld, Neal, Snow, and Stephens, *Brother Jonathan*, p 137.

131 "the foremost American institutional legal treatise of its time": Parisian, Catherine M. 2010. *The first White House library: A history and annotated catalog*. University Park, Pa: Published by the Pennsylvania State University Press for the Bibliographical Society of America and the National First Ladies' Library, p. 218. (I might also note that in creating a biographical sketch of Judge William Kent, I also relied on Lawson's *American State Trials*, pp. 457–458.)

132 "This is the first time I have been engaged on the part of the People": Lawson, *American State Trials*, p. 458. (There was no shortage of resources excerpting trial testimony. I tried to gauge each source on its own merit and match each up against the next. Some of these sources were peppered with rhetoric and "penny press" racism and the subjective thoughts

and prejudice of the writer. With all that in mind, Lawson's *American State Trials* was a good, clean source, seemingly free of any creative additions and predisposition.)

132   **"Baltimore [was] where he taught mathematics for a while"**: Ibid. (footnote at bottom of page)

133   **"On a table were two black hats"**: Ibid., p. 469.

133   **"saw Mr. Colt in Chambers Street near Church, the morning of the 18th September, about nine o'clock"**: Ibid., p. 462.

134   **"The same excitement prevailed about the Court"**: Publication: *Brooklyn Eagle*, "Colt's Trial: Third Day," Jan. 24, 1842; Section: None; p. 2.

135   **"Am Mayor of New York"**: Lawson, *American State Trials*, p. 463.

135   **"Went over to the building and examined several persons"**: Ibid.

136   **"Did not hear anything about the salt in the box"**: Ibid.

136   **"[O]n seeing which,"** the *Eagle* reported: Publication: *Brooklyn Eagle*, "Colt's Trial: Fourth Day," Jan. 26, 1842; Section: None; p. 2.

137   **"Saw spots on the wall"**: Lawson, *American State Trials*, p. 465.

137   **"Her appearance produced a great sensation"**: Publication: *Brooklyn Eagle*, "Colt's Trial: Fourth Day," Jan. 26, 1842; Section: None; p. 2.

137   **"I did not see the body at the dead house"**: Lawson, *American State Trials*, p. 466.

137   **"We spoke of his brother"**: Ibid., p. 469.

138   **"purchased a pair of Colt's pistols"**: Ibid.

CHAPTER 18: A BROTHER'S SINS

139   **"Sam's submarine battery . . . was exactly what every member of Congress would have ordered"**: Rohan, *Yankee arms maker*, p. 137.

139   **"who saw [Sam] as a publicity-seeking charlatan"**: Tucker and Tucker, *Industrializing antebellum America*, pp. 62–63.

139   **"[M]any scientists viewed the battery as an auxiliary"**: Ibid.

140   **"Although his political acquaintances had enough self interest"**: Rohan, *Yankee arms maker*, p. 147.

140   **"violent and adventuresome years in our nation's"** history: Hosley, *Colt: The making of an American legend*, p. 67.

141   **"dispose of all the goods and chattels"**: Keating, *The flamboyant Mr. Colt and his deadly six-shooter*, p. 57.

141   **"Sir: I am very sorry"**: Ibid.

141   **"I am perfectly satisfied that the principle"**: Ibid.

142   **"The chancery suit part of the wrangling"**: Ibid., p. 58.

142   **"Sam also wrote to his attorney"**: Ibid.

142   **"Gentlemen of the jury"**: Lawson, *American State Trials*, p. 470.

143   **"While you have sympathy for him"**: Ibid.

143   **"A man will fight for his life"**: Ibid.

143   **"eloquent"**: Publication: *Brooklyn Eagle*, "Colt's Trial: Fourth Day," Jan. 24, 1842; Section: None; p. 2.

144   **"Adams was killed by blows from the confiscated hatchet"**: Smith, Tom. "John Colt Trial: 1842." Great American Trials. 2002. *Encyclopedia.com*. (November 15, 2010). www.encyclopedia.com/doc/1G23498200057.html.

144   **"Am the inventor of Colt's patent firearms"**: Lawson, *American State Trials*, p. 471.

144   "asked to show some experiments": Ibid.
145   "Never made pistols with more than one barrel": Ibid.
145   "penetrated by a ball propelled only by cap": Ibid.
145   "I was never able but once even to indent a fireboard": Ibid.
145   "The impression did not appear to be so great at five feet": Ibid.
146   "It is impossible to say what particular degree of injury would be necessary": Ibid.
146   "Made paper to order and on account of Mr. Colt in July and August, 1841": Ibid., p. 472.
147   "The head of Mr. Adams was . . . brought into court by the physicians and coroner":
       Ibid.
147   "Have examined the head of Mr. Adams": Ibid.
147   "We move, Your Honor, that the skull and axe should be shown to the jury" (and subse-
       quent conversation): Ibid.
148   "crowded to excess": Ibid.
148   "Trial coverage was a staple in the so-called 'penny press'": Hall, Dennis, and Susan G.
       Hall. 2006. *American icons. An encyclopedia of the people, places, and things that have shaped
       our culture Volume one*. Westport, Conn.: Greenwood Press; p. 167.
149   "use them to make sense of their world": Ibid., p. 166.
149   "He placed the corner of the axe in the hole over the left ear": Lawson, *American State
       Trials*, p. 472.

CHAPTER 19: BORN FOR BLOOD

150   "interesting" . . . "dreadful sight": Sun, The. 1842. *Trial of John C. Colt for the murder
       of Samuel Adams*, Colt, JC. New York (State). Court of Oyer and Terminer (New York
       County), p. 8.
150   "went on to explain the nature of the wounds": Dunphy, Thomas, and Thomas J.
       Cummins. 1878. *Remarkable trials of all countries particularly of the United States, Great
       Britain, Ireland, and France: with notes and speeches of counsel: containing thrilling narratives
       of fact from the court room, also historical reminiscences of wonderful events*. New York: Ward
       & Peloubet; p. 260.
150   "Am indebted to Mr. Colt": Sun, The. *Trial of John C. Colt for the murder of Samuel Adams*,
       p. 8.
150   "Is Miss Henshaw in the courtroom": Ibid.
150   "created quite a sensation among the audience": Ibid.
150   "aroused acute public discourse": Tucher, Andie. 1994. *Froth & scum: Truth, beauty, good-
       ness, and the ax murder in America's first mass medium*. Chapel Hill [u.a.]: Univ. of North
       Carolina Press; p. 104.
151   "dark bonnet, black veil, and light cloth cloak": Sun, The. *Trial of John C. Colt for the
       murder of Samuel Adams*, p. 8.
151   "Have been acquainted with John C. Colt": Ibid.
152   "First became acquainted with Colt at Philadelphia": Ibid., p. 9.
152   "Am a mother by Mr. Colt": Ibid., p. 10.
152   "Did not know there was a watch in the trunk when Justice Taylor took it": Ibid.
152–153 "[My client's] relation with her": Ibid.
153   "Unless the character of a witness is impeached": Ibid.
154   "easy, lucid, and spoke without confusion": Lewis, "The Broadway-Chambers Street
       Murder," p. 48.

154   "We will admit that Colt took the life of Adams": Lawson, *American State Trials*, p. 475.

155   "We had intended to state the facts to the public": Ibid., p. 476.

155   "Are such a course of remarks proper?": Ibid., p. 483.

156   "My remarks shall not extend to a length unnecessarily": Ibid., p. 483.

156   "Do you suppose": Ibid.

156   "I believe the wounds were given before the body of Mr. Adams was struck down": Ibid., p. 484.

157   "Yet the means had nothing to do with the offence unless collected for that purpose": Ibid., p. 487.

158   "The learned counsel said this morning that Caroline Henshaw's testimony": Ibid.

158   "Caroline Henshaw had access to the trunk": Ibid., p. 488.

158   "Now for the quarrel": Ibid.

159   "When the wife was here": Ibid.

159   "A charge was made that a pistol had been used": Ibid., p. 490.

160   "Gentlemen, after nearly a fortnight's trial": Ibid.

Chapter 20: A Bloodthirsty Heart

161   "Blood has been spilt": Lawson, *American State Trials*, p. 490.

162   "As to the last gentleman who has spoken": Ibid., p. 491.

162   "As to the threats of the other gentleman": Ibid.

163   "practicing medicine without a license" (along with the following quotes in this paragraph regarding Fowler's arrest): *The New York Times*. January 16, 1886. "A Warrant for Dr. O.S. Fowler," (no page available).

163   "study of the shape and protuberances of the skull": phrenology. Answers.com. Britannica Concise Encyclopedia, Encyclopædia Britannica, Inc., 1994–2010. www.answers.com/topic/phrenology, accessed November 20, 2010.

163   "indication of mental abilities and character traits": Ibid.

164   "I recollect perfectly well": *The American phrenological journal and miscellany*. 1838. Philadelphia: A. Waldie; p. 312.

164   "[T]he whole organization": Ibid.

164   "You would not hesitate fighting a duel in defense of yourself": Ibid., p. 313.

164   "Approbativeness and Self Esteem are both very large": Ibid.

165   "Mr. Colt, I have one word of caution to give you": Ibid.

165   "As far as I am informed": Ibid.

166   "time to write a confession": Lawson, *American State Trials*, p. 491.

166   "You are to remove all doubts from your minds": Ibid., p. 492.

166   "If he killed Samuel Adams to get rid of a debt": Ibid.

167   "This gentleman is represented to be everything mild": Ibid., p. 494.

167   "Had there been no improper intention": Ibid., p. 495.

167   "It does not matter when Adams came into the room": Ibid.

167   "I have done everything that has been asked of me": Ibid., p. 496.

167   "Had a quarrel taken place": Ibid., p. 497.

168   "no substantial amount of time need elapse": Emanuel, Steven. 2007. *Criminal law*. Austin: Wolters Kluwer Law & Business/Aspen Publishers; p. 262.

168   "Most modern courts": Ibid.

168   "Gentlemen, I have endeavored to do my duty": Lawson, *American State Trials*, p. 499.

169   Judge Kent was next to address the jury: Ibid.

169   "Some allusion has been made to the excitement out of doors": Ibid., p. 500.

169   "The degrees of homicides are four": Ibid.

170   "Such as correcting a servant and death ensues": Ibid., p. 501.

170   "difficult to exclude": Ibid., p. 502.

171   "The question, then, is as to murder or manslaughter": Ibid.

171   "In regard to the latter": Ibid.

171   "Now, as to the occurrence itself" (and the remainder of Kent's instructions to the jury): Ibid., pp. 504–507.

CHAPTER 21: "DEATH HATH NO TERRORS"

173   "There is a world above this": Colt, *Life and letters of John Caldwell Colt; condemned to be hung on the eighteenth of November, 1842, for the murder of Samuel Adams*, p. 7.

173   "Gentlemen, what is your verdict?": Lawson, *American State Trials*, p. 507.

174   "We find the prisoner": Ibid.

174   "Although I stand condemned by *twelve men*": Colt, *Life and Letters*, p. 8.

174   "fiendish appetite . . . burning in the bosom of many witnesses": Ibid.

175   "2,700 and 3,200 pistols in various models": Hosley, *Colt: The making of an American legend*, p. 21.

175   "I have employed my leisure": Colt to President John Tyler, 19 June 1841, retained copy, Colt Papers, box 5.

176   "The idea of Submarine explosions": Samuel Colt to Representative Henry C. Murphy, House Committee on Naval Affairs, 3 June 1844, Samuel Colt Papers (manuscripts, Connecticut Historical Society, Hartford), box 6.

176   "revolving pistol": Gallien, Gail. *Association of Ohio Long Rifle Collectors*, 2 August 1993. "Henry Humbarger: Gunmaker of Perry Co. Ohio and Whitely Co. Indiana"; p. 3.

176   "Adam, Henry and . . . Peter II": Ibid.

177   "completed the double-action": Ibid.

177   "to apply for a patent": Ibid., p. 4.

177   "It amounts to nothing": Ibid.

177   "anyone could visit his shop and watch the progress he was making": Ibid.

178   "Justice is but a name": Colt, *Life and Letters*, p. 8.

178   "the evidence of the least importance in the case": Ibid.

178   "unfortunate, foolish man": Ibid., p. 13.

178   "Because I defended myself": Ibid., p. 11.

178   "I cannot blame counsel": Ibid.

179   "beautiful pack of questions": Ibid., p. 12.

179   "When you had killed Adams" (and the remainder of this Q&A): Ibid., pp. 12–13.

179   "It was five or six days after the catastrophe": Ibid.

179   "Why did you strip the body of its clothing": Ibid.

179   "The clothing would have identified it years afterwards": Ibid.

179   "Why did you ship the body to New Orleans": Ibid.

179   "Because it was a warm climate": Ibid.

180   "Thank God I do not feel myself culpable and never shall": Ibid., p. 14.

180   "This misfortune is using me up fast": Ibid.

180   "Were it not for my child": Ibid.

180   "Do you read and believe in the Bible?": Ibid.

180   "a curious book. . . . As a book of history": Ibid.

181   "If you wish to know": Ibid.

181   "Christ's Sermon on the Mount": Ibid.

181   "Be careful not to parade your uprightness in public to attract attention": *The New Jerusalem Bible*. 1985. Garden City, N.Y.: Doubleday; p. 1618.

CHAPTER 22: ENGINE OF DESTRUCTION

185   "the Navy stopped honoring his drafts for the submarine mine": Keating, *The flamboyant Mr. Colt and his deadly six-shooter*, p. 58.

185   "harbor defense battery" [...] "revolutionary iron-hulled Stevens Battery": Lundeberg, *Samuel Colt's submarine battery: The secret and the enigma*, p. 25.

186   "split the gate from the demonstration": Keating, *The flamboyant Mr. Colt and his deadly six-shooter*, p. 59.

186   "Colt's sub-marine battery created much attention": New York *Evening Post*, 5 July 1842.

187   "The case containing the combustibles was sunk under the hulk": *New York American*, quoted in *Niles' National Register*, volume 62 (16 July 1842), p. 310.

187   Sam's "battery" had been "placed under": New York *Herald*, 6 July 1842.

187   "[I]t strikes us that the great difficulty": *New York Sun*, quoted in *Niles' National Register*, volume 62 (16 July 1842), p. 310.

189   "experts think he was": Keating, *The flamboyant Mr. Colt and his deadly six-shooter*, p. 61.

CHAPTER 23: BLOOD ON HIS HANDS

192   "aglow with happiness": Lewis, "The Broadway-Chambers Street Murder," p. 49.

192   "solemn protest against the legal competency of the court": Edwards, Charles. 1867. *Pleasantries about courts and lawyers of the state of New York*. New York: Richardson; p. 323.

193   "convulsed with tears": Devens, R. M. 1878. *Our first century: Being a popular descriptive portraiture of the one hundred great and memorable events of perpetual interest in the history of our country, political, military, mechanical, social, scientific and commercial: Embracing also delineations of all the great historic characters celebrated in the annals of the republic; men of heroism, statesmanship, genius, oratory, adventure and philanthropy.* Springfield, Mass.: C.A. Nichols & Co.; p. 531.

193   "Rooms were prepared in Brooklyn for the reception of Colt": Lawson, *American State Trials*, p. 510.

194   "A doctor of the city undertook to resuscitate Colt": Ibid.

194   "Colt's wife, and his brother Samuel": Devens, *Our first century*, p. 531.

194   "I want to see the sheriff": Ibid., p. 532.

194   "I am innocent of the murder of Adams": Ibid.

194   JC "begged the sheriff not to execute the sentence": Ibid.

195   "Banish all hope of that kind": Ibid.

195   "I want to see Doctor Anthon": Ibid.

195   "If there are any gentlemen present who wish to see Mr. Colt": Ibid.

195   "with one or two exceptions": Ibid.

195   "Can I be left alone until the last moment?": Ibid.

195   "God bless you, and may you prosper in this life": Ibid., p. 385.

196   "the excitement . . . increased tremendously": Ibid.

196   "a rush of feet, attended by a clangor of bells": Lewis, "The Broadway-Chambers Street Murder," p. 49.

196   "In the midst of the riot": Ibid.

196   "Colt is dead in his cell": Ibid.

196   "tower over the vestibule of the prison" burned: Edwards, *Pleasantries about courts and lawyers of the state of New York,* p. 323.

196   "On the keeper opening the door": Ibid.

197   "As I thought" (and subsequent quotes): Devens, *Our first century,* p. 532.

197   "[John Colt] had stabbed himself about the fifth rib": Ibid.

CHAPTER 24: A DREADFUL CUP OF VENGEANCE

198   "expression changed to something nearly approaching joy": Tucher, *Froth & scum:* p. 106.

198   "Thank God!": Ibid.

199   "In another part of this day's paper": Lewis, "The Broadway-Chambers Street Murder," pp. 49–50.

199   "did impanel a jury": Ibid., p. 50.

200   "The rumor continued that the hastily assembled coroner's jury": Goldberg, Stone, "John Caldwell Colt: A Notorious Accountant," pp. 128–129.

200   "She speaks and understands German and can best be cared for in the German countries": Rywell, *Samuel Colt: a man and an epoch,* p. 139.

201   "To-day, I cannot write of beauty": *The United States magazine and Democratic review.* 1843. Washington, D.C.: Langtree and O'Sullivan; p. 443.

201   "We were to have had an execution yesterday": Ibid., p. 444.

202   "He was precisely in the situation of a man": Ibid.

202   "And so the chapter ended": Lewis, "The Broadway-Chambers Street Murder," p. 50.

202   "He was sentenced to be hanged": Walling, George W. 1887. *Recollections of a New York chief of police.* New York: Caxton Book Concern; p. 26.

CHAPTER 25: MOVING ON

203   "Everything on my part was conducted as privately as possible": Lundeberg, *Samuel Colt's submarine battery,* p. 30.

204   "[I]t was apparent to John Quincy Adams": Ibid.

204   "He [Adams] was as fully conscious that the system would be useless to the United States": *Congressional Globe,* Volume 11 (1842), p. 930; Barnard, *Armsmear,* pp. 282–284 [note 21].

205   "Undaunted": Lundeberg, *Samuel Colt's submarine battery,* p. 37.

205   "believed that sending messages over a wire was the work of Satan": Holbrook, Stewart Hall. 1946. *Lost men of American history.* New York: Macmillan Co.; p. 99.

206   "The first person who made any practical use of electricity": Lundeberg, pp. 37–38.

206   "mutinied rather than continue sailing": Keating, *The flamboyant Mr. Colt and his deadly six-shooter*, p. 67.

207   "with mixed results": Ibid., p. 67.

207   "[starve] to death the inventors": Rohan, *Yankee arms maker*, p. 153.

208   "something like a mathematical certainty": no byline given, 2005. *Free LanceStar*, the (Fredericksburg, VA), "The Forgotten Tragedy: The 1844 Explosion on the USS Princeton …"

208   "the patriotic ardor": Ibid.

209   "Twenty feet of the ship's bulwark": Ibid.

209   "Though the Peacemaker accident had killed his most powerful and sympathetic supporter": Keating, *The flamboyant Mr. Colt and his deadly six-shooter*, p. 68.

Chapter 26: The Tail of a Lion

211   "sowed his mines on the Anacostia River": Keating, *The flamboyant Mr. Colt and his deadly six-shooter*, p. 68.

212   "[T]he whole populace was in a fidget of satisfaction": Ibid.

212   "I strolled down to the shores of the Eastern Branch about three o'clock": *Washington Daily National Intelligencer*, 15 April 1844 (also reprinted in its entirety in Lundeberg's booklet on Colt's submarine battery, an invaluable resource if one wanted to study Sam's obsession with receiving government grants to continue his research.)

212   "an elevated bluff": Ibid.

213   "In the middle of the stream": Ibid.

214   "Every eye was turned toward the ship": Ibid.

214   "This exhibition rose as if by the touch of magic": Ibid.

214   "Ah!" the crowd said in unison: Ibid.

214   "Oh, he has missed her": Ibid.

214   "The words were scarcely uttered when a third explosion took place": Ibid.

215   "momentary pause of gratified suspense": Ibid.

215   "[T]he shores resounded with heartfelt plaudits": Ibid.

215   "on the opposite bank of the river": Lundeberg, *Samuel Colt's submarine battery*, p. 45.

216   "As experiments, these, as many others have been, were very beautiful": Ibid., p. 46.

216   "Mr. Colt may, perhaps, not attempt to found his claims to originality": Ibid., p. 47.

217   "Movements are making to kill me of[f]": Ibid.

218   "[I]n no single instance have I failed": Ibid., p. 48.

218   "together … in postponing submarine mine development": Ibid., p. 52.

218   Sam's "novelty [was] sufficient to sustain a patent": Ibid., p. 54.

219   "Unhappily for Colt": Ibid.

219   "invention is entitled to the favorable consideration of government": Ibid., p. 55.

219   "…[I]t is better to be at the head of a louse": Tucker and Tucker, *Industrializing Antebellum America*, p. 64.

Chapter 27: Saved by the Indians

220   "Sam sent him a hundred dollars and advised him to avoid duels": Rohan, *Yankee arms dealer*, p. 159.

221   "striking [a man] several times in the face with his fist": Keating, *The flamboyant Mr. Colt and his deadly six-shooter*, p. 74.

221   "He was immediately struck with its possibilities": Ibid.

222   **"Powder-burn them"**: Ibid., p. 75.

222   **"a shot for every finger on the hand"**: Ibid.

222   **the "bow and arrow"**: Ibid.

223   **"Whereas, the Congress of the United States of America"**: Texas. 1846. *Laws passed by the ... Legislature of the state of Texas.* Houston: Telegraph Office; p. xlvi.

223   **"a barefaced steal of its territory"**: Rohan, *Yankee arms dealer,* p. 163.

223   **"tried vainly to buy the northern provinces of Mexico"**: Rywell, *Samuel Colt: a man and an epoch,* p. 86.

224   **"As war exists, and notwithstanding all our efforts to avoid it"**: *AR; The American review.* Vol. 3, 1973. New York: Bantam Books; p. 577.

224   **"Colt Sir ... *The pistols which you made for the Texas Navy*"**: Rosa, Joseph G. 1995. *Age of the gunfighter: Men and weapons on the frontier, 1840–1900 : With artifacts from the Gene Autry Western Heritage Museum and the Buffalo Bill Historical Center.* Norman: University of Oklahoma Press; p. 22.

225   **"Although Colt was not destined to fight in the Mexican War"**: Grant, *The Colt Armory,* p. 21.

226   **"Without your pistols we would not have had the confidence"**: Ibid., p. 21.

226   **"I regret exceedingly that you cannot lend a helping hand"**: Hosley, *Colt: The making of an American legend,* p. 24.

227   **"Whitney and a group of machinists and technicians"**: Ibid.

227   **"Cost overruns and production delays piled up"**: Ibid., p. 23.

228   **"as late as 11 or 12 o'clock at night"**: Ibid., p. 24.

228   **"based more on the availability of credit"**: Ibid.

228   **"establish an Armory in Hartford"**: Ibid.

228   **"This was one wave Sam Colt was determined to ride"**: Ibid., p. 23.

CHAPTER 28: HOUSE OF HOPE

229   **The building he found was a "medium-sized, three-story" tenement**: Rohan, *Yankee arms dealer,* p. 168.

229   **Edwin Wesson ... "erected a three-story brick building"**: Ibid.

230   **"already a centre of arms-making"**: Witzel, Morgen. 2005. *The encyclopedia of the history of American management.* Bristol: Thoemmes Continuum; p. 86.

230   **he was "granted a controversial renewal of the patent"**: Hosley, *Colt: The making of an American legend,* p. 25.

230   **"The invention for the construction of these arms being patented"**: United States, and James D. Richardson. 1896. *A compilation of the messages and papers of the presidents, 1789–1897.* Washington: Government Printing Office, p. 2331.

230   **"The right to use this patent by the United States"**: Ibid.

230   **"They are close cronies"**: Rywell, *Samuel Colt: a man and an epoch,* p. 99.

231   **"I am working on my own hook"**: Grant, p. 21.

231   **"his pockets bulging with orders"**: Rohan, *Yankee arms dealer,* p. 179.

231   **"year of new beginnings"**: Hosley, *Colt: The making of an American legend,* p. 25.

232   **a "central figure," as Hosley noted, "in the Colt legend"**: Ibid.

232   **"the important thing is that you come to me at the earliest possible moment"**: Ibid., p. 26. Please note that although I use Hosley's book at times as a resource for Sam's letters, I did go back and read the letters myself where possible. The problem is, the handwriting of the era is extremely difficult to read at times. It's messy, or, in some cases, too crisp.

Not only that, but Hosley's book is an irreplaceable and unmatched Colt resource—a true canon of Colt history.

232 **Sam had "lured [Elisha Root] away":** Grant, p. 21.

232 **"He was a clever designer":** Smith, Anthony. 2004. *Machine gun: The story of the men and the weapon that changed the face of war.* New York: St. Martin's Paperbacks; p. 41.

233 **"He knew all about those floods":** Rohan, *Yankee arms dealer,* p. 179.

234 **"If his fellow citizens had regarded him as merely stupid":** Ibid., p. 180.

234 **"The attempt to protect the South Meadow":** Barnard, *Armsmear,* p. 65.

234 **"but he is a practical man":** Ibid.

234 **"He thumbed his nose at society":** Leavenworth, Jesse, "Arms, Art and the Man ...," *The Hartford Courant,* September 20, 2006, p. D1.

235 **"Now, sir," Sam wrote to one newspaper:** Barnard, *Armsmear,* p. 66.

Chapter 29: Fortune Smiles

236 **"Unlike her entrepreneurial husband-to-be":** Hosley, *Colt: The making of an American legend,* p. 28.

237 **"New England's fabled resort community":** Ibid., p. 29.

237 **"Stunning, poised, well-connected":** Ibid.

237 **"quick, high-tempered, impulsive":** Barnard, *Armsmear,* p. 306.

237 **Sam "never forgot to be generous":** Ibid.

238 **One "passion" of Sam's, Barnard pointed out in his memorial to Sam** (along with the following quote): Ibid.

238 **"There was a majesty in his forbearance":** Ibid.

238 **"I am a rather elderly man":** This and the remainder of the quotes from "Bartleby, the Scrivener" in this brief section were excerpted from Melville, Herman, and Pierre Leyris. 1978. *Bartleby.* Montpellier, France: Université Paul Valéry.

240 **"the largest private Armory in the world":** Barnard, *Armsmear,* p. 308.

240 **"The compound was the most ambitious":** Hosley, *Colt: The making of an American legend,* p. 98.

241 **"Its extent," Henry Barnard observed:** Ibid.

Chapter 30: Life Springs and Death Blows

243 **"glorified bachelor's party":** Hosley, *Colt: The making of an American legend,* p. 30.

243 **"draped in bunting and flags" [...] "grand salute of rifles was fired form the cupola of the Armory":** Ibid.

244 **"long, grand, impressive, contradictory, beautiful, strange":** Rywell, *Samuel Colt: a man and an epoch,* p. 136.

244 **"Armsmear" [...] "was a mold":** Ibid.

244 **"His stage was not Hartford":** Leavenworth, Jesse, "Arms, Art and the Man ...," *The Hartford Courant,* September 20, 2006, p. D1.

245 **"For ten months":** Barnard, *Armsmear* (memoir section), p. 312.

245 **"a little son was given ...":** Ibid., p. 314.

246 **"Dark-eyed baby Lizzie":** Ibid.

246 **"[W]hen the chill October winds were blowing":** Ibid., p. 316.

246 **"a death-blow":** Ibid.

246   The "agony" on Sam's gaze: Ibid.

246   "little train of mourners": Ibid.

246   "The prayers were said": Ibid., p. 317.

246   "convulsed with such grief as one seldom sees": Ibid.

247   "He," Elizabeth wrote, "who had borne unflinchingly every ill": Ibid., p. 316.

247   "when his body was suffering so unspeakably": Ibid., p. 317.

247   "brought to him increased cares": Ibid., p. 318.

248   "He was always a democrat": Ibid.

248   "Had he received a military education": Ibid., p. 320.

249   "Like little Lizzie": Ibid.

249   the "children bright and well": Ibid.

249   "a slight attack": Ibid.

250   "[He] seemed so proud to show him his boy of three summers": Ibid., p. 321.

250   "sit up all day": Ibid.

250   "[O]ur hopes were very sanguine": Ibid.

250   "the queen ... of Hartford society": *The Connecticut magazine: An illustrated monthly*. 1899. Hartford, Conn.: The Connecticut Magazine Co.; p. 128.

251   "must have" [...] "touched an answering chord in his soul": Barnard, *Armsmear* (memoir section), p. 321.

251   "noticing that he was much flushed": Ibid.

251   "quiet and cheerful": Ibid.

251–253 Beginning with "His mind began to wander" until the conclusion of this chapter, including the conversations between Elizabeth and Sam during the final moments of his life, please see Ibid., pp. 322–323.

For more information about the relationship between Sam and his illegitimate son with Caroline Henshaw, see Rywell, *Samuel Colt: a man and an epoch*, pp. 139–140. Also see: Rohan, *Yankee arms dealer*, pp. 259–263.

CHAPTER 31: HIS FATHER'S SON

254   "The funeral of Samuel Colt": Grant, *The Colt Legacy*, p. 15.

255   "Hartford knew that day it had lost one of its noblest sons": Barnard, *Armsmear* (memoir section), p. 324.

255   "His prophecy had been fulfilled": Rohan, *Yankee arms dealer*, p. 295.

255   "several remarkable original models": Trumbull, J. Hammond. 1886. *The memorial history of Hartford County, Connecticut, 16331884*. Boston: E.L. Osgood; p. 566.

255   "No one learned the cause": Smith, Anthony. 2004. *Machine gun: the story of the men and the weapon that changed the face of war*. New York: St. Martin's Paperbacks; p. 54.

255   "a facsimile of that destroyed": Trumbull, *The memorial history of Hartford County, Connecticut, 1633-1884*, p. 566.

256   "emotional and artistic focal point of the church": Hosley, *Colt: The making of an American legend*, p. 204.

256   "The Lord which is in the midst of the Throne shall Feed them": This quote can, obviously, be viewed from inside the church; or see Hosley, p. 204.

257   "a group of young ladies and gentleman in costume": Grant, p. 66.

257   "Collie grew up a gay blade": Rohan, *Yankee arms dealer,* p. 295.

258   "were wild enough to inspire tales of orgies": Grant, p. 66.

Chapter 32: A Final Blow

260   "large-hearted man with generous impulses": Grant, p. 68.

260   "[t]his is absurd and pure fabrication": Hosley, *Colt: The making of an American legend,* p. 207.

261   "one of the eccentric masterpieces of Victorian American architecture": Ibid.

261   "spent the equivalent of $30 million building three of what today rank among Hartford's ten most significant architectural treasures": Ibid., 209.

261   "I have tried to honor their memories always": Ibid., p. 222.

261   "group of Connecticut capitalists": Rohan, *Yankee arms dealer,* p. 295.

262   "One can survive everything": Wilde, Oscar. 1905. *The plays of Oscar Wilde.* Boston: J.W. Luce & Co.; p. 20.

262   "as many impoverished but refined and educated gentlewomen as the buildings" would support: Hosley, *Colt: The making of an American legend,* p. 226; and Smith, *Machine gun,* p. 55.

262   "Elizabeth Colt's death marked the end of an era": Hosley, *Colt: The making of an American legend,* p. 227.

Selected Bibliography

I found the following list of texts, published books, magazines, and newspaper accounts helpful when gathering my research on the Colt family, John Colt's life, and the legacy that Samuel Colt left behind. I am in awe of a few late-eighteenth- and nineteenth-century writers who were unafraid to write with an iron fist. I can relate in a lot of ways to the tone and sometimes sarcastic context some of these writers put their subjects into, as I often do myself. There's an inherent honesty within the writings of our past that, when we look beyond the obvious overblown and sometimes purple prose used to relate this information, a genuine feeling of integrity emerges from the page; writers had no trouble expressing how they felt about a particular subject.

Anyone interested in New York history should have a look at, especially, Edwin Burrows and Michael L. Wallace's *Gotham: A History of New York City to 1898* (Oxford University Press, 1999). Any fan of history should own this doorstop. It is expertly written and thoroughly researched. There are sections that read like a novel.

I would be remiss not to mention Bill Hosley's incredible book on Sam Colt one last time. Hosley's research is exhaustive and outstanding; it's hard to look beyond what Hosley has done with the Colt story and find things missing from the record. I used *Colt: The Making of an American Legend* as a guide, often quoting from it and becoming lost in the sheer beauty and grace of Hosley's prose and illustrations. If any reader of mine wants to learn more about the Colt family, and dig into the subplots and subjects I merely touched upon in this book, please purchase Hosley's book.

I could go on and on citing all the books I found to be exciting and some of the best scholarship I have ever studied on the era, but I'll step aside and allow my bibliography to showcase those works.

Ackroyd, Peter, and Edgar Allan Poe. 2008. *Poe: a life cut short.* London: Chatto & Windus.
The American law review. 1866. Boston: Little, Brown, and Co.
AR; The American review. Vol. 3, 1973. New York: Bantam Books.
Barnard, Henry. 1973. *Armsmear: The home, the arm and the armory of Samuel Colt. A memorial.* New York: [Alvord, Printer].

Bennett, James Arlington. 1826. *The American system of practical book-keeping, Adapted to the commerce of the United States in its domestic and foreign relations, comprehending all the modern improvements in the practice of the art; : and exemplified in one set of books kept by double entry, embracing five different methods of keeping a journal. : Designed for the use of schools. : To which are added Forms of the most approved auxiliary books; and a copperplate engraving, exhibiting, at one view, the final balance of the leger.* New York: Collins & Hannay.

Burrows, Edwin G., and Michael L. Wallace. 1999. *Gotham: a history of New York City to 1898.* New York: Oxford University Press.

Carter, Gregg Lee. 2002. *Guns in American society: An encyclopedia of history, politics, culture, and the law.* Santa Barbara, Calif: ABC-CLIO.

Chisholm, Hugh. 1910. *The encyclopædia britannica; a dictionary of arts, sciences, literature and general information.* Cambridge, Eng: University of Cambridge Press.

Colt, John Caldwell. 1842. *Trial of John C. Colt for the murder of Samuel Adams.* New York: Benj. H. Day.

Connecticut, James P. Andrews, John M. Comley, Richard Henry Phillips, William S. Locke, and William P. Aspell. 1897. *Cases argued and determined in the Supreme Court of Errors of the State of Connecticut.* New York: Published for the State of Connecticut by Banks & Brothers.

The Connecticut magazine: an illustrated monthly. 1899. Hartford, Conn.: The Connecticut Magazine Co.

Davies, John D. *Phrenology: Fad and science: A nineteenth-century American crusade.* New Haven, Conn.: Yale University Press, 1955.

De Puy, W. H., and A. S. Packard. 1898. *The People's cyclopedia of universal knowledge: with numerous appendixes invaluable for reference in all departments of industrial life, with the pronunciation and orthography conformed to Webster's International dictionary.* New York: Eaton & Mains.

Devens, R. M. 1878. *Our first century: Being a popular descriptive portraiture of the one hundred great and memorable events of perpetual interest in the history of our country, political, military, mechanical, social, scientific and commercial: embracing also delineations of all the great historic characters celebrated in the annals of the republic; men of heroism, statesmanship, genius, oratory, adventure and philanthropy.* Springfield, Mass: C.A. Nichols & Co.

Dickens, Charles. 1842. *American Notes.* London: Chapman and Hall.

Dillingham, William B. 2008. *Melville's short fiction, 1853-1856.* [S.l.]: University of Georgia Press.

Dizard, Jan E. 1999. *Guns in America: A reader.* New York, N.Y. [u.a.]: New York University Press.

Dolan, Jay P. 2010. *The Irish Americans: A history.* New York: Bloomsbury Press.

Dunphy, Thomas, and Thomas J. Cummins. 1867. *Remarkable trials of all countries; particularly of the United States, Great Britain, Ireland and France: with notes and speeches of counsel. Containing thrilling narratives of fact from the court-room, also historical reminiscences of wonderful events.* New York: Diossy & Cockcroft.

Edwards, Charles. 1867. *Pleasantries about courts and lawyers of the state of New York.* New York: Richardson.

Edwards, William B., and Samuel Colt. 1953. *The story of Colt's revolver; the biography of Col. Samuel Colt.* Harrisburg, Pa.: Stackpole Co.

Ellis, Edward Robb, and Jeanyee Wong. 1997. *The epic of New York City*. New York: Carroll & Graf.

Emanuel, Steven. 2007. *Criminal law*. Austin: Wolters Kluwer Law & Business/Aspen Publishers.

Evans, Harold, Gail Buckland, and David Lefer. 2004. *They made America*. New York, N.Y. [u.a.]: Little, Brown.

Fowler, Orson S. *The American phrenological journal and miscellany*. 1838. Philadelphia: [A. Waldie].

Fowler, Orson S. *The Practical Phrenologist: A Compendium of Phreno-Organic Science*. Boston: O. S. Fowler, 1869.

Gallien, Gail. *Association of Ohio Long Rifle Collectors*, 2 August 1993. "Henry Humbarger: Gunmaker of Perry Co. Ohio and Whitely Co. Indiana."

Goldberg, Louis, and Stone, Willard. "John Caldwell Colt: A Notorious Accountant," *The Accounting Historians Journal*, Vol. 12, No. 1, Spring 1985.

Grant, Ellsworth S. 1995. *The Colt Armory: A history of Colt's Manufacturing Company, Inc.* Lincoln, R.I.: Mowbray Pub.

Grant, Ellsworth S. 1982. *The Colt legacy: The Colt Armory in Hartford, 1855-1980*. Providence, R.I.: Mowbray Co.

Grant, Ellsworth S. 2006. *Connecticut disasters: True stories of tragedy and survival*. Disasters series. Guilford, Conn.: Globe Pequot Press.

Great stories of American businessmen, from American heritage, the magazine of history. 1972. New York: American Heritage Pub. Co.

Hall, Dennis, and Susan G. Hall. 2006. *American icons. An encyclopedia of the people, places, and things that have shaped our culture Volume one*. Westport, Conn.: Greenwood Press.

Haswell, Chas. H. 1896. *Reminiscences of New York by an octogenarian (1816 to 1860)*. New York: Harper.

Hazlett, James C., Edwin Olmstead, and M. Hume Parks. 2004. *Field artillery weapons of the Civil War*. Urbana: University of Illinois Press.

Holbrook, Stewart Hall. 1946. *Lost men of American history*. New York: Macmillan Co.

Hosley, William N. 1996. *Colt: The making of an American legend*. Amherst: University of Massachusetts Press.

Houze, Herbert G., Carolyn C. Cooper, Elizabeth Mankin Kornhauser, and Samuel Colt. 2006. *Samuel Colt: Arms, art, and invention*. New Haven [u.a.]: Yale Univ. Press [u.a.].

Jackson, Kenneth J., ed. 1995. *The Encyclopedia of New York City*. New Haven: Yale University Press.

Keating, Bern. 1978. *The flamboyant Mr. Colt and his deadly six-shooter*. Garden City, N.Y.: Doubleday.

Lamb, Martha J. 1879. *The homes of America*. New York: D. Appleton.

Lardner, James, and Thomas A. Reppetto. 2000. *NYPD: A city and its police*. New York: Henry Holt and Co.

Lawson, John Davison. 1972. *American state trials: A collection of the important and interesting criminal trials which have taken place in the United States, from the beginning of our government to 1920: with notes and annotations*. Wilmington, Del.: Scholarly Resources.

Laxton, William. 1838. *The Civil engineer and architect's journal*. London (PUBLISHED FOR THE PROPRIETOR, 57 KING STREET, WESTMINSTER).

Lewis, Alfred Henry, "The Broadway-Chambers Street Murder," *Pearson's Magazine*. 1899. New York, N.Y.: Pearson Pub. Co.

Lundeberg, Philip K. 1974. *Samuel Colt's submarine battery: The secret and the enigma.* Smithsonian studies in history and technology, 29. Washington: Smithsonian Institution Press.

Marshall Cavendish Corporation. 2008. *Inventors and inventions.* New York: Marshall Cavendish.

McCabe, James Dabney. 1872. *Lights and shadows of New York life, or, The sights and sensations of the great city a work descriptive of the city of New York in all its various phases: with full and graphic accounts of its splendors and wretchedness, its high and low life, its marble palaces and dark dens, its attractions and dangers, its rings and frauds, its leading men and politicians, its adventurers, its charities, its mysteries, and its crimes.* Philadelphia, Pa.: National Pub. Co.

McComb, David G. 2010. *Texas, a modern history.* Austin: University of Texas Press.

McPherson, James M. 2003. *The illustrated battle cry of freedom: The Civil War era.* Oxford [U.K.]: Oxford University Press.

The Merchants' magazine and commercial review. 1861. New York: Freeman Hunt.

Monkkonen, Eric H. 2000. *Murder in New York City.* Berkeley: University of California Press.

The New Jerusalem Bible. 1985. Garden City, N.Y.: Doubleday.

New York State Historical Association. 1895. *The memorial history of the city of New York: Biographical.* New York: New York History Co.

Oehlschlaeger, Fritz. 2003. *Love and good reasons: Postliberal approaches to Christian ethics and literature.* Durham, N.C.: Duke University Press.

Parisian, Catherine M. 2010. *The first White House library: a history and annotated catalog.* University Park, Pa: Published by the Pennsylvania State University Press for the Bibliographical Society of America and the National First Ladies' Library.

Parton, James. 1889. *The life of Horace Greeley, editor of "The New-York tribune," from his birth to the present time.* Boston: Houghton, Mifflin & Co.

Poe, Edgar Allan. 2004. *The collected tales and poems of Edgar Allan Poe.* Hertfordshire, Ware: Wordsworth Editions.

Poe, Edgar Allan. 1975. *The complete tales and poems of Edgar Allan Poe.* New York: Vintage Books.

Poe, Edgar Allan, Stuart Levine, and Susan F. Levine. 1990. *The short fiction of Edgar Allan Poe: An annotated edition.* Urbana: University of Illinois Press.

Poe, Edgar Allan, *The Works of Edgar Allan Poe,* Vol. III (New York: WJ Widdleton; 1849).

Powell, C. Frank, *An authentic life of John C. Colt, now imprisoned for killing Samuel Adams, in New York, on the seventeenth of September, 1841.* 1842. Boston: s.n. Dickinson.

Rohan, Jack. 1935. *Yankee arms maker: The incredible career of Samuel Colt. [Illustr.]* New York: Harper and Brothers.

Rosa, Joseph G. 1995. *Age of the gunfighter: Men and weapons on the frontier, 1840–1900: with artifacts from the GeneAutry Western Heritage Museum and the Buffalo Bill Historical Center.* Norman: University of Oklahoma Press.

Rose, Joel. 2008. *The blackest bird: A novel of murder in nineteenth-century New York.* [Toronto]: Anchor Canada.

Rywell, Martin. 1955. *Samuel Colt, a man and an epoch.* Harriman, Tenn.: Pioneer Press.

Sizer, Nelson. *Forty years in phrenology; embracing recollections of history, anecdote, and experience.* New York: Fowler and Wells, 1882.

Smith, Anthony. 2004. *Machine gun: The story of the men and the weapon that changed the face of war.* New York: St. Martin's Paperbacks.

Smith, Tom. "John Colt Trial: 1842." Great American Trials. 2002. *Encyclopedia.com*. (November 15, 2010). www.encyclopedia.com/doc/1G2-3498200057.html.

Sokal, Michael M. "Practical Phrenology as Psychological Counseling in the 19th-Century United States." In *The Transformation of Psychology: Influences of 19th-Century Philosophy, Technology, and Natural Science*. Edited by Christopher D. Green.

Spann, Edward K. 1981. *The new metropolis: New York City, 1840-1857*. New York: Sur.

Sun, The. 1842. *Trial of John C. Colt for the murder of Samuel Adams*, Colt, JC. New York (State). Court of Oyer and Terminer (New York County).

Stashower, Daniel. 2007. *The Beautiful Cigar Girl: Mary Rogers, Edgar Allan Poe, and the Invention of Murder*. New York: Berkley Books.

Stern, Madeleine B. 1971. *Heads and headlines: The phrenological Fowlers*. Norman: University of Oklahoma Press.

Sutton, Charles, James B. Mix, and Samuel Anderson Mackeever. 1874. *The New York Tombs; its secrets and its mysteries. Being a history of noted criminals, with narratives of their crimes*. San Francisco, Cal: A. Roman & Co.

Trumbull, J. Hammond. 1886. *The memorial history of Hartford County, Connecticut, 1633-1884*. Boston: E.L. Osgood.

Tucher, Andie. 1994. *Froth & scum: Truth, beauty, goodness, and the ax murder in America's first mass medium*. Chapel Hill [u.a.]: Univ. of North Carolina Press.

Tucker, Barbara M., and Kenneth H. Tucker. 2008. *Industrializing antebellum America: The rise of manufacturing entrepreneurs in the early republic*. New York: Palgrave Macmillan.

United States, and James D. Richardson. 1896. *A compilation of the messages and papers of the presidents, 1789-1897*. Washington: Government Printing Office.

The United States magazine and Democratic review. 1837. Washington, D.C.: Langtree and O'Sullivan.

Van Rensselaer, Stephen. 1947. *American firemarms; an histology of American gunsmiths, arms manufacturers & patentees with detailed description of their arms*. Watkins Glen, N.Y.: Century House.

Walling, George W. 1887. *Recollections of a New York chief of police*. New York: Caxton Book Concern.

Weld, H. Hastings, John Neal, George M. Snow, and Edward Stephens. 1842. *Brother Jonathan*. New York: Wilson & Co..

Witzel, Morgen. 2005. *The encyclopedia of the history of American management*. Bristol, Eng: Thoemmes Continuum.

Woodberry, George Edward. 1885. *Edgar Allan Poe*. American men of letters. Boston: Houghton, Mifflin.

INDEX

About the Author

Crime expert, lecturer, television personality, and investigative journalist M. William Phelps is the national best-selling, award-winning author of nineteen nonfiction books and the host of the Investigation Discovery channel show *Dark Minds*, which debuts in early 2012. Winner of the 2008 New England Book Festival Award for *I'll Be Watching You*, Phelps has appeared on CBS's *Early Show, tru TV,* The Discovery Channel, Fox News Channel, CN8, ABC's *Good Morning America,* The Learning Channel, Biography Channel, History Channel, *Montel Williams,* Investigative Discovery, *Geraldo at Large,* USA Radio Network, Catholic Radio, EWTN Radio, Ave Maria Radio, ABC News Radio, and Radio America, which calls him "the nation's leading authority on the mind of the female murderer." You might recognize Phelps as a featured and recurrent expert guest on the hit Investigation Discovery channel show *Deadly Women.* He's also written for the *Providence Journal, Hartford Courant,* and the *New London Day,* and he has consulted for the Showtime cable television series *Dexter.* He lives in a small Connecticut farming community. Phelps can be reached at www.mwilliamphelps.com.